Jews and Christians

in Twelfth-Century Europe

D1452564

Notre Dame Conferences in Medieval Studies

NUMBER X

Institute of Medieval Studies
University of Notre Dame

JOHN VAN ENGEN, *Director*

Jews

and

Christians

in Twelfth-Century Europe

Edited by

Michael A. Signer

and

John Van Engen

University of Notre Dame Press
Notre Dame, Indiana

Designed by Wendy McMillen
Set in 10.8/13.6 Goudy by Stanton Publication Services, Inc.
Printed in the U.S.A. by Sheridan Books, Inc.

Manufactured in the United States of America

Library of Congress Cataloging-in-Publication Data
Jews and Christians in twelfth-century Europe / Michael A. Signer and John
    Van Engen, editors.
        p.   cm. — (Notre Dame conferences in medieval studies ; 10)
    Includes bibliographical references and index.
    ISBN 0-268-03253-x (cloth : alk. paper)—ISBN 0-268-03254-8 (pa : alk. paper)
        1. Jews—Europe—History—To 1500—Congresses.   2. Jews—Germany—
History—1096–1147—Congresses.   3. Crusades—First, 1096–1099—Jews—
Congresses.   4. Christianity and other religions—Judaism—Congresses.
5. Judaism—Relations—Christianity—Congresses.   6. Europe—Ethnic relations—
Congresses.   I. Signer, Michael Alan.   II. Van Engen, John H.   III. Series.

DS124 .J52 2000
940'.04924—dc21
                                                                00-056799

∞ *This book was printed on acid-free paper.*

Contents

Acknowledgments

This volume originated as a conference held at the University of Notre Dame in October 1996. The organizers are deeply grateful to the Crown-Minow Foundation, to Robert Conway, to the Medieval Institute, and to the Department of Theology for generously making the conference possible. More particularly, the editors would like to thank Christoph Cluse and Sharan Newman for their work on the English translation of Alfred Haverkamp's essay; Gabriel Ash and Robin Vose for the English translation of Gérard Nahon's essay; and David Mengel, together with James Mixson, for careful work preparing the essays for the Press.

Abbreviations

CCCM
Corpus Christianorum Continuatio Mediaevalis. Brepols.

CCSL
Corpus Christianorum, Series Latina. Brepols.

CSEL
Corpus Scriptorum Ecclesiasticorum Latinorum. Vienna, 1866– .

MGH
Monumenta Germaniae Historica. Hannover, Leipzig, Weimar, Munich, 1826– .

PL
Patrologia Cursus Completus, Series Latina. Ed. J. P. Migne. 221 vols. Paris, 1841–1864.

Rolls Series
Rerum Britannicarum Medii Aevi Scriptores, or, Chronicles and Memorials of Great Britain and Ireland during the Middle Ages. London, 1858–1896.

Introduction:
Jews and Christians Together
in the Twelfth Century

JOHN VAN ENGEN

Medieval society fostered intimacy and distance at the same time. Princes and beggars stumbled over one another in the same street, masters and servants lived in the same household, men and women were bound into the same family: each moved suffocatingly close to the other, and yet experienced a different world. So it was with Jews and Christians. They lived together in northwestern Europe between the years 1000 and 1200, inhabiting similar places and spaces. Within city walls, most commonly renascent towns with princely or ecclesiastical residences, they walked through the same narrow streets, interacted in merchants' shops or marketplaces, and lived in the same sorts of houses. They spoke the same local language, whatever role each reserved for their sacred and learned languages, Hebrew and Latin. Exceptions grew out of political or social situations which they shared: the Jews who moved into England with the Norman conquerors spoke Anglo-Norman French, not English, and the Jews who moved east out of the Rhineland into Slavic territories, with their Christian counterparts, retained a Germanic tongue. For Jews this marked the origins of Yiddish, which would become their common language for the next millenium. In common, just as importantly, Jews and Christians experienced disruption and unsettling change throughout the eleventh and twelfth centuries, disturbances that grievously exacerbated tensions within and between their communities.

Yet they lived in different worlds. Each religious community located its adherents in an altogether different universe. Jews lived, exiled from Zion, in Ashkenaz, a term of uncertain origin and meaning, but in any case in diaspora. They moved as a protected minority within the rules and powers of an alien religious community, which boldly claimed to have replaced them as the true inheritors of God's covenant and promises. In Ashkenaz, in exile, they awaited the Messiah and return to Jerusalem. Christians, by contrast, lived in Christendom. They saw Europe as their inheritance, the antique world-part given Japheth after the Flood and ultimately promised to Christ's spiritual heirs. In Christendom, following the end of the Roman persecutions, they lived in a period of "peace," in effect, of Christian dominance in society and culture. They expected this to last until the coming of Anti-Christ.

Everyday life in these two universes, in practice, overlapped. Relations proceeded relatively untroubled between the eighth and eleventh centuries, though the balance of social and cultural power leaned decidedly in one direction. Christians expected to set the framework for this cohabitation. From the Christian perspective, Ashkenazi Jews inhabited Christendom as historical relics, as living witnesses to the Old Testament and the catastrophic repudiation of Jesus as the Messiah. In principle, therefore, Jewish magistrates might not rule over Christian subjects, or Christian slaves serve Jewish masters. In reality, nothing like consistency obtained: Christian servants, including wet-nurses, served Jewish families, and Christian princes or patricians became deeply beholden to Jewish merchants. The communities, much of the time, pursued their own ends with minimal interference. Neither side, for the most part, seriously questioned either intimacy in the world or coexistence in two cultural universes. Indeed neither expected, or entirely trusted, movement from one community to the other. For Jews and for Christians, uniformity, that is, a final reckoning and a kingdom of peace, would come only at the end of time.

This mixture of intimacy and distance suffered disruption during the twelfth century. As never before in living memory, each community was forced to reconsider and redefine its boundaries and its points of intersection. Those disruptions served as a point of departure for the essays gathered here and the conference from which they originated. In the opening paragraphs of a thematic statement circulated prior to the conference, the two editors put it this way:

In the summer of 1096 marauding Crusaders attacked the Jewish communities resident in the Rhineland cities of Speyer, Worms, and Mainz. This violence disrupted what had been, for two centuries and more, a relatively peaceful coexistence between Jews and Christians in western Europe. Chronicles written in Latin and in Hebrew record the destruction wrought within the Jewish quarters, the baptisms demanded and sometimes effected, and the martyrdom of numerous Jews, some at their own hands. The most common telling of these events goes on to a narrative of deteriorating relations between both communities and hastening decline for the Jewish community. The majority community increasingly asserted itself against the only significant religious minority within its midst: charges of ritual murder in England a half century later, imposed restrictions at Lateran IV another half century later, and the attack on the Talmud a generation later. In counterpoint to this narrative, other scholars have constructed a narrative that emphasizes enhanced and generally beneficial interaction: Jewish and Christian scholars working together on the Hebrew Scriptures, especially in Paris, kings and bishops protecting and privileging Jewish communities in their kingdoms and dioceses, with expulsions from whole territories not beginning until the end of the thirteenth century.

Both narratives, true as they are, have assessed the interaction between Jews and Christians almost entirely in terms of a majority and minority community, and measure their relations on a scale of persecution and privilege. This is important, but not the whole story. In the course of the twelfth century both communities (each in fact a congeries of many different local communities) found themselves caught up in larger changes, social, cultural, and religious, some of these apparently common to both, some peculiar to each. In Christian communities the reform of the church, for instance, unleashed its own internal violence in the form of a virtual civil war in some German and Italian bishoprics, while setting reformers against traditionalists in numerous chapters and monasteries. In Jewish communities recent studies have highlighted the development of communal autonomy and new forms of rabbinic scholarship and congregational piety, permitting Jewish life to flourish within northern Europe.

With this statement the editors intended neither to exaggerate nor to understate the murderous riots of 1096 and their aftermath. For the

conference, and for this volume, the editors looked toward a different
goal: to "mainstream" Jewish communities and their experience as an
integral part of medieval European history. Within the inherited histori-
ographies, the events of 1096 and their consequences have often framed,
or become paradigmatic for, a persistent and steadily worsening enmity
between two hostile communities. This story-line has made it nearly impossible even to imagine Jews and Christians living together in twelfth-
century Europe. It is due as much to a ghettoization of historical writing
as to the historical ghettoization of Jews behind walls—itself more a
phenomenon of later medieval and early modern Europe. Christian or
gentile authors, down nearly to the present generation, did not include
Jews as part of the European story except in cases where their presence
helped account for some other piece of the story, thus, as the victims of
spectacular violence in the First Crusade, or as merchants and moneylenders, or as translators and intellectual interlocutors. Otherwise Jews
were largely ignored, even by fine and sophisticated historians, as if they
simply did not form part of the medieval or European story. Such a narrative makes Jews into silent participants, obliterating or distorting their
actual presence.

Jewish historians, on the other hand, writing after the Enlightenment and during the period of romanticism, made their story of Jewish
martyrdom and survival the whole story, complete in itself. Since the
nineteenth century each set of historians, accordingly, has pursued different questions. Christians asked about medieval Jews only at points of
intersection with what they accounted the master narrative. These were
all too often negative encounters with Jews regarded as objects of economic competition in moneylending, the "positive" coming at best in
moments of intellectual exchange. Jewish historians in turn focused upon
medieval Christians only as they impinged on their community's story,
again in mostly negative or threatening forms that, in addition, became
linked to superstition or hatred. Neither group of historians, until recently, gave much thought to elements that might contribute to a common history, illumine similar patterns of life, or take up parallel problems
and achievements. And neither could imagine—or perhaps tolerate—
notions of "influence" going either way, especially any that affected or
shaped their own community apart from its internal dynamics. More recently, efforts to include Jews in the European story as the "marginal-

ized" or the "fantastic other" risk replicating one-sidedly, as the historical whole, a particular dimension of the medieval distancing dynamic.

This volume aims to encourage approaches that attend closely to both intimacy and distance, and thereby attempt to integrate the Jewish and Jewish-Christian stories into a larger European story. It means, at the level of mundane affairs, taking seriously scattered evidence that points toward routines of intimacy and intense interaction. Beyond commercial and juridical relations, conversation and confrontation, there were adjoining neighborhoods, servants going both ways, instances of intermarriage, and arrangements for burial places. In towns and marketplaces, and at court, Jews were increasingly part of Christian experience in the century and a half broadly labeled as the twelfth century (1050–1200). Nor could Jews live without an awareness of the Christian society and culture around them. In Speyer, the synagogue and ritual bath, with their surrounding Jewry, functioned a city block or so from the cathedral, the burial place of the Salian emperors; and in Cologne they directly adjoined the city hall. Mainz, the primatial see for Christians in German lands, was for Jews a key center of rabbinic culture. Much the same urban topography obtained in northern France and in England. From this physical and spatial closeness an easy informality could arise. Indeed Pope Innocent III claimed in Lateran Council IV that he wanted Jews distinguished by clothing, lest Christians enter into intimate relations with them unknowingly.

Within their respective communities the intellectual and social dynamics are suggestive of comparable elements at work. In religious life, for instance, each set of communities engendered a new piety and a new focus upon intentionality, characterized by new efforts to interpret Scripture in its plain sense and to treat matters of belief with an instrumental reason. In the public sphere both communities acted in a common but changing environment: more assertive monarchies, more self-consciousness about law in society, more active commercial enterprises, more money and credit, more urbanization. Jews began to seek a special status of "immunity" from envious or greedy local powers, and to this end employed a version of the means that privileged Christian communities such as monasteries had adopted before them. In such privileges, the strong arm of a higher and distant authority extended protection, usually in exchange for tribute, and always at the risk of

inciting local resentments or rendering the group more dependent upon
a distant power—as true for monastic houses as for Jewries. Princes who
granted collective privileges of protection blithely referred to the
people as "our Jews." In the document that set the standard for papal
protection (*Sicut Judaeis*), going back to Pope Callixtus II (1119–24)
but surviving from Alexander III (1159–83), Jews were placed, at their
request, under papal protection. Specifically, popes promised to "shield"
them from threats of coerced baptism, from random violence, and from
harassment during their worship services and holy days; offending
princes were threatened with loss of office and Christians generally with
excommunication.[1]

Twelfth-century Jews and Christians also presumed and maintained
great distances. Some factors were of long standing, most obvious in
matters of public practice and the differences in cult: circumcision or
baptism, Passover or Easter, Torah or Scripture, Sabbath or Lord's Day.
Also of long standing were the stories, myths, and conceptual notions
whereby one community categorized the other, many passed down from
late antiquity. Most were unexamined and taken for granted, whether
they were sophisticated accounts of the other group's positions and er-
rors or simply vulgar slurs. Both communities reinforced their people
and protected their offspring with these elaborated stories and myths
about the other, thus, in their cruelest forms, stories about "the crucified one" or about the "crucifiers." And, while both communities lived
broadly under the aegis of Christian kingdoms, each lived more immediately within the structures of its own specific laws, practices, and customs—this was as true for various Christian communities as for the
Jewish.

Beyond these inherited distances, twelfth-century Europe set in motion a new dynamic of deepened and more violent hostility, exacerbat-
ing relations between communities. This has received much of the
attention in past literature, and indeed receives plenty of attention in
this volume, too. Rumormongering, new charges, and occasional waves
of violence made it harder to sustain routine patterns of interaction and
to live alongside one another. Both new hostilities and new understand-
ings arose in part from new factors, several peculiar to one community
or region, some common to the era and to many communities. One factor, still under discussion, may be that the Jews of northwestern Europe

represented relatively recent arrivals; their communities thus were not holdovers from Roman and early medieval settlements but rather families scattered from their Mediterranean homelands in pursuit of new opportunities. The twelfth-century interactions would thus represent in some sense the first large-scale encounter between the two communities in this region. Another factor may be a much fuller personal and intellectual engagement in this era with what one group thought they knew about the other, that is, with both an alien community and its claims about the other group. Too often these historical events, affecting the whole of medieval Europe, are treated primarily in terms of one community: a "persecuting church" (Moore), Christians acting pathologically out of "religious doubt" (Langmuir), and Jews exposed to danger as recent "immigrants" (Chazan) or to envy as successful moneylenders. Unfortunately, debates that focus on the origins of anti-Semitism or the character of the medieval church illumine only one part of a complex historical dynamic that was shared in some sense by all communities. The results, then, impressive or suggestive, fail to satisfy hopes for a history which might integrate the common and the unique experience in a comprehensive understanding of medieval Europe.

Another approach to writing this history would presume interaction and take a different point of departure: Did greater interaction engender greater conflict? Did more conflict produce, and was it produced by, new and more hostile images of the other community? From the perspective of the editors and authors in this volume, this sense of complementarity, of interaction or action and reaction—evident in the recent controversial essays of Israel Yuval—needs to better inform the medieval story. The essays in this volume, therefore, intentionally highlight areas of common or parallel activity: in vernacular literature, in biblical exegesis, in piety and mysticism, in the social context of conversion, in relations to prelates and monarchs, in coping with a time of change, renewal, and upheaval. This requires nuanced accounts that will move in both directions and are open to the parallels and to the differences among the communities. And this approach must be sensitive to the possibilities of mutual influence, direct and indirect. Christians wrote or argued or acted, even restructured their own tradition, with Jews and the challenge of an alternative faith and practice, derived from the same Scriptures, in mind. Jews did the same with the Christian community in mind.

Historians now commonly identify the twelfth century as the crucial turning point, as laying down a pattern of relations between Jews and Christians that would affect European history to modern times.[2] Authors in this volume take varying positions on this interpretation, but none fail to deal with it in some way. If historians are to make both communities properly a part of the story and thus move toward a more integral history of twelfth-century Europe, they must begin by posing similar or at least parallel questions: Were there dynamics common to both communities? How did these play themselves out in interaction? What do the heightened hostilities reveal about intimacy and distance? Was it less possible after the confrontations of the twelfth century for Jews and Christians to live together, to inhabit separate universes and yet in some sense the same world? Or was an increased level of vituperation and violence, ironically, a mark of their living more closely together? The hope is that present-day work, including the essays in this volume, will contribute to a more powerful and fuller integration of Jews and Christians in the story of medieval Europe.

NOTES

1. Shlomo Simonsohn, *The Apostolic See and the Jews: Documents, 492–1404,* Studies and Texts 94 (Toronto, 1988), 51 (no. 49).

2. See especially Robert Chazan, *Medieval Stereotypes and Modern Antisemitism* (Berkeley, 1997), with a good bibliography; David Berger, "From Crusades to Blood Libels to Expulsions: Some New Approaches to Medieval Antisemitism," *Second Annual Lecture of the Victor J. Selmanowitz Chair of Jewish History, Touro College* (New York, 1997); and Gilbert Dahan, *Les intellectuels chrétiens et les Juifs au moyen âge* (Paris, 1990). Each of these works looks back at the main patterns of recent study, in effect providing a bibliographical orientation, which has not been attempted here.

one

A 1096 Complex?
Constructing the First Crusade
in Jewish Historical Memory,
Medieval and Modern

JEREMY COHEN

Let the ears hearing this and its like be seared; for who has heard or
seen the likes of it? Inquire and seek: Was there ever such a mass sacrificial offering (*Aqedah*) since the time of Adam . . . ? On a single day . . .
one thousand one hundred holy souls were killed and slaughtered,
babes and sucklings who had not sinned or transgressed, the souls of
poor innocent people. . . . That day the diadem of Israel fell, the students of the Torah fell, and the outstanding scholars passed away. . . .
Gone were the sin-fearers, gone were the men of virtuous deed; ended
were the radiance of wisdom and purity and abstinence, the glory of the
priesthood and the men of perfect faith; diminished were the ranks of
those who give charity in secret. Gone was truth; gone were the expli-
cators of the Word and the Law; fallen were the people of eminence
and the sage—all on this day, on which so many sorrows befell us. . . .
Since the day on which the Second Temple was destroyed, their like
had not arisen, *nor shall there be their like again*—for they sanctified and
bore witness to the unity of God's name with all their heart and with all
their soul and with all their might.[1]

Thus the twelfth-century Hebrew chronicler recalled how nine hundred years ago, at the end of the spring and beginning of the summer of

1096—during the earliest months of the First Crusade—bands of armed crusaders attacked Jewish settlements in western and central Germany; those Jews whom they could the crusaders converted, while others who fell in their path they killed. Jewish communities of the Rhine valley—in Speyer, Worms, Mainz, Cologne and its suburbs, Metz, and Trier—and others, including Regensburg and Prague to the east, suffered serious losses in life and property upon this, the first widespread outbreak of anti-Jewish violence in medieval Christian Europe.

When compelled by their attackers to choose between conversion to Christianity and death, the Jews of Ashkenaz compounded the novelty and singularity of the events of 1096 in no less striking a fashion: To be sure, there evidently were attempts to flee the crusaders, to bribe them, to seek refuge with the local potentates, to flee altogether, and even to take up arms. A significant number opted for baptism, although many of these—very probably most of them—returned to Jewish life within several years of the violence. Yet many others, perhaps a majority of those attacked in 1096, elected to die a martyr's death; and of these, very many took their own lives and those of their loved ones in order to avoid capture, torture, forced conversion, and/or death at the hands of the enemy. In such rampant willingness to forfeit life ʿal qiddush ha-Shem (in sanctification of God's name, as they put it) and, perhaps, in violation of rabbinic strictures against suicide, many students of Jewish history have beheld a distinctive hallmark of medieval Ashkenazic Jewish culture, one which contrasts sharply with the frequent preference of Sefardic/Spanish Jewry for conversion (to Christianity or Islam) in the face of religious persecution.

Equally novel are the Jewish documents which narrate the events of these persecutions in general and numerous scenes of such self-inflicted martyrdom in particular. For centuries the ancestors of these Ashkenazic Jews had recalled and lamented moments of national tragedy in liturgical poetry (piyyut), and an impressive number of extant piyyutim bemoan the suffering and casualties of 1096.[2] Alongside poetic laments of this sort, however, three Hebrew chronicles of the First Crusade survive, among the earliest instances of local Jewish historiography in medieval Europe.[3] Apart from Abraham ibn Daud's Sefer ha- Qabbalah, the Hebrew crusade chronicles are often considered the sole examples of genuinely historical literature produced by medieval Jews, and they have

figured centrally in academic debate concerning the ahistorical consciousness of medieval Jewish civilization.[4]

In the twelfth century and again in the nineteenth and twentieth
centuries, these novel dimensions to the persecutions of 1096 contributed to their singular prominence in Jewish historical memory. Our
twelfth-century Hebrew chronicler committed his story to writing out of
the conviction that exilic Jewry had neither suffered nor valiantly withstood the trials of suffering as the Jews of Mainz did in 1096; for
Solomon bar Samson, the chronicler, not only did they outshine those
who had preceded them, but never "shall there be their like again."
Following the lead of their medieval predecessors, modern historians of
medieval Jews have commonly viewed the persecutions of 1096 as a critical turning point in medieval Jewish history:[5] Until the First Crusade,
runs this argument, Jews fared relatively well in the Latin West, living
alongside their Christian neighbors with minimal interference from
church or state, the targets of physical persecution in only a few, isolated
instances; after the violence of 1096, however, the status of medieval
Jews declined steadily. Massacres of Jews in the name of Christian piety
revealed the inadequacy of existing safeguards for the person and property of the Jew. His need for greater protection enhanced his dependence
on, and weakness before, Christian princes, without whose goodwill he
remained at the mercy of an increasingly hostile European society; at
the same time, the physical persecution of the Jews, albeit technically il-
legal, awakened Latin Christendom to their anomalous situation. Why
were the enemies of Christ permitted to remain and to thrive within the
domains of Christianity, far beyond the limits dictated by Christian leg-
islators and theologians of old? Churchmen and jurists responded by repeatedly reevaluating the Jews, their Judaism, and their contemporary
situation during the twelfth and thirteenth centuries, by the end of
which period a constellation of principled and practical considerations
induced the political rulers of medieval Europe to begin expelling Jews
from their lands. In the wake of 1096, Israeli historian Haim Hillel
Ben-Sasson has concluded, "the Jews now realized that charters alone
could not provide absolute security against mob fury. Christian religious
fervor had kindled a fire in the tents of Jacob and had led to slaughter
in his habitations. The blood of the Jews had, as it were, been made free
for the Christian masses. In respect to legal formulations, security and

possibilities of livelihood, the First Crusade inaugurated a new and harsh epoch for Jews in Christian lands."[6] And in his oft-reprinted and translated survey of Jewish history, Cecil Roth offered a still more definitive appraisal:

> The effects of the Crusades upon the Jew . . . the passions and the tendencies which they set in motion continued to dominate his history for at least four centuries, and left traces upon it which are discernible even today. They influenced his political position, his geographical distribution, his economic activity, his forms of literary expression, even his spiritual life. It may be added that, in almost every direction, the influence was for the bad. Take any realistic description of the position of world Jewry down to the close of the last century; take any indictment drawn up by an anti-Semite in our own times; take any contemporary analysis of the weakness of the Jewish position or the alleged shortcomings of the Jewish character; and in almost every instance it will be possible to trace the origin, if not actually to the crusades, to the currents which they stirred.[7]

Various investigators have endeavored to modify or to refute this notion that the persecutions of 1096 constituted a virtual watershed in medieval European Jewish history, but only a few have sought to understand the basis for the theory and its popularity in modern scholarship. We have before us a historiographical tradition that has repeatedly, in varying contexts and modes since 1096, edited, reformulated, and reoriented current memories of the persecutions in response to the changing needs and temperament of the prevailing Jewish culture. Not all the links in this tradition are known to us; especially in the medieval period, many agents of historical memory—or "phantoms of remembrance," as Patrick Geary has recently dubbed them—remain highly elusive.[8] I therefore propose a new examination of several stages in the development of this tradition, the first of them medieval, the remainder more recent.

First, however much we might like to use the twelfth-century Hebrew chronicles to document what actually transpired in the Rhineland in 1096, I have argued the contrary in several previous papers. I can only summarize my argument here:[9] that their narratives of the events—and the phenomenon of self-inflicted martyrdom above all—elucidate the perspective of those Jews who survived much more than they explain the behavior of those who died. On the one hand, these chronicles empowered Ashkenazic Jews of the early twelfth century to respond in kind, not to the knights of the crusade, but to the polemical overtones of crusading ideology, which, Jonathan Riley-Smith has shown, matured only in the twelfth-century Christian chronicles of the First Crusade.[10] Quite simply, the Jewish chroniclers' message read: Our martyrdom, the atonement it effected, and the salvation it secured were genuine; yours are not. Our martyrs surpass your martyrs, even your Martyr *par excellence*. Our holy war, in which we readily died as martyrs, was greater, more meritorious, than yours. We must recall, on the other hand, that Jews who survived the persecutions of 1096 generally did so by converting to Christianity, which most abandoned once the violence had subsided. Imagine the guilt that must have plagued the communities of these survivors and their children when contrasting their survival with the martyrdom of their brethren. *Their* memories imbue the chronicles, and it should not surprise us that such memories project the survivor's conflicts and doubts onto the martyr, helping to resolve the dissonance between the ostensive weakness of the former and heroism of the latter.

The persecutions of 1096 received but scanty attention in Jewish historical literature of the late medieval and early modern periods, and the second phase in our story brings us to the nineteenth century. Arguing that reliable historical evidence concerning the massacres and their lasting impact upon Ashkenazic communities does not justify the portrayal of 1096 as a watershed in Jewish history, Simon Schwarzfuchs has recently characterized that portrayal as the creature of Jewish historiography in nineteenth-century Germany. Romanticism then conditioned European historical thought, and the "charms of the East and the birth of colonialism" sparked renewed interest in the crusades. Products of the *Haskalah* or modern Jewish enlightenment, and wedded to the philological program of the *Wissenschaft des Judentums* (their movement of the Science of Judaism) for rehabilitating Judaism in modern European society, medieval Jewish historians of the time confronted a serious problem: Precious little material offered documentation of Jewish life in medieval Europe, such that the history of medieval Jewry became chiefly a literary history, which seemed to predominate over any other concern.

Non-literary evidence was scanty and largely non-Jewish, so that there existed no continuity between ancient Jewish history and the subsequent reappearance of the Jewish people in the history of Europe. The discovery of the Hebrew crusade chronicles, reasoned Schwarzfuchs,

> allowed for relating the annals of the Jews in Western Europe in the terms of *Jewish* historical experience. . . . These stories became history; they allowed for explaining the decline of the condition of European Jews, for which they cast blame on the rabble and thus allowed for fruitful dialogue with the heads of the church and with political rulers. They also testified to the antiquity of Jewish settlement in Europe and transformed the Jews of the Rhine valley into Europeans. Overnight, the tragedy of the crusades became one of the high points in the entirety of Jewish history.[11]

Schwarzfuchs has rightly concluded that nineteenth-century Jewish historians bequeathed their perspective to their successors, but one can profitably pursue such an analysis of this interpretation further, both among its progenitors in the nineteenth century and among its proponents in our own. Scholars of the nineteenth century like Heinrich Graetz, Moritz Güdemann, and Simon Dubnow attributed multifaceted significance to the persecutions of 1096.[12] In one respect, Hebrew documentation of the events accorded authenticity to the *Jewish* experience in Germany during its earliest stages and thus proved suggestive for the predicament of the modern German Jew as well. The massacres demonstrate that along with Jews themselves, unjustified hatred for them had a long history in Germany. Frightful though the accounts of martyrdom might be, one can understand—and even applaud—the steadfast resistance of Ashkenazic Jews to Christianity, and their resolute protest against the moral bankruptcy of the Christian church. In a different vein, however, the events of 1096 demonstrate how, for better and for worse, the destiny of Germany's Jews is enmeshed in that of the German civilization in which they live. Their tragic results notwithstanding, declared Graetz, the crusades ultimately wrought beneficial changes in Western history for which Jews of the present day must be thankful, too. As for these Jews' medieval ancestors, Graetz, Güdemann, and Dubnow all linked the ethos that underlay their enthusiasm for *qiddush ha-Shem* to the pernicious influence of contemporary Christian asceticism and religious mysticism. Such influence wore on in the case of Ashkenazic Jewry, resulting in a truly dark, primitive age that suppressed healthy cultural creativity, that stifled the poetic spirit and serious exegesis of the Bible and Talmud, that substituted a backward pietism for the inquisitive rationalism of medieval Sefardic Jews, and that, as Güdemann would have had it, effectively postponed the onset of Jewish cultural awakening and *Haskalah* in Germany. "Everything that we now see and encounter among our people—the flight from the world, dejection of the spirit, anxiety, petty-mindedness in matters of religion, superstition, and esotericism—all these are products of that terrible time, which, with repeated, periodic recurrences, has become deeply ensconced in their memory, never to be forgotten."[13]

While the manifold contributions of these early generations of modern Jewish scholarship endure, the past generations have produced a new historiography—and a third phase in our tradition—that has altered the meaning to be found in the persecutions of 1096. More than to Graetz and company, present-day students of Jewish history turn to the voluminous writings of Yitzhak Baer, Benzion Dinur, Bernhard Blumenkranz, Cecil Roth, Salo Wittmayer Baron, Haim Hillel Ben-Sasson, Jacob Katz, and others for their basic understanding of the medieval Jewish experience. To be sure, the intervening decades of research unearthed additional documentary sources to illuminate the events and impact of the crusades, and these historians also benefited from an array of new scholarly ideas and interpretations bearing on the analysis of this data. No less important, these authors themselves lived through two momentous transitions in Jewish history which the nineteenth-century students of the *Wissenschaft* school could never have anticipated: the Nazi Holocaust, and the establishment of a Jewish state in the land of Israel. One must beware of overly facile connections between their personal experiences and their understanding of 1096. But it would be equally misguided to suppose the absence and/or unimportance of such interdependence. How have the giants of twentieth-century Jewish historical research evaluated the persecutions?

Following in the footsteps of the *Wissenschaft* school, most Jewish historiography of the present century deems the 1096 massacres a critical turning point in the medieval Jewish experience.[14] Reacting against a "lachrymose" conception of Jewish history, some historians may have challenged the characterization of the First Crusade as the beginning of the process that culminated in the decline and virtual disappearance of European Jewry by the end of the Middle Ages. Yet that characterization has remained prevalent, and even Salo Baron, who hastened to reject the lachrymose conception of Jewish history, retained the notion of 1096 as a critical juncture.[15] Twentieth-century Jewish scholars have remained responsive to the centrality of crusade-related research among "general"/Christian medievalists; whether one considers the crusades a congenial or deplorable byproduct of medieval civilization, the judgment of Sidney Painter (who himself believed the crusades' impact overrated) remains typical. "They are at once the chief proof of the tremendous vitality and expansive power of medieval civilization and the most concrete illustration of the meaning of the common expression 'an Age of Faith.'"[16] Just as the crusades exemplify the Middle Ages for many general medievalists, so do the persecutions of 1096 and their aftermath embody much that is special about medieval Jewish history for its twentieth-century investigators. These more recent historians continued to read the Hebrew crusade chronicles primarily as accurate documentary evidence of what occurred in 1096, and only secondarily as noteworthy developments in Jewish literary history. Furthermore, like their European forerunners, they have perceived in the new Ashkenazic pattern of qiddush ha-Shem both a conscious rejection and an unconscious adaptation of Christian cultural norms.

This point warrants elaboration. Preference for martyrdom over religious conversion clearly entails an unmitigated rejection of the values of the oppressor, and, in the case of the self-inflicted killings in 1096, qiddush ha-Shem represents an expression of ultimate commitment to the distinguishing norms of the minority. As Yitzhak Baer wrote in the epilogue to the English translation of Galut, published in 1947,

> We taught the world the idea of martyrdom, and in the third great age of our history—the real age of the Galut—this idea was realized in the very body of the people [i.e., in 1096]. For two thousand years we suffered for the sake of the redemption of mankind; we were driven forth and scattered over every part of the earth because of the fateful interaction of the religious and political factors determining our history.[17]

Yet, as much as Baer accentuated the exclusivist idealism implicit in *qiddush ha-Shem*, he also took the lead in developing an impression that his nineteenth-century predecessors suggested but did not pursue: that the new extreme to which Ashkenazic Jews took such idealism in 1096 derived, at least in part, from the influence of the Christian environment upon them. What induced Ashkenazic Jews to martyr themselves as they did? Baer drew upon Carl Erdmann's groundbreaking work, *The Origin of the Idea of Crusade*,[18] as well as various studies of Cluniac monasticism in the tenth and eleventh centuries, to argue that just as external cultural influences regularly led to the appearance of new institutions and even new legal norms among medieval Ashkenazic Jewish communities,

> thus did such influences bear also on their inner life and the collective religious spirit itself. The tradition of martyrdom in sanctification of God's name reappeared among the Jews in France and western Germany from the beginning of the eleventh century, and it was infused with an exceptional enthusiasm in the face of widespread persecution. The parallel with the religious movement that was then awakening among the Christians and that emerged from the French monastery of Cluny should be evident.[19]

No matter that violent persecution and martyrdom naturally aggravated the distance between members of rival religious communities; a common cultural environment yielded parallel constellations of ideas and behavior even as communities struggled virulently for an exclusive claim to the status of God's chosen.[20] So, too, with the written records of the persecutions. Baer grounded his argument that the three Hebrew chronicles derive from a (lost) common source, composed in the immediate aftermath of the violence of 1096 and therefore embodying impeccable, eyewitness accounts of what transpired, on an array of similarities between the extant Hebrew texts and contemporary Christian accounts of the First Crusade. Information as to what had transpired traveled freely between Jewish and Christian communities, in strikingly similar documentary media: letters, stories, and, finally, more extensive, more carefully edited chronicles.

Despite these various avenues along which Baer and his mid-century colleagues pursued the lead of nineteenth-century Jewish historiography, they took issue with their forebears on vital aspects of the persecutions of 1096. The influences of the surrounding Christian environment notwithstanding, mid-twentieth-century Jewish historians have rarely interpreted the events of the First Crusade as a catalyst for the synthesis of Jewish and German/Christian experiences. They have depicted the Jewish minority as capable of adaptation from the culture of the majority in whose midst they lived; but such influence or adaptation did not threaten the national distinctiveness of the minority, the probity of its Judaism. The persecutions of 1096 did not render the annals of the Jewish experience a subset of German or Christian history; they did not inaugurate a period during which Ashkenazic Judaism succumbed to backward, pernicious cultural influences from the larger, Christian world around it. Rather, these persecutions demonstrated the reciprocal, *healthy* interactions of medieval Jewish and Christian communities, even as each preserved its independence and hostility vis-à-vis the other. Most historians had already read the violence of 1096 as an expression of an ethos of *Adversus Judaeos* deeply ingrained in Latin Christendom. Identifying with this common consensus, many have since accepted the judgment of Jacob Katz, that "the attitude of the Jewish martyrs, perhaps more than any other factor, bears out the assertion that the Jewish community at this time conceived its position and religious mission in terms of its own antagonism to Christianity."[21]

Katz's formulation hints at the application of the new historiographical consensus to the specific issue of *qiddush ha-Shem*. Not only did that which medieval Ashkenazic Judaism assimilate from Christian civilization fail to stunt its independent growth, but intercultural exchange stopped short of tainting the essential, distinguishing religious principles of northern European Jewry. Unlike the Jews of medieval Spain, praised by Graetz, Dubnow, and others for their urbaneness, their rationalism, and their involvement in the scientific endeavors of the non-Jewish culture around them, Ashkenazic Jews zealously defined and maintained limits to such cross-cultural interaction. The aloofness that their predecessors had deemed obscurantist and primitive, Baer, Dinur, Ben-Sasson, Katz, Haym Soloveitchik, and others subsequently hailed as that which facilitated the continued survival of traditional rabbinic Judaism through the ages. As opposed to Sefardic Marranism, the Ashkenazic preference for martyrdom over apostasy epitomized the remarkable achievement of medieval European Jewish civilization: its steadfast commitment to its spiritual ideas even under the threat of physical destruction. Thus Baer: "The persecution of 1096 was no passing incident, but a momentous catastrophic event, the finale to the first and classic movement in the history of rabbinic Judaism and liturgy in the Rhineland."[22] Dinur: "Ashkenazic Jews . . . , as they died in this manner, bequeathed to future generations the belief that Israel is indeed the nation of God and that the generation of self-inflicted martyrdom (*qiddush ha-Shem ha-ʿaqedati*) is a generation of the elect."[23] And Ben-Sasson: "This hallowing of the Holy Name by martyrdom (*qiddush ha-Shem*) strengthened Jewry from within, enriched it spiritually, crystallized the concepts of honour and heroism among the Jews and gave them the strength to face later trials."[24]

One can rightly discern in these twentieth-century investigations an attempt to correct prejudicial judgments of the nineteenth-century *Wissenschaft* school. Scholars of this century construed the interaction between Ashkenazic Judaism and the surrounding Christian civilization as a natural, healthy one, which did not violate the true, unique spirit of Judaism but actually perpetuated it. At the same time, they beheld limits to the extent of this interaction and thus accentuated the glorious singularity of self-inflicted Jewish martyrdom in 1096. From the perspective of the generation of the Holocaust and the struggle for Israeli independence, this might appear perfectly sensible. But is there not inconsistency here, perhaps fueled by ideological concerns no less prevalent than those which characterized Graetz and his colleagues? The horrors of the Holocaust notwithstanding, what justifies the glorification of the peculiarities of Ashkenazic Jewish culture any more than their disparagement by earlier scholars, in their preference for a Sefardic, Maimonidean sort of Jewish rationalism? Why should martyrdom, passive or self-inflicted, *ʿal qiddush ha-Shem* remain sacrosanct, immune to the same literary, historical, and cultural criticism typically applied in the study of any community's normative religious practice?

Perhaps one can discern yet another incipient phase in the unfolding of our historiographic tradition in various scholarly works of the last fifteen or twenty years. Against the background of a sharpened historiographical self-consciousness, exemplified in David Myers's book, *Re-Inventing the Jewish Past*, and alongside initial efforts to enrich Jewish studies with a postmodernist critical perspective,[25] some investigators have begun to challenge the consensus view that typified the previous generation and still enjoys much support, as in the work of Robert Chazan and Avraham Grossman.[26] Granted, many readers of the Jewish crusade chronicles had already acknowledged their apologetic and ideologically grounded agenda, and Isaiah Sonne earlier in this century had discerned "fruits of fabrication" in passages from Solomon bar Samson's Hebrew narrative.[27] Yet a new leaf in research on the persecutions of 1096 was turned by Ivan Marcus, when he proposed to apply Victor Turner's paradigm theory to an analysis of that same text, and when he called for approaching the Hebrew chronicles primarily as "fictions: imaginative reorderings of experience within a cultural framework and system of symbols."[28] Furthermore, recent writers have sought to mitigate the long-hallowed contrast between activist Sefardic involvement in the surrounding Gentile culture and self-imposed Ashkenazic isolation from it, thus tampering with some of the basic assumptions advanced in influential works like Jacob Katz's *Exclusiveness and Tolerance*. Some have argued that mutual awareness, shared traditions and symbols, and dynamic intellectual exchange characterized medieval Jewish-Christian relations in northern Europe much more than hitherto acknowledged, and that this perspective must inform our appreciation of the persecutions of 1096. Israeli scholar Israel Yuval has linked the study of Jewish martyrdom during the First Crusade to the possibility that Jews bore a measure of responsibility for subsequent Christian accusations of ritual murder against them;[29] he quickly prompted heated responses from those who would label such studies methodologically misguided, "consciously post-Zionist," and liable to promote antisemitic slander.[30] Thus accused, Yuval has lashed out at the prejudicial partiality, "the ahistorical method," and "the excessively positivistic interpretations" of his detractors, arguing that at the root of one critic's charges against him lies

> his fear, "what will the Gentiles say?" This fear has led him completely to disqualify accepted models for research and to view him that uses them in the present context a dangerous person. . . . Ought we to convert our historical studies into a broadsheet for propaganda because of the distortions of Antisemites? Shall we destroy our world on account of fools?[31]

The emotional stakes in this historiographical debate might appear surprisingly high, and they testify yet again to the formative impact of our own frame of reference upon present-day constructions of the past. Nonetheless, the recent receptiveness to greater cultural exchange between medieval Christians and Ashkenazic Jews can prove fruitful for our study of the persecutions of 1096 and their written records. Yuval has proposed that the new paradigm of Jewish martyrdom derived from an eschatological hope for revenge upon the enemies of Israel; thus expressed in acts and discourse of *qiddush ha-Shem*, such messianic expectation fueled new Christian suspicions concerning Jews: If hope for their redemption and our punishment led them to kill their own children, how can we expect them to behave toward our children? Mary Minty has pursued this line of inquiry further, documenting reactions to self-inflicted Jewish martyrdom in German literature and art of the later Middle Ages.[32] Ivan Marcus has suggested that the Christian willingness to dedicate one's life to the crusade and Ashkenazic enthusiasm for martyrdom manifest essentially the same phenomenon: the crusaders' conviction that, the perils of their endeavor notwithstanding, "*Deus vult*," which twelfth-century Ashkenazic Jewish pietists expressed as the ultimate fulfillment of *retson ha-Bore'*, the will of the creator.[33] And, as I have begun and will continue to argue, one must understand the new paradigm and discourse of Ashkenazic martyrdom as evidence of Jewish self-expression in the idiom of twelfth-century Christendom. The ideology and narratives of *qiddush ha-Shem* fit squarely into that cultural milieu, and their significance relates directly to the history of the Christian idea of the crusade and its literature.

The unconventional title of my paper, "A 1096 Complex?", derives from my sense that one can draw an instructive parallel between the historiographical career of the 1096 persecutions and the interpretation of the fall of Masada in twentieth-century Israeli culture. In the summer of 1971, *Newsweek* columnist Stewart Alsop criticized Israel and Prime Minister Golda Meir for their intransigence in Middle East peace negotiations, which, argued Alsop, derived from a "Masada complex," an epithet to which Meir subsequently retorted at a Washington press corps luncheon: "it is true, we do have a Masada complex; we have a pogrom complex; we have a Hitler complex."[34] As sociologist Nachman Ben-Yehuda explains, the Masada myth "revolves around the ideas of proud and self-conscious Jews fighting for their own cultural identity and freedom, in their own land, to the bitter end. It is a narrative of the few against the powerful many, struggling against tremendous odds. It is the story of preference for a liberating and violent death as opposed to a despicable life."[35] The element of Jews fighting *in their own land* is critical here. For the Masada complex manifests a twentieth-century, secular Zionist mentality that negates the value of a religiously defined Jewish civilization in *Galut*, in the exile, as it looks to the modern independent State of Israel as the fulfillment of Jewish history. From this perspective, literary critic Yael Zerubavel elaborates, "exile displays the Jews' choice to prove their devotion to the Jewish faith through a martyr's death. Kiddush ha-Shem . . . , the traditional Jewish concept of martyrdom, represents the Jews' failure to offer armed resistance to their persecutors and actively defend themselves."[36] In this spirit, the tank corps of the Israel Defense Forces for years conducted its swearing-in ceremony on the top of Masada; Israeli schools and youth movements regularly have made pilgrimages to the ancient fortress; and the synagogue discovered within Masada's ruins became a favorite site among tourists for Bar and Bat Mitzvah celebrations.

The persecutions of 1096 have hardly evoked a similar popular concern; yet I believe that the Masada complex and myth can enrich the elucidation of their significance in Jewish historiography. We remember both 1096 and Masada as singular expressions of Jewish heroism, when outnumbered bands of Jews slaughtered themselves rather than surrender to their enemies. In either case, those responsible for our memories of these events—the survivors of the pogroms, on the one hand, the first-century Jewish historian Josephus, on the other—themselves capitulated before their attackers and undoubtedly used their chronicles to explain their own behavior as much as to record historical information. Both narrative traditions experienced long periods of relative neglect before evoking a new, intense interest among modern Jewish readers. In the case of Masada, as Ben-Yehuda and Zerubavel have demonstrated, the narrative tradition has been consciously edited, reformulated, and exploited in Israeli society in order to nurture commitment to national ideals; resulting popular concern and debate have in turn generated diverse alternative or "counter-commemorative" narratives, even concerted efforts at "myth-wrecking," which compete for acceptance in Israeli collective memory.[37]

Our own study has revealed a similar phenomenon in the case of modern historiography on the persecutions of 1096. The first generations of modern Jewish scholars used the plight of Ashkenazic Jewry during the crusade to highlight both noble and deplorable aspects of the German Jewish experience, and thus to promote their own quasi-messianic vision of a cultural symbiosis. During and after the Holocaust, Israeli historians presented an opposing interpretation of these events, which transformed the self-sacrificing piety of the martyrs and their heirs from primitive barbarism into glorious achievement; it bespoke that "which was, ultimately, most formative and decisive in the development of the character of the Jewish people throughout history."[38] Baer and company, we might suggest, not only revised their predecessors' evaluation of 1096 but also defended the exemplary character of its martyrs against the disparaging challenge of the Masada myth. And, finally, the present generation has rescrutinized these and other milestones of Jewish history, challenging regnant assumptions, rethinking the relationship between historical event and text, and perhaps contributing to what the social scientist would term myth-wrecking. Nonetheless, we conclude with the observation that, while the significance of the persecutions of 1096 might vary in the wake of current research and while the glamour of its *qiddush ha-Shem* may appear to have abated, our conference testifies that their rightful claim to the historian's attention has not diminished.

NOTES

1. A. Neubauer and M. Stern, eds., *Hebräische Berichte über die Juden-verfolgungen während der Kreuzzüge*, Quellen der Geschichte der Juden in Deutschland 2 (Berlin, 1892), 8; English translation by Shlomo Eidelberg, *The Jews and the Crusaders: The Hebrew Chronicles of the First and Second Crusades* (Madison, Wisc., 1977), 33.

2. For an enumeration of the extant *piyyutim*, see Avraham Grossman, "Shorashav shel Qiddush ha-Shem be- Ashkenaz ha-Qedumah," in *Sanctity in Life and Martyrdom: Studies in Memory of Amir Yekutiel*, ed. Isaiah M. Gafni and Aviezer Ravitzky (Jerusalem, 1992), 102–103, nn. 7–9.

3. On the composition and interrelationship of these three texts, see, above all, Isaiah Sonne, "Nouvel examen des trois rélations hebräiques sur les persécutions de 1096," *Revue des études juives* 96 (1933): 137–152, and "Which Is the Earlier Account of the Persecutions during the First Crusade" [Hebrew], *Zion*, n.s. 12 (1947–1948): 74–81; Yitzhak Baer, "Gezerat TaTN"U" [Hebrew], in *Sefer Asaf*, ed. M. D. Cassuto et al. (Jerusalem, 1953), 126–40; Robert Chazan, "The Hebrew First-Crusade Chronicles," *Revue des études juives* 133 (1974): 235–254, and "The Hebrew First-Crusade Chronicles: Further Reflections," *Association for Jewish Studies Review* 3 (1978): 79–98; and Anna Sapir Abulafia, "The Interrelationship between the Hebrew Chronicles of the First Crusade," *Journal of Semitic Studies* 27 (1982): 221–239.

4. Cf. the opposing viewpoints of Haim Hillel Ben-Sasson, "Li-Mgamot ha-Khronografiah ha-Yehudit shel Yemei ha-Beinayim u-Vaʿayoteha," in idem, *Continuity and Variety*, ed. Joseph R. Hacker (Tel Aviv, 1984), 379–410, 485–487; and Yosef Hayim Yerushalmi, "Clio and the Jews: Reflections on Jewish Historiography in the Sixteenth Century," in *American Academy for Jewish Research Jubilee Volume*, ed. Salo W. Baron and Isaac E. Barzilay, 2 vols. (Jerusalem, 1980), 2:607–638, and *Zakhor: Jewish History and Jewish Memory* (Seattle, 1982), ch. 2.

5. See, for example, Simon Schwarzfuchs, "The Place of the Crusades in Jewish History" [Hebrew], in *Culture and Society in Medieval Jewry: Studies Dedicated to the Memory of Haim Hillel Ben-Sasson*, ed. Menachem Ben-Sasson et al. (Jerusalem, 1989), 251–269; Jeremy Cohen, "Recent Historiography on the Medieval Church and the Decline of European Jewry," in *Popes, Teachers, and Canon Law in the Middle Ages: Essays in Honor of Brian Tierney*, ed. James Ross Sweeney and Stanley Chodorow (Ithaca, N.Y., 1989), 251–262; Grossman, "Shorashav shel Qiddush ha-Shem," 100–105. See also Kenneth R. Stow, "Ha-Keneisiyyah ve-Historyografyah Neutralit," in *Studies in Historiography: Collected Essays*, ed. Joseph Salmon et al. (Jerusalem, 1987), 101–115.

6. Haim Hillel Ben-Sasson, *A History of the Jewish People* (London, 1976), 414.

7. Cecil Roth, *A Short History of the Jewish People*, rev. ed. (London, 1969), 185.

8. Patrick J. Geary, *Phantoms of Remembrance: Memory and Oblivion at the End of the First Millennium* (Princeton, 1994). Some consideration of the tradition in question appears in Robert Chazan, *In the Year 1096: The First Crusade and the Jews* (Philadeophia, 1996).

9. Jeremy Cohen, "*Gezerot Tatnu*: Martyrdom and Martyrology in the Hebrew Chronicles of 1096" [Hebrew], *Zion*, n.s. 59 (1994): 169–208, and "The Hebrew Chronicles of the First Crusade in Their Christian Cultural

Context," in *Juden und Christen zur Zeit der Kreuzzüge*, ed. Alfred Haverkamp, Vorträge und Forschungen 47 (Sigmaringen, 1999), 17–34.

10. Jonathan Riley-Smith, *The First Crusade and the Idea of Crusading* (London, 1986).

11. Schwarzfuchs, "The Place of the Crusades," 266–267.

12. Heinrich Graetz, *Geschichte der Juden von den ältesten Zeiten bis auf die Gegenwart*, vol. 6 (Leipzig, 1861), ch. 4; Moritz Güdemann, *Geschichte der Erziehungswesens und der Cultur der abendländischen Juden während des Mittelalters und der neueren Zeit*, 3 vols. (1880–1888; reprint, Amsterdam, 1966), 1:127 ff.; Simon Dubnow, *Weltgeschichte des jüdisches Volkes*, 10 vols. (Berlin, 1925–1930), 4:271 ff.

13. Güdemann, *Geschichte der Erziehungswesens*, 1:127–128.

14. See n. 5 above.

15. Salo Wittmayer Baron, *A Social and Religious History of the Jews*, 2d ed., 18 vols. (New York, 1952–1983), 4:89 ff.

16. Sidney Painter, *A History of the Middle Ages, 284–1500* (New York, 1953), 219.

17. Yitzhak Baer, *Galut*, trans. Robert Warshow (New York, 1947), 122.

18. Carl Erdmann, *The Origin of the Idea of Crusade*, trans. Marshall W. Baldwin and Walter Goffart (Princeton, 1977).

19. Yitzhak Baer, "The Religious-Social Tendency of Sefer Hassidim" [Hebrew], *Zion*, n.s. 3 (1937): 3.

20. Jacob Katz, *Exclusiveness and Tolerance: Studies in Jewish-Gentile Relations in Medieval and Modern Times* (1961; reprint, New York, 1962), pts. 1–2; Haim Hillel Ben-Sasson, "Mavo le-Toledot 'Am Yisra'el," in idem, *Continuity and Variety*, 342–349.

21. Katz, Exclusiveness and Tolerance, 90.

22. Baer, "Gezerat TaTN"U," 126.

23. Benzion Dinur, *Israel in the Diaspora* [Hebrew], 2 vols. in 10 pts. (Tel Aviv, 1958–1972), 2, 1:4.

24. Ben-Sasson, *History of the Jewish People*, 414.

25. Among others, see David Myers, *Re-Inventing the Jewish Past: European Jewish Intellectuals and the Zionist Return to History* (New York, 1995); and Steven Kepnes, ed., *Interpreting Judaism in a Postmodern Age* (New York, 1996).

26. Robert Chazan, *European Jewry and the First Crusade* (Berkeley, 1987), and "The Facticity of Medieval Narrative: A Case Study of the Hebrew First-Crusade Narratives," *Association for Jewish Studies Review* 16 (1991): 31–56; Grossman, "Shorashav shel Qiddush ha-Shem."

27. Sonne, "Which Is the Earlier Account," 76.

28. Ivan G. Marcus, "From Politics to Martyrdom: Shifting Paradigms in the Hebrew Narratives of the 1096 Crusade Riots," *Prooftexts* 2 (1982): 40–52.

29. Israel J. Yuval, "Vengeance and Damnation, Blood and Defamation: From Jewish Martyrdom to Blood Libel Accusations" [Hebrew], *Zion*, n.s. 58 (1993): 33–90.

30. See Mordechai Breuer, "The Historian's Imagination and Historical Truth" [Hebrew], *Zion*, n.s. 59 (1994): 317–324, at 318; and Ezra Fleischer, "Christian-Jewish Relations in the Middle Ages Distorted" [Hebrew], *Zion*, n.s. 59 (1994): 267–316.

31. Israel J. Yuval, "'The Lord Will Take Vengeance, Vengeance for His Temple'—Historia sine Ira et Studio" [Hebrew], *Zion*, n.s. 59 (1994): 351–414, 352, 395–396, 402.

32. Mary Minty, "*Kiddush ha-Shem* in German Christian Eyes in the Middle Ages" [Hebrew], *Zion*, n.s. 59 (1994): 209–266.

33. Ivan G. Marcus, "Mi-'Deus vult' li-'Retson ha-Bore'—Ide'ologyot Datiyyot Qitsoniyyot u-Metsi'ut Historit be-TaTN"U," paper delivered at conference of the Zalman Shazar Center for Jewish History, Jerusalem, May 1996.

34. Stewart Alsop, "The Masada Complex," *Newsweek*, 12 July 1971, 92, and "Again, the Masada Complex," *Newsweek*, 19 March 1973, 104.

35. Nachman Ben-Yehuda, *The Masada Myth: Collective Memory and Mythmaking in Israel* (Madison, Wisc., 1995), 294–295.

36. Yael Zerubavel, *Recovered Roots: Collective Memory in the Making of Israeli National Tradition* (Chicago, 1995), 19.

37. Among many others, see, for example, Robert Alter, "The Masada Complex," *Commentary* 56:1 (July 1973): 19–24; and Benjamin Z. Kedar, "Masada: The Myth and the Complex," *Jerusalem Quarterly* 24 (Summer 1982): 57–63.

38. Baer, "Gezerat TaTN"U," 140.

T W O

The Dynamics of Jewish
Renaissance and Renewal in
the Twelfth Century

IVAN G. MARCUS

These reflections on the dynamics of Jewish renaissance and renewal in the twelfth century are offered as a framework within which to place not only such important narratives as the Hebrew accounts of 1096, but also the various other creative achievements that different elites in the medieval Jewish and Christian cultures produced in the twelfth century. What Salo Baron called the lachrymose conception of Jewish history[1] correctly linked the dominant perspective of modern Jewish historians to an earlier one preserved in medieval Jewish chronicles. But most modern Jewish interpretations of medieval Jewish history missed the mark, not only, as Baron emphasized, by ignoring medieval Jewish self-government and political activism, but also by interpreting what medieval Jews remembered in the narratives and liturgical poems that they wrote as depictions only of Jewish passive suffering. Rather, such narratives portrayed symbolic acts in which Jews fashioned a positive religious identity for themselves under duress, offered as a model for how other Jews could live or die as Jews in a Christian society. Moreover, by reading these narratives as representations of violent Jewish-Christian interaction with the positivist assumption that what mattered about the narratives was ferreting out what happened, most modern Jewish historians accepted the medieval narratives not only as reflecting typical medieval Ashkenazic historical experience, but also as reliable factual accounts.

The narratives about 1096 are but one strand in a complex skein of cultural constructions that emerge for the most part in twelfth-century Europe and that are related to the European phenomenon sometimes referred to as "the renaissance of the twelfth century." By that I refer not only to Charles Homer Haskins's specific analysis of the recovery in the Christian schools of ancient texts and methods of learning, but also to the larger issues of change raised by such works as Richard Southern's *The Making of the Middle Ages*[2] and summarized in Robert Benson and Giles Constable's commemorative volume, *Renaissance and Renewal in the Twelfth Century*.[3] Perhaps there is a connection between the kinds of Christian culture that emerged in the twelfth century and the history of Jewish-Christian relations. Such a link has been proposed as a consequence of a renewed emphasis on rationalism in the schools. Especially influential was the pioneering essay by Amos Funkenstein, originally published in Hebrew, summarized in English in *Viator* in 1971, and now available in an expanded translation as "Changes in the Patterns of Christian Anti-Jewish Polemics in the 12th Century."[4] To this seminal essay, one should add Jeremy Cohen's comprehensive and very stimulating analysis, "Towards a Functional Classification of Jewish Anti-Christian Polemic in the High Middles Ages,"[5] and Anna Sapir Abulafia's study, *Christians and Jews in the Twelfth-Century Renaissance*.[6] Abulafia has analyzed in detail the rationalist features of the Latin renaissance of the twelfth century and posited a causal link between it and the emergence of irrational accusations against European Jews. Her work builds on that of students of anti-Jewish polemics and of medieval Jewish attacks, notably, the important work of Gavin Langmuir and the studies of Robert Moore.[7]

Ironically, Jewish historians have posited a peaceful period of coexistence between Jews and Christians precisely during the early Middle Ages, which Southern and others characterized as an age of warfare and brutality. In contrast, as Christian society and culture became more urbanized, peaceful, and refined, from the eleventh century on, Jews confronted the Crusade riots in the Rhineland, followed by allegations that they ritually killed Christian children, used Christian blood in their celebrations, stabbed the consecrated Host, and endangered Christian society by practicing usury and by poisoning wells or other sinful acts. A superficial comparison might suggest that just as the Christian Middle

Ages were getting "made," to use Southern's idiom, the Jewish Middle Ages were getting "unmade." For when we compare the flourishing Christian culture, on the one hand, and growing Jewish insecurity, on the other, it seems that the curves of Christian security and Jewish insecurity were moving in opposite directions and crossed sometime in the twelfth century.

To add to this picture of two apparent reversals of fortune, however, several scholars have noted that Jewish culture, too, flourished precisely in the twelfth century, not only in northern France and Germany, but also in southern France and in Muslim lands. One wonders how Hebrew and Latin creativity are related to each other and how both might have affected Jewish-Christian social relations. That there was a flourish of Jewish culture in the twelfth century was pointed out by Salo Baron in 1957. In his broad historical survey he explicitly alluded to the renaissance of the twelfth century and noted, "there is no question of the great economic and cultural upsurge of Spanish and other European Jewries in the course of the twelfth century."[8] A bit later, in a Hebrew lecture delivered in Jerusalem in 1969, Haim Hillel Ben-Sasson called attention to the creativity of the twelfth century in Christian Europe and indicated that even though Jews suffered during the Crusades in the north and from the Almohad invasion in southern Spain, they still had been creative in various ways by shaping a new chronography/historiography; Tosafism, that is, the dialectical glossators of the Babylonian Talmud; the ascetic German-Pietist movement known as *hasidei ashkenaz;* as well as plain-sense Bible exegesis, all in the north, and the philosophy of Maimonides, Hebrew courtier poetry, Hebrew grammar, and philological biblical exegesis, all in the Muslim south. Apart from drawing a brief comparison with Haskins, Ben-Sasson was trying to revisit the familiar twin emphases in nineteenth-century Jewish historiography on Jewish persecution and culture by suggesting that the latter existed either despite or even because of the former. The Jewish cultural creativity of the twelfth century was a response to an oppressive challenge, and Jews rose to the occasion at the same time Christian culture flourished nearby. He did not press the implications of this comparative approach.[9]

Focusing on the relationship among various medieval Jewish cultural developments and the place of law in Jewish culture, Isadore Twersky also pointed to the flowering of different modes of culture that appeared in separate centers in the twelfth century. He referred to them as the meta-halakhic disciplines of the plain sense of Scripture, the study of philosophy, as in Maimonides, of Qabbalah, of the Tosafist Talmud glossators, and the German Hasidim or Pietists. By meta-halakhic, Twersky meant that each mode made a claim that something other than religious practice was at the center of Jewish spirituality, even though, as he put it, medieval "Judaism is halakhocentric."[10] Although he did not directly refer to Haskins's *Renaissance of the Twelfth Century*, he did cite Stephan Kuttner's classic, *Harmony from Dissonance: An Interpretation of Medieval Canon Law*,[11] and Giles Constable's important essay, "Twelfth Century Spirituality and the Late Middle Ages."[12]

Like Twersky's article, Ephraim Urbach's masterly study of the northern French Tosafist glossators of the twelfth century also pointed to the Christian cultural context, this time the similarities between the Roman and canon law compilations of the eleventh and twelfth centuries, such as Gratian's *Decretum*, and the commentaries of Jewish dialecticians in Champagne. Without really pressing the matter, he suggested parallel cultural developments rather than any direct influence in either direction.[13] This lead has not been followed up, even though there is evidence of such an awareness among those who opposed some aspects of the Tosafists. Thus, as Yitzhaq Baer noted, the Latin term *dialectica* appears in Hebrew characters in the German Pietist work, *Sefer Hasidim* (Book of the Pietists), written in late-twelfth- or early-thirteenth-century Germany.[14] Nor, for that matter, have Yitzhaq Baer and Haym Soloveitchik's comparisons of the religious sensibilities of the German Pietists with twelfth- and thirteenth-century Christian spirituality been pursued further.[15]

Robert Chazan has emphasized the similarities between Jewish and Christian cultural vitality in the eleventh and twelfth centuries and explicitly pointed to certain comparisons between them. His emphasis challenged primarily the historiographical point that the existence of Jewish creativity belies the convention that 1096 was a catastrophic watershed in Jewish culture leading to a decline. But Chazan also referred to such Jewish elites in the twelfth century as the Tosafists, the Bible exegetes of northern France, and the German Pietists in the Rhineland, and suggested that Jewish culture was much closer to Christian culture than had been thought before. In relation to the early

Qabbalah in Provence, Moshe Idel wrote that it was but one "arena in which the great renaissance of twelfth-century Jewish learning took place. . . ."[16]

Among many problems still to be considered is an analysis of the interrelationships, not only between the Christian cultural revival and Jewish-Christian security, but also between newer modes of Jewish and Christian letters, on the one hand, and changes in Jewish-Christian social relations, on the other. These are complex matters, but it would be helpful to seek inclusive perspectives that could enable us to examine the various strands of research about the Jewish and Christian cultures and their social relations as they changed over time.

We should suspend a predisposition to view medieval Jewish history first and foremost as the story of growing insecurity from the twelfth century on, and instead compare Jewish culture and the revival that scholars have mapped out for Christian culture. This surely includes the schools, but also the proliferation of new religious orders and reformed instances of older ones, such as the Cistercians recommitting to the Rule of St. Benedict. Perhaps we can find a basis for comparison between the two cultures that also is related to how members of both interacted in the society they inhabited together. Identifying a dynamic pattern that obtained in twelfth-century Europe would offer us several points of comparison between Jews and Christians and possibly even suggest why, if it is the case, the security curves crossed then.

Recently I have tried to work out in some detail a case study of Jewish ritual revival and transformation in medieval Germany and France. The Jewish elementary school initiation rite selectively recaptured earlier Jewish elements and themes and appropriated Christian theological motifs and rites to fashion a Jewish anti-Christian social polemic. In *Rituals of Childhood,* I suggest that other studies of public ritual and ceremony, gestures and celebrations, as well as narratives, images, and other sources, may offer a way of bridging the gap that usually exists between the study of Jewish and Christian comparative cultural history and the study of Jewish-Christian social interactions.[17] I would like to look further at the comparative cultural side of the picture. It seems to me that a similar dynamic is at work in many of the Jewish cultural movements that emerged in the twelfth century, not only in northern Europe, but also in the south and Muslim east as well. This dynamic exhibits the process of recovering ancient traditions and of reshaping them in a twelfth-century context familiar from Christian culture, be it in the schools or in the new monastic movements and thinking.

The coincidence in both Latin Christendom and medieval Jewish culture of a similar dynamic of retrieving ancient sources of authority and adapting them to new shared circumstances resulted paradoxically in two opposite trends in Jewish-Christian social relations. One trend was an increase in the possibilities for individuals to make new choices among different religious groups. Such a choice might also include crossing over the boundary to join the other religious culture as a convert. The other trend, which occurred at the same time, and in some ways was stimulated by the dangers perceived in the first, involved an upsurge of each religious culture's sense of group solidarity and identity. This included an increased hostility toward members of the other camp. Even if both sides could not act out that hostility in equal measure, there are signs that it existed in both. Within this dynamic of revival and adaptation exhibited by several features of the Jewish and Christian cultures in the twelfth century, the peculiarities of a society at once more open to individual choices and yet more hostile become more understandable.

Consider the dimension of individual choice. Giles Constable has stressed the new individual will that colors much of twelfth-century Christian spirituality: "The twelfth century saw the emergence of a more subjective and individual concept of virtue, which was closely related to the voluntarism of its spirituality."[18] Caroline Bynum has noted that individual Christians now had more choices than before, as conflicts arose from revived modes competing with recent custom and tradition: scholastic with monastic, new monks with Benedictines, and so on. Such conflict presented individuals with new options for choosing among them, even if this is not the same thing as modern individualism.[19]

In some cases, members of one culture even found members of the other attractive, especially those of the opposite sex. This straying of individuals over the border could result not only in increased individual uncertainty and insecurity but also in collective insecurity. The individual's problem of decision making is found in evidence that some Jews hesitated before resisting persistent efforts to convert them, reflected in the ironic Hebrew narrative about Rabbi Faithful or Amnon of Mainz.[20]

And like Judah who became "Hermannus quondam Judaeus," some Jews did convert in the twelfth century.[21] In addition, several cases arise of Christian men becoming romantically involved with young Jewish women, as John Mundy observed. This is mentioned in Latin chronicles such as the *Annales Egmundani* from Germany in 1152, referring to a romance between a priest and a young Jewish woman;[22] in ecclesiastical cases, as at the Council of the Province of Canterbury, held in Oxford in 1222, which condemned to death a deacon who had converted to Judaism over a Jewish woman;[23] in *exempla,* such as those of Caesarius of Heisterbach's *Dialogus Miraculorum* from the early thirteenth century, which also depict some young Jewish women in romantic affairs with Christian clerics;[24] and in *responsa,* such as those of Rabbi Meir b. Barukh of Rothenburg, in the second half of the thirteenth century, which refer to instances of Jewish women becoming involved with Christian men.[25]

In addition to promoting more inner conflict, accompanied by individual choices, the revivals of early religious textual authorities also rehearsed the ancient sources of competition between Judaism and Christianity in antiquity. Members of each culture became more aware of themselves in contrast to the other. This awareness played a part in increasing the mutual distrust and hostility between both camps, even as it also increased some members' knowledge about and attraction to the other. Thus, a close examination of the Jewish cultural movements that appeared in twelfth-century Germany and northern France, as well as in southern France and Spain, reveals a dynamic or pattern of development similar to that renaissance and renewal of the twelfth century described by scholars like Haskins and Benson-Constable. Both cultures exhibit a dynamic of reaching back into earlier or ancient times for relatively neglected early sources and transforming the immediate cultural landscape by reviving and adapting ancient learning in a way that appears to be revolutionary but is actually conservative and revolutionary at the same time.

In the south, as Twersky has shown, the *Mishneh Torah,* Maimonides' Code of Jewish law completed around 1178, is not only a remarkable synthesis and reinterpretation of all of Jewish law within the Muslim-Jewish sphere, but also represents the culmination of the early medieval genre of law codification begun in eighth-century Baghdad.

Despite its originality as a synthetic treatment of Jewish law, arranged according to fourteen new categories, it recapitulates the sweep of the first book of Jewish law from late antiquity, the Mishnah of Rabbi Judah the Patriarch from around the year 200. In name and language and scope, Maimonides' *Mishneh Torah* is a revival of the Mishnah, and at the same time transformation of the Talmud, as well as the Geonic and Muslim-Spanish Jewish legal opinions and traditions. Like the Mishnah, the *Mishneh Torah* claims to be the exhaustive expression of rabbinic Oral Tradition. Like the Mishnah, the *Mishneh Torah* is written in classical rabbinic Hebrew—Mishnaic Hebrew, in fact; and like the Mishnah, the *Mishneh Torah* is comprehensive in scope, including a review of the complex but obsolete laws of the Temple and Purities found in the Mishnah but not in other Jewish codes since the third century. It is presented as the Mishnah for Maimonides' time. That achievement was carried out by a Spanish Jew who had been exiled in his youth by the Almohad invasion, which drove Maimonides' family from Cordoba, first to Fez, and then to Fustat, Egypt.

A similar pattern or dynamic is found in the earliest traces of the theosophical Qabbalah which emerged in another twelfth-century Jewish community, Provence. Claiming to be ancient, the early Qabbalah was written down for the first time in the twelfth century, perhaps to refute the Maimonidean claim in Provence that esoteric Jewish truth lay in a philosophical approach to Scripture, perhaps for reasons not yet clear. Whatever the immediate causes of the appearance of the written forms of the theosophical Qabbalah in twelfth-century Provence, some of the traditions and motifs, including a theurgic approach to a multifaceted Godhead, were in part derived from German Pietist traditions that held the Godhead to be compound. Pietists in a state of purity were thought further to affect it theurgically, as Elliot Wolfson's painstaking research has demonstrated. The Rhineland Pietists, in turn, were reviving and developing ancient ascetic customs and theological motifs, some possibly attested in Philo of Alexandria, that they claimed had been transmitted for generations from southern Italy and before that from the east. As in the case of Maimonides' Code, a creative transformation occurred in twelfth-century Provence, which was at least in part a revival and in part a reshaping of earlier lore.

In the north, the German-Jewish cases include the collecting of local customs, fashioning the historiographic narratives about 1096, and the writings of the German Pietists. A northern French case is the dialectical Talmud glossators or Tosafists. Although the degree to which each of these is a revival of ancient lore or an innovation has been hotly debated, I think that they are both. That is, the dynamic of revival and transformation which is claimed for Latin Christian culture in the twelfth century is exhibited in these cases as well. The German-Jewish examples look and claim to be conservative in focus, and they are, but they are also adaptations of older material in a new setting within Christian Europe. Similarly, the French Tosafists see themselves as belonging to a new time, and yet they are reviving an ancient mode of rabbinic discourse.

Consider the Rhineland. The culture of early Ashkenaz began in the Rhineland towns of Mainz and Worms, to which Jewish merchant families migrated from Italy and northern France in the tenth century. Settlements are reflected in Jewish sources only toward the end of the tenth century. Jews in northern France who were moved to continue their elementary education went off to school in the east, to Mainz and Worms, as Rashi of Troyes did in his youth in the 1060s. At the end of the eleventh century, first in Mainz before 1096 and continuing in Speyer afterwards, the four sons of Rabbi Makhir, the great grand-nephews of Rabbenu Gershom ben Judah of Mainz (d. 1028), collected the local Jewish customs of the Rhineland. As Avraham Grossman has shown, these corpora represent the accumulated customary laws of the early Rhineland Jewish subculture, their *consuetudines*, but some of them went back to early Byzantine southern Italy and Muslim Iraq, others to ancient Palestine. These collections, in turn, were copied and appropriated by Jewish legal authorities from the twelfth century on, adding to the self-image of Rhineland Jews as the bearers of ancient customs and lore.

The dynamic to recover and collect recent, ancient, and early medieval traditions is also reflected in the way the narrators and editors of the events of 1096 went about their work, and anticipates the same dynamic cultural process of collecting and transforming various early traditions that we see in the Rhineland from the middle of the twelfth century by the Jewish Pietists of Germany (*hasidei ashkenaz*). The narratives of 1096 reflect the events of Christian attacks and Jewish political and martyrological responses, but in particularly stylized ways. For many years historians have argued over the reliability of these narratives and their details. It is clear to me that despite their general reliability in preserving memories of actual carnage and of different ways Jews took their own lives or those of their families as sacrifices to Judaism, the texts that have come down are literary constructions.

To get the full sense of this, one need only read David Nirenberg's *Communities of Violence*,[26] which includes a new study of the fourteenth-century Shepherd's Crusade of 1320 and the Lepers' Plot of 1321, for which both archival and Jewish chronicle writings exist, to see how the archives challenge many details and constructions in the narratives. Would that we had archival data on the events of 1096, but it simply is not possible to treat literary historical narratives, shaped by literary motifs and allusions, as are the 1096 texts, as though they were archival records. Instead, we have to consider the ways the narratives are shaped and constructed, and how the narrators made sense of their informants and written sources, which in turn depended on witnesses, reports, and interpretations at every level. For even field workers, as anthropologists know, interpret what they see when they see it. When the narrators of the three accounts wrote them down, they made use of ancient typologies and traditions and applied them to the material in front of them, omitting whatever did not apply. They shaped them, as Israel Yuval and Jeremy Cohen have shown, in an anti-Christian adaptation of Jewish and Christian motifs, that is, the same process of cultural subversion that I illustrated in *Rituals of Childhood*.[27]

Among the ancient traditions that reappear in the 1096 account of martyrdom is the tradition of ancient Jerusalem Temple priests committing suicide and homicide when the Temple or holy city is burning. As David Goodblatt and Avraham Grossman have argued, this tradition, as well as the acts of homicide and suicide remembered from Masada in 73, are attested in first-century sources and were transmitted in literary traditions to southern Italy and the Rhineland.[28] Because Jews in Ashkenaz did not differentiate between what they considered sacred literary models and Jewish legal texts, they acted out the literary typology of the Temple Priests which made homicide and suicide a religious commandment, not a religious problem. Haym Soloveitchik's attempt to accommodate this peculiarity of Ashkenazic German mentality to the norms of rabbinic legal traditions about suicide and martyrdom are anachronistic and unnecessary.

Although the anti-Jewish riots of the spring and summer of 1096 did not destroy the Jewish communities of the Rhineland, they did hit especially hard those at Mainz, already hurt in 1084 by a fire that broke out in the Jewish quarter, and at Worms. It is significant that Speyer, which mainly survived the killing, became an important center of Jewish culture in the twelfth and early thirteenth centuries. In this respect, there was a significant difference in the Rhineland after 1096, despite other continuities. And Mainz Jews who survived in Speyer became the ancestors of the German Pietists. The German-Jewish Pietists traced their lineage back to northern Italy, although their Greek family name, Qalonimos, indicates southern Italian Byzantine roots. The first written sources seem to have been composed in the middle of the twelfth century and with greater volume after 1217, when master Judah the Pietist died and his student R. Eleazar of Worms wrote hundreds of pages of a special kind of numerical exegesis. This process of writing down and transforming ancient and early medieval lore was part of a conservative trend found in the Rhineland Jewish elites from the end of the eleventh century, which includes writing down local customs by the sons of Makhir and assembling and editing the narratives about 1096.

German Pietists claimed that their traditions were "ancestral customs" (*minhag avoteinu*), the early customs of Ashkenaz and southern Italy, and they in fact did include lore and practices going back to ancient Palestine. These traditions did not emerge in writing until after the Tosafists had appeared. Haym Soloveitchik's proposal that the Pietists' world view can be understood as a response to the Tosafists' scholastic challenge is correct, but primarily because it makes sense of the timing of the writing down of the German Pietists' traditions. The Tosafists' appearance alone does not explain the content and substance of most of Pietism. For example, one can claim that the Pietists' emphasis that Torah study should be of the practical codified laws of behavior, not dialectic, is a reaction to the Tosafists' emphasis on dialectic. But the Pietists were not inventing this curriculum as a consequence of the Tosafists' insisting on dialectic. Rather, the Pietists were reiterating the older method of practical study that had been the custom in early Ashkenaz, which the Tosafists had challenged by reviving the even more ancient method of dialectic that characterizes the ancient Talmud itself.[29] Like the Tosafists, the German Hasidim were recovering, adapting, and writing

down for the first time older traditions, including such departures from
Talmudic law as requiring Jews who sin to confess their sins to another
Jew of a higher spiritual status, a practice we find in the *Manual of
Discipline* in the Dead Sea Scrolls, or the expectation that small children
of one or two years old fast all day on the Day of Atonement.

This last practice is one ancient pietistic custom among many that
can be shown to have been transmitted to Europe from ancient sources.
The Mishnah of Rabbi Judah the Patriarch, published in the beginning
of the third century in Palestine, states (Yoma 8:4): "We do not make
young children (*tinoqot*) fast on the Day of Atonement, but we get them
used to doing so one year or two before [they are of age] so that they may
become accustomed to [doing] the commandments." Is this prohibition
a theoretical matter or is it intended to criticize and oppose an existing
practice in Palestine where the Mishnah was written? As Yitzhaq Gilat
has shown, there was an ancient Palestinian tradition that even very
small children should fast, probably based on the verse in Leviticus
23:29 about the Day of Atonement: "Indeed, any person (kol ʾish) who
does not practice self-denial [i.e., fasting] throughout that day shall be
cut off from his kin."[30] The practice was in force among Samaritans, for
example.[31] In the early rabbinic legal collection called the *Tosefta* (Yom
ha-Kippurim 5:2), there is an explicit tradition that reports about the
first-century Palestinian sage, "Shammai the Elder did not want to feed
his son (on the Day of Atonement) and the other rabbis issued a decree
forcing him to so with both hands."[32]

The existence of an ancient Palestinian-Jewish custom that very
small children should be required to fast on the Day of Atonement,
which the Mishnah implies is to be enforced no earlier than one or two
years before one reaches the majority of age thirteen, is reflected in an
early medieval compilation of laws and customs called *Masekhet Soferim*.
There we find the following: "It also was an accepted custom in Jerusalem [for Jews] to train their young sons and daughters on a fast day,
one year olds [to fast] half a day, and two year olds, all day. . . ."[33] Although six out of seven manuscripts contain this reading of the text,
emphasizing age one and two, not one or two years before the age of
thirteen, that is, eleven and twelve, the editor of the book ignored them
and put in their stead a single manuscript witness that agreed with the
Mishnah, that is, that one trains a child to fast at age eleven or twelve,

one or two years before his majority. In criticizing the editor for privileging the harmonizing single manuscript over the six that disagreed, Saul
Lieberman noted in his review that the editor had nearly wiped out an
ancient custom in the body of the text but fortunately had preserved it
in the variant readings.[34]

The practice of young children fasting appears again in the Rhineland, among the German Pietists and among some Jews in Normandy
who were influenced by German Pietist ascetic traditions.[35] Jews in the
town of Pontoise, which was in royal France but near Normandy, sent
a query to Rabbenu Jacob of Ramerupt, known later as Rabbenu Tam
(d. 1171), the preeminent Tosafist of the twelfth century: "May our master
teach us further. Those [Jews] who serve God have become numerous,
they who separate themselves in purity and pietism from other Jews, and
do not want to feed their small children on the Day of Atonement, even
though they have not yet reached the age of education."[36] In his *responsum*, Rabbenu Tam criticizes these Jews for not feeding their small children and affirms that their practice was contrary to Talmudic law, his
standard, as indeed it was. Here, as in many other cases, the German
Pietists revived, preserved, and adapted ancient or early medieval practices and wrote them down only in the mid-twelfth century.

Why so late? This brings us again to the Tosafists or Talmud glossators of northern France, whose work so resembles the methods of
scholastic theology and of Roman and canon law, and of whom
Rabbenu Tam was the foremost figure. Compared to the way the Talmud
had been studied in the schools of Mainz and Worms in the eleventh
century, the Tosafists' use of dialectic looks and is revolutionary. But in
fact they were not inventing a new method of study in twelfth-century
Europe. Rather, they were recovering and adapting the ancient method
of comparing earlier legal sources and resolving imputed contradictions
in them by making distinctions, the method that characterizes the
Babylonian Talmud itself. Is the Tosafist method, then, new? Yes and no.
When it appeared after hundreds of years of opposition and neglect, first
by the early medieval Geonic masters of Baghdad, and later by reliance
in early Ashkenaz on local oral tradition and practice grounded in custom, the Tosafist emphasis on books, dialectic, logical consistency, and
reason seemed a threatening innovation. The motto "truth versus custom" comes to mind.[37]

In some ways, as Ephraim Kanarfogel has noted, the German
Pietists prior to the advent of the Tosafists were a Jewish monastic culture in the Rhineland. It was largely based on their *minhagim* or customs
(*consuetudines*), grounded in special running commentaries on texts
such as Scripture, the Talmud, the liturgy, and on ascetic practices of
pietism and atonement. The Tosafists, in turn, resembled the Latin
scholastics, the schoolmen who challenged the regnant monastic religious culture. The appearance in writing of the Pietists' works in the
mid-twelfth century should be compared to the reactionary monastic responses of figures like Peter the Venerable or Bernard of Clairvaux, who
spoke for the earlier monastic culture that tried to persist in competition
with the legacy of the Peter Abelards.[38] Both cultures, then, underwent
a similar transformation in the twelfth century from a more monastic or
synagogue- and chapel-based practice, grounded in custom, to a more
school-based, dialectical one, grounded in reason and logic, with which
the older culture now had to come to terms.[39]

This dynamic process of recovery and transformation made waves
in twelfth-century Ashkenaz. The Tosafits upset the German Pietists
enough that they began to write down their traditions which they held
to be ancient and ancestral. Several of the Pietists' elaborate *exempla*
deal with the Pietist's inner struggle between competing loyalties and
principles. Now, German Jews had new choices as never before, including going to France to follow a Tosafist master, or following German
Pietism with or without any exposure to Tosafism in Germany. Many
Jewish students now went west to France, in contrast to Rashi, who had
gone east to Mainz from Troyes two generations or more earlier. A
German-Jewish student en route to Champagne and Rabbenu Tam
might well have agreed with the sentiments expressed in the Latin
poem, "Hospita in Gallia," that begins: "Vale, dulcis patria, suavis
suevorum Suevia, salve dilecta Francia, philosophorum curia! Suscipe
disciplinum in te peregrinum, quem post dierum circulum remittes
Socratinum!" ("Dear my fatherland, to you, sweet Swabian Swabia
adieu, beloved France to which I roam, all hail Philosophy's your home!
Take a foreign student up to your bosom, please, and when the time's
ripe, send him back well trained like Socrates!").[40]

In addition to having new choices, however, the recovery of ancient
pietistic traditions by the martyrs of 1096 and their interpreters, as well

as by the German Pietists, increased some Jews' self-image as a pure and holy people who must resist contact with impure Christians.[41] The imagery and rhetoric of the ancient and early medieval "*Toledot Yeshu*" or Life of Jesus traditions, those Aramaic and Hebrew parodies of the Gospels that circulated throughout the Middle Ages and depicted Jesus and Mary in the most unflattering terms, permeate the narratives about 1096 and inform the German Pietists' writings as well.[42] Jews are pure, Christians are polluting and are to be avoided unless a Jew is in a position of relative strength and power, a case of "right order" applied to Jewish-Christian social relations from the Jewish side.[43] Choices, yes, but also heightened solidarity and antipathy in both camps.

Thus, an increase in individual choice among religious groups, including those not in one's own culture—Judah-Hermannus became a Premonstratensian monk—and an intensification of group solidarity played upon each other. This complex process of choice and attempted repression, involving hesitation, attraction, contrition, or anger, accompanied the proliferation of cultural revivals and transformations in both Jewish and Christian cultures in twelfth-century Europe. The shared dynamic in both Latin and Hebrew cultures contributed to a stronger sense of the individual will and thereby to increased religious defensiveness and hostility, both of which are central features of the renaissance and renewal of twelfth-century spirituality and society.

NOTES

1. Robert Liberles, *Salo Wittmayer Baron: Architect of Jewish History* (New York, 1995), 159–160; cf. William Chester Jordan, *The French Monarchy and the Jews* (Philadelphia, 1989), 20.

2. R. W. Southern, *The Making of the Middle Ages* (New Haven, 1953).

3. Robert L. Benson and Giles Constable, eds., *Renaissance and Renewal in the Twelfth Century* (Cambridge, Mass., 1979). See also Giles Constable, *The Reformation of the Twelfth Century* (Cambridge, 1996).

4. *Zion* 33 (1968): 125–144; "Basic Types of Christian Anti-Jewish Polemics," *Viator* 2 (1971): 373–382; reprint in Funkenstein, *Perceptions of Jewish History* (Berkeley, 1993), 172–219, with a new introduction.

5. In *Religionsgespräche im Mittelalter*, ed. Bernard Lewis and Friedrich Niewöhner (Wiesbaden, 1992), 93–114.

6. (London, 1995).

7. Gavin Langmuir, *Toward a Definition of Antisemitism* (Berkeley, 1990); R. I. Moore, *The Formation of a Persecuting Society* (Oxford, 1987).

8. Salo W. Baron, *A Social and Religious History of the Jews*, 18 vols. (New York, 1952–1983), 4:311.

9. Haim Hillel Ben-Sasson, "The Uniqueness of the Jewish People According to the Twelfth Century Figures" [Hebrew], *Peraqim* 2 (1974): 145–218, esp. 145–150, where Haskins is mentioned in n. 1; also his "On the Tendency of Medieval Jewish Chronography and its Problems" [Hebrew], in Haim Hillel Ben-Sasson, *Rezef U-Temurah* (Tel Aviv, 1984), 384–385.

10. Isadore Twersky, "Religion and Law," in *Religion in a Religious Age*, ed. S. D. Goitein (Cambridge, Mass., 1974), 70.

11. (Latrobe, Pa., 1960).

12. *Medieval and Renaissance Studies* 5 (1971): 27–60.

13. Ephraim E. Urbach, *Ba'alei ha-Tosafot*, 2 vols. (Jerusalem, 1980), 17–31.

14. R. Judah b. Samuel, he-hasid, *Sefer Hasidim*, ed. Jehuda Wistinetzki (Frankfurt am Main, 1924), par. 752, 1931; Yitzhaq Baer, "The Social-Religious Tendencies of *Sefer Hasidim*" [Hebrew], *Zion* 3 (1938): 11.

15. Haym Soloveitchik, "Three Themes from the *Sefer Hasidim*," *AJS Review* 1 (1976): 311–357.

16. Robert Chazan, *European Jewry and the First Crusade* (Berkeley, 1987), 194; Moshe Idel, *Kabbalah: New Perspectives* (New Haven, 1988), 251.

17. (New Haven, 1996).

18. Constable, "Twelfth-Century Spirituality," 35.

19. Caroline Walker Bynum, "Did the Twelfth Century Discover the Individual?" in her *Jesus as Mother: Studies in the Spirituality of the High Middle Ages* (Berkeley, 1982), 88–89; Colin Morris, *The Discovery of the Individual*, 1050–1200 (New York, 1972).

20. See Ivan G. Marcus, "Une communauté pieuse et le doute," *Annales: Histoire, Sciences Sociales* 5 (September–October 1994): 1031–1047.

21. *Hermannus Quondam Judaeus: Opusculum de Conversione Sua*, Gerlinde Niemeyer, MGH Quellen zur Geschichte des Mittelalters 4 (Munich, 1963); trans. Karl F. Morrison, *Conversion and Text* (Charlottesville, 1992), 39–113. R. Jacob b. Meir, *Sefer ha-Yashar* (Berlin, 1898), 45 (par. 25), refers to twenty converts to Christianity in Paris alone in the mid-twelfth century.

22. John Mundy, *Europe in the High Middle Ages, 1150–1309* (New York, 1973), 210; *Annales Egmundani*, ed. G. H. Pertz, MGH, Scriptores 16, Anno 1152, 458, cited in Baron, *Social and Religious History*, 4:148.

23. Cecil Roth, *A History of the Jews in England*, 3d ed. (Oxford, 1964), 41. See Frederick William Maitland, "The Deacon and the Jewess; or, Apostasy at Common Law," in H. A. L Fisher, ed., *The Collected Papers of Frederick William Maitland*, vol. 1 (Cambridge, 1911), 385–406.

24. *Dialogus miraculorum*, ed. Josephus Strange, 2 vols. (Köln, 1851; reprint, Ridgewood, N.J., 1966), bk. 2, ch. 23–26; Ivan G. Marcus, "Jews and Christians Imagining the Other in Medieval Europe," *Prooftexts* 15 (1995): 222, 226 n. 40. See too Susan L. Einbinder, "Pucellina of Blois: Romantic Myths and Narrative Conventions," *Jewish History* 12:1 (Spring 1998): 29–46.

25. This conclusion was reached by Jeffrey Nadamer in a seminar paper, "Aspects of Jewish-Gentile Relations as Revealed in the Responsa of Rabbi Meir of Rothenburg," Yale University, Spring 1996. Compare Yom Tov Assis, "Sexual Behaviour in Mediaeval Hispano-Jewish Society," in *Jewish History: Essays in Honour of Chimea Abramsky*, ed. Ada Rapoport-Albert and Steven J. Zipperstein (London, 1988), 25–59.

26. (Princeton, 1996).

27. (New Haven, 1996). In referring to the 1096 Hebrew narratives as a special kind of "fiction," I mean not that they are fabrications but, as I wrote, that they are literary reshapings of oral and written reports. See Ivan G. Marcus, "From Politics to Martyrdom: Shifting Paradigms in the Hebrew Narratives of the 1096 Crusade Riots," *Prooftexts* 2 (1982): 42. For this sense of "fiction" as "forming, shaping, and molding," see Natalie Zemon Davis, *Fiction in the Archives* (Stanford, 1987), 3. A recent important study of the Trier episode described in the Latin and Hebrew parallel sources has demonstrated the remarkable reliability of *realia* in those texts, at least so far as the Trier units are concerned. Accurately reported *realia* do not enhance the factual reliability of the martyrologies and other stories in that or the other community episodes in the three Hebrew accounts, unless there is corroboration of the stories themselves. The distinction between *realia* and stories is an important one to keep in mind. See Eva Haverkamp, "'*Persecutio*' und '*Gezerah*' in Trier während des Ersten Kreuzzugs," in *Juden und Christen zur Zeit der Kreuzzüge*, ed. Alfred Haverkamp (Sigmaringen, 1999). In addition, see Ivan G. Marcus, "The Representation of Reality in the Sources of the 1096 Anti-Jewish First Crusade Riots," *Jewish History* 13:2 (Fall 1999): 37–48, especially n. 2. Robert Chazan's comments in his *God, Humanity, and History: The First Crusade Narratives* (Berkeley, 2000), 138–139, and my study, "From Politics to Martyrdom," are in essential agreement as to the literary and historical character of these fascinating texts.

28. David Goodblatt, "Suicide in the Sanctuary: Traditions on Priestly Martyrdom," *Journal of Jewish Studies* 46:1–2 (1995): 10–29; Avraham Grossman, "The Origins of Martyrdom in Early Ashkenaz" [Hebrew], *Qedushat ha-Hayyim ve-Heiruf ha-Nefesh*, ed. Isaiah Gafni and Aviezer Ravitzki (Jerusalem, 1993), 99–130.

29. For Soloveitchik's views, see "Three Themes from *Sefer Hasadim* (n. 15 above), passim. On the clash of methods of study, see Israel Ta-Shema, "The Commandment of Torah Study as a Social-Religious Problem in *The Book of the Pietists*" [Hebrew], *Sefer Bar Ilan* (1977): 98–112; Ivan G. Marcus, *Piety and Society: Jewish Pietists in Medieval Germany* (Leiden, 1981), 102–106; Israel Ta-Shema, "Ashkenazi Hasidism in Spain: R. Jinah Girondi—the Man and His Work" [Hebrew], in *Galut Ahar Golah [Haim Beinart Jubilee Volume]*, ed. Aharon Mirsky, Avraham Grossman, and Yosef Kaplan (Jerusalem, 1988), 165–194; Ephraim Kanarfogel, *Jewish Education and Society in the High Middle Ages* (Detroit, 1992), 86–88.

30. Yitzhaq Gilat, "Age Thirteen: Is One Responsible for Performing the Commandments?" [Hebrew], in *Mehqerei Talmud* 1, ed. Yaakov Zusman and David Rosenthal (Jerusalem, 1990), 39–53.

31. Ibid.

32. *Tosefta, Mo'ed*, ed. Saul Lieberman (New York, 1962), 249.

33. *Masekhet Soferim* 18:7, ed. Michael Higger (1937; reprint, Jerusalem, 1970), 318–319.

34. Saul Lieberman, Review [Hebrew] of *Masekhet Soferim*, ed. Michael Higger, *Qiryat Sefer* 15 (1938–39): 56–57.

35. *Sefer Hasidim*, par. 1540.

36. R. Jacob b. Meir of Ramerupt (Rabbenu Tam), *Sefer ha-Yashar*, ed. Shraga Rosenthal (Berlin, 1898), 106–108, 111 (see 106 for Pontoise source); on the Tosafot of Evreux, see Urbach, *Ba'alei ha-Tosafot* 1:483–484, and Kanarfogel, *Jewish Education*, 75–78.

37. See Constable, "Twelfth-Century Spirituality," 39 and notes.

38. Jacques Le Goff, *Intellectuals in the Middle Ages*, trans. Teresa Lavender Fagan (French ed., 1957; Oxford, 1993), 35–48.

39. See Kanarfogel, *Jewish Education*, 71–72.

40. "Narrative Fantasies in *Sefer Hasidim*," trans. Ivan G. Marcus, in *Narrative Fantasies in Rabbinic Literature*, ed. David Stern and Mark Mirsky (1990; reprint, New Haven, 1998); *Vagabond Verse: Secular Latin Poems of the Middle Ages*, trans. Edwin H. Zeydel (Detroit, 1966), 75.

41. Robert Chazan, "The Early Development of *Hasidut Ashkenaz*," *Jewish Quarterly Review* 75:3 (January 1985): 199–211, pointed to the motif of divine will in both 1096 Hebrew Crusade narratives and in the German Pietist writ-

ings. There are ancient traditions in both as well as a similarity with the Latin reports about Urban II's speech that inspired the First Crusade. See Ivan G. Marcus, "From 'Deus Vult' to 'the Will of the Creator' . . ." [Hebrew], conference volume on 1096 to be published by the Merkaz Dinur of the Hebrew University of Jerusalem.

42. Samuel Krauss, *Das Leben Jesu nach jüdischen Quellen* (1902; reprint, Hildesheim, 1977); Herbert W. Basser, "The Acts of Jesus," in *The Frank Talmage Memorial Volume I,* ed. Barry Walfish (Haifa, 1993), 273–282; Jordan, *French Monarchy,* 16–17.

43. Ivan G. Marcus, "Hierarchies, Religious Boundaries and Jewish Spirituality in Medieval Germany," *Jewish History* 1:2 (Fall 1986): 2–26; Jacob Katz, *Exclusiveness and Tolerance* (New York, 1961), 98–99, where necessity rather than hierarchy is proposed for explaining the Pietists' contacts with Christians.

ᴛʜʀᴇᴇ

From the First Crusade to the Second: Evolving Perceptions of the Christian-Jewish Conflict

ROBERT CHAZAN

The call of Pope Urban II at Clermont evoked exhilarated responses across all sectors of society in western Christendom and set in motion a campaign that ended in one of the signal victories in the history of the Christian world. The First Crusade has fascinated the Western world—and indeed other sectors of the globe as well—from then till now. Although the First Crusade has been carefully analyzed for more than a century, major issues remain to be clarified.[1] High on the agenda of historians of medieval western Christendom is delineation of the impact of this remarkable undertaking. To what extent did the First Crusade create new realities that must be carefully tracked? Or, alternatively, to what extent does it simply serve as a convenient marker for ongoing developments in a rapidly evolving European society?

The subgroups of researchers concerned with the history of Christian-Jewish relations or the place of the Jewish minority within the medieval Christian majority have regularly focused on the impact of the First Crusade. Often the events of 1095–99, in particular the sanguinary assaults of 1096, have been projected as a watershed in Christian-Jewish relations, radically altering Jewish circumstances.[2] I and others have recently argued against this view, urging that the violence of 1096 was hardly so destructive as to alter the demographic realities of northern-European Jewish existence and that, in fact, twelfth-century Jewish life in northern Europe shows considerable evidence of security, economic progress, and

46

cultural flourishing.[3] What I have suggested as an alternative is that 1096 serves as "a portent of things to come," in effect, a marker of the evolution—more accurately the deterioration—of Christian-Jewish relations in western Christendom.[4] This essay is devoted to further explication of this ongoing change. I shall attempt to clarify the ways in which Christian perceptions of Jews evolved from the First Crusade through the Second Crusade, as well as the ways in which Jewish views of Christians shifted.

Let us begin with changing Christian perceptions of Jews.[5] My thesis is that the spiritual environment of the First Crusade moved some participants and bystanders—to be sure, a minority of participants and bystanders—to a heightened sense of Jewish enmity. This sense of Jewish animus was rooted in the traditional Christian emphasis on historic, even cosmic, Jewish opposition to Christianity. As we move from the First Crusade to the Second Crusade, and as crusading in a more general way proceeds from the sublime to the increasingly earthly, perceptions of Jewish enmity became more firmly anchored in the here-and-now, with accelerating concern over Jewish economic activity, over Jewish blasphemy against Christianity and its symbols, and over murderous Jewish hostility to Christian neighbors.

Recent research on the ideas and ideals that undergirded the First Crusade has emphasized the diversity of operative concepts and symbols. Extension of these diverse rationales for the violence of the late 1090s into an argument for assault on Jews was by no means ubiquitous in crusader ranks. Only a small minority of those who took the cross saw in the motifs that animated them the grounding for anti-Jewish actions. The minority of crusaders who engaged in anti-Jewish violence seem to have interpreted the call to holy war against the Muslim unbelievers as justification for attack on what was perceived as an older and more heinous foe. Perhaps more compellingly, the call for an armed pilgrimage to the Holy Sepulcher seems to have been refracted against the Jews, allegedly responsible for the crime that created this key Christian shrine.[6]

The earliest source for the anti-Jewish assaults, the well-constructed Hebrew narrative often identified as the *Mainz Anonymous*, provides a rationale for crusader violence:

> It came to pass, in the year one thousand twenty eight after the destruction of the [Second] Temple [1096], that this calamity befell Israel. The

barons, nobles, and commonfolk in France first stepped to the fore, deliberated, and decided to go up, to rise like an eagle, to do battle, to clear the way to Jerusalem the Holy City, and to reach the sepulcher of the crucified, a trampled corpse that can neither aid nor save because he is vanity. They [the crusaders] said to one another: "Behold we travel to a distant land to do battle with the kings of that land. [We take] our lives in our hands to kill or to subjugate all the kingdoms which do not believe in the crucified. How much more [should we subjugate or kill] the Jews who killed and crucified him."[7]

Note here the twin themes of holy war and armed pilgrimage, and the sense of the Jews as historic enemies. The Jews under assault do not seem to have been viewed in their immediate reality; rather, in this period of intense exhilaration, of high-blown rhetoric, and of potent imageries, the Jews were abstracted into profound and eternal enemies.

Two of the most important mid-twelfth-century figures in western Christendom reinforced the First-Crusade sense of the Jews as historic enemies, although with significant shifts. In his famous letter calling the warriors of western Christendom to the Second Crusade, Bernard of Clairvaux addressed overtly the place of the Jews in the crusading enterprise. Recalling the bloodshed of 1096 and disquieted over signs of renewed agitation, Bernard warned unequivocally against anti-Jewish violence.[8]

Bernard's warning by no means rejected the conviction expressed by the 1096 anti-Jewish crusaders of historic Jewish enmity. By basing his powerful scriptural argument on Psalm 59, Bernard in fact reinforced the sense of age-old Jewish hostility. The psalm, viewed as divinely inspired and predictive of future developments, antedated the crucifixion by many centuries. God, according to Bernard, had already seen and proclaimed the Jewish propensity to malevolence. "Save me from my enemies, O my God; secure me against my assailants. Save me from evildoers; deliver me from murderers. For see, they lie in wait for me; fierce men plot against me for no offense of mine, for no transgression, O Lord; for no guilt of mine do they rush to array themselves against me" (Ps. 59:2–4). Writing with divinely inspired foreknowledge, the psalmist already discerned the Jews as enemies, as assailants, as fierce men moved by groundless hatred. The occasional crusader sense of Jews as the

worst of the enemies of Christianity and Christendom was therefore
hardly unwarranted.

Bernard parted company with the anti-Jewish thinking of 1096 and
1146, however, with respect to the actions which historic Jewish enmity
should entail. For some of the crusaders of 1096 and for the agitators of
1146, historic Jewish enmity served as legitimation for violent Christian
revenge. For Bernard, by contrast, such violence was illegitimate, not
because it was undeserved, but because God had decreed against it. In
his infinite wisdom, God had preferred a more painful punishment for
the Jews, the punishment of degradation in this earthly life. Further, in
his infinite mercy God anticipated the eventual repentance of these
Jewish foes and was prepared to accept such repentance. In the course of
his complex argumentation, Bernard offers further rationales for non-
violence against Jews. He notes specifically that the Jews of his own day
lived peacefully in their subjugation and that such acquiesence required
Christian restraint. Jews who accepted their degrading punishment
should by no means be subjected to assault.[9]

Bernard's important contemporary, Peter the Venerable, likewise re-
capitulated the 1096 sense of the Jews as historic enemies, although
again introducing important alterations. Like Bernard, Peter wrote an
important letter in the course of which he treated at length the issue of
the Jews within the crusading context.[10] The entire thrust of Peter's mis-
sive differed from that of Bernard, however. Whereas Bernard had added
his observations on the Jews to his general crusade epistle in order to
forestall anti-Jewish actions, Peter the Venerable addressed the king of
France with the specific goal of eliciting anti-Jewish actions, actions
that he viewed as reasonable and legitimate rather than violent and
irresponsible.

How did Peter the Venerable come to a different set of conclusions
with respect to crusading and the Jews? Like Bernard, Peter felt deeply
the sense of historic Jewish enmity, and, again like Bernard, he rejected
the popular violence that had cost so many Jewish lives in 1096 and that
once more threatened in 1146. Peter diverged, however, from Bernard's
assessment of their Jewish contemporaries as living peacefully under
Christian domination. Like Bernard and Peter, the violent crusaders of
1096 and the agitators of 1146 considered the Jews of Jesus' day as standing in profound opposition to Jesus; these crusaders and agitators paid

scant heed to the actual contours of Jewish life in their own day. For
Bernard, the Jews of the 1140s were resigned to docile subjugation to
their Christian masters; for Peter, however, the Jews in mid-twelfth-
century northern Europe continued to manifest intense hostility to Jesus
and his people. According to Peter, the Jews of his day took every opportunity to bring harm to Christianity through blasphemy and through
misuse of objects sacred to the Christian community. Jewish economic
endeavor, problematic in itself, became for Peter yet one more means
exploited by the Jews as a part of their campaign of animosity and blasphemy. Such ongoing Jewish enmity could hardly be dismissed or over-
looked. Yet, physical assault was not the proper response. Rather, Peter
urged the French monarch to punish his Jews by forcing them to contribute their allegedly ill-gotten and ill-used goods to the great crusading
venture. Evident even in this cursory treatment of Peter the Venerable
is the transition from an earlier sense of Jews as an abstract historical
enemy to this perception of contemporary Jewish neighbors as devoured
by hatred, poised at every moment to bring harm on the Christian society that hosted them.[11]

These new stereotypes of malevolent contemporary Jews were not
spun out among the elites of northern Europe and then promulgated to
the masses. Just as in 1096 the sense of the Jews as historic enemies had
developed fairly spontaneously and had cut across societal lines, so too
the new perception of contemporary Jewish hostility emerged at all levels of society and affected all classes.[12] Perhaps the most accurate gauge
for the development of these new stereotypes is the rapid emergence and
spread of the accusation of gratuitous Jewish murder, of the Jewish
propensity to take Christian lives groundlessly whenever and wherever
possible.

Two well-known instances of this malicious-murder accusation stem
from the decade of the Second Crusade. The first case involves the
death of the young tanner, William of Norwich, in 1144. In discussing
this famous incident, I am not at all interested in the claim of ritualized
murder, specifically murder by crucifixion, which Gavin Langmuir has
so convincingly associated with the subsequent writing of Thomas of
Monmouth in 1150.[13] Rather, I wish to draw attention to the evidence
that, upon discovery of the body of the youngster, some—although by
no means all—of the Christian populace of Norwich immediately con-

cluded that the murderers must have been the Jews of that city.[14] Similarly, the discovery of a dismembered corpse in Wurzburg on the eve of the Second Crusade was spontaneously viewed by many crusaders and burghers as evidence of Jewish misdeed.[15] During the ensuing decades, the conviction that a Christian corpse should readily be interpreted as evidence of Jewish foul play became widespread across northern Europe. This conviction was far more common than the more complex and imaginative stereotype of ritualized Jewish murder.[16]

The malicious-murder accusation and the conviction of Jewish malevolence that underlay it in turn aroused anxiety among the Jews themselves. The Blois incident of 1171 constitutes a radical instance of the malicious-murder accusation.[17] It was extreme in that no physical evidence of a crime was ever unearthed. The Blois incident did not begin with the discovery of a corpse; it opened with the unsubstantiated allegation that Jews had deposited a cadaver in the fast-flowing Loire river. The situation, with its lack of a *corpus delecti*, was exacerbated by the outdated trial method invoked by the count of Blois in dealing with the allegation. He chose to submit the witness to the purported crime to a trial by ordeal. Finally, and most distressingly to the Jews, the witness's success in the trial by ordeal was followed by the execution of more than thirty Jews in Blois, representing the first time that the new accusation was dignified by acceptance in a court, in fact in the court of a major northern-French baron. Frightened by the potential impact of this formal condemnation on the credibility of the malicious-murder stereotype, the Jews of northern France embarked on a wide-ranging diplomatic effort aimed at combating the new allegation. Happily, a number of letters from this diplomatic effort survive. The evident excitement of the Jewish negotiators over their successes reflects the deep anxiety occasioned by the new perception. Thus, the leaders of Parisian Jewry report enthusiastically on the response of King Louis VII to their concerns: "Now, all you Jews in my land, be aware that I harbor no suspicions in this regard. Even if Christians discover a slain Christian either in town or in the countryside, I shall say nothing to the Jews on that score."[18] The leaders of Troyes Jewry reported with parallel satisfaction that the count of Champagne, a brother of Theobald, had declared: "Nowhere in the the law of the Jews have we found that it is permitted to kill a Christian. Yesterday, on the eve of Passover, a rumor spread in

Epernay, and I accorded it no reliability."[19] That the Jews of northern France should have found it necessary to undertake such a counter-campaign indicates clearly the spread of the new stereotype and the dangers that it posed.

Thus, what was at the time of the First Crusade a sense of historic and cosmic conflict between Jews and Christians had descended into the realm of the everyday. Contemporary Jews were now perceived as consumed by anti-Christian hostility, as exploiting available opportunities to harm the Christian faith, and as expressing their animus in acts of violence against unsuspecting Christian neighbors. The broad tendency for crusading excitement and aggression to be expressed in increasingly mundane fashion is well reflected in the evolution of Christian anti-Jewish sentiment during the half century between the First Crusade and the Second.

Jewish perceptions of the Christian-Jewish conflict also evolved. In this area, the data are hardly so copious. The evidence of the Hebrew crusade narratives and of their chronology lays bare changing patterns of Jewish perception of Christianity and Christians.[20]

As is well known, three Hebrew narratives detailing the assaults of 1096 have survived.[21] Paradoxically, the least interesting of the three to modern historians is the most widely preserved. The account written by Eliezer bar Nathan, in all likelihood the famous halakhist of that name, is simply a resumé of the lengthiest of the narratives that we possess with the addition of liturgical poems celebrating each of the Jewish communities depicted in the prose account. This reworking of the lengthiest of the narratives stems from the middle or closing decades of the twelfth century.[22]

The longest of the three Hebrew narratives and the richest in theological rumination has survived in but one manuscript. It includes a brief but important passage that seems to identify its author as one Solomon bar Simson and the date of its composition as 1140. While there is much that is troubling about this passage, researchers have had little choice but to accept it as reliable, thus dating the editing of this composite narrative with its numerous independent strands to the eve of the Second Crusade.[23]

In many ways the most valuable of the narratives is the so-called *Mainz Anonymous*, likewise extant in but one manuscript. When first published at the close of the nineteenth century, this narrative was considered the latest of the three because of the fifteenth-century copyist's opening identification of the text as "the tale of the persecutions of yore" and because of the reference to an accusation of well-poisoning at Worms.[24] Both these bases for late dating have properly been dismissed. The copyist's sense of the persecution as lying far in the past obviously tells us nothing of the time of composition of the text copied. Similarly, the emergence of the well-poisoning accusation as a common motif during the fourteenth century hardly implies that the charge could not have been leveled some centuries earlier. The more recent tendency has been to date the *Mainz Anonymous*, like its lengthier counterpart, to the middle decades of the twelfth century, in effect to the eve of the Second Crusade.[25] However, two considerations have led me to argue that the *terminus ad quem* for the composition of the *Mainz Anonymous* must be fairly close to the events themselves: the author's intense and sustained interest in the specifics of the anti-Jewish assaults, an interest not manifest in the later *Solomon bar Simson Chronicle*, and the accuracy of the author's information on the early evolution of the crusade.[26] Views of the Christian-Jewish conflict appropriate to the crusade years themselves, rather than to mid-twelfth-century hindsight, serve to buttress my sense of an early dating for the *Mainz Anonymous*.[27]

A profound sense of Christian-Jewish conflict lies at the core of the *Mainz Anonymous*. The Jewish author makes no effort to minimize the religious motivation that lay at the heart of the crusading enterprise. While he detests the crusaders and their burgher allies, he does not see them as anything but religiously motivated. For the Jewish narrator, the crusade is not material cupidity masquerading under the pretense of high ideals. The crusaders, according to our Jewish observer, are in fact moved by very high ideals, ideals that are of course in his eyes hopelessly misguided.[28] In the *Mainz Anonymous*'s opening depiction of the onset of the crusade, the crusade is portrayed as a genuine religious undertaking, an effort to clear the way to the Holy City and to reach the central shrine of the Christian faith. For our early Jewish narrator, there are no ulterior earthly motives; the crusade is really about Jerusalem and its sacred sites. More significantly, the Jewish writer, in so describing the crusade, flies in the face of venerable Jewish historiographic stances. In the classics of Jewish historical writing, there are no foes moved by such profound motives; earlier enemies are regularly portrayed as motiveless, serving merely as the rods of divine wrath, or else as moved by the basest of human jealousy and lust for power.

While the Jewish author leaves no doubt as to the essential religiosity of the crusade, he at the same time is utterly dismissive of the enterprise. It is a religious campaign undertaken in the name of vanity and futility. The very sentence that highlights the core ideals of the crusade, which culminate in the conquest of the Holy Sepulcher, identifies the crusade's objective as "the sepulcher of the crucified, a trampled corpse that can neither profit nor save, because it is vanity." Every element in this depiction resonates. Identification of the shrine as the sepulcher of the crucified (*kever ha-zaluv*) introduces an immediate note of denigration. The Hebrew *zaluv* does not carry any positive connotation; it connotes an ignominious death.

This crucified figure is a trampled corpse (*peger muvas*), an image taken from Isaiah 14, one of the prophet's lengthy diatribes against Babylonia. Isaiah contrasts tellingly the arrogance of the mighty Babylonia, which had visited so much destruction upon the world, with its ignominious end:

> All the kings of nations
> Were laid, every one, in honor,
> Each in his tomb;
> While you were left unburied,
> Like loathsome carrion,
> Like a trampled corpse. . . . (Isaiah 14:18–19)

On one level, the power and the arrogance of the Christian world are, for the Jewish narrator, contrasted with the ignominy of its slain messiah figure. For our Jewish observer, the Isaiah image highlights the essential flaw of the Christian religious vision, its focus on a central figure who represents the opposite of divine majesty. At the same time, the Isaiah citation suggests that the seeming strength and power of the Christian world, so strikingly expressed in the crusading venture, are in fact chimeric. This massive undertaking is destructive in the extreme, the very embodiment of arrogance. For all the grandeur of the crusade, its eventual fate will be the undoing prophesied by Isaiah, with the peoples of the world rejoicing at the downfall of the haughty.

There is yet a second pointed biblical resonance in the dismissive depiction of the crusader goal. The figure whose sepulcher the crusaders seek is depicted as a power that "can neither profit nor save, because it is vanity." This combination of terms comes directly from the well-known speech in 1 Samuel 12. There the aged judge upbraids his people for requesting a king, that is to say, a human leader to usurp the place of God himself. God sends a miracle to chastise the people, who cry out in remorse over their lack of faith in asking for such a human leader. Samuel, in the face of Israelite contrition, reassures his people:

> Have no fear. You have indeed done all these wicked things. Do not, however, turn away from the Lord your God, but serve the Lord with all your heart. Do not turn away toward vanities which can neither profit nor save, for they are vanity. For the sake of his great Name, the Lord will never abandon his people, seeing that the Lord undertook to make you his people. (1 Sam. 12:20–22)

There is a double message here, negative with respect to Christianity and positive with respect to the Jews. Christianity is depicted as yet another sinful search for a human intercessor, along the lines of the Israelites of Samuel's days. At the same time, the Jewish readers are reassured that the God who had remained loyal to them in days of old would continue to hold them dear as his own special people, all seeming Christian power and success notwithstanding.

Central to the *Mainz Anonymous* is the constant distinction between Jews with their unerring religious sensitivity and Christians with their unremitting attraction to what is intellectually unacceptable and morally repugnant. Again, the conflict is conceived at the highest possible level. The aggressive speech of the Mainz Jew, David Ben Netanel, provides one striking instance of this sense of Jewish rectitude and Christian error. This Jew and his family had avoided the general bloodbaths that had destroyed most of Mainz Jewry by hiding out with a friendly cleric. In view of the slaughter of most of Mainz's Jews, the cleric urged upon David what he saw as the only feasible option, conversion. The Jew resolved to die the death of a martyr, but in a special way, that is, by gathering a crowd of crusaders and burghers through the ruse of readiness for conversion and then using his last breaths for excoriating the Christian faith. Following is the *Mainz Anonymous*'s reconstruction of David's speech, highlighted by contrasts:

You are children of whoredom! You believe in one born out of whoredom! But I believe in the eternal God, who exists in the highest heavens. In him have I trusted to this day and to the expiration of my soul.
You are going to kill me. My soul will repose in paradise, in the living
light. But you shall descend to the nethermost pit, to eternal damnation, to hell, where you will be judged along with your deity, who was a
child of lust and was crucified.[29]

The Christian-Jewish conflict, as reflected in this striking speech, involved right belief versus wrong belief, with concomitant salvation versus damnation. As was the case with the Christian sense of the Jews,
immediate issues are absent; the sense of conflict reflected here is at the
most fundamental and the most abstract levels.

Just as the Christian sense of conflict crystallized quickly into the
realm of the mundane, so too did the Jewish sense of engagement move
into the realm of the immediate and the historical. Israel Yuval has argued that both the speeches attributed to the Jews of 1096 and the
third-person reflections of the subsequent Jewish narrators reflect a
vengeful messianism, a call for divine redemption for the Jews accompanied by destruction of the Christianity that had brought so much suffering on the Jewish people.[30] In fact, however, when we look closely at the
Mainz Anonymous, which I have argued is our earliest Hebrew narrative
of the events of 1096, there is not a single speech in which the Jewish
victims call down vengeance upon their Christian persecutors. The central themes of the speeches included in the *Mainz Anonymous* involve
the distinction in belief patterns of the two faiths and the diversity of
otherworldly fates awaiting the adherents of these two faiths. Even the
narrator in his third-person observations rarely alludes to this-worldly
revenge. In the entire *Mainz Anonymous*, there is only one direct outburst asking for divine revenge. At the close of the description of Jewish
behavior in the courtyard of the archbishop's palace in Mainz, one of
the high points of Jewish heroism from the narrator's perspective, the
author breaks out into an exclamation: "At such things will you restrain
yourself, O Lord! May you take vengeance for the blood of your servants
that has been spilled!"[31] Both statements have biblical roots. The first is
a quotation from Isaiah 64, in which the prophet laments the destruction suffered by the Jews and asks God how long he will restrain himself.

Revenge is not the central motif in this passage or sentence. The second sentence is an adaptation from Psalm 79, and the central theme is in fact vengeance. This, however, is the only such outburst in the *Mainz Anonymous*. Again, the author's sights are set on the more sublime dimensions of the Christian-Jewish conflict.

The atmosphere in the later *Solomon bar Simson Chronicle*, seemingly edited half a century later, is substantially altered. While the Speyer-Worms-Mainz segment of the narrative is rooted in the *Mainz Anonymous*, in other segments even the martyrs' speeches show signs of what Yuval has labeled vengeful messianism.[32] The lengthiest and richest of all the reconstructed speeches in the Hebrew narratives is the address of Moses *ha-Cohen* to the Cologne Jews assembled in Xanten. This remarkable address focuses on the Jewish imagery of Jerusalem and the exhortation that Jews make the true pilgrimage to the Holy City. The Holy Sepulcher is supplanted in this speech by the Temple, which the Jews gathered in Xanten are to reconstruct through their acts of heroic self-sacrifice. Toward the end of this exhortation, Moses introduces the normal grace after meal, which is embellished with themes from the events about to take place. In the section of the grace devoted to extolling the actions of the All-Merciful, the Jewish leader adds the following: "May the All-Merciful avenge in the days of those who remain after us and before their eyes the blood of your servants that has already been shed and that is yet to be shed."[33] The Jews assembled at Xanten are fated to die. The request is for almost immediate revenge upon their persecutors.

More striking is the ubiquity of pleas for revenge in the third-person reflections of the author/editor of the *Solomon bar Simson Chronicle*. Such appeals are peppered throughout the narrative. For instance, the entire Speyer-Worms-Mainz segment of the lengthy narrative ends with a plea for divine retribution upon the Christian persecutors and recompense for the Jewish victims. The calls for retribution begin with citation of a series of biblical verses that highlight God's vengeance upon the enemies of Israel. These verses are succeeded by the following petition: "May the Lord our God provide us with vengeance. May vengeance for the blood of his servants that has been spilled be made known speedily to all before our eyes, for the sake of your great Name which has been bestowed upon us, so that all creatures may know and understand their [the crusaders'] sin and guilt for what they did to us. Bring down upon them in accordance with what they did to us. Then they will comprehend and understand and take to heart that for vanity they threw our corpses to the earth, and that for frivolous teachings they killed our saintly ones, and that for a trampled corpse they spilled the blood of our saintly women, and that for the words of an enticer and heretic they spilled the blood of infants and sucklings."[34] The sense of conflict between Christians and Jews has been decisively shifted here to the earthly realm, to the historical scene. The victory at the walls of Jerusalem in 1099 convinced many of the truth of Christianity. According to the author of the *Solomon bar Simson Chronicle*, the punishment that God must and will mete out to the Christian world will convince all of the truth of the Jewish faith.

The manner in which the so-called *Solomon bar Simson Chronicle* closes is revealing. The author/editor chose to end his narrative with the first evidence of divine retribution as he perceives it, namely, the disasters suffered by the crusading forces of Peter the Hermit and Emicho of Flonheim. News of this crusading catastrophe made its way westward "and gladdened our hearts, for the Lord showed us vengeance against our enemies." There follows a powerful set of biblical verses through which the narrator beseeches yet further revenge against Israel's enemies.[35] The reality of divine vengeance and the plea for its intensification constitute the note on which the narrrator chose to conclude his account.

Thus, on the Jewish side as well, the sense of cosmic confrontation apparent in the 1090s gave way, with the passage of time, to a more mundane concern with the here-and-now, with God's actions on the contemporary scene that might reverse the impression of the victory in 1099 and prove to all objective observers that the beleaguered and persecuted Jews express the true faith and that God's favor is ultimately reserved for them.

The First Crusade was primarily a war against Muslims, not Jews. For those who understood the call to Jerusalem as justifying anti-Jewish violence, and for their victims, the Christian-Jewish conflict was focused on the historic, the cosmic, the otherworldly level. With the dampening of passions and the dissipation of exhilaration, the flare-up of anti-Jewish animosity might well have abated. But it did not. Like so many aspects of crusading, the otherworldly and cosmic tone was lost, and a more earthly, here-and-now temper developed. For Christians, this meant a growing sense of the Jews as immediate enemies, poised to strike at any moment; for Jews, this meant a heightened sense of contemporary confrontation, with ever enhanced need for divine intervention to rectify the skewed realities of Christian power and Jewish subjugation.

NOTES

1. A striking new perspective on lay enthusiasm reflected in the First Crusade has been provided by Marcus Bull, *Knightly Piety and the Lay Response to the First Crusade: The Limousin and Gascony c. 970–c. 1130* (Oxford, 1993).

2. This traditional view is reflected in such standard works as Haim Hillel Ben-Sasson, ed., *A History of the Jewish People* (Cambridge, Mass., 1976), 386, and Leon Poliakov, *The History of Anti-Semitism*, trans. Richard Howard et al., 4 vols. (New York, 1965–85), 1:41–46. Even Salo W. Baron makes some strong statements in this direction in the opening pages of his chapter entitled "The Age of the Crusades," *A Social and Religious History of the Jews*, 2d ed., 18 vols. (New York, 1952–83), 4:89–149; to be sure, in the course of this chapter, Baron mitigates the traditional view considerably.

3. Robert Chazan, *European Jewry and the First Crusade* (Berkeley, 1987), 197–210; Simon Schwarzfuchs, "The Place of the Crusades in Jewish History" [Hebrew], in *Tarbut ve-Hevrah be-Toldot Yisra'el bi-Me ha-Benayim*, ed. Menahem Ben-Sasson et al. (Jerusalem, 1989), 251–267.

4. Chazan, *European Jewry and the First Crusade*, 210–217. The phrase "a portent of things to come" is taken from R. W. Southern, *The Making of the Middle Ages* (London, 1953), 13.

5. See my study of this subject in Robert Chazan, *Medieval Stereotypes and Modern Antisemitism* (Berkeley, 1997).

6. For a recent overview of the thinking that underlay the First Crusade, see Jonathan Riley-Smith, *The First Crusade and the Idea of Crusading* (London, 1986), and Bull, *Knightly Piety and the Lay Response to the First Crusade*.

7. The *Mainz Anonymous* was published in a scholarly edition by Adolf Neubauer and Moritz Stern (henceforth N&S), *Hebräische Berichte über die Judenverfolgungen während der Kreüzzuge* (Berlin, 1892), 47–57; republished by Abraham Habermann (henceforth Habermann), *Sefer Gezerot Ashkenaz ve-Zarfat* (Jerusalem, 1945), 93–104; English translation in Shlomo Eidelberg

(henceforth Eidelberg), *The Jews and the Crusaders* (Madison, Wisc., 1977), 99–115, and in Chazan, *European Jewry and the First Crusade*, 225–242. I have reexamined the *Mainz Anonymous* in considerable detail in "The *Mainz Anonymous*: Historiographic Perspectives," in *Jewish History and Jewish Memory: Essays in Honor of Yosef Hayim Yerushalmi*, ed. Elisheva Carlebach, John Efron, and David Myers (Hanover, N.H., 1998), 54–69. The opening passage cited can be found in N&S, 47; Habermann, 93; Eidelberg, 99; and Chazan, *European Jewry*, 225.

8. *Sancti Bernardi opera*, ed. Jean Leclercq and Henri Rochais, 8 vols. (Rome, 1957–77), 8:311–317.

9. I have analyzed the position of Bernard in some detail in *Medieval Stereotypes and Modern Antisemitism*, chap. 3.

10. *The Letters of Peter the Venerable*, ed. Giles Constable, 2 vols. (Cambridge, Mass., 1967), 1:328–329.

11. I have likewise analyzed the stance of Peter the Venerable toward the Jews in *Medieval Stereotypes and Modern Antisemitism*, chap. 3.

12. In *Medieval Stereotypes and Modern Antisemitism*, I take issue with the position developed by R. I. Moore in *The Formation of a Persecuting Society* (Oxford, 1987). Moore argues that the anti-Jewish, anti-heretic, anti-leper motifs in twelfth-century European society were created by the ruling elites as a way of augmenting their political power. My study suggests, in contrast, that the anti-Jewish perceptions were self-generated across the entire spectrum of northern-European society.

13. See Gavin I. Langmuir, "Thomas of Monmouth: Detector of Ritual Murder," *Speculum* 59 (1984): 822–846, reprint in G. I. Langmuir, *Toward a Definition of Antisemitism* (Berkeley, 1990), 209–236.

14. Thomas of Monmouth, *The Life and Miracles of St. William of Norwich*, ed. and trans. Augustus Jessopp and Montague Rhodes James (Cambridge, 1896). My analysis of the early reaction of the burghers of Norwich is found in chapter 4 of *Medieval Stereotypes and Modern Antisemitism*.

15. *Annales Herbipolenses*, in MGH, Scriptores 16 (Hanover, 1859), 3–4.

16. In a 1985 essay, "Historiographic Crucifixion," *Les Juifs au miroir de l'histoire: Melanges en l'honneur de Bernhard Blumenkranz*, ed. Gilbert Dahan (Paris, 1985), 109–127, reprint in Langmuir, *Toward a Definition of Antisemitism*, 282–298; Langmuir notes (111 and 282, respectively) that the crucifixion slander, upon which much of his attention is focused, was in fact overshadowed by the charge of murder.

17. I have studied the Blois incident in detail in "The Blois Incident of 1171: A Study in Jewish Intercommunal Organization," *Proceedings of the American Academy for Jewish Research* 36 (1968): 13–31. I have more recently

examined the Hebrew sources for this incident from a historiographic perspective in "The Timebound and the Timeless: Medieval Jewish Narration of Events," *History and Memory* 6 (1994): 5–34.

18. N&S, 34; Habermann, 145.

19. N&S, 35; Habermann, 146.

20. The two halves of this essay are somewhat disparate. While the first half draws on a recently completed book-length study (*Medieval Stereotypes and Modern Antisemitism*) and is thus quite fully documented, the second half is tentative, drawn from work in a very early stage. While I believe that my contrast between the early *Mainz Anonymous* and the later *Solomon bar Simson Chronicle* is well founded, the next step is to investigate other sources and ascertain whether the same divergence obtains.

21. The publication details for the *Mainz Anonymous* have been indicated above, in n. 7. The *Solomon bar Simson Chronicle* can be found in N&S, 1–30; Habermann, 24–60; Eidelberg, 21–72; Chazan, *European Jewry*, 243–297. The epitome authored by Eliezer bar Nathan can be found in N&S, 36–46; Habermann, 72–82; Eidelberg, 79–93.

22. The dependence of the Eliezer bar Nathan abridgement upon the *Solomon bar Simson Chronicle* seems to me patent. Given the dating of the latter to 1140, to be discussed shortly, the abridgement must be later. The famed halakhist Eliezer bar Nathan is assumed to have been born around 1090; he was active in the 1140s and 1150s; the date of his death is not clear. For full details on this important figure, see Ephraim E. Urbach, *Ba'aley ha-Tosafot*, 5th ed., 2 vols. (Jerusalem, 1986), 1:173–184.

23. See N&S, 21; Habermann, 48; Habermann, 55; Chazan, *European Jewry*, 280.

24. For the copyist's introductory remark, see N&S, 47; Habermann, 93; Eidelberg, 99; Chazan, *European Jewry*, 225. For the well-poisoning accusation, see N&S, 49; Habermann, 95; Eidelberg, 102; Chazan, *European Jewry*, 228.

25. See, for example, the recent study by Jeremy Cohen, "The 'Persecutions of 1096'—From Martyrdom to Martyrology: The Sociocultural Context of the Hebrew Crusade Chronicles" [Hebrew], *Zion* 59 (1994): 169–208.

26. See my essay in *Jewish History and Jewish Memory*. In addition, I adduce there two specific passages that suggest early provenance.

27. That is to say, the tentative findings of the present essay serve ultimately to buttress my sense of the early provenance of the *Mainz Anonymous*.

28. My essay entitled "The First Crusade as Reflected in the Earliest Hebrew Narrative," *Viator* 29 (1998): 25–38, examines the *Mainz Anonymous* perception of the crusading phenomenon, as experienced by Rhineland Jews.

29. N&S, 56; Habermann, 104; Eidelberg, 114; Chazan, *European Jewry*, 241–242.

30. Israel Yuval, "Vengeance and Damnation, Blood and Defamation: From Jewish Martyrdom to Blood Libel Accusations" [Hebrew], *Zion*, n.s. 58 (1993): 33–90.

31. N&S, 54; Habermann, 101; Eidelberg, 110; Chazan, *European Jewry*, 237.

32. Perhaps the most controversial suggestion of the Yuval essay cited above, in n. 30, is the linkage of the Jewish propensity toward vengeful messianism and the mid-twelfth-century Christian perceptions of the Jews as murderous. If my suggestion that Jewish emphasis on vengeance develops somewhat slowly between 1096 and the middle of the twelfth century is correct, Yuval's suggestion is weakened considerably. More precisely, the fact that the *Mainz Anonymous* does not attribute calls for vengeance to the 1096 martyrs themselves serves to vitiate the force of the Yuval connection.

33. N&S, 22; Habermann, 49; Eidelberg, 57; Chazan, *European Jewry*, 282.

34. N&S, 16–17; Habermann, 43; Eidelberg, 48; Chazan, *European Jewry*, 272.

35. N&S, 30; Habermann, 59; Eidelberg, 71; Chazan, *European Jewry*, 297.

The Discovery of the Self:
Jews and Conversion in the
Twelfth Century

JONATHAN M. ELUKIN

Jews who converted to Christianity in the Middle Ages often confronted Christians who refused to believe that they had truly effaced their Jewish identity.[1] From late antiquity on, many Jewish converts never completely escaped the perceived stigma of their Jewishness. After the millennium, examples of this antagonism toward Jewish converts increased markedly in the documentary record. This increase provokes several questions. Is the larger dossier of evidence about converts a result of the increased level of all literary and documentary evidence as record keeping in the Middle Ages improved? Was anxiety about the efficacy of Jewish conversion an offshoot of the more intense antagonism expressed against all Jews after the twelfth century?[2] Were there simply more converts—and thus more ambivalence among Christians—as conversionary pressure on the Jews increased during the thirteenth century? Finally, did Christians increasingly project their sense of the immutability of Judaism and the Jewish people onto individual Jews who wished to convert, effectively trapping them in their Jewish identity?[3]

These factors may all have influenced the anxiety of Christians towards Jewish converts after the millennium and thus how that anxiety was expressed in the documentary evidence. It would be unwise to put too much explanatory pressure on any one.[4] Answers to some of the questions raised above may be impossible to discover, given the fragmentary and idiosyncratic nature of medieval evidence. However, it may now be possible to find one factor that offers a better explanation than the others for the apparent intensification of anxiety about the efficacy of conversion after the millennium—and a better likelihood of having enough surviving evidence to make a real connection between intellectual changes in Christian culture and their impact on attitudes about the conversion of Jews.

Amidst the cultural, economic, and political developments that energized European society in the twelfth century, the human being—or rather a self-awareness of the individual—received new attention from medieval intellectuals. Scholars have given this movement of thought the contested shorthand label "the discovery of the individual," although "discovery of the self" may be more accurate. Richard Southern, Colin Morris, John Benton, and others have sketched out a mosaic of medieval Christian thought about the individual and his identity.[5] Despite reservations about the specific terms of the discussion and even disagreements among participants in the debate, it is reasonable to conclude that men and women in the twelfth century saw themselves more intensely as individuals in relation to each other, as well as in relation to God. They looked with obsessive interest into the workings of their interior selves, and they began to study and reflect systematically upon their own minds, hearts, and souls. Carolyn Bynum has rightly provided a crucial corrective to the tenor of this discussion when she urged scholars on the trail of the "individual" not to ignore the corporate or communal nature of twelfth-century society.[6] Still, if it is not overstated, this new interest in the individual allows us to approach Christian perceptions of Jews from a new angle.

How then did Christians imbued with this sensibility about human identity see the Jews who lived among them in medieval European society during and after the twelfth century? How did they fit Jews into this pattern of thought which created a new awareness of the interior dynamics of human beings? The new sensibility of the interior human being played a crucial role, I will argue, in undermining the confidence of Christians in the effectiveness of Jewish conversions to Christianity.

It would be inaccurate to think that ambivalence about converts sprang fully formed in the *mentalité* of the twelfth century. Christianity was a religious culture particularly sensitive to concerns about true conversions from the very beginning; it was a faith built upon conversion.

Robin Lane Fox has described, at least for the early centuries of Christianity, the long process of initiation for the catechumen: "It is certainly not a process dominated, or largely explained, by sudden miracles. . . . The years of instruction and preparation became, in their turn, one of the faith's particular appeals. People felt that they were exploring a deep mystery, step by step. They were advancing with a group of fellow explorers along a route which required a high moral effort."[7] Other Christians might very well ask: "But how could those whose minds had not been impregnated with divine love be won from their depraved and animal understanding to true belief?"[8] This implicit suspicion tainted all Christians: "Insofar as converts aroused suspicion, the entire community of believers was shot through with universal and mutual suspicion . . . [and] the suspicion of crypto-belief in former ways was endemic in a society of converts."[9]

Still, the evolution and intensification of this suspicion of converts depended, I believe, upon the larger shift in attitudes toward the interior person—itself a process still not fully understood. That change in attitude might become clearer through looking at the dynamics of conversion in the early Middle Ages. Even though individual converts were sometimes still identified as former Jews, little attention was paid to the interior dynamics of a Jew's shifting identity. In particular, where large groups of Jews were concerned, they seemed to integrate fully into Christian society; there was no reference to a residual Jewish identity that might have suggested an incomplete internal conversion. And, too, there was no need for the conversion to be accompanied by a miracle that legitimized the conversion. The presence of a miracle only became an important element in later conversions where Christians, more sensitive to the inner process of conversion, needed some external confirmation of the change in a Jew's identity.

Most of the accounts of conversion that have survived from the early Middle Ages tell the story of a bishop confronting a local Jewish community with the stark choice of conversion or expulsion. In other words, clerics—at least at the local level—did not seem particularly concerned with the internal sensibilities of the Jews when they converted. Gregory the Great, for example, had to reprimand one Italian bishop for expelling the Jews from the accustomed place in which they had celebrated their *festivitates*.[10] Gregory insisted that such strategies would not work to bring the Jews to Christianity. While he may have wanted to see the Jews convinced with sweet preaching and persuasion, the local bishop was obviously taking a harsher line.[11] Later in the tenth century, Pope Leo VII apparently had lost Gregory's compassion; he responded to Frederick, archbishop of Mainz (937–954), and agreed that the bishop could give the Jews a choice of conversion or exile.[12] There were other similar stories. Ademar of Chabannes (988–1034) relates that Audouin, bishop of Limoges, compelled the Jews of Limoges to come to baptism or leave the city. After a month of disputing with the Jews, only three or four Jews became Christians. The rest hastened to disperse to other cities with their wives and children.[13]

A more famous and elaborate but fundamentally similar situation is preserved in great detail in Gregory of Tours' account of the events surrounding the conversion of the Jews of Clermont in the sixth century. It is the story of Avitus, the bishop of Clermont, and his effort to bring the Jews to baptism. After a convert had been attacked by fellow Jews, the Christians were agitating for an attack on the Jews:

> On the blessed day on which our Lord ascended in glory into heaven after the redemption of man, while psalms were being sung and the bishop was processing from the cathedral to one of the local churches, the crowd following him attacked the Jewish synagogue, destroyed it down to its very foundations and levelled it to the ground.

After this massive intimidation, the Jews of Clermont were apparently more receptive to the urgings of the bishop. Gregory's account continues with a report of how Avitus entreated the Jews to convert or be expelled:

> On another occasion the Bishop sent this message to the Jews: 'I do not use force nor do I compel you to confess the Son of God. I merely preach to you and I offer to your hearts the salt of knowledge. I am the shepherd set to watch over the sheep of the Lord. It was of you that the true Shepherd, who suffered for us, said that He had other sheep, which are not of His fold, but which he must bring, so that there might be one flock, and one shepherd. If you are prepared to believe what I believe, then become one flock, with me as your shepherd. If not, then leave this place.'

It was after this ultimatum that the Jews, or at least a sizeable number of them, chose to be converted:

> They argued among themselves and hesitated for some time; but on the third day, persuaded by the bishop, or so I believe, they gathered in a group and sent this answer to him: 'We believe that Jesus Christ is the son of the living God, promised to us by the pronouncements of the prophets.' The bishop rejoiced at the news. He celebrated nocturns on the holy eve of Pentecost and then went out to the baptistery without the city wall. There the whole company of Jews lay prostrate before him, begging for baptism. Saint Avitus wept with joy. He washed them all in water, anointed them with chrism and brought them together into the bosom of the Mother Church. Candles flamed, lamps burned and the whole city shone bright with the white-robed flock. The joy felt in Clermont was not less than that experienced long ago in Jerusalem when the Holy Spirit descended on the Apostles. More than five hundred were baptized. Those who refused to accept baptism left the city and made their way to Marseille.[14]

This fascinating account can tell us much about the perception of Jews in the culture of late antique Gaul. Gregory preserves the reality that Avitus and the Christian population set out upon a carefully conceived program of intimidation to bring about the Jews' conversion. In Gregory's memory, the destruction of the synagogue and the hectoring of sermons serve as stepping stones for the deliberative—one might say miraculous—change of heart among many Jews. While the conversion of the Jews was presented as a quasi miracle that attested to Avitus's holiness and the new Christian nature of Clermont, Gregory's narrative emphasizes the deliberative nature of the Jews' decision. In Gregory's account, their decision is taken as sincere. The interior workings of the Jewish mind evoke no interest, nor is there any anxiety that the decision to convert had provoked half-hearted conversions. Neither is there apparently a need for a miracle to confirm the conversion, which would have suggested some qualms about the validity of the interior change of heart. Clermont had truly become—at least in Gregory's vision—one flock.

This "pragmatism" was not universal. Occasionally, the conversion of Jews before the millennium was remembered as provoked by miracles. In several stories of conversions, Jews converted after witnessing miraculous

actions of the host. Gregory of Tours himself preserves, for example, the
story of the Jew who threw his son into an oven after discovering he had
been to mass. The boy survived unharmed, and the father and other
Jews then converted to Christianity.[15] The same kind of story is found in
the Life of St. Syrus, a third- or fourth-century bishop of Pavia. It reap-
peared in Radbertus of Corbie's treatise on the Eucharist in the ninth
century as well as the eucharistic treatise by Geza of Tortona in the late
tenth century. The story runs like this: a Jew attends a mass celebrated by
bishop Syrus in order to obtain a host that he then intends to throw into
an outhouse. The Jew takes the host in his mouth but cannot remove it
because it burns inside his mouth like fire. Only after the bishop prays
for him does the host come free. At that moment the Jew converts.[16]

While these stories of miraculous conversion might suggest that
Christians before the millennium were searching for miracles to confirm
the conversion of the Jews, they were intended primarily to demonstrate
the power of the Eucharist rather than emphasize the miraculous origins
of Jewish conversions. Radbertus, for example, treated such miracles as
ways to convince those who doubted that Christ was really present
in the host.[17] Indeed, as Gavin Langmuir has noted, "when Geza of Tortona retold the story, he was more worried about the danger of profanation than eager for miraculous conversions, for he recommended that
Jews be kept away from masses since they always tried to profane the
host."[18]

The intriguing story of the conversion of the Jews of Minorca provides a larger-scale conversion scenario where the miracle of the conversion also seems an offshoot of the real point of the account—the
power of the relics. When the relics of St. Stephen were discovered and
transported to Minorca in 417 AD, the Christian community began an
aggressive campaign to convert the Jews.[19] The Jews, after much internal debate and intimidation by Christian mobs, finally converted. They
continued to hold privileged positions in the community; their allegiance had simply shifted to the bishop. The account does not emphasize, however, the miraculous nature of the conversion. The conversion
was part of a general sea-change in the local society when the relics appeared. There seemed to be no concern in the narrative that the Jewish
conversions were incomplete. The Jews appeared as good Christians
even if they saw Stephen work what Peter Brown has characterized as

"Jewish" miracles, like the appearance of manna or the rush of sweet water from a rock.[20]

All in all, then, the conversions of Jews in the early Middle Ages reflect a landscape where changes in religious identity were not subjected to searching scrutiny. Nor was there a need for an external miracle to confirm the conversion. A laissez-faire approach to conversion makes sense given the general pattern of ethnic and tribal conversions in early medieval Europe. Conversion was an ongoing phenomenon, and it would have been impossible and unwise to question the validity of each conversion. Identity in early medieval Europe was such a fluid thing that conversion to Christianity may have been less important than ethnic allegiance, adherence to Latin culture, or the articulation of a particular kind of Christian belief—or heresy. In short, the cultural and psychological pressures of the early Middle Ages helped to create an environment in which conversion from Judaism was generally accepted as legitimate without an accompanying examination of the interior conversion of the individual—or a miracle to substantiate that shift.

After the millennium, conversion was no longer an ever present event in the core countries of European medieval society. When it did occur, there seemed an ever increasing need for some confirmation that the interior person had truly changed. I take this to be the effect of medieval culture's new emphasis on the interior self. How could other people know if someone had truly changed their identity? Perhaps a more visible Jewish community and steady confrontation with Islam and heresy may have sparked this increased need for inner knowledge or, at least, greater certainty of one's interior religious identity. To be sure, conversions without accompanying miracles were still possible and were accepted as legitimate, as evidenced by Jewish men, women, and adolescents who embraced Christianity. These individuals were accepted to varying degrees by the communities in which they found themselves. But in the stories that became representative of post-twelfth-century culture, the most secure conversions were those accompanied by a miracle. Divine signals testified to the changes in the interior identity of the Jews. They confirmed that the journey to God, which Christians knew to be hazardous and difficult, had divine guidance.

When Innocent III, for example, wanted to attest to the sincerity of a certain convert—in the milieu of a society that expressed doubt about the sincerity of converts—he related the story of this Jew's conversion as stimulated by a miraculous appearance of hosts.[21] Other men of this time, preoccupied with searching out the recesses of the interior person, responded to the conversions of Jews by looking for miraculous testimony for conversions.

Guibert of Nogent, whose sense of his interior self was hyperactive, to say the least, recounts the forced baptism of a Jewish child seized in Rouen during the First Crusade. Guibert was told: "After the ritual prayers were recited, they reached the point where a candle is lit and liquid wax is dropped into the water. There was one drop in particular that traced in the water such a perfect sign of the cross that no human hand could ever have managed to trace anything of the kind with such a tiny piece of matter." Guibert was still suspicious, even though the sign was verified by the boy's patron and "by a priest, and both of them swore several times in God's name that the story was true." Guibert admits that he would not have "paid much attention to this matter if I had not witnessed this child's extraordinary progress." In the context of the boy's religious career—he went on to become a monk—the meaning of the tiny wax cross was clear: "The appearance of the cross at his baptism, then, was not a chance event but was divinely willed. It was a sign of the faith that would develop in this man of Jewish stock, a rare event in our time."[22] The miracle confirmed the interior change in the Jew's identity and helped to suppress Guibert's doubts.

Sometimes a miracle was unavailable, and this made conversion a long and painful process. That seemed to be the case in the conversion of Herman-Judah, whose controversial twelfth-century autobiography is one of the most important texts of the perceived experience of conversion. Even without the miracle, Herman's account displays an obsessive concern with the interior life of the individual and its impact on Jewish identity. Herman, a young Jew in the Rhineland, prayed constantly for some divine sign that would support his growing attraction to Christianity. He embraced the offer of a holy man who had befriended him to show Herman such a sign: "He proposed to me, with the greatest steadfastness, this bargain: that if, in proof of his faith, he sensed no burning while carrying (as is customarily done) a scorching iron in his bare hand, I would faithfully submit to the cure of holy baptism, the dark cover of all unbelief washed from my heart."[23]

Unfortunately, the bishop stopped the ceremony and rebuked the holy man for trying to solicit a sign from God. The bishop instructed them:

"You are never to ask or, above all, to yearn for some sign from God to promote this change. Certainly, it would be the easiest thing for his omnipotence to convert whomever he wished without any miracle, but only by the secret visitation of his grace. A sign which is displayed visibly to the external sight would be idle if he did not work invisibly through grace in the heart of a human being. And, indeed, we read that many have been converted without signs but also that countless others have stayed fast in infidelity after seeing miracles. Besides," he added, "it has to be known that faith which is won over by miracles has either no or very little merit but that faith which is undertaken without any incitement of miracles, but with simple piety and pious simplicity, has the most excellent merit before God and the highest praise."[24]

After countless hours spent listening to Christian clergy explain the christological meaning of the Old Testament, after hours of fasting and prayer, and invoking the sign of the cross, Herman felt no closer to becoming a Christian. He was trapped in some kind of limbo, neither Jew nor Christian. There was no way to actualize or see what the bishop had described: "the action of God's grace in the heart of a human being." In the end, only the intercession of the prayers of two holy women—representing for Herman the church itself—gave him somehow the confident awareness of his faith. "Not at all much later," he wrote, "by their merits and prayers, so great a brightness of Christian faith suddenly shone in my heart that it entirely put to flight from it the shadows of all former doubt and ignorance." Herman knew that his conversion was difficult to understand: "Look at me," he exclaimed, "neither the explanation given by many concerning the faith of Christ nor the disputation of great clerics could convert me to the faith of Christ, but the devout prayer of simple women did."[25] The intercession of the women seems to me a rather weak attempt to replace a miraculous sign. The workings of the inner person, his mind, soul, and heart were still hidden from the eyes of Herman's fellow Christians. His autobiography was, as Sander

Gilman has written, a way to justify his new identity.[26] Such an effort was necessary because the same question remained: Could a Jew really change his interior identity?

By the twelfth century, then, the landscape of conversion to Christianity had changed. It was harder for a Jew to be accepted as a true Christian. Many factors played a role in this shift, but the discovery of the interior self among Christians, with their increasingly ambivalent ideas about the interior self of Jewish converts, must be considered a key factor. It is deeply ironic that the very human quality of his or her interior self now made it so difficult for a Jew to become a Christian in the eyes of other Christians. It distorts the complexity of Christian thought to indict Christian intellectuals of the twelfth century for describing the Jews as irrational and essentially non-human because they refused to accept Christian truth.[27] Jews were condemned to remain apart from Christians not because Jews were perceived to be fundamentally different kinds of human beings or less than human, but precisely because they were human beings who had to cross what seemed an insurmountable distance to come to a fuller understanding of God. Whether that is comforting or tragic is not for a historian to say.

NOTES

I would like to thank John Van Engen and Michael Signer for their kind invitation to contribute to the conference at the University of Notre Dame and to this collection of essays.

    1. See my "From Jew to Christian? Conversion and Immutability in Medieval Europe," in Varieties of Religious Conversion in the Middle Ages, ed. James Muldoon (Gainesville, Fla., 1997), 171–89.
    2. For different theories about the origins of this intensification of antagonism, see Amos Funkenstein, "Changes in the Pattern of Christian Anti-Jewish Polemics in the 12th Century" [Hebrew], Zion 33 (1968): 125–44; Jeremy Cohen, The Friars and the Jews: The Evolution of Medieval Anti-Judaism (Ithaca, N.Y., 1982); R. I. Moore, The Formation of a Persecuting Society: Power and Deviance in Western Europe, 950–1250 (Oxford, 1987); Gavin Langmuir, "Doubt in Christendom," in his History, Religion, and Antisemitism (Berkeley, 1990), as well as his larger argument about the evolution of anti-Semitism in Toward a

Definition of Antisemitism (Berkeley, 1990); and Anna Sapir Abulafia, *Christians and Jews in the Twelfth-Century Renaissance* (London, 1995).

3. I tried to elucidate this in my dissertation, "The Eternal Jew in Medieval Europe: Christian Perceptions of Jewish Anachronism and Racial Identity" (Ph.D. diss., Princeton University, 1993).

4. As I now believe I did in the dissertation by trying to link anxiety about converted Jews exclusively to perceptions of the immutability of Jews and Judaism.

5. See, for example, Richard Southern, *The Making of the Middle Ages* (New Haven, 1959), 219–57; Colin Morris, *The Discovery of the Individual: 1050–1200* (1972; reprint, New York, 1973); John Benton, "Individualism and Conformity." in *Individualism and Conformity in Classical Islam*, ed. A Banani and S. Vryonis, Jr. (Wiesbaden, 1977), 145–58; and Walter Ullmann, *The Individual and Society in the Middle Ages* (Baltimore, 1966).

6. Caroline Walker Bynum, "Did the Twelfth Century Discover the Individual?" in her *Jesus as Mother: Studies in the Spirituality of the High Middle Ages* (Berkeley, 1982), 85: "Yet current research on the twelfth-century religious revival in fact underlines nothing else so clearly as its institutional creativity. It depicts a burgeoning throughout Europe of new forms of communities, with new rules and custumals providing new self-definition and articulating new values. . . . For twelfth-century religion did not emphasize the individual personality at the expense of corporate awareness. Nor did it develop a new sense of spiritual and psychological change, of intention, and of personal responsibility by escaping from an earlier concern with types, patterns, and examples. Rather twelfth-century religious writing and behavior show a great concern with how groups are formed and differentiated from each other, how roles are defined and evaluated, how behavior is conformed to models." I take up the impact of this corporate model on attitudes toward Jews in an article, now being revised for publication, tracing the perceived evolution of Judaism from a collection of heresies to a monolithic and unchanging religion of the Pharisees.

7. Robin Lane Fox, *Pagans and Christians* (New York, 1987), 314.

8. Karl Morrison, *Understanding Conversion* (Charlottesville, Va., 1992), 45.

9. Morrison, *Conversion*, 73.

10. Gregory the Great, *Registrum Epistularum*, ed. Dag Norberg, CCSL 140, vol. 1, ep. 34, p. 42.

11. Gregory, *Registrum*, ep. 34, p. 42: "Hos enim qui a christiana religione discordant, mansuetudine, benignitate, admonendo, suadendo, ad unitatem fidei nccesse est congregare, ne, quos dulcedo praedicationis et praeuentus futuri iudicis terror ad credendum inuitare poterat, minis et terroribus repellantur."

12. Pope Leo VII, ep. 14, PL 132, 1083–84. Like Gregory he was concerned that the Jews convert with a full heart; but he seemed perfectly willing to believe that conversion even under such pressure would be legitimate. "Et si credere et baptizari toto corde voluerint, immensis laudibus omnipotenti Domino referimus gratias; si autem credere noluerint, de civitatibus vestris cum nostra auctoritate illos expellite, qui non debemus cum inimicis Domini societatem habere. . . ."

13. Ademar of Chabannes, PL 141, 60.

14. Gregory of Tours, *Histoire des Francs: Texte des manuscrits de Corbie et des Bruxelles*, ed. Henri Omont and Gaston Collon, 1886, 1895, rev. ed. René Poupardin (Paris, 1913), 5.11, pp. 161–63. English translation by Lewis Thorpe, *History of the Franks* (Baltimore, 1986), 265–67. In a forthcoming article (in a collection of papers given at the International Congress of Medieval Studies, Kalamazoo, Mich., 1997), Emily Rose tries to link the Clermont episode with the earlier account by Sulpicius Severus of the conversion of the Jews in Minorca. I am grateful to Ms. Rose for sending me a copy of her paper.

15. Gregory of Tours, *Liber in Gloria martyrum*, MGH Scriptores rerum merovingicarum, ed. Bruno Krusch (Hannover, 1885), 2:51 (21); cited by Gavin Langmuir, "The Tortures of the Body of Christ," *Christendom and Its Discontents*, ed. Scott L. Waugh and Peter D. Diehl (Cambridge, 1996), 294–95.

16. Langmuir, "Tortures," 295. The fourth-century *Life of St. Basil* also recounted how a Jew who attended a mass celebrated by Basil saw in Basil's hand a slaughtered child and perceived the host to be real flesh and the chalice to be filled with real blood. He, too, converted. (PL 73, 301–2, cited by Langmuir, "Tortures," 295).

17. Langmuir, "Tortures," 295.

18. Ibid.

19. For a discussion of the Minorca episode, see Peter Brown, *The Cult of the Saints* (Chicago, 1981), 103–5. See too, most recently, Carlo Ginzburg, "The Conversion of Minorcan Jews (417–418): An Experiment in History of Historiography," in Waugh and Diehl, *Christendom and Its Discontents*, 207–20, as well as the article by Emily Rose (n. 14).

20. Brown, *Cult of the Saints*, 105.

21. Innocent III wrote to Peter of Corbeil, archbishop of Sens, on behalf of a convert formerly named Isaac. Shlomo Simonsohn, *The Apostolic See and the Jews: Documents, 492–1404*, Studies and Texts 94 (Toronto, 1988). See no. 93, Rome, June 8, 1213, p. 98. Peter was apparently reluctant to help support the new convert and his family, so Innocent tried to make him more attractive by relating the story of their conversion, which involved the multiplication of the

host hidden in the family's home by a Christian servant. This kind of story was certainly in the tradition of the earlier miraculous Eucharist accounts. However, the story was not part of the discourse of the Eucharist, but rather related specifically to the nature of one convert's identity.

22. ". . . ubi, accenso lumine, liquens in undam cera dimittitur, gutta singulariter ibidem visa est cecidisse, quae per se solam in ipsis aquis adeo accurate sua, ut sic dicam, quantitatula effigiem crucis expressit, ut ex tantilla materie simile quid manu fieri humana non possit"; "hoc etiam ipse presbyter pariter non sine divini nominis plurima contestatione dixerunt. Quem ego eventum satis leviter accepissem, nisi successus egregios pueruli indubie pervidissem"; "Crux igitur in ejus baptismate non fortuitu, divinitus autem facta jure apparuit, quae insolitam nostro tempori in judaici generis homine credulitatem futuram innotuit," Guibert of Nogent, *Autobiographie*, ed. and trans. into French by Edmond-René Labande (Paris, 1981), 248–52, book 2.5; trans. into English by Paul J. Archambault, *A Monk's Confession: The Memoirs of Guibert of Nogent* (University Park, Pa., 1996), 112–13.

23. ". . . hanc mihi constantissime proposuit conditionem, ut si ferrum ignitum nuda, ut fieri solet, manu in fidei sue argumentum baiolans nullum sensisset incendium, ego de corde meo totius infidelitatis detersa caligine sacri baptismatis fideliter subirem remedium," Hermannus Quondam Judaeus, *Opusculum de conversione sua*, ed. Gerlinde Niemeyer, MGH Quellen zur Geistegeschichte des Mittelalters 4 (Weimar, 1963), 84; trans. into English by Karl F. Morrison, in *Conversion and Text: The Cases of Augustine of Hippo, Herman-Judah, and Constantine Tsatsos* (Charlottesville, 1992), 86.

24. "Ceterum autem, ait, huius rei gratia signum aliquod a Deo tibi nec petendum nec magnopere exoptandum est, cum utique eius omnipotentie facillimum sit absque omni miraculo sola occulta gratie sue visitatione convertere, quem voluerit, et otiosum sit signum, quod visibiliter foris exhibetur, si ipse per gratiam in corde hominis invisibiliter non operetur. Et multos enim absque signis conversos, innumeros vero etiam post visa miracula legimus infideles perstitisse. Sciendum, ait, praeterea est, fidem, qui miraculis persuadetur, vel nullum vel minimum meritum habere, illam vero, que sine ullo miraculorum incitamento simplici pietate et pia simplicitate suscipitur, excellentissimi coram Deo meriti summeque laudis existere," Niemeyer, *Opusculum*, 85–86; Morrison, *Text*, 86.

25. "Haud multo enim post tempore meritis ipsarum et precibus tanta repente cordi meo christiane fide claritas infulsit, ut ab eo totius pristine dubietatis et ignorantie tenebras penitus effugaverit"; "Ecce enim me, quem ad fidem Christi nec reddita mihi a multis de ea ratio nec magnorum potuit clericorum convertere disputatio, devota simplicium feminarum attraxit oratio," Niemeyer, *Opusculum*, 108; Morrison, *Text*, 101.

26. Sander L. Gilman, *Jewish Self-Hatred* (Baltimore, 1986), 31.

27. See Abulafia, *Jews and Christians*, passim. This is not the place for a full critique of Abulafia's provocative book. It can be challenged on various grounds, including the extent to which her authors believed in the metaphors they were using to describe the Jews in polemical texts, the very limited number of references to the Jews' inhumanity, and the extent to which such thoughts penetrated other social classes. Ultimately, though, if Christian elites in the twelfth century thought the Jews were so inhuman, why did they expend so much energy in the thirteenth trying to convert them?

Adolescence and Conversion in the Middle Ages: A Research Agenda

WILLIAM CHESTER JORDAN

The conversion of Jews to Christianity in the European Middle Ages is an issue where emotions have clouded research and interpretation. One need not like converts or the process of conversion to realize that not all converts were necessarily unprincipled opportunists.[1] I have argued elsewhere that historians have to articulate carefully a taxonomy of plausible reasons for conversion and have to take seriously the psychological pressures on the adolescent and young men who converted.[2] Why adolescent and young men? Although scholars have identified a number of Jewish female converts to Christianity in the Middle Ages,[3] males appear to have constituted the vast majority of voluntary and individual converts.[4] And, the evidence is reasonably strong that these males were youthful at the time of conversion. The demographic profile was far more varied, of course, for forced and mass converts.[5]

The relative frequency or salience of adolescent converts among all voluntary converts is perhaps inferable from the existence of distinctive rules concerning their conversion. Specifically, in David Abulafia's words, "teenagers were given several days to think over what they were planning to do before going to the font"; this tradition was followed—or, at least, was articulated—in both southern and northern Europe.[6] Even if the existence of these rules cannot be taken as evidence of a preponderance of adolescent converts, it nonetheless demonstrates that adolescent conversion was perceived as an express category of conversion experience. Special study of it therefore is justified.[7]

One implication of the existence of this tradition is that the age which we would call adolescence (when first, as the *Sachsenspiegel* puts it, the male youth "has hair in his beard and down below and beneath each arm")[8] was subject to putatively irrational mood swings. To be sure, literary texts (at least those Middle High German literary texts studied recently by James Schultz) do not support this conclusion. They do present conversion in fictional narratives as occurring at the end of childhood or in what I am calling the adolescent stage, but they represent no such psychological profile ("irrational mood swings") for adolescents.[9] Fortunately, Schultz himself admits that "it would be foolish to think that [these texts] represent the real children of the German Middle Ages."[10] Indeed, in real life the emotional roller coaster of adolescence promoted caution among medieval Christian authorities, making them hesitant without considerable deliberation to accept an adolescent's decision to convert. This caution was as much in evidence in the face of expressed desires to convert from Judaism to Christianity as it was when the issue was conversion within Christianity from the secular to the religious life.

An anecdote told in the *Liber restorationis* of Saint-Martin of Tournai, a twelfth-century description of Odo of Tournai's reform of the church of Saint-Martin, makes this point well. The *Liber* tells of a youth or adolescent (*iuvenis*), Alufus by name, who experienced a spiritual conversion from what might be called conventional to zealous Christian devotion and wanted to join the canons of Saint-Martin in order more fully to embrace the apostolic life. His father, Siger, clearly regarded the decision as unreflective if not silly. He went to Saint-Martin's and dragged his son out by the hair, treating him like a naughty child. But the boy persisted; and the next day his father repeated the humiliation. Time and again the scene was repeated, until the boy's resolve finally convinced the old man that his son had made a considered decision, and he relented in his efforts to restrain him. (Indeed, late in life Siger himself joined his son's community at Tournai.)[11]

Although the parallel in this episode with popular expectations about adolescence today—moodiness, indecisiveness, unthinking audacity; the necessity of parental firmness as a restraint—is patent, it is not my point to argue that the category of adolescence then (in the Middle Ages) and now were precisely the same. Expectations about this time of life presumably changed many times during the course of the Middle Ages, from region to region, from social group to social group, and between the sexes. Barbara Hanawalt, for one, argues persuasively that medieval communities admitted the existence of the adolescent stage, although she acknowledges that opinions about that stage differed over time and that the word *adolescentia* cannot be translated unreflectively by our "adolescence."[12] Despite these concessions and her recognition that many of the "signs" or "markers" indicating entrance into adolescence in the Middle Ages were unique to that period, she sees a number of consistencies between medieval and modern notions of the adolescent phase in the life cycle.[13]

If we are willing to grant, with Hanawalt, that certain structural similarities between medieval and modern adolescence are strong, some cautious comparisons may be made. Boys in their teenage years were on the threshold of adulthood, marriage and fatherhood being the principal seals of the transition. Without invoking bar mitzvah (in any case a largely post-medieval ceremony),[14] it is still accurate to say that in Jewish circles twelve or thirteen was a crucial date for entering this transitional phase.[15] The age of twelve or thirteen was important among Christians as well. It was a commonplace, after all—one repeated, for example, by that completely mediocre German friar, Johannes Klenkok—that adolescence began at age thirteen.[16] Granted that people at such a juncture may react in ways similar to people in other quite distinct traditions facing the same transition, it should be possible to test the insights gleaned from the study of adolescence in early modern and modern situations (where the evidence is lavish) against what can be recovered from the medieval historical record.[17]

Presumably, it is not unreasonable to suggest that these young men, like their modern counterparts, wanted what most men on the edge of maturity in structurally similar cultural processes appear to want. One rather common desire focused on women with whom they might find emotional and sexual pleasure. One Antoine Demorgin, "having recently converted to the Christian faith" in late medieval Dijon, seems immediately to have become affianced.[18] There can be little doubt that conversion afforded him or appeared to afford him the opportunity—whether it worked out or not is irrelevant—to enter into a relationship that he thought would bring him gratification and stability. Although the desires impelling him to his conversion ought not necessarily to be identified with "romantic love," they were far closer to this sentiment than what was likely to occur, if Bonfil can be believed, within the con-strained arrangements characteristic of the Jewish community.[19]

Besides freedom of choice in marriage, Jewish youths on the thresh-old of adulthood sought broader autonomy or relative autonomy from the constraints of adults, along with material satisfactions and spiritual peace. Yet, in every case, the norms of behavior in the medieval Jewish community put tremendous pressures on these young men to submit to community and parental authority. The routinized responses to these pressures in acts of submission are what compel Bonfil to conclude that "there was no youth or adolescence as we understand it in the premodern [Jewish] world"—for males or females.[20] What he means, I think, is that adolescent impulses were restrained by community and parental forces, creating a tension that sometimes had grave consequences (conversion is a case in point) for a youth and for his community.

Jewish norms which emphasized hierarchy did not imply that emo-tional well-being with a marriage partner was something that should be put aside completely or that autonomy was not to be treasured or that comfort in a material sense was not to be desired or, finally, that spiritual peace was not valued. What Jewish community norms—recoverable from so-called ethical wills and poetry, among other sources—did insist upon was the "properly" narrow range of options for the achievement of these goals. The woman of choice was to conform to the standards of the family; indeed, in many cases was to be the choice of the family. The southern French Jewish maiden who told her grandfather she would rather die than marry the man for whom she was chosen shows the dilemma from one woman's point of view.[21] (And she was not alone.)[22] Perhaps her potential husband would rather have converted than tie himself to a life partner who held him in contempt. The fact that her grandfather relented reveals the possibility of compromise, even in such a society of constraints.[23] Moreover, the pressures were such over time that some historians see a secular increase in the freedom of young Jews to say no to parental choices of spouses in the course of the late Middle Ages and Renaissance.[24]

It is also possible to look at autonomy in the context of conflicting social and personal impulses. Autonomy or relative autonomy could not be quite so high a priority in a community that depended almost absolutely *for its very survival* on kinds of corporate unity that necessarily narrowed choice. Bonfil is almost certainly correct when he asserts that the leaders of the Jewish community of sixteenth-century Verona were registering a commonplace order of priorities when they made "provision for all dangers that may eventually threaten the community, and for matters of public utility" before also addressing "the individual misfortunes to which any member of the community may fall a victim."[25] I, for one, would like to know what psychological (and, by repetition, social) effects this had on the life of young males. Obviously the achievement of power was a distinguishing characteristic of the achievement of maturity. But the quality and quantity of power obtained by the new adult would have been far different from what moderns in Europe or America might take for granted or view as "natural." It might also have been viewed as inadequate by some of those medieval young men to whom it came. Conversion could have been seen—accurately or inaccurately—as an escape route by these individuals.

The point was well made by the Muslim diarist, Ibn Jubayr, who discussed conversion (in this instance from Islam to Christianity) in the context of late-twelfth-century Christian-dominated Norman Sicily. His travel diary for 1184–1185 focuses both on family dynamics as the key set of circumstances in understanding conversion and on the assertion of power against marital and patriarchal authority as being at the very center of the conversion impulse. "Should a man show anger," he writes,

> to his son or his wife, or a woman to her daughter, the one who is the object of displeasure may perversely throw himself into a church, and there be baptised and turn Christian. Then there will be for the father no way of approaching his son, or the mother her daughter.[26]

No one who has suffered the rejection of his or her ideals from a beloved child can fail to be affected by this observation.

Empathy, of course, is a very dangerous historical method. Yet, if we fail to take into consideration the possibility that a set of desires for power and autonomy—even if different from ours—could have been much more intense than the normative sources allow, we are caught in the bind of regarding every aberrant behavior that departs from those prescribed in normative or idealized sources as idiosyncratic. The contrary view—that the normative sources reflect normal activity and beliefs and, since these are so different from our own behavior and beliefs, that medieval Jews are quintessentially "Other"—that they could under no conditions have the same expectations as we do—is too hard for me to accept. The survival of the community did depend on the subordination of the individual will, but that does not mean that such subordination as was accomplished was achieved with equanimity. Enough explicit evidence survives to suggest that conversion was seen fairly frequently (again, accurately or not) as a way out of the bind.[27]

One other desire associated routinely with the transition to adulthood is the achievement of some decent and stable level of material comfort. Jewish medieval poetry, like most traditional poetry, is explicit about the uncertainty of wealth, not just because material possessions are transitory and we all die, but specifically because, in the kind of world in which Jews lived in the Middle Ages, they were always vulnerable to having material possessions suddenly ripped away.[28] We—like the poets—may advise courage and steadfastness or resignation and fatalism,[29] but we ought to do so with a sufficient notice of another cluster of human desires, namely, to surrender and escape further indignities. The repeated seizure of goods painstakingly acquired and the humiliation of parents and elders in the process could easily impress upon young minds the desire to escape the ever recurrent pattern by allying with the other side. The justification for doing so might not have been crass materialism per se, but the belief that God was punishing an errant adherence to the Old Law. Were such mental articulations by would-be converts mere window dressing to crass materialism? Sometimes, no doubt, they were, and sometimes they were cankers on the consciences of those who entertained them. But in a world that so often equated material prosperity with God's blessing, repeated humiliation might rationally be construed as God's punishment—either for failing in one's faith (being a bad Jew) or, perhaps, for persevering in the wrong faith, if Christianity's dominance was construed as the blessing of God.

Conversion seen in the context of these comments becomes not a tale of inducements and constraints imposed upon a few weak Jews and the overwhelming but flat heroism of the majority, it becomes a real and human story. To be sure, many times pressures which otherwise made conversion seem a rational choice were overcome. In part, this was due to personal courage; at other times it was owed to community coercion or community sustenance, to charity, or to fear of alienation of the affection of parents and grandparents, brothers and sisters, and on and on. But those who did choose conversion did so for equally varied reasons. At least, in the scenarios I have described, the converts no longer seem like an undifferentiated mass of traitors. Some were clearly principled. Others were resentful and wanted to dispel the extraordinary psychological pressures on them, the daily pressures of a thousand demands generated both from within and without the community.

By conceptualizing the issue of conversion in this way, we can begin to ask ourselves better questions about the outlook of the converts, and that awful, simplistic phrase, "the zeal of the convert," would at last begin to be nuanced. For the assumption almost always seems to be that every convert became a fiend—like, say, Nicholas Donin (the instigator of the mid-thirteenth-century attack on the Talmud)[30]—when in fact the overwhelming majority of converts—all those *Ludovici conversi* and *Philippi conversi* in French documents—never show up again in the records. They may have been mentally tortured all their lives with regret or they may have lived happily ever after. But whatever they did, their fate and their understanding of themselves or Christians' understanding of them ought not to be conflated uncritically with that of the arch-traitors like Donin.

One may well ask just how scholars will be able to discuss matters of this sort, given the relative paucity of data. The easy answer is that medievalists are medievalists usually because they like the paucity of data and have developed techniques—once they ask the right questions—to exploit fragmentary data with great success. That is the easy answer and, in this case, I think that it is the best one. We need especially to reread the treatises written by converts for the hints they provide of the social and psychological turmoil that informed their conversion or perhaps even of the principled nature of their act.

It is fortunate that we are able to anchor ourselves in at least one text, the twelfth-century autobiographical memoir of Herman the Convert. To be sure, Avrom Saltman has argued that the text is a pious Christian forgery.[31] But even if he were correct, the memoir would inform us generously on Christians' expectations about the forces affecting and the chronology of a male Jew's conversion in the twelfth century. The truth, however, is that the text is authentic. Saltman's arguments are tendentious and unconvincing, as Aviad Kleinberg has demonstrated.[32] It can still be argued that a genuine convert wrote a fiction, one telling twelfth-century Christians what they wanted to hear.[33] We would in this and any case have to seek other evidence to confirm or nuance conclusions based on analysis of Herman's memoir alone, but research must begin somewhere. As tentative as our conclusions must be, that research may as well begin with Herman's little book.

His story of the Jew, Judah, who converts to Christianity and takes the baptismal name Herman is now reasonably well known to an English-reading audience because of Karl Morrison's translation of the convert's letter (or memoir as I called it above) to a friend explaining his conversion.[34] From the beginning the very structure of the text emphasizes the critical role of the threshold and passage of adolescence.[35] The conversion narrative, properly speaking—that is, after the brief introduction (pp. 76–77)—commences with a dream which Judah dreamed at the age of twelve or thirteen ("in the thirteenth year of my age," p. 77). It is a dream which, in hindsight, he will regard as "a most joyful premonition [of] the blessings of (God's) grace that were to come to me" (p. 77).[36]

The specific content of the dream raises innumerable problems of interpretation, not all of which can be addressed here. But a few images seem central to any interpretation. From confiscated properties, the German Christian king-emperor, Henry V, gives Judah "a horse, white as snow and wonderfully muscled, and a belt woven of gold with consummate craftsmanship, and a silk purse hanging from it that had seven very heavy coins" (p. 77). The king-emperor also endows the dreamer in his dream with an inheritance (hereditas, p. 77). Whatever the symbolic significance of precisely seven coins, the overall image is one of coming of age. To be sure, neither the Jewish sage whom Judah first engages to interpret the dream (pp. 77–78) nor Judah himself years later (pp. 110–12) interprets the dream this way, but the meaning of the symbolism, as we shall now see, is almost patent and would have been lost on no disinterested medieval interpreter. (A Jewish sage would hardly have been disinterested; a Jewish boy's dream about his exhilarating partici-

pation in Christian rites of passage and his co-option by Christian society, which is what this dream is about, was repugnant. It behooved a
Jewish interpreter in the twelfth century to gloss the dream as a prophecy
of continued and enriched attachment to his native confessional community.[37] Judah's own later retelling of the dream as premonition of his
spiritual growth is self-serving.)

The horse—and the gift of the horse—along with the belt signify
Christian knighthood and its willing acceptance (Judah buckles on the
belt and mounts the steed, p. 77). A horse which was "white as snow
and wonderfully muscled" and also a stallion (*equus*) was obviously a
war-horse.[38] Gifts of horses were a customary part of the knighting protocol.[39] The golden belt, one might think, was merely an expensive belt
(*cingulum* is the word used when the dream is first described), but an alternate word, *balteus*, is employed later in the text (pp. 110–11) and
clinches the association with knighthood, since *balteus* means 'sword-
belt'.[40] The giving of other gifts, like the seven heavy (gold?) coins, were
also customary aspects of celebrations of knighthood. The inheritance
as a marker of the transition to full adulthood hardly needs further explanation. After receiving the gifts, the dreamer joins the king at a great
feast (p. 77), which would have been standard for the celebration of
knighthood (typically at age twenty-one).[41]

The wakened Judah is neither child nor adult; or, rather, he is a
child on the verge of putting away childish things. He makes this point
explicitly:

> And so, awakening, still in the joy of this vision, I did not—even
> though a child (*puer*)—judge the most extraordinary things that I had
> seen to be empty, as the lightheartedness of a child (*levitate puerili*)
> might have indicated. Instead, I was sure that I had foreseen by that
> premonition some great thing in store for me (p. 77).

The Judah within the dream and the Judah awakened from the dream
are both on the threshold of adulthood and autonomy: "even though a
child," yet no longer judging with "the lightheartedness of a child."

If we had any doubt of this interpretation, Judah himself removes it
by insisting that the next phase of his conversion opens seven years
later (p. 78)—in (the symbolism is patent) his twenty-first year. The

intervening years of which he gives us almost no details were in fact not without crucial developments. Sometime in this period Judah was betrothed, and by the time he was twenty-one pressures had built up for him to go through with the marriage (pp. 94–96). His resistance is all the more remarkable, since the Jewish sage from whom he had first sought an interpretation of his youthful dream had seen in the gift of the horse a sign of a wonderful bride to come (p. 78). One is tempted to see the Jewish interpretation of the dream and the arranged betrothal as linked events. If so, apprehension about marriage hung over Judah's head for years.[42]

However this may be, further events unsettled the youth and his family circle. These commenced when his parents learned that Judah in carrying on some business for them in a different city had failed to secure a loan with a pledge from the bishop who received the money. He was immediately instructed to seek out the bishop, remind him of his obligation, and indeed persevere in the bishop's company until the loan was repaid. At the same time, parents and friends of young Judah were afraid, in his words, "that going about with Christians, I might be turned away by their stimulus from following our fathers' tradition" (p. 78). To be sure, these fears were not necessarily grounded in evidence on Judah's own part of suspicious "curiosities" expressed earlier.[43] But soon, which is to say in the period of his association with the bishop, his emotional topsy turvy did reveal itself openly: his interest in Christianity was, he writes, "led on by a friendly inquisitiveness common to the young (*amica adolescentibus curiositate illectus*), or rather by a brazen impudence" (p. 79).

The fears of his parents and friends had caused the former to appoint a companion for Judah to accompany him to the bishop and make sure he persevered in the faith of his fathers. The tension between childhood and adulthood, tutelage and autonomy, comes out time and again. Judah, being curious (*curiosus*) about Christianity, crosses the "threshold of churches" (*ecclesiarum limina*), a spatial liminality that mirrors his emotional and developmental liminality (p. 80). His companion therefore rebukes him "as one given over to his custody," and threatens him as a child might be admonished (although Judah is twenty-one): "he affirmed that he was going to report to my parents' ears all the follies of my illicit curiosity" (*illicite curiositatis*, p. 80).

What sort of person, finally, was Judah? In Jeremy Cohen's words, he was "the child . . . searching for security and meaning in life as his adolescence drew to a close."[44] He was, as Cohen puts it in another place, the very type of "the groping adolescent,"[45] frightened, apprehensive before the possibility of poverty and degradation by adhering to a faith which God Himself appeared to have rejected.[46]

> If observance of the legal rites still pleased [God], he would not have so deprived the Jews, who observed those rites, of the aid of his grace that he would have dispersed them, proscribed from all goods and homeland, far and wide through all the nations of the world. . . . [I]f he cursed the sect of the Christian religion, he would not have suffered it to spread and prosper so greatly throughout the earth (p. 90).

This observation is not the final 'proof' for Judah.[47] He was not a mere materialist, but it evokes still another consideration in the plethora of reasons that provoked young men of Judah's age to imagine what it might be like to convert and sometimes to act upon that image and abandon the faith of their fathers.

The remainder of the story of how Judah the Jew becomes Herman the Christian and enters into an ecclesiastical career—ironically, of voluntary poverty and a return to celibacy from his coerced marriage— need not delay us. It is a remarkably interesting tale and it makes a challenging text on many levels. The text reveals under close scrutiny some of the ways in which male Jewish adolescents in the twelfth century constructed (or how Christians supposed that they constructed) new identities as converts in the emotional struggles they endured. To recover these constructions and the struggles that underlay them is not to understand with perfect satisfaction why any single Jew converted or refused to convert, but it does humanize the story both of conversion and resistance. Any research agenda that wants to pursue these issues will have to go back to texts far less explicit on the surface than Herman's memoir to do so. The task will not be easy; the rewards will seldom be as abundant as the enchantments of knighthood glimpsed in Judah's dream. But, to invoke Spinoza, all things excellent are as difficult as they are rare.

NOTES

I want to acknowledge a critical and very fruitful reading of this paper by Elspeth Carruthers of the Department of History at Princeton University. A much shorter and schematic version of the paper was presented at the Eighteenth International Congress of Historical Sciences (Montreal, August 1995).

1. An excellent step forward in reopening the question of medieval conversion is Joseph Shatzmiller's "Jewish Converts to Christianity in Medieval Europe, 1200–1500," in *Cross Cultural Convergences in the Crusader Period: Essays Presented to Aryeh Grabois on His Sixty-Fifth Birthday*, ed. Michael Goodich et al. (New York, 1995), 297–318.

2. William Jordan, *The French Monarchy and the Jews from Philip Augustus to the Last Capetians* (Philadelphia, 1989), 138–39.

3. Cf. Robert Stacey, "The Conversion of Jews to Christianity in Thirteenth-Century England," *Speculum* 67 (1992): 271–73; Shatzmiller, "Jewish Converts," 307–8.

4. Roger Kohn, *Les Juifs de la France du Nord dans la seconde moitié du XIVe siècle* (Louvain, 1988), 183.

5. A good discussion of the pressures on French Jews and Spanish immigrant Jews in France in the 1380s and 1390s to convert en masse may be found in Kohn, *Juifs de la France du Nord*, 184–87.

6. The quotation (which refers to southern European traditions) is from Abulafia's article, "From Privilege to Persecution: Crown, Church and Synagogue in the City of Majorca, 1229–1343," in idem, *Church and City* (Cambridge, 1992), 122. For northern European traditions, see Ivan Marcus, "Une Communauté pieuse et le doute: Mourir pour la Sanctification du Nom (*Qiddouch ha-Chem*) en Achkenaz (l'Europe du Nord) et l'histoire de rabbi Amnon de Mayence," *Annales: Histoire, Science sociales* (September–October 1994): 1044.

7. Ivan Marcus, "Jews and Christians Imagining the Other in Medieval Europe," *Prooftexts* 15 (1995): 222: ". . . the notion of adolescence as a time of vulnerability toward conversion for Jewish and Christian men and women needs to be studied further."

8. Quoted in Robert Bartlett, "Symbolic Meanings of Hair in the Middle Ages," *Transactions of the Royal Historical Society*, 6th series, 4 (1994): 44.

9. James Schultz, *The Knowledge of Childhood in the German Middle Ages, 1100–1350* (Philadelphia, 1995): in his words, "many conversions occur at the end of childhood" (166), but there is no evidence in fictional narratives that medieval German children "engage in the process of identity formation, including role experimentation and vocational choice, which experts and nonexperts

expect of modern adolescents" (131). Conversion also fails, for Schultz, as a formal rite of passage to adulthood (see 166), since the act (or process) is not necessarily confined to a specific life-stage; however, as we shall see when we turn to the case of Herman the Convert (below), conversion certainly can play a fundamental role in rites of passage.

10. Schultz, *Knowledge of Childhood*, 13.

11. The anecdote is retold in the introduction to Irven Resnick's edition of Odo of Tournai's *On Original Sin* and *A Disputation with the Jew, Leo, Concerning the Advent of Christ, the Son of God* (Philadelphia, 1994), 14–15. Blessed Odo, the head of the community, had a role in the story. Although Saint-Martin of Tournai had become known as a zealous community, it was still a community of canons at the time the boy wanted to enter. Odo resolved to transform his followers from canons to monks who would better represent the adolescent's aspirations but also confront him with the stark character of his desire to abandon the world. Alufus, even after being made aware of the rigorous self-denying life of the monks, maintained his determination in the face of his father's opposition. This was what induced the father to accept his son's decision.

12. Barbara Hanawalt, *Growing Up in Medieval London: The Experience of Childhood in History* (New York, 1993), 5, 8, 10–13, 109–14.

13. Hanawalt, *Growing Up*, 10–13 (structures of adolescence), 109–14 (medieval markers of the adolescent threshold).

14. It was unknown or virtually so in Renaissance Italy. Robert Bonfil, *Jewish Life in Renaissance Italy*, trans. A. Oldcorn (Berkeley, 1994), 131.

15. Cf. Simcha Goldin, "Die Beziehung der jüdischen Familie im Mittelalter zu Kind und Kindheit," in *Lebensräume für Kinder*, ed. Christian Büttner and Aurel Ende, Jahrbuch der Kindheit 6 (Weinheim, 1989), 214, 223.

16. Christopher Ocker, *Johannes Klenkok: A Friar's Life, c. 1310–1374*, Transactions of the American Philosophical Society 83, part 5 (Philadelphia, 1993), 8 n. 5. For Ocker's characterization of Klenkok as "mediocre" and therefore typical, see 3–6.

17. Among the numerous studies of early modern and modern adolescence in Europe, see Ilana Ben-Amos, *Adolescence and Youth in Early Modern England* (New Haven, 1994), 10–38, according to whom images of adolescence in the period she studies emphasized propensity to sin, excess piety, insubordination, high hopes, extraordinary vigor, and wit.

18. Kohn, *Juifs de la France du Nord*, 186.

19. Bonfil, *Jewish Life in Renaissance Italy*, 259 ("in our period nobody [in the Jewish community] married for love") and 260 ("even if the possibility of a love story was not out of the question, nothing could be done without parental

consent"). Contrast the views of Shatzmiller on cross-confessional liaisons, "Jewish Converts," 308: "Romance, too, may have been reason for conversions in the Middle Ages. Although difficult to detect, romance between Jews and Christians did exist in our period."

20. Bonfil, *Jewish Life in Renaissance Italy*, 255, 257.

21. Monique Wernham, "Une Rupture de promesse de mariage, 1430," *Provence historique* 115 (1979): 73.

22. For similar examples, see Shatzmiller, "Jewish Converts," 307–8.

23. Kenneth Stow, "Marriages Are Made in Heaven: Marriage and the Individual in the Roman Jewish Ghetto," *Renaissance Quarterly* 48 (1995): 467, offers ("suspects") a rather different interpretation of this incident, preferring to see the family manipulating the situation ("masterminding the 'plot'," in his words) for its own purposes. There is no explicit evidence for this suspicion.

24. See, for example, Stow, "Marriages Are Made in Heaven," 458.

25. The translation of the text of the ordinance quoted accompanies Bonfil's discussion, *Jewish Life in Renaissance Italy*, 188.

26. The travel diary entry is quoted in David Abulafia, "Ethnic Variety and Its Implications: Frederick II's Relations with Jews and Muslims," in *Intellectual Life at the Court of Frederick II of Hohenstaufen*, ed. William Tronzo, Studies in the History of Art 44; Center for Advanced Study in the Visual Arts: Symposium Papers 24 (Washington, D.C., 1994), 215.

27. Kohn, *Juifs de la France du Nord*, 184–87; Stacey, "Conversion of Jews," 270–72.

28. Jordan, *French Monarchy and the Jews*, passim.

29. For examples, see T. Carmi, *The Penguin Book of Hebrew Verse* (Harmondsworth, 1981), 415–16.

30. On Donin, see Jordan, *French Monarchy and the Jews*, 138 and accompanying notes.

31. Avrom Saltman, "Hermann's *Opusculum de Conversione Sua*: Truth or Fiction?" *Revue des études juives* 147 (1988): 31–56. Simon Schwarzfuchs allied himself with (and cites Shlomo Simonsohn as another supporter of) Saltman's argument in "Religion populaire et polémique judéo-chrétienne au 12e siècle," in *Medieval Studies in Honour of Avrom Saltman*, ed. Bat-Sheva Albert et al., Bar-Ilan Studies in History 4 (Ramat-Gan, 1995), 196. Gerd Mentgen offers no firm opinion, but cites Saltman and a number of his critics (see also below, n. 32) in "Jüdische Proselyten im Oberrheingebiet während des Spätmittelalters: Schicksale und Probleme einer 'doppelten' Minderheit," *Zeitschrift für die Geschichte des Oberrheins* 142 (1994): 130–31. I want to thank Professor Alfred Haverkamp for bringing this article to my attention and for securing an offprint of it for me.

32. Aviad Kleinberg, "Hermannus Judaeus's *Opusculum:* In Defence of Its Authenticity," *Revue des études juives* 151 (1992): 337–53. See also Jean-Claude Schmitt, "La Question des images dans les débats entre juifs et chrétiens au XIIe siècle," in *Spannungen und Widersprüche: Gedenkschrift für František Graus,* ed. Susanne Burghartz et al. (Sigmaringen, 1992), 254; idem, "La Mémoire des Prémontrés: A propos de l'autobiographie' du Prémontré Hermann le Juif," in *La Vie quotidienne des moines et chanoines réguliers au Moyen Age et temps modernes,* ed. Marek Derwich (Wroclaw, 1995), 440; and Anna Abulafia, "The Ideology of Reform and Changing Ideas concerning Jews in the Works of Rupert of Deutz and Hermannus Quondam Iudeus," *Jewish History* 7 (1993): 50, 55. At the conference for which the present essay was prepared, Alfred Haverkamp alluded with acquiescence to Jean-Claude Schmitt's views, namely, that the text is authentic though it may have been written down in its present form by a different scribe (after Herman's death).

33. Cf. Jeremy Cohen, "The Mentality of the Medieval Jewish Apostate: Peter Alfonsi, Hermann of Cologne, and Pablo Christiani," in *Jewish Apostasy in the Modern World* (New York, 1987), 31. If it is a fiction, however, it differs considerably from normative fictions in the Middle High German literary tradition as analyzed by Schultz, *Knowledge of Childhood.* Whether this difference in and of itself supports the narrative's claim to authenticity is moot.

34. Karl Morrison, *Conversion and Text: The Cases of Augustine of Hippo, Herman-Judah, and Constantine Tsatsos* (Charlottesville, Va., and London, 1992), pp. 76–113. The critical edition is *Hermannus quondam Judaeus, Opusculum de Conversione sua,* ed. Gerlinde Niemeyer, MGH, Quellen zur Geistesgeschichte des Mittelalters 4 (Weimar, 1963). All quotations in English are to the Morrison translation and page numbers in the text are given for that translation; quotations from Latin are from the critical edition whose page references are provided as marginalia in the Morrison edition.

35. Cf. Marcus, "Jews and Christians," 216 (drawing on Momigliano, "A Medieval Jewish Autobiography").

36. In constructing a psychological profile of Judah, Cohen ("Mentality of the Medieval Jewish Apostate," 34, following the late Bernhard Blumenkranz, "Jüdische und christliche Konvertiten,") insists on the coincidence of the date of the dream and the bar mitzvah (and also the fact that Judah's father had probably recently remarried at the time of the dream). But there is no explicit mention of bar mitzvah in the memoir; and even if the bar mitzvah was practiced in Judah's circle at the time, his phrase, "in the thirteenth year of my age," could easily mean that he was twelve.

37. This obligation of the interpreter, Willis Johnson, now John Nuveen Instructor of the Divinity School, University of Chicago, informs me, finds a

prooftext in the Talmud (*Berakot* 55b) and was endorsed by Rashi (d. 1105). (I want to thank Dr. Johnson for this information.) The *Sefer Hasidim*, produced within a twelfth-century Rhenish Jewish community (or sect; on which, see Ivan Marcus, *Piety and Society: The Jewish Pietists of Medieval Germany* [Leiden, 1981]), also stresses the necessity of a Jewish interpreter of dreams deliberately misleading a client when the plain meaning of the dream is, in Jewish terms, sinful (as, for example, when it points to a successful career as a Christian preacher; the citation is to Judah b. Samuel, he-Hasid, *Sefer Hasidim*, 3 vols. (Toronto, 1955–1965), 1:210, para. 389). I owe this reference to the generous help of Professor Susan Einbinder of Hebrew Union College.

38. Cf. Bradford Broughton, *Dictionary of Medieval Knighthood and Chivalry: Concepts and Terms* (New York, 1986), 252.

39. For examples, see Broughton, *Dictionary*, 171, and Maurice Keen, *Chivalry* (New Haven, 1984), 65–66.

40. *Cingulum* was a perfectly acceptable word for the sword belt, as Boulton makes clear, but it had a wider semantic field. This is why the use of *balteus* is valuable confirmation. The article by Boulton is a wonderful evocation of the early history of knighthood with particular reference to England. His conclusions cannot be readily extrapolated to the Rhineland, since England was relatively slow in adopting the formal protocols of knighthood. Nonetheless, the article is full of useful information; see D'A. J. D. Boulton, "Classic Knighthood as Nobiliary Dignity: The Knighting of Counts and Kings' Sons in England, 1066–1272," in *Medieval Knighthood V*, ed. Stephen Church and Ruth Harvey (Woodbridge, Suffolk, 1995), 41–100. On the use of *cingulum*, see 78; on England's belated adoption of knighting protocols, cf. 48–49. I wish to thank Professor Maureen Boulton for bringing this article to my attention.

41. On feasts as part of the protocol of knighting, see the examples marshalled in Broughton, *Dictionary*, 201, 294–95, and Keen, *Chivalry*, 65, 69. On the convention (though by no means requirement) of knighting at age twenty-one, see Broughton, *Dictionary*, 293.

42. As Bonfil points out (*Jewish Life in Renaissance Italy*, 257), "it was considered perfectly natural for [Jewish] parents to draw up marriage contracts when the children were thirteen or fourteen years old."

43. The words *curiositas* and *curiosus* occur, as we shall see, repeatedly in the memoir. By the time Herman wrote he would have imbibed the rich literature on *curiositas*, which had both positive and negative valences. The *curiositas* which leads people to frivolities (even heresy) is evil; that which leads them to self-knowledge or greater knowledge of the Catholic faith is virtuous. It is certainly possible that Herman means to play with this dichotomy, which, in itself, takes on a somewhat ironic flavor since his *curiositas* was to be characterized as

"illicit" by a Jewish acquaintance (text in Morrison, *Conversion and Text*, 80; and Richard Newhauser, "Towards a History of Human Curiosity: A Prolegomenon to Its Medieval Phase," *Deutsche Vierteljahrsschrift für Literaturwissenschaft und Geistesgeschichte* 56 [1982]:570). On the rich history of *curiositas*, see also Newhauser, "The Sin of Curiosity and the Cistercians," in *Erudition at God's Service*, ed. John Sommerfeldt (Kalamazoo, Mich., 1987), 71–95; "Augustinian *Vitium Curiositatis* and Its Reception," in *Saint Augustine and His Influence in the Middle Ages*, ed. Edward King and Jacqueline Schaefer (Sewanee, Tenn., 1988), 99–124; Edward Peters, "Transgressing the Limits Set by the Fathers: Authority and Impious Exegesis in Medieval Thought," in *Christianity and Its Discontents*, ed. Scott Waugh and Peter Diehl (Cambridge, 1996), 338–62; Gunther Bös, *Curiositas: Die Rezeption eines antiken Begriffes durch christlichen Autoren bis Thomas von Aquin* (Paderborn, 1995), 138–75.

44. Cohen, "Mentality of the Medieval Jewish Apostate," 34.

45. Ibid., 41.

46. Cf. ibid., 30.

47. There were many steps on the road to Herman's conversion (including inconclusive discussions with the intellectual giant, Rupert of Deutz; see John Van Engen, *Rupert of Deutz* [Berkeley, 1983], 243–44), and the range of possible motivations for him to take the final step can never be known for sure. Nevertheless, it is undoubtedly the case that the stability of the monastic life offered an attractive alternative to the dizzying uncertainties of his spiritual journey and, ironically, locked Herman into a structure of obedience not unsimilar to that in which he had been embedded in the Jewish society he abandoned. (I owe this last speculation to some stimulating comments of Mr. David Bachrach following the initial presentation of this paper at Notre Dame.)

S I X

The Expulsion of the Jews as History and Allegory in Painting and Sculpture of the Twelfth and Thirteenth Centuries

WALTER CAHN

On being asked by the organizers of this conference to explore images of Christians and Jews in the art of the twelfth century, I found myself stimulated and challenged, though made mindful at the same time
that explorers do sometimes come home empty-handed or lose their
way. Something like a general map of the territory to be covered may be
found in Bernard Blumenkranz's *Le Juif médiéval au miroir de l'art chrétien*, published with a simultaneous German edition in 1966.[1] This was,
as the author himself noted with a certain surprise, the first broad overview of the subject, for neither writers on the Christian side nor the
major Jewish histories of Graetz, Dubnow, and Baron had paid much attention to this material. It is not my intention to summarize, let alone to
criticize, Blumenkranz's pioneering venture, all the more so since he
himself was aware of its somewhat tentative and provisional nature. His
documentation came primarily from illuminated manuscripts, and he
deliberately excluded illustrations of legends in which Jews played a
part, as well as depictions of a historical or pseudo-historical character,
this on the questionable grounds that such subjects "only follow the data
of the written sources."[2]

I subscribe to one of his central observations: there is a distinction
between the way Jews are depicted in Christian art during the earlier

94

Middle Ages, and representations from the eleventh century and after, corresponding roughly to the early phases of Romanesque art in our terminology. In early medieval times, Jews are not visually differentiated from other people. "Art was [at this time] incapable," Blumenkranz writes a little helplessly, "to express by graphic means the connection of individuals to a particular group."[3] His example is the illustration preceding Exodus in the ninth-century Bible to Moutiers-Grandval (fig. 1) and showing (in the lower half of the page) Moses communicating the Law to the assembled Israelites, an assembly of stolid, vaguely senatorial Romans, whose identity as Jews—biblical Jews, in this instance—is made apparent to us only through the presence of inscriptions.[4] In the high and later Middle Ages, on the other hand, Jews were singled out pictorially through the ascription to them of distinctive physiognomical traits, elements of dress, or symbolic attributes. Blumenkranz makes this point, in an understated fashion perhaps, by comparing the image in the Grandval Bible with a miniature in a late fourteenth-century Parisian manuscript containing a collection of Miracles of the Virgin. The painting refers to a miracle involving a Christian merchant and a Jew from whom he had borrowed a sum of money. The Christian is bareheaded and smooth-skinned, while the Jew is bearded and of a darker complexion. His head is covered by a hood, and he wears the tell-tale badge.[5]

The point is made even more vividly by contrasting the illustration in the Carolingian Bible with the corresponding subject in a thirteenth-century German World Chronicle, drawn here from Ruth Mellinkoff's ample and informative recent study of pictorial devices of denigration in the art of the later Middle Ages (fig. 2).[6] Here, the assembled Israelites all wear a version of the peculiar conical hat that came to be one of their principal distinguishing marks in Romanesque and Gothic art, with Moses' headgear smartly strung over his shoulder in order to expose his face, irradiated by the light of divine inspiration. Thus, whereas Jews in early medieval art are all but invisible, later they are hard to miss and indeed endowed with an extravagant, hyper-visibility, as if their Jewishness, for the intended viewer, was all that mattered, and everything else flowed from this unfortunate condition. Blumenkranz does not pronounce in detail on the reasons for this momentous change, but in designating 1096, the year of the First Crusade, as a turning point, he no doubt intended to associate it with those manifold contemporaneous developments in the relations between Christians and Jews to which this conference is devoted.

This paper focuses on a monument which, though hardly unknown, has not, to my knowledge—and for reasons that will become apparent shortly—been mentioned in the growing body of studies concerned with the subject at hand: the sculpture which once graced the Porta Romana, one of the monumental gates of Milan, whose remains are now displayed in the Museo Civico of the city, housed in the Castello Sforzesco.[7] Among the preserved fragments of this sculpture, there is a long, contemporaneous inscription that proclaims that the Porta Romana was erected in 1171, following the return from exile of the Milanese after the conquest of the city four years earlier at the hands of the German emperor Frederick Barbarossa. It also gives the name of the builder, a certain Girardus de Mastegnianega, and of two assistants. Still other inscriptions identify the sculptors responsible for different parts of the work, one man named Gerald and another called Anselm, who is praised in conventional fashion as another Daedalus. The monument, which stood at the point of entry of a major road along the city's south-eastern side, was dismantled in 1793. Its design is recorded in a later eighteenth-century engraving (fig. 3), and can be further visualized with the help of other, still-standing gates of Milan, like the Porta Ticinese.[8] It had a double-arched opening, with the sculptural decoration disposed in the form of friezes along the capital zone of the middle pier and, ap-parently, the two lateral sides. This, though, remains somewhat uncer-tain, since the left doorway as it appears in the engraving is walled up and truncated, and the surviving sculpture does not suffice for a recon-stitution of the decoration of both arches.

The monument has recently received a comprehensive and compe-tent monographic treatment by Andrea von Hülsen-Esch, and I shall concern myself only with the frieze that, according to current recon-structions, occupied two adjacent sides of the pier along the right side of the portal (figs. 4–5). It shows St. Ambrose, the fourth-century bishop of Milan, armed with a whip and driving away a procession of men and women who carry bundles and other possessions. The carving is worn and certain details are now difficult to make out, but the general sense of the composition is clear enough. The frieze is made up of five sections of

stone, with the action unfolding from left to right. Ambrose, wearing
episcopal vestments and a miter, is preceded by a deacon or crucifer
bearing a processional cross. With his extended right arm, expressively
enlarged, he grasps a cat-o'-nine-tails whose lashes fall on the head and
back of a man, the first of a sequence of processing, squatly-proportioned
figures advancing toward the right. Their more-or-less uniform dress, a
kind of robe tightly encasing the upper body but flaring out in tubular
folds below, sets them apart as laymen from the pair of clerics at the left,
and the vessels, pouches, or sacks that they carry on poles or balance on
their heads characterize them as travelers. On the shorter, concluding
section of the frieze on the outer face of the arch, a woman carrying a
child, accompanied by an animal, can be seen (fig. 5, right).

Two sets of inscriptions purport to identify these proceedings for the
viewer, but the information they provide fails to accord on an important
point. In the narrow abacus zone immediately above the frieze, the figures driven out by Ambrose are called Arians (*Arriani*). The larger, more
formally composed text incised on the curving surface of the surmount-
ing impost block, on the other hand, calls them Jews: AMBROSIUS CELEBS
IUDEIS ABSTULIT EDES, which can be translated as "The celibate Ambrose
expels the Jews from their houses."[9] Medieval art rarely rewards our curiosity so richly, while leaving us without a wholly reliable method for
resolving inconsistency or apparent contradiction. It might be conjec-
tured that the inconsistency is due to a revision, the correction of one
assertion by another, perhaps made after a short interval in time,[10] or
the result of a simple error, a slip of the chisel, as it were, and nothing
more. Most scholars have in any case concluded that only one of these
assertions could be the intended one, and having to choose, have judged
it more likely that the scene depicts the expulsion of the Arians from
Milan.[11] This judgment builds its case on inference rather than hard
fact, for although Ambrose had adversarial dealings with the Jews as
well as the Arians, there is no historical evidence that, in a literal sense
at least, he expelled either one or the other from the city.

What actually happened, however, to the extent that it can be se-
curely established, does not in the present instance much help us, for we
are dealing with the shadowy processes of legendary elaboration, for
which images like the frieze of the Porta Romana may well themselves
be primary witnesses. Pierre Courcelle, whose work on Ambrosian

iconography is the most authoritative treatment of the subject to date,
interprets the Porta Romana relief as the expulsion of the Arians, chiefly,
so far as I can see, on the basis of the pictorial cycles of the life of
St. Ambrose in late medieval and Renaissance art, where such scenes
are said to appear. But an examination of several examples that Courcelle cites and discusses is by no means decisive on this point. Are the
turbaned, dark-haired, and long-robed victims of the saint's ire in a
fourteenth-century wall painting at Mocchiroli in Lombardy, one of
these examples, unambiguously heretics rather than Jews?[12] I would not
want to press the issue too far, but my reading of the secondary literature
on St. Ambrose, which is now fairly voluminous, suggests to me that, for
recent authors at least, an anti-heretical or anti-Arian Ambrose is a
more congenial figure than an anti-Jewish one, and this, too, may be a
distorting factor in the adjudication of cases that are less than clear-cut,
like the one before us.

The choice between contending interpretations may not have been
so urgent or even wholly meaningful to the medieval viewer. It is time,
however, to turn to Ambrose himself, and to the materials, literary and
pictorial, from which the highly militant image of the Porta Romana
was fashioned. What we know of the saint's life and career comes almost
entirely from the *vita* written at the request of St. Augustine by Paulinus
of Milan, who had been a cleric or a notary in Ambrose's service.[13] It is
Paulinus who mentions that when Ambrose attempted to flee from
Milan in order to avoid having to accept his election, he was miraculously prevented from leaving the city just as he reached the Porta
Romana—something that might have been a factor in the choice of the
portal's later, Romanesque imagery, as has been suggested.[14] Paulinus
next relates the struggles of Ambrose against the Arians, who had been
dominant in Milan and whose machinations against Ambrose he attributes to the evil designs of the Empress Justina. The high moment of this
struggle is the dispute over the possession of one of the major churches
of the city, the Basilica Portiana, miraculously resolved in favor of
Ambrose and the Catholic side. In his narration of these events,
Paulinus makes the telling observation that the mockery of Ambrose by
his Arian enemies, who claimed that the divine favor shown to the saint
was of demonic inspiration, followed the accusations against him of the
Jews. "Theirs was the language of the Jews, their allies," he writes.[15] In

this highly polemical context, the Arian doctrine's tendency to enlarge the role of God the Father in relation to the other persons of the Trinity would have suggested one more charge to hurl against heresy: its proximity to Judaism, or worse, its collusion with it.[16]

While the provocations of Justina and the events around the attempted seizure of the Basilica Portiana exemplify for Paulinus Ambrose's dealings with the Arians, the affair of the synagogue of Callinicum exemplifies Ambrose's involvement with the Jews. Paulinus bases his narration of this affair on the account given by the saint himself in his Epistles 40 and 41.[17] This incident has often been recounted: the Christians of Callinicum, a fortified settlement near the Euphrates in present-day Syria, set fire to the synagogue as well as to a sanctuary of Valentinian Gnostics because the Jews and Valentinians, according to Paulinus, who once again here conjoins Judaism with heresy, had insulted some Christian monks. The emperor Theodosius ordered the local bishop to reconstruct the synagogue and to punish the monks. When the news reached Ambrose, he protested against what he perceived to be an injustice, for in his view, the actions of the Christians should be seen as a manifestation of divine Providence, and the punishment of the culprits would be tantamount to giving aid and comfort to their enemies. Modern scholarship on St. Ambrose has tended in its more apologetic moments to interpret his actions in this case as a reflection of his interest in the proper exercise of political authority in religious matters rather than as a sign of an ingrained hostility toward Judaism.[18] However this may be, the Callinicum affair must have been in twelfth-century Milan the principal grounds for his reputation as an anti-Jewish champion. The statement inscribed on the Porta Romana that "he expelled the Jews from their houses" cannot in a literal way be connected with this incident, yet something like a distant echo of it reverberates in the monument.

Students of the life of St. Ambrose have had at their disposal a second Latin *vita*, datable to the ninth century, and represented by a single manuscript that Monsignor Paredi discovered in the library of the abbey of Saint-Gall.[19] As might be expected, it follows Paulinus on the "factual" outline of the saint's life, but it has not escaped attention that it considerably sharpens his anti-Jewish convictions. Thus, a kind of panegyric that follows the relation of the edifying circumstances of his death concludes with the following words of praise: "Among mortals, it would be difficult to find another man so prudent as he in his total avoidance of contacts with Jews and heretics, not to speak of other marks of familiarity and even a simple salutation. In his uncompromising rejection of the enemies of the Catholic faith, he execrated the festivals of the Jews and their fasting days, just as he avoided the evil councils of the heretics and the temples of the pagans, in order not to provide, in the words of the Psalmist, 'an occasion for scandal'" (Psalm 105:36). This conception of heroic virtue, requiring a total rupture of one's social ties with a pariah group, can be found also in the writings of a contemporary of the anonymous author, Agobard of Lyon.[20] This seems worth pondering in the present context, since pushed to its logical conclusion, it would render the coexistence of different religious persuasions at close range impossible or, at any rate, unthinkable.

For the sculptor of the Porta Romana, as well as for his putative audience, the categories of Jew and Arian—*Iudeorum vel hereticorum*, as the Carolingian *vita* has it—however distinguishable they might be in the abstract, could be comfortably amalgamated. The outbreak of heresy in the twelfth century, particularly strong in and around Milan, and often conceptualized in contemporary writings as a resurgence of Arianism,[21] might also have stimulated hostility toward the Jews, though in concrete factual terms, little is known about the Jewish population of the city at this time.[22] Yet whatever the monument might owe to history, theology, or the contemporaneous social reality, its conception and design are of biblical inspiration and follow a visual model. It is indeed all too apparent that the composition casts Ambrose in the role of Christ driving the merchants and money changers from the Temple. The sources are Matthew 21:12, Mark 11:15, and John 2:13–16, the latter best accounting for the major features of the relief: "The Passover of the Jews was at hand, and Jesus went up to Jerusalem. In the temple he found those who were selling oxen and sheep and pigeons, and the money changers at their business. And making a whip of cords (*quasi flagellum de funiculis*), he drove them all, with their sheep and oxen, out of the temple; and he poured the coins of the money changers and overturned their tables. And he told those who sold pigeons, 'Take these things away; you shall not make my Father's house a house of trade.'"

These verses have a rich exegetical history which, to the best of my knowledge, has not yet received detailed scholarly scrutiny. Ambrose himself cites them in his tract *Sermo contra Auxentium*, where he compares the firm, but in his view, mild demeanor of Jesus toward the merchants of the temple with the cruelty of the armed men in the service of the Arians, wielding not the whip but the sword.[23] St. Augustine, close here to the spirit of the bishop of Milan, asserts in his commentary on St. John's Gospel that Jesus' wrath was directed against the Jews and the blasphemies of those he terms "false Christians."[24] In the period of the Gregorian movement, the cleansing of the temple came to be understood as a charge to rid the church itself of abuses. Thus, according to the *Glossa ordinaria*, the pigeon sellers driven out by Christ are those who have stained themselves with the heresy of simony, "those who for the imposition of hands, by which the gift of the Holy Spirit is received, demand a payment."[25]

If the temple merchants prefigure error, enmity, or pollution of true doctrine, Christ's enactment of an energetic, cleansing violence is taken in Milan to exemplify or to justify a certain militant ideal or style of episcopal conduct in defense of the faith. Righteous, cleansing anger is concretized in the figure of the scourge, understood simultaneously as a weapon and its anthropomorphic embodiment—as Augustine expresses it when he speaks in his commentary of both Jesus and his whip as "*flagellum Iudeorum.*"[26] Beyond the relief of the Porta Romana, there is another witness of this hagiographic appropriation on behalf of St. Ambrose now attached to the north doorway of the basilica of Sant'Ambrogio, where he is depicted in a severely frontalized, iconic stance, holding the episcopal crozier in one hand, and in the other a ceremonial staff from which four lash-like, fluttering straps extend (fig. 6). The date of the work is not known, but I am inclined to think that it originated in the later decades of the twelfth century, and thus not too distant in time from the Porta Romana.[27] No older instance of the scourge as the saint's attribute has thus far been discovered, though examples in later art abound.[28] On the other hand, we know on the basis of a Milanese source datable to around 1130, the *Ordo Ecclesiae ambrosianae mediolanensis* of Beroldus Vetus, that at this time, it was customary for the bishop of Milan to carry a *flagellum* in the procession from the cathedral to Sant'Ambrogio that took place on the anniversary of the saint's ordination (December 7).[29] The cross-bearing acolyte who precedes Ambrose on the Porta Romana relief evidently makes reference to this liturgical practice.

Depictions of the expulsion of the merchants and money changers from the temple are comparatively uncommon in early medieval art. One of the oldest examples of the subject is found on a famous Milanese monument, the Carolingian golden altar of Sant'Ambrogio. A somewhat more sustained production of images of the Expulsion appears in both northern and southern Europe during the eventful times of reform and upheaval following the year 1000.[30] Whatever their style or material constitution, these images have certain elements in common, exemplified by the colored drawing in the early twelfth-century Gospels of Mathilda of Tuscany in the Pierpont Morgan Library (fig. 7): a figure of Christ wielding a whip, a setting of arches or turrets designating the sacred precinct of the temple, and a more or less expansive display of people engaged in profane activities—bird sellers, dealers in cattle, men at counting boards or gaming tables.[31] This summary inventory of basic components brings to the fore the distinctive features of the Porta Romana relief. The emphasis is here not on the varied acts of profanation, but on the forced exodus of the evildoers, whose attributes allude to mercantile activities in only a generalized sense and make no reference at all to money transactions. There is also no architectural marker of any kind. All this, of course, is explained by the sculptor's need to recast his model for the purposes at hand, erasing those details that point to the specifics of the biblical narrative, reshaping the rest into a somewhat different story, the apocryphal uprooting of religious dissidence carried out in a manner that conveys the effect of an exorcism.

Ambrose himself has something to say on this topic in the treatise *De officiis*, where, in fact, he argues vigorously on moral, social, and economic grounds against the practice in his time of expelling strangers (*peregrini*) from Rome at times of famine.[32] Nevertheless, in a number of recorded instances, Jews were offered the choice of conversion or expulsion by saintly bishops of sixth- and seventh-century Gaul.[33] In a late, legendary elaboration that is reminiscent of the case of St. Ambrose in Milan, the Jews of Rome were presented with the same choice during the pontificate of Boniface IV (608–15), when this pope proceeded with the cleansing of the Pantheon and its transformation into a church under the patronage of the Virgin Mary.[34] The letter that Frederick, archbishop of Mainz from 937 to 939, sent to Pope Leo VII in order to ask for advice on how to deal with the Jews of the city is often cited by students of Christian-Jewish relations in the early Middle Ages concerned especially with the historical antecedents and background of the later, mass expulsions of the Jews carried out in 1290 by Edward I in England and not long after by Philip the Fair in France. Leo's answer was to direct the archbishop to preach Christian doctrine in vigorous and untiring fashion to the Jews and seek to induce them to accept baptism, though without the use of force. "If they refuse to believe," his reply goes on, "you are authorized by us to expel them from your cities, since we cannot live in community with the enemies of God, as the Apostle says: 'Do not bear the yoke of the unbelievers. For what has justice in common with iniquity? Or what fellowship has light with darkness?'" (2 Cor. 6:14).[35] The monument in Milan, I would argue, is a symptom of the growing appeal of this policy, heretofore not explicitly sanctioned and applied in only episodic fashion.

It is pertinent to ask whether St. Ambrose's combative posture is an isolated and purely Milanese phenomenon, or whether the art of the twelfth and thirteenth centuries registers other examples of such heightened apostolic or patristic militancy. The formation of a knightly ideal and the justification it provided for combat in defense of the faith gave to soldier-saints a certain iconographic currency. The image of St. James as a warrior on horseback setting off for battle (*Santiago matamoros*) makes its initial appearance, so far as we know, with the relief within the church at Santiago de Compostela, which must be roughly contemporaneous with the Porta Romana sculpture.[36] It has been noted that from the middle of the twelfth century, Paul is depicted bearing or wielding a sword, and his conversion is staged as a fall from a horse, the customary attribute of knighthood.[37] As these examples suggest, this process of militarization affected saintly and adventuresome preachers of the Gospels, but not bishops, men in clerical orders whose conduct was subject to different expectations or cast into other hagiographic molds. Among the Fathers, Augustine stood as the model exponent of Christian doctrine against Judaism and heresy, not the man that modern scholarship permits us to envisage, but a figure of much more ample and fluctuating contours, to whom all sorts of anti-Jewish tracts by lesser or anonymous authors were attributed.[38] Although it is the fashion in historical scholarship to seek to strip away these inauthentic accretions, they are telling evidence of the high reputation achieved in this role by the bishop of

Hippo in medieval eyes. Artists generally show him as the Christian ora-
tor or controversialist *par excellence*, taking on learned and contentious
adversaries whose arguments he refutes in duel-like confrontations. But
such triumphs may take quite virulent forms, as in a drawing of an
eleventh-century Norman manuscript, exceptional for its violence even
as allegory, in which Augustine thrusts his crozier into the throat of the
defeated Manichee Faustus.[39]

Augustine has a place in this discussion since the expulsion of the
Jews from their homeland and their dispersion throughout the world is a
significant element in his theological reflection.[40] In the Pseudo-
Augustinian *De altercatione Ecclesiae et Synagogae*, known to have had a
wide diffusion and an impact on the liturgy of Holy Week, the personi-
fied Church cites the Jews' degradation as proof of her divine election in
the place of a discredited Synagogue.[41] Within the very large body of
images that this polemical dialogue directly or indirectly inspired, it
seems pertinent to single out for attention in the present context a certain number which, like the composition of the Song of Songs in the
Cîteaux Bible (fig. 8), depict the defeat of *Synagoga* as a forcible ejection
by the Lord from His presence (an action compounded in the illu-
mination by her, presumably later, physical erasure).[42] We meet here a
motif with some currency in exegesis, the attribution of contrasting fates
and moral significance to conceptually symmetrical pairs of men and
women, wives or sons, like Rachel and Leah, Jacob and Esau, Hannah
and Peninnah (1 Sam. 1:1–28), the older, rebellious Vashti, and her
young and fair successor, Esther. The pictorial treatment of these anti-
thetical pairings in Romanesque art may, like the Cîteaux *Synagoga* and
Ecclesia, take the form of almost emblematic, judgment-like scenes, in
which the Lord's blessing or embrace is conferred on the favored side,
and dismissal inflicted on the reprobate (fig. 9).[43]

Among these Old Testament foreshadowings of the future separation of Jews and Christians, the figures of Sarah and Hagar have the
pride of place, expulsion being integral to the story and no mere meta-
phorical manner of speaking. In St. Paul's treatment of the story in the
Epistle to the Galatians (4:22–27) and for some authors after him, the
two women stand for the two covenants, Hagar the slave for the Lord's
pact with Israel on Mt. Sinai, and Sarah, the free woman, for his promise of the New Jerusalem.[44] Paul concludes (Gal. 4:30) by citing the
words addressed by Sarah to Abraham: "Drive out the slave woman and

her son, for the son shall not share in the inheritance of the free woman's son." Reflecting this exegesis, the initial letters in a group of thirteenth-century Bibles, to which Luba Eleen has called attention, show Paul carrying out this expulsion in person (fig. 10).[45] Paul's doctrine of the supercession of the Old Covenant by the New is expressed in the Hebrews initial of another Parisian Gothic Bible belonging to the same series, which exhibits the Apostle driving the Synagogue away with the help of a cross (fig. 11).[46] The rhetoric of allegory, sometimes hermetic beyond its textual confines, converges here in ominous fashion upon the realities of the contemporaneous history.

NOTES

1. B. Blumenkranz, *Le Juif médiéval au miroir de l'art chrétien* (Paris, 1966); idem, *Juden und Judentum in der mittelalterlichen Kunst* (Stuttgart, 1965).

2. Blumenkranz, *Le Juif médiéval*, 13.

3. Ibid., 15.

4. London, British Library Add. 10546, fol. 25v; Blumenkranz, *Le Juif médiéval*, 21–22.

5. Paris, Bibliothèque Nationale Fr. 820, fol. 192; Blumenkranz, *Le Juif médiéval*, 21–22.

6. Munich, Bayerische Staatsbibliothek Clm. 6404, fol. 68; R. Mellinkoff, *Outcasts: Signs of Otherness in Northern European Art of the Later Middle Ages* (Berkeley, 1993), 1:74; and C. Kratzert, *Die illustrierten Handschriften der Weltchronik des Rudolf von Ems* (Ph.D. diss, Berlin, 1974), 24–30.

7. L. Beltrami, "I bassorilievi commemorativi della Lega Lombarda già esistenti alla antica Porta Romana," *Archivio Storico Lombardo* (1895): 395–416; T. Binaghi Olivari, "I rilievi di Porta Romana e alcune sculture milanesi del XII secolo," *Contributi dell'Istituto di Storia dell'Arte Medioevale e Moderna*, Pubblicazioni dell'Universita Cattolica del Sacro Cuore, Scienze Storiche, ser. 3, 14 (Milan, 1972), 2:44–52; M. T. Fiorio, "'Opus turrium et portarum': Le sculture di Porta Romana," *Milano e la Lombardia* (Milan, 1993): 189–92, 471–73, nos. 404–5; A. von Hülsen-Esch, *Romanische Skulptur in Oberitalien als Reflex der kommunalen Entwicklung im 12. Jahrhundert* (Berlin, 1994).

8. On these gates, see F. Reggiori, "L'architettura militare a Milano e nel territorio durante l'età medioevale e rinascimentale," *Storia di Milano*, vol. 8 (Milan, 1957), 777–820, and J. Gardner, "An Introduction to the Iconography

of the Medieval Italian City Gate," *Dumbarton Oaks Papers* 41 (1987): 199–213.

9. Hülsen-Esch, *Romanische Skulptur*, 42–43, 83 ff; P. Courcelle, *Recherches sur Saint Ambroise: "Vies" anciennes, culture, iconographie* (Paris, 1973), 187–88.

10. A. von Hülsen-Esch, "Mailand: Skulptur im Spannungsfeld der kommunalen Entwicklung," *Studien zur Geschichte der europäischen Skulptur im 12./13. Jahrhundert*, ed. H. Beck and K. Hengevoss-Dürkop (Frankfurt, 1994), 257.

11. Hülsen-Esch, *Romanische Skulptur*, and Courcelle, *Recherches*, 187–88. R. Jullian, *Les Sculpteurs romans de l'Italie septentrionale* (Paris, 1952), pl. XXVIII, 7, calls the scene "Saint Ambroise chassant les Ariens et les juifs." J. P. Puricellis, *Ambrosianae mediolani basilicae ac monasterii, hodie cistertiensis, monumenta* (Milan, 1645), 925 (cited by Hülsen-Esch, *Romanische Skulptur*, 52), holds that Ambrose expelled not only the Arians, but also the Jews, because of their evil usurious practices, while G. L. Barni, *Storia di Milano*, vol. 4 (Milan, 1955), 85, supposes that the Milanese resented Barbarossa's concession of privileges to them and regarded the Jews as covert allies of the imperial side. Courcelle (*Recherches*, 188) sees in the inscription concerning an expulsion of the Jews from the city only a reflection of "l'antisémitisme croissant du IXe au XIIe siècle."

12. Courcelle, *Recherches*, 192.

13. PL 14, 27–46; E. Lamirande, *Paulin de Milan et la 'Vita Ambrosii'* (Paris, 1983). For the life of Ambrose and its historical background, see J.-R. Palanque, *Saint Ambroise et l'empire romain* (Paris, 1933), and most recently, N. B. McLynn, *Ambrose of Milan: Church and Court in a Christian Capital* (Berkeley, 1994).

14. PL 14, 29. Hülsen-Esch, *Romanische Skulptur*, 86.

15. PL 14, 32.

16. B. Blumenkranz, *Les Auteurs chrétiens latins du moyen âge sur les juifs et le judaisme* (Paris, 1963), 196, 16, remarks in connection with the Pseudo-Augustinian sermon *Contra Iudaeos, Paganos, et Arianos* that the comparison between Jews and Arians was commonly made. Athanasius calls the latter "New Jews."

17. PL 14, 34; McLynn, *Ambrose of Milan*, 298–315.

18. See, for example, P. Courcelle, "Des sources antiques à l'iconographie médiévale de Saint Ambroise," *Ambrosius episcopus*, ed. G. Lazzati (Milan, 1976), 1:197–99, and Courcelle, *Recherches*, 235, where the "prétendu antisémitisme d'Ambroise" is mentioned.

19. *Vita e meriti di S. Ambrogio: Testo inedito del secolo nono illustrato con le miniature del Salterio di Arnolfo*, ed. A. Paredi (Milan, 1964). Courcelle, *Recherches*, 49 ff.

20. Courcelle, *Recherches*, 103, 139. Agobard, *De cavendo convictu et societate Judaica* (PL 104, 107–14), on which see also the commentary of H. Schrecken-berg, *Die christlichen Adversus-Judaeos-Texte und ihr literarisches und historisches Umfeld (1.–11.Jh.)*, Europäische Hochschulschriften, ser. 23, vol. 172 (Frankfurt, 1982), 491 ff. This connection was pointed out to me by Jeremy Cohen at the Notre Dame conference.

21. Y.M.-J. Congar, "'Arriana Haeresis' comme désignation du Néo-manichéisme au XIIe siècle. Contribution à l'histoire d'une typification de l'hérésie au moyen âge," *Revue des sciences philosophiques et théologiques* 43 (1959): 449–61.

22. S. Simohnson, *The Jews of the Duchy of Milan* (Jerusalem, 1982) 1:xiii–xvi.

23. PL 16, 1014, cited by Courcelle, *Recherches*, 158.

24. *In Iohannis evangelium* (CCSL 36, 102): "Flagellatus est flagellis Iudaeorum, flagellatur blasphemiis falsorum christianorum."

25. PL 104, 153. The relevance of this interpretation for depictions of the Cleansing of the Temple in the period of Gregorian Reform was noted by R. Rough, *The Reformist Illuminations in the Gospels of Mathilda, Countess of Tuscany* (The Hague, 1973), 25.

26. See above, n. 24. The parliamentary designation of a Whip (or Chief Whip) perpetuates this usage.

27. Binaghi Olivari, "I relievi di Porta Romana," 51; Courcelle, *Recherches*, 158–59, assigns it to the eleventh century, which seems too early.

28. The study of E. Callegaris, "Il flagello di Sant'Ambrogio e le legende delle lotte Ariane," *Ambrosiana: Scritti vari pubblicati nel XV centenario dalla morte di S. Ambrogio* (Milan, 1897), was not available to me. On the history of this attribute, see also E. Cattaneo, "Il flagello di Sant'Ambrogio," *Studi storici in onore di Ottorino Bertolini* (Pisa, 1972), 1:93–103.

29. Hülsen-Esch, *Romanische Skulptur*, 87, and earlier, Cattaneo, *Il flagello*, 93–94.

30. V. H. Elbern, *Der karolingische Goldaltar von Mailand*, Bonner Beiträge zur Kunstwissenschaft 2 (Bonn, 1952), 35–36.

31. New York, Pierpont Morgan Library, M. 492, fol. 84; G. F. Warner, *Gospels of Mathilda, Countess of Tuscany, 1055–1115* (Oxford, 1917); Rough, *The Reformist Illuminations*, 25.

32. E. Faure, Saint Ambroise et l'expulsion des pérégrins de Rome," *Etudes d'histoire du droit canonique dédiées à G. Le Bras* (Paris, 1965), 1:523–40.

33. B. Blumenkranz, *Juifs et chrétiens dans le monde occidental, 430–1096*, Paris, 1960, 99 ff; G. A. Langmuir, "From Ambrose of Milan to Emicho of Leiningen: The Transformation of Hostility against Jews in Northern Christen-

dom," *Gli ebrei nell'alto medieoevo*, Settimane del Centro italiano di studi sull'alto medieoevo 26 (Spoleto, 1980), 313–68, reprint in Langmuir, *Toward a Definition of Antisemitism* (Berkeley, 1990), esp. 75 ff; K. R. Stow, *Alienated Minority: The Jews of Medieval Latin Europe* (Cambridge, 1992), 46–47.

34. Blumenkranz, *Juifs et chrétiens*, 104.

35. S. Simonsohn, ed., *The Apostolic See and the Jews*, vol. 1, *Documents, 492–1404* (Toronto, 1988–91), 33, no. 34; K. R. Stow, "Hatred of the Jews or Love of the Church," *Antisemitism through the Ages*, ed. S. Almog (Jerusalem, 1988), 76–77; Schreckenberg, *Adversus-Judaeos-Texte*, 527–28.

36. S. Alcolea, *La catedral de Santiago* (Madrid, 1958), 114, and the exhibition catalogue *Santiago de Compostela. 1000 ans de pèlerinage européen* (Ghent, 1985), 362–63, no. 359. For the development of militant sanctity in relation to St. James, see C. Erdmann's now classic *Die Enstehung des Kreuzzugsgedankens* (1935; reprint Darmstadt, 1965), 254–55.

37. L. Eleen, *The Illustrations of the Pauline Epistles in French and English Bibles of the Twelfth and Thirteenth Centuries* (New York, 1982), 38 ff.

38. B. Blumenkranz, *Die Judenpredigt Augustins, Ein Beitrag zur Geschichte der jüdisch-christlichen Beziehungen in den ersten Jahrhunderten*, Basler Beiträge zur Geschichtswissenschaft 25 (Basel, 1946); idem, *Auteurs chrétiens*, 20–22, 35, 39–42, 52, 54–55; idem, "Augustins et les juifs, Augustins et le judaisme," *Recherches augustiniennes* 1 (1958): 225–41, reprint in Blumenkranz, *Juifs et chrétiens: Patristique et moyen âge* (London, 1977), no. 3, esp. 237 ff.

39. Paris, Bibliothèque Nationale lat. 2079, fol. 55; Exh. Catal. *Trésors des abbayes normandes* (Rouen 1979), 113, no. 126.

40. Augustine, *De civitate Dei* 4.34, and 18.18; Blumenkranz, *Augustin et les juifs*, 230 ff; M. R. Cohen, *Under Crescent and Cross: The Jews in the Middle Ages* (Princeton, 1994), 20–21.

41. PL 42, 1131–40; Blumenkranz, *Auteurs chrétiens*, 39–42, no. 23.

42. Dijon, Bibl. Mun. Ms. 14, fol. 60; W. Cahn, *Romanesque Manuscripts: The Twelfth Century*, A Survey of Manuscripts Illuminated in France, vol. 2 (London, 1996), 70–72, no. 58. On the theme of *Synagoga* and *Ecclesia*, see M. Schlauch, "The Allegory of Church and Synagogue," *Speculum* 14 (1939): 448–64, and P. Bloch, "Nachwirkungen des Alten Bundes in der christlichen Kunst," *Monumenta Judaica: Handbuch* (Cologne, 1963), 751 ff. H. Jochum, in a study that came to my attention after the completion of this paper ("Ecclesia und Synagoga. Antijudaismus in der christlichen Kunst des Mittelalters," *Das Erste Kreuzzug 1096 and seine Folgen*, Schriften des Archivs der Evangelischen Kirche im Rheinland, 9 [Düsseldorf, 1996], 123–38, devotes some remarks to the theme of the ejected ("Verstossene") Synagoga.

43. My illustration is drawn from a manuscript of Glossed Minor Prophets, most probably from Anchin, in the Pierpont Morgan Library, M. 962 (Cahn, *Romanesque Manuscripts*, 2:132, no. 109).

44. Schreckenberg, *Adversus-Judaeos-Texte*, 89, 99 ff., 245–46, 306, 402, 426.

45. Eleen, *Illustrations of the Pauline Epistles*, 118 ff. The manuscript here illustrated, a small Bible from the Grands-Augustins (Paris, Bibliothèque Mazarine, Ms. 20), should be added to the list of codices grouped by that author under the heading "Prologue Cycle."

46. Paris, Bibl. Sainte–Geneviève, Ms. 1180; Eleen, *Illustrations of the Pauline Epistles*, 120, no. 10.

Fig. 1. Exodus Frontispiece, Moutiers-Grandval Bible (ninth century).
London, Brit. Lib. Add. 10546, fol. 25v (British Library). By permission
of the British Library.

Fig. 2. Moses addresses the Israelites, Rudolf of Ems, *World Chronicle* (thirteenth century). Munich, Bayer. Staatbibl. Clm. 6406, fol. 68 (Marburg Bildarchiv). By permission of Foto Marburg/Art Resource, New York.

Fig. 3. Milan, Porta Romana, eighteenth century. Engraving (after Carotti, *Archivio Storico Lombardo*, 1896, 423).

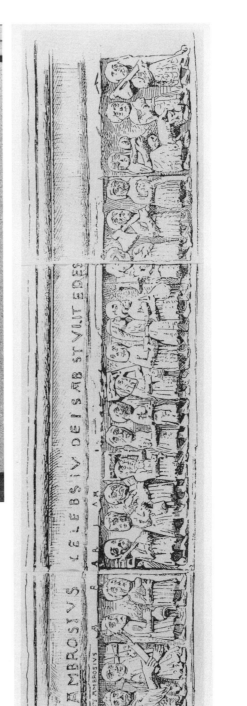

Fig. 4 (*right*). St. Ambrose expels the Jews, relief from the Porta Romana (1171). Milan, Castello Sforzesco (Foto Saporetti, Milan). By permission of the Civico Museo d'Arte Antica-Milan, Castello Sforzesco.

Fig. 5 (*below*). St. Ambrose expels the Jews, relief from the Porta Romana (1171), reconstruction (after Beltrami, *Archivio Storico Lombardo*, 1895, 404–6).

Fig. 6. St. Ambrose, relief from the atrium of Sant'Ambrogio, Milan, twelfth century (after F. Reggiori, *La Basilica di Sant'Ambrogio*).

Fig. 7. Cleansing of the Temple, Gospels of Mathilda of Tuscany
(twelfth century). Pierpont Morgan Library, New York, M. 492, fol. 84.
By permission of the Pierpont Morgan Library.

Fig. 8. The Lord between the Church and the Synagogue, Song of Songs initial, Cîteaux Bible (1109). Bibliothèque Municipale de Dijon-France, Ms. 14, fol. 60. By permission of the Bibliothèque Municipale.

Fig. 9. The Lord with Jacob and Esau, Malachy initial, Glossed Minor Prophets, Anchin (twelfth century). Pierpont Morgan Library, New York, M. 962, fol. 133. By permission of the Pierpont Morgan Library.

Fig. 10. St. Paul drives out Hagar and Ishmael, Galatians initial of a thirteenth-century Bible. Paris, Bibl. Mazarine, Ms. 20, fol. 412 (Haseloff Collection, Bildarchiv zur Buchmalerei, Universität des Saarlandes). By permission of the Bildarchiv zur Buchmalerei.

Fig. 11. St. Paul drives out the Synagogue, Hebrews initial of a thirteenth-century Bible. Paris, Bibl. Sainte-Geneviève, Ms. 1180, fol. 353v (Haseloff Collection, Bildarchiv zur Buchmalerei, Universität des Saarlandes). By permission of the Bildarchiv zur Buchmalerei.

s e v e n

Put in No-Man's-Land: Guibert of Nogent's Accusations against a Judaizing and Jew-Supporting Christian

JAN M. ZIOLKOWSKI

Conversions of both Christians to Judaism and Jews to Christianity took place in the early Middle Ages. But the only document from any such convert was left by a Christian who became a Jew: the well-known and fascinating case of Bodo, the ninth-century Alemannic nobleman who set out from the imperial court of Louis the Pious (814–840) in France ostensibly to make a pilgrimage to Rome but actually to flee to the religious freedom of Spain. He had himself circumcised, took up the name Eleazar, married a Jewish wife, adopted the dress of a knight and the hair style of a Jew, and not only practiced his new religion openly but even entered into a polemic correspondence in Latin with Paul Alvarus, who was his mirror image: a Jewish-born Christian.[1] In the twelfth century and later in the Middle Ages the situation could not differ more acutely. Whereas not a single first-hand account of a convert to Judaism survives, such figures as Petrus Alfonsi (who had been Rabbi Moses Sephardi until his conversion and who lived from 1062 to ca. 1140), the Premonstratensian Hermann of Cologne (who went by the name Judah until his baptism and who lived from 1107 or 1108 until after 1181), and the Dominican Pablo Christiani (also known as Friar Paul Christian) left or inspired substantial written records that dealt at least implicitly with the experiences and motivations of their apostasies from Judaism to Christianity.[2]

The reasons behind any possible change in the direction of conversions from the early Middle Ages to the twelfth century are too complicated to be reduced to a single explanation that would hold valid for the whole of Europe or for all of the personalities involved—a host of psychological, political, theological, and economic factors could have come into play in the decisions of individuals to renounce one faith and adopt another. But whatever the specific motivations of individual converts, it is apparent that, at the latest from the end of the eleventh century, the stakes in converting to Judaism from Christianity grew dangerously high. A Jew who turned Christian might expect to win considerable rewards; in contrast, a Christian—whether a person born into a Christian family or a Jew who had accepted baptism under duress—who abandoned the Christian faith and became Jewish ran the risk of capital punishment, because in church law apostasy came to be considered heresy, and heresy was punishable by death.[3] In the succinct wording of *Las siete partidas,* "Where a Christian is so unfortunate as to become a Jew, we order that he shall be put to death just as if he had become a heretic; and we decree that his property shall be disposed of in the same way that we stated should be done with that of heretics."[4] Converts to Judaism would have had to take flight from their homelands so as to keep hidden their Christian origins.

These intensified circumstances in the twelfth century would have worked at least two effects on people who adopted Jewish customs and beliefs—that is, people who Judaized—or who were perceived as favoring Jews in their behavior or policies. The first would be to reduce still further the number of outright converts from Christianity. If even in less intolerant times a Christian who wished to give up his faith and profess Judaism felt obliged to emigrate from Christendom to Muslim Spain before publicizing his intention, a Christian in the twelfth century who wanted to do the same could hardly have been more open about his inclinations. The second would be to render the accusation of "Judaizing" a most threatening weapon wielded against a person by enemies.

Thanks to the availability of databases for two of the largest text series of Medieval Latin theological writings (namely, the *Patrologia latina* and the *Corpus Christianorum*), it would seem on the face of it an easy matter to build a dossier of medieval reports about Judaizing or Judaeophile Christians. The difficulty lies in finding the words under which to

conduct a lexicographic search. The verb *iudaizare*—which would appear to have been the natural candidate to describe the types of behavior
and outlook under discussion here—was established in Latin through its
single appearance in the Vulgate Bible almost as a terminus technicus,
meaning "to live in the Jewish way," but with reference exclusively to
Christian antiquity.[5] Paul, who declared that before his own conversion
he was especially advanced in his knowledge of Judaism and in his
standing in the Jewish community, employed the verb in his letter to the
Galatians (2:14). When Paul tells of rebuking Peter for refusing to eat
with Gentile members of the church at Antioch, he implies that Peter
would have eaten with them if they had conformed to Jewish sumptuary
rules and that Peter's action was an attempt to "compel the Gentiles to
Judaize":

> But when I saw that they walked not uprightly unto the truth of the
> gospel, I said to Cephas [= Peter] before them all: If thou, being a Jew,
> livest after the manner of the Gentiles, and not as the Jews do, how
> dost thou compel the Gentiles to live as do the Jews?[6]

The verb *iudaizare*, used most often in interpretations of this verse in the
Bible, seems to have taken on associations with the remote past—as if
once the Christian faith had become established, no one would have
dreamt of judaizing. Thus there is a definite shock-value when Eleazar
(né Bodo) adduces precisely the verb *iudaizare* at the end of his text to
describe his decision to become a Jew.[7] He can use it and acknowledge
his conversion with impunity, however, only from the safe haven of
Muslim Spain. Within Latin Christendom itself, the verb may appear in
the second and third person—in accusations of discouraged behavior
leveled against another—but not in the first person. *Judaizing* was a form
of conduct no Christian could afford to admit.

Which Christians would have been most likely to spend enough
time with Jews to become attracted to their beliefs, or most likely to
incur suspicion of favoring Jewish interests and therefore accused falsely
of Judaizing? Three groups come to mind. First, scholars who are known
to have made special efforts to learn Hebrew and become conversant
with Jewish Bible exegesis. Little evidence is forthcoming that any so-
called Christian Hebraist of the twelfth century was led by his linguistic

or exegetic researches to consider adopting Judaism or to show a special supportiveness toward the Jews, such that he was rendered suspect to Christian authorities. Perhaps, however, the Christian Hebraist Archbishop Gerard of York (1100–08) acquired his reputation as a practitioner of the black arts partly because he possessed Jewish psalters.[8] There is also the evidence of wavering monks and clerics mentioned as background to Ralph of Flaix's commentary on Leviticus.[9] Because of the great reverence attached to Hebrew—the first of the *tres linguae sacrae* and the basis of the *hebraica veritas* to which Jerome's authority added no small weight—there was no danger that Hebraizing (a verb that did not exist in the Middle Ages)[10] and Judaizing would be routinely conflated.

Another group likely to have judaized or been suspected of judaizing comprises servants of Jews, about whom the Christian legal system had been preoccupied from the early fourth century at the latest. Here it is interesting to note the particular concern about such servants that Rigord (ca. 1158–1208) voiced in his entry for the year 1182 in the *Gesta Philippi Augusti*: "When they [= the Jews] had made a long sojourn there, they grew so rich that they claimed as their own almost half of the whole city, and had Christians in their houses as menservants and maidservants, who were open backsliders from the faith of Jesus Christ, and *judaized* with the Jews."[11]

The third group was made up of those rulers, noblemen, and their agents who through financial dealings had more contact with Jews than did most other medieval Christians. Even a king such as Louis VII, the first French king to be tagged *rex christianissimus*, was taxed with having shown undue favor to the Jews. The proxy of Richard Lionheart, William Longchamp, who was bishop of Ely as well as chancellor and chief justiciar of England, incurred harsh criticism for his attempts— entirely unsuccessful—to bring to justice the persons responsible for the York Massacre in 1190.

The most peculiar source in which the verb *iudaizare* occurs—applied to a nobleman—is the *Liber monodiarum mearum* (which could be translated as "The Book of My Solo Songs") by Guibert of Nogent (1053–1124). The *Liber* has been plumbed repeatedly and deservedly by historians for (among other things) the very full account it gives of the communal uprising in Laon in 1111 and for the briefer one of a massacre of Jews which took place before the First Crusade. What seems to have slipped notice is the unusual description it gives of Jean, count of Soissons. This particular section of the *Monodiae*, it is my conviction, is as curiously revealing of twelfth-century attitudes toward a sometimes pro-Jewish aristocracy as the image of the dwarf on the giant's shoulder is of the twelfth-century relation to the classical past.[12]

Guibert holds considerable promise for such an investigation because of his uncanny ability to record bits of information that are extraordinarily revealing of contemporary attitudes, even though he does not betray any particular awareness of their importance. For instance, when relating the story of a forced convert who eventually became a monk after suffering the loss of his parents in a pogrom, Guibert quotes the sorts of reasoning that the instigators of the massacre elaborated to justify their actions. He recounts:

> In that monastery of Fly there is a monk of Jewish origin. At the time when talk of a crusade to Jerusalem began to reverberate throughout the Latin world for the first time he was rescued from his superstition in the following manner. At Rouen one day, some men who had taken the cross with the intention of leaving for the crusade began complaining among themselves. '*Here we are,*' they said, '*going off to attack God's enemies in the East, having to travel tremendous distances, when there are Jews right here before our very eyes. No race is more hostile to God than they are. Our project is insane!*' Having said this they armed themselves, rounded up some Jews in a church—whether by force or by ruse I don't know—and led them out to put them to the sword regardless of age or sex. Those who agreed to submit to the Christian way of life could, however, escape the impending slaughter. It was during this massacre that a nobleman saw a little boy, took pity on him, whisked him away, and took him to his own mother.[13]

However much weight one places on the accuracy of Guibert's report about this incident, the central sentence in this passage—which I have italicized in the English translation—is invaluable in conveying with almost crystal-like symmetry how the Crusading mentality could escalate from hostility toward an external infidel to hostility toward an internal infidel.

This Jewish-born monk—a kind of proto-Hermann of Cologne or Pablo Christiani—became, notably, the recipient of a special volume composed by Guibert. Guibert tells us:

> To increase the fervor of his already robust faith I sent him a little book of mine that I had written almost four years earlier against the count of Soissons, who was a Judaizer and a heretic.[14]

Once again, the sense of symmetry is overpowering: in tending like a physician to a patient, Guibert prescribes for this unnamed Christianized Jew the treatise *De incarnatione contra Judaeos* that he wrote in 1111 against the Judaizing Christian, Count Jean of Soissons.[15]

Jean is a particular bugbear for Guibert, who devotes to him an entire chapter later in the *Monodiae* (3.16). Apart from Guibert's chapter, there exists no real prosopographic information about him and his activities. In the words of Edmond-René Labande, who produced the standard edition, "On est fort mal informé sur cet homme."[16] Without much to support Guibert's picture of Jean, it is reasonable to suppose that Guibert's picture is just that: a picture that lies far from any actuality. Guibert, thus, in my argument, distorted any underlying reality about Jean's lineage, beliefs, and personal habits to suit his own stereotypes of anyone who would have doubts about Christianity and curiosities about Judaism.

The chapter on Jean is a kind of triptych in which the first panel deals with his parentage, the second with his own perversities in religion and sexuality, and the final with his consequent demise. In the first panel Guibert touches lightly upon the bad character that Jean inherited on the paternal side but lavishes substantial attention upon the nefarious deeds of his mother. The maternal minihistory of the mother has an almost geometrically regular shape, as it relates how she "had ordered a deacon's tongue pulled out of his throat and his eyes gouged out";[17] how she collaborated with a Jew to poison her own brother; how the Jew was burned at the stake for this crime; how she suffered a stroke from overeating just before Lent; and how her subsequent illness almost led to the removal of her tongue in an attempted cure. The events can be charted as follows:

1. Persecution of deacon through extraction of tongue and eyes
2. Poisoning of brother with help of a Jew

3.   Burning of the Jew at the stake
4.   Suffering of stroke after gluttony at end of Shrovetide
5.   Nearly undergoing extraction of tongue

This chiastic structure takes to an extreme the biblical *lex talionis* of "eye for eye, tooth for tooth." Indeed, it suggests crime and punishment—or sin and punishment—of an almost Dante-esque form: the punishments are *contrappassi* of a truly infernal sort, fitted to correspond to the sin. Yet this is not to say that the symmetry of this episode was purely the creation of Guibert's fantasy. Rather, it could have resulted from exaggeration and selectivity on his part in deciding what to pick and choose from the certainties and rumors about Count Jean's mother; and there is simply not enough information on Guibert's psychology to infer with confidence whether his reshaping of reality was conscious or unconscious. Nonetheless, Guibert believed the events of this mother's life revealed a kind of cosmic tit for tat, in which her affronts against God— aided by a Jew—led to the punishment by God first of the Jew and then of her. Although there is no explicit textual evidence, the Count's mother appears to become in Guibert's mind the antithesis of his own mother, whom Guibert idolized with a peculiar intensity.[18]

After describing Jean's conduct at the funeral of his mother, Guibert concludes with a biblical citation (Ezekiel 16:3) that on one level sums up the barbarous lineage from which the Count arose and on another equates him with an ungrateful Jerusalem—which is to say, with Jews as Guibert regarded them: "In sum Count Jean, of whom it might have been said: 'Your father was an Amorite and your mother a Hittite,' not only duplicated his parent's wickedness; he did things far worse."[19] The parallel drawn between Jean's ancestry and Jerusalem's ancestry lays the groundwork for the possibility that the Judaism in which his mother was implicated—a Judaism of stealthy murder—is a kind of family weakness or illness. Guibert builds massively upon this basis in the section that follows.

As it turns out, Jean's viciousness even exceeds that of his parents. In the second panel of this triptych, Guibert faults the Count first for his religious beliefs and then for his sexual practices, which he presents as closely related to each other—and connected to the dalliance with Judaism that lurks in the background of Jean's mother's life. Guibert accuses Jean of having advanced the beliefs of Jews and heretics, especially in blaspheming against the savior. His treatise *De incarnatione contra Judaeos* clarifies his view that Jean's specific blasphemy is adherence to the Jewish rejection of the divine incarnation of Christ. The Count's trampling of Christian beliefs earns him no friends in the Jewish community, according to Guibert: not even the Jews accept him. Jean's incredulity runs the gamut from the incarnation through the resurrection, as the rest of the section reveals. Guibert tells us that Jean's display of humility during Christmas and Passiontide is pure show, since Jean affirms that he disbelieved the resurrection. When asked why he goes to church and pretends to be humble, Jean tells Guibert that his motive is nothing but lust: he relishes the opportunity to watch attractive women. This observation leads to a set of anecdotes about shortcomings in Jean's morality which are implicitly linked with his pro-Jewish leanings. Although Jean has a gorgeous young wife—and although Guibert has just documented his fondness for looking at beautiful women—Guibert now tells us that Jean spurns his spouse so as to expend his time and sexual energies on an ugly old hag.

Jean's preference in paramours runs against a small torrent of medieval literature, in which the lucky heroes are blessed with aged wives or loathly ladies who miraculously turn young and comely—the wish fulfillment given best-known shape by the Wife of Bath in the story that she tells in Chaucer's *Canterbury Tales*.[20] It also conflicts with the image of the "Wife Mill," a kind of Land of Cockaigne factory that took in worn-out old wives and turned out rejuvenated young ones.[21] What would have induced Jean to fancy this crone? Late medieval and early modern art, which arose out of an older textual tradition, were clear in asserting that only one enticement would draw the youthful to the aged, namely, money. According to the tradition of "unequal lovers," the old crave the bodies of the young, while the young want the coins that the old are willing to give.[22] This conduct is presented not just as foolish on the part of the young—in one picture a fool's cap associates the young man with a donkey at his side—but even as diabolic.[23] Perhaps it is here that the question of Judaism comes in, since Jews were so often equated with devils.

Guibert never states that the old woman is Jewish. The Jewish connection emerges in Guibert's assertion that the trysting place of this odd couple is primarily the house of a Jew, although he avers that in the heat of desire Jean will settle for any corner or closet. If there was a paramour in Jean's life, I suspect, she was not a Jew, and though Guibert dared not tamper with the incontrovertible fact that she was a Christian, he could at least give her the taint of Jewishness by presenting her as somehow associated with Jews by having her misconduct facilitated—maybe even pimped and certainly pandered—by a Jew.

Both iconographically and ideologically the contrast that Guibert constructs is fascinating. Behind him he had in the exegetic tradition all sorts of oppositions that depicted the rivalry between Christianity and Judaism as a choice between two women. One such antithesis would be between Church and Synagogue. But although this pairing appears frequently in medieval literature and art, it was not cast in most cases as a choice between an old woman and a young—which would seem to have been a natural possibility through conflation with the concepts of the Old and New Testaments or the Old and New Laws—but rather as a beauty contest between two competitors who differ mainly in their attributes and certainly not in their ages.[24] The same principle holds for portrayals of the expulsion of Hagar, which illustrate Galatians 4:22–30 (indebted to Genesis 21:10–14).[25] Paul's metaphor understands Hagar and Sarah as embodying two dichotomies, corresponding to Synagogue and Church or Law and Grace. Artists, although they do allude to Hagar's lower social status, never seem to have played upon the possibility of making her look older. But what served the purposes of exegetes and the illustrators who collaborated with them failed to function in Guibert's mind or times. For him, the notion of turning away from Christianity toward Judaism was not so much shocking as revoltingly abhorrent, and it required him to envisage the person so perceived as a monster who deviated from normality in every way.

Accordingly, as the section on Jean's sexual practices continues, Guibert reverses another major motif of twelfth-century literature, in this case the involuntary adultery of King Mark with Brangane in the story of Tristan and Isolde.[26] Guibert reports that Jean endeavored to trick his wife into committing adultery by arranging for another man to enter her bed. Typically, in describing what forestalls Jean from succeeding in his wicked design, Guibert seizes the opportunity to anatomize an even more detestable aspect of his antagonist:

> His wife immediately sensed from the feel of the man's body that this was not the count—her husband's skin was covered with pustular

boils—and she began striking this rascal with all her strength, with the help of her women-in-waiting.[27]

Guibert concludes this section of his account by mentioning that Jean's sexual abusiveness extended even to nuns and other religious women. That circumstance is undoubtedly what stirs the Virgin Mary into action. Guibert's devotion to the cult of the Virgin ran strong, and it made great sense for him to show Mary taking an active stand against a woman who was her opposite in age and piety, who appears as an anti-Virgin and unfruitful.[28] In the final panel of the triptych that Guibert's chapter on Jean constitutes, the Virgin Mary strikes back. Whether by dispatching a diabolic force herself or merely by withholding her protection, she causes Jean to be afflicted by a swarm of demons. Though fearful, Jean is not so intimidated that he refuses to sleep with the old hag, an act which leads in turn to the onset of his terminal illness.

To the end Jean shows himself an advocate of freethinking. To Guibert it was evidently impossible to accept that anyone would choose not to believe in a god of some sort. A person who rejected Christianity had to have been seduced by another faith. In this case the religion that Guibert had in mind—no matter whether it corresponded to reality—was Judaism. Jean undergoes at the hands of Guibert the same Frankenstein-ification as the Muslims do in *chansons de geste* contemporary with him: his human elements are detached, distorted, and reassembled in inhuman dimensions.[29] It is very revealing that in his *Tractatus de incarnatione contra Judaeos* Guibert places Jean in a category neither male nor female, neither masculine nor feminine: for wavering between Christianity and Judaism, Jean becomes *Neutericum*.[30] From Guibert's perspective, Jean's Judaizing puts him in a no-man's-land and makes him close to the lepers, both moral and real, who inhabited such spaces. What the realities of Jean's conduct and circumstances were we will never know: only Guibert's image of a Judaizer remains for us to analyze.

Notes

1. For the Latin text, see Bernhard Blumenkranz, "Un pamphlet juif médiolatin de polémique antichrétienne," *Revue d'histoire et de philosophie*

religieuses 34 (1954): 401–413. For discussion, see Solomon Katz, *The Jews in the Visigothic and Frankish Kingdoms of Spain and Gaul* (Cambridge, Mass., 1937), 27, 40–41, 45–46, and 69; Arthur Lukyn Williams, *Adversus Judaeos: A Bird's-Eye View of Christian Apologiae until the Renaissance* (Cambridge, 1935), 225–227.

2. For the most recent information on Petrus Alfonsi's *Dialogi, in quibus impiae Judaeorum opiniones refutantur*, see Petrus Alfonsi, *Dialogo contra los judíos*, ed. John V. Tolan, Klaus-Peter Mieth, Esperanza Ducay, and Maria Jesus Lacarra, Larumbe 9 (Huesca, 1996). For a translation of Hermann of Cologne, see Karl F. Morrison, *Conversion and Text: The Cases of Augustine of Hippo, Herman-Judah, and Constantine Tsatsos* (Charlottesville, Va., 1992), 39–113 and 165–176 (notes). For a translation of the Latin protocol of the Barcelona disputation in 1263 between Pablo Christiani and Ramban (Nachmanides), see Robert Chazan, *Church, State, and Jew in the Middle Ages* (New York, 1980), 266–269. For a translation of the account by Ramban (Nachmanides), see Ramban, *Writings and Discourses*, trans. Charles B. Chavel (New York, 1978), 2:656–696.

3. For example, Ralph of Coggeshall describes how an apostate to Judaism was burned at the ecclesiastical council at Oxford in 1222; see *Radulphi de Coggeshall Chronicon anglicanum*, ed. Joseph Stevenson, Rolls Series 66 (London, 1875), 190–191.

4. *Las siete partidas del Rey don Alfonso el Sabio* (1265), ed. Academia de la Historia, 3 vols. (Madrid, 1807), 7.24.7, 3:673; trans. Samuel Parsons Scott, *Las siete partidas* (Chicago, 1931), 1433–1437.

5. F. V. Filson, "Judaizing," in *The Interpreter's Dictionary of the Bible*, ed. George Arthur Buttrick et al., 4 vols. and 1 supplementary (Nashville, 1962), 2:1005–1006.

6. "Sed cum vidissem quod non recte ambularent ad veritatem evangelii, dixi Cephae coram omnibus: 'Si tum cum Iudaeus sis gentiliter et non iudaice vivis, quomodo gentes cogis iudaizare?'" *Biblia sacra iuxta vulgatam versionem*, ed. Robert Weber et al., 4th ed. (Stuttgart, 1994); translated into English, *The Holy Bible: Douay Rheims Version* (Baltimore, 1899).

7. Blumenkranz, "Un pamphlet juif," 413.

8. For the Latin, see Henry Knighton, *Chronicon Henrici Knighton: vel, Cnitthon, monachi leycestrensis*, Great Britain Public Records Office, Rolls Series 92 (London, 1889–1895), 1:114, and William Henry Dixon, *Fasti Eboracenses*, ed. J. Raine (London, 1863), 158–163. For discussion, see Raphael Loewe, "The Medieval Christian Hebraists of England, Herbert of Bosham and Earlier Scholars," *Transactions of the Jewish Historical Society of England* 17 (1953): 234, and R. B. Dobson, *The Jews of Medieval York and the Massacre of March 1190*, Borthwick Papers 45 (York, 1974), 5 nn. 16–17.

9. See in this volume John Van Engen, "Ralph of Flaix: The Book of Leviticus Interpreted as Christian Community."

10. It is found in none of the major Medieval Latin dictionaries.

11. Rigord, *Gesta Philippi Augusti*, parts 6, 12–13, and 15–16, ed. H. François Delaborde in *Oeuvres de Rigord et de Guillaume le Breton, historiens de Philippe-Auguste*, Société de l'histoire de France 210 (Paris, 1882), 1:15–29; English translation in James Harvey Robinson, *Readings in European History* (Boston, 1904), 1:426–428.

12. Of the many articles devoted to this metaphor, I will single out Édouard Jeauneau, "Nains et géants," in *Entretiens sur la Renaissance du 12e siècle*, ed. Maurice de Gandillac and Édouard Jeauneau (Paris, 1969), 21–38.

13. "In ipso monasterio monachus quidam est genere hebraeus. Is Hierosolymitani itineris per latinum orbem personante primordio, sic est a sua superstitione sublatus. Rothomagi, quadam die, hi qui, illam ituri expeditionem, sub eadem crucis professione susceperant, inter se coeperunt queri: '*Nos Dei hostes Orientem versus, longis terrarum tractibus transmissis, desideramus aggredi, cum ante oculos nostros sint Judaei, quibus inimicior existat gens nulla Dei; praeposterus,*' inquiunt, '*labor est!*' His dictis, arma praesumunt et in quandam ecclesiam compellentes, utrum vi nescio an dolo inde recutiunt, et gladiis indiscrete sexus et aetates addicunt, ita tamen, ut qui christianae conditioni se subderent, ictum mucronis impendentis evaderent. In qua digladiatione vir quidam nobilis puerulum vidit, misertus eripuit et ad matrem suam detulit." Guibert of Nogent, *Autobiographie/De vita sua* 2.5, ed. Edmond-René Labande, Les Classiques de l'histoire de France au Moyen Age 34 (Paris, 1981), 246–248; trans. Paul J. Archambault, *A Monk's Confession: The Memoirs of Guibert of Nogent* (University Park, Pa., 1996), 111 (my italics).

14. "Ad hunc, ob augendum infractae fidei suae robur, libellum quendam direxi, quem contra Suessorum comitem, judaizantem pariter et haereticum, ante quadriennium ferme scripseram. . . ." Guibert 2.5, ed. Labande, 252; trans. Archambault, 113.

15. PL 156, 489–528.

16. Labande, 422, n. 3.

17. Guibert 3.16, ed. Labande, 422 ("linguam diacono cuidam a gutture exemptam succidi fecit oculosque convelli"); trans. Archimbault, 193.

18. On Guibert's attitude toward his mother, see Chris D. Ferguson, "Autobiography as Therapy: Guibert de Nogent, Peter Abelard, and the Making of Medieval Autobiography," *Journal of Medieval and Renaissance Studies* 13 (1983): 187–212, at 194.

19. Guibert 3.16, ed. Labande, 424 ("Denique comes ipse, cui recte dici posset: 'Pater tuus Amorreus, et mater tua Cettea', non modo ad parentem regeneravit utrumque, sed multo deteriora peregit"); trans. Archambault, 194.

20. The motif is also found in "The Weddynge of Sir Gawen and Dame Ragnell," ed. Bartlett J. Whiting, in F. W. Bryan and Germaine Dempster, eds., *Sources and Analogues of Chaucer's Canterbury Tales* (New York, 1958), 242–264.

21. For information and illustrations, see Lutz Röhrich, *Das grosse Lexikon der sprichwörtlichen Redensarten*, 3 vols., 2d ed. (Freiburg, 1990), 3:1707–1708.

22. For examples, see Alison G. Stewart, *Unequal Lovers: A Study of Unequal Couples in Northern Art* (New York, 1978), 10, 62, and 82.

23. See Stewart, *Unequal Lovers*, 135.

24. The standard study is Wolfgang S. Seiferth, *Synagogue and Church in the Middle Ages: Two Symbols in Art and Literature* (New York, 1970).

25. For examples in which Hagar and Sarah are contrasted, see Luba Eleen, *The Illustration of the Pauline Epistles in French and English Bibles of the Twelfth and Thirteenth Centuries* (Oxford, 1982), plates 268 and 273.

26. R. S. Loomis, *Arthurian Legends in Medieval Art* (London, 1938), pl. 88.

27. "Quae cum non esse comitem ex corporis qualitate sentiret,—erat enim comes foede pruriginosus,—suo quo valuit nisu et pedissequarum auxilio, scurram dure cecidit." Guibert 3.16, ed. Labande, 426; trans. Archambault, 195.

28. On Guibert's devotion to the Virgin, see Anna Sapir Abulafia, "Twelfth-Century Humanism and the Jews," in *Contra Iudaeos: Ancient and Medieval Polemics between Christians and Jews*, ed. Ora Limor and Guy G. Stroumsa, Texts and Studies in Medieval and Early Modern Judaism 10 (Tübingen, 1996), 161–175, at 166–167.

29. For background on medieval Christian stereotypes of Muslims, see Philippe Sénac, *L'Image de l'autre: L'occident médiéval face à l'Islam* (Paris, 1983).

30. *Tractatus de incarnatione contra judaeos*, PL 156, 490C: "Plane hunc non incongrue Neutericum novo vocabulo dicam, qui neutrum sectatur. . . ."

God's Love for Israel: Apologetic and Hermeneutical Strategies in Twelfth-Century Biblical Exegesis

MICHAEL A. SIGNER

Jews in France and Germany in the eleventh and twelfth centuries continued the custom of their ancestors reciting the biblical verses from Deuteronomy 6:4, "Hear O Israel, the Lord our God the Lord is one," twice a day. Immediately preceding this biblical declaration of the unity of God, they also recited a prayer affirming, "With a great love you have loved us, O Lord Our God." Reading this prayer assured the Jews that God's love for them was manifest in the commandments and statutes which guided their lives. In the concluding formula these Jews affirmed, "Blessed are You O God who chooses His People Israel in love."[1]

This liturgical formulation of God's election of Israel in love consti-tutes the principal theme of community formation for the Jewish popu-lations in Northern Europe during the Middle Ages. They lived in Christian lands where ecclesiastical buildings proclaimed the message that God's love for Israel had been extended to another people, who had adapted the biblical narratives of the Hebrew Bible for their own pur-poses.[2] Episodic outbreaks of violence from Christian communities dur-ing the eleventh century and the riotous upheavals in the Rhineland created a challenge for those Jewish intellectuals who set the instruction of future generations of Jews as their task.[3] How would it be possible to maintain the continuity of Jewish communal identity grounded in God's freely chosen election of the Jewish people in love? The experience of violence and the assertions of Christian triumph might plant doubt in the hearts of many in the Jewish community. Can we presume that there might have been the same doubt about God's election and love of the Jews which Gavin Langmuir and others have asserted motivated intellectual activity among Christians?[4]

That some doubt had arisen among Jews about God's justice and faithfulness to his covenant is evident in the chronicles and poetry written by Jews in the aftermath of the First and Second Crusades. David b. Meshullam of Speyer's poem, "God do not be silent to my blood," calls upon the Almighty to demonstrate some sign of favor.[5] Lengthy passages in the concluding portions of Solomon b. Samson's account of the First Crusade implore the divine to look upon the activities of the "saintly members of the congregations" and wreak vengeance upon those who brought proud communities of observant Jews to annihilation.[6] Israel J. Yuval has described this theme as a "vengeful messianism" which reveals the depths of hatred for the surrounding Christian society that permeated Jewish literature.[7] There was little serenity or self-assured sentiment among the authors of religious poetry or those who sought to put contemporary events into the context of God's continuous covenant with the Jews as expressed in Scripture.

The existence of apostate Jews during this period provided occasion for another doubt. There has been a tendency in the historiography of Ashkenazi Jewry to minimize the extent of lost bodies and souls.[8] Yet the literature we possess indicates that apostates were a matter of concern to the Jewish community. There was anxiety about their participation in Jewish divorce; there was concern as to whether or not children of apostates who had returned to Judaism might be permitted to participate in Jewish public liturgical ceremonies such as the priestly blessing. These apostates, whether they returned to Judaism or not, constituted a challenge to a homogeneous Jewish community.[9]

The return of an apostate to the Jewish community through interaction with a Rabbi and his biblical exegesis may indicate that "preaching" Scripture was an appropriate path. This interaction is illustrated by a passage in the thirteenth-century book of Joseph the Zealot, *Sefer Yosef HaMeqqaneh*, by Joseph ben Nathan Officiel.

An apostate who was very orthodox came before Rabbi Joseph Bekhor Shor. Rabbi Bekhor Shor said to him, "Fool! Let your ears hear what your mouth says. 'Lo my servant shall prosper.' If [Jesus] is truly God, why does [Isaiah] call him 'servant?'" Immediately, the apostate tore his clothing, rolled in the dust, and returned [to the Jewish community] in repentance.[10]

This narrative about Rabbi Joseph Bekhor Shor, also known as Joseph of Orléans, is embedded in a thirteenth-century Jewish manual for disputing with Christians.[11] The originality of the exegesis on Isaiah 53 is not important for our purpose here. What is significant is the interaction between the Rabbi and the apostate. Rabbi Joseph of Orléans wrote biblical commentaries which contained sharp refutations of Christian interpretations of Scripture.[12] In the passage from the *Book of Joseph the Zealot*, the Rabbi encounters an intensely pious apostate and with a single word of interpretation brings him back to Judaism. This incident provides an ironic reversal of many occasions in Christian Latin dialogues where Jews convert upon hearing their Scripture "properly" interpreted.[13] What this passage may really indicate, however, was the sense of purpose that Jewish interpreters of Scripture had in their composition of exegetical works. A passage of Scripture fitly interpreted could maintain the loyalty of a Jewish community shaken in its faith; it might also bring back those who had left the community.[14]

The Rabbis who took upon themselves the task of biblical exposition in France during the eleventh and twelfth centuries followed in the footsteps of Rabbi Solomon b. Isaac of Troyes, known by his acronym, Rashi. Known in the tradition as *"Parshandata," the* expounder of Scripture, Rashi composed exegetical treatises on nearly every book of the Hebrew Bible.[15] In addition, his commentary on the Babylonian Talmud provided guidance on many difficult passages from Scripture.[16] These commentaries emphasized the *peshat* or "plain meaning" of Scripture as the firm foundation for understanding the rabbinic interpretations in a later era. Rashi's colleagues and students, such as Joseph b. Simeon Kara, Rabbi Samuel b. Meir, Rabbi Joseph of Orléans [Bekhor Shor], and Rabbi Eliezer of Beaugency, continued to develop and refine his method.[17] An investigation of their exegesis has led scholars since the nineteenth century to focus on how these authors refined their idea of "plain meaning" in order to negotiate the tension between the traditions of biblical exegesis they received from earlier generations and the necessity of expounding Scripture within its own context. But were the efforts of these scholars exclusively the result of developments within the Jewish community, which called for improvements in pedagogy? Or, were there elements in the broader culture of Northern European civilization that motivated this development? There is evidence that both internal and external forces were present. M. Banitt has demonstrated that the internal demand of scriptural pedagogy for younger students required greater attention to the individual terms within Scripture.[18] The external Christian cultural environment also was significant. In a rather extreme formulation, Yitzhak Baer proposed that the refutation of Christian claims to Scripture was the primary motivation for the focus on *peshat* or plain meaning, while Sara Kamin and Eliezer Touitou have continued the analysis of the *peshat/derash* or plain meaning/tradition tension as in parallel with a sharpened Christian investigation of the *sensus litteralis* of Scripture.[19] Their research as well as my own indicates that changes in methods of scriptural exegesis in both Jewish and Christian communities brought greater attention to both the meaning of individual words and a more intense scrutiny of how these words could be properly constructed into a narrative.[20]

It is the shaping of larger communal narratives that I want to emphasize in this essay. By "communal narrative" I mean a narrative grounded in Scripture that provides the community with a sense of solidarity with their ancestral traditions and a hope for their ultimate salvation in the future.[21] We can begin with a brief survey of the Christian community and then direct our attention to the Jewish community.

The late eleventh and first half of the twelfth century witnessed new efforts by Christian scholars to shape and refocus their community on Scripture and the economy of salvation.[22] Anna Sapir Abulafia's recent book demonstrates that Anselm of Canterbury's *Cur Deus Homo* generated the composition of several treatises which focused on the nature of the incarnation.[23] It is not just the reasonableness of the incarnation which is significant for Anselm, but the fact that it was necessary for the salvation of humankind. Toward that purpose Anselm's treatise is a hermeneutical key to the reading of the narrative of Christian Scripture, both Old and New Testament. The *Cur Deus Homo* situates the reader in the biblical drama of the history of salvation.[24] Alternatively, one can turn to the writings of another early-twelfth-century master, Rupert of

Deutz.[25] His multivolume commentary "On the Trinity and Its Works" provides a guide to the workings of the trinity throughout the biblical canon. Rupert argues that the trinity is present in the Old Testament and that the narratives of the Hebrew Bible provide the Christian reader with evidence of the triune God's grace from the origins of our created world until the parousia.[26]

Another master who focused on creating a coherent meaning for Scripture from Creation to the end of time was Hugh of St. Victor.[27] Hugh insisted on the value of *historia* or narrative, "the first use of the words of Scripture properly constituted according to their order," as the foundation of all allegorical or moral reading.[28] His treatises on the ark reveal his attention to the smallest detail of its physical structure to reveal God's saving grace for fallen humanity.[29] For Hugh, all of the divine plan is constituted in the work of creation and the work of restoration. The salvation narrative of humankind receives its most thorough treatment in Hugh's work *On the Sacraments of Christian Faith*.[30] Efforts at creating Christian narratives for Scripture extend beyond Hugh of St. Victor. Other efforts at constructing the Hebrew Scripture as a narrative are to be found in Richard of St. Victor's *Liber Exceptionum*[31] and Peter Comestor's *Historia Scholastica*.[32] Joachim of Fiore completes the group of theologians who created coherent Christian narratives for Scripture, with his *Liber de Concordia Novi ac Veteris Testamenti* and other writings.[33] All of these authors provided a narrative which would supply the syntax to explain any particular biblical pericope. Therefore, when Jewish philological and "historical" arguments were offered, no matter how convincing they might be, it was possible to claim that the Jews simply did not have the appropriate context for their grammatical exploration. Richard of St. Victor's *De Emanuele* provides an example of the refutation of this type of argument.[34]

Do we find a similar attempt within the Jewish community to create a coherent narrative that provides a context for scriptural exegesis? Do the Rabbis develop a "counternarrative" which might immunize Jews from their doubts? The answer is not easy. Rabbinic literature in classical antiquity provided the models for literary discourse in the medieval period. Investigations of the Mishnah, Talmuds, and Midrashim in their historical setting reveal precisely how difficult it is to wrest from the Rabbis any precise indication of the specific identity of their adversaries.[35]

The use of the term *minim* or "sectarians" has provided the opportunity for argument about precisely what religious grouping in antiquity may have been the object of rabbinic animus.[36] However, uncensored texts of the Talmuds indicate that the Rabbis did not hesitate to develop strategies to demean the power of Jesus and his disciples.[37]

In the Passover Haggadah, a narrative of Israel's deliverance from Egypt read on the first night of the holiday in Jewish homes, we observe the retelling of the book of Exodus with a strong emphasis on divine intervention and miracle.[38] Israel J. Yuval has demonstrated that in the deliberations of the proper date of celebrating the Passover/Pascha or in significant details of the Passover ritual, the Rabbis develop their own counternarrative to the Christian appropriation.[39] The Passover Haggadah of the Rabbis would, according to Yuval, then constitute a primary example of a seamless Jewish story which would strengthen the hearts of the faithful in the absence of the Temple and the still anticipated presence of the Messiah who would redeem Israel.

Both Abraham Grossman and Israel J. Yuval have also demonstrated that medieval Jewish authors developed coherent narratives of the historical situation of the Jewish people.[40] Their studies of how these Rabbis interpreted the eschatological justification of the Jewish people fall into two complementary narratives. Yuval points toward a fiery end in which the arrogant gentile nations are utterly destroyed. God's messiah acts as the champion of the people of Israel, who have sacrificed their blood to evoke God's wrath upon the Gentiles and mercy upon Israel. Grossman indicates that the horrific end of Israel's enemies will ultimately bring about the conversion of the gentile nations. The narratives emplotted both by Yuval and Grossman are consistent with passages in the biblical prophetic literature that speak about the end of days. The biblical prophets provided both for the horrible end of the enemies of Israel and for the restoration of Jerusalem and its Temple as the object of veneration by all the nations of the world.

Eschatological aspirations might provide hope for the future. What about the patent discontinuity of Israel's glorious past with its current lowly state in dispersion? Was there a break in Israel's covenant which was so serious that it had brought about a change in the relationship with God? Had the calling of the nations been a turning point for Israel's fate? These questions create the framework for the remaining parts of this study, which will focus on the biblical commentaries by Rashi. I will argue that Rabbi Solomon ben Isaac of Troyes created a series of counternarratives to those created by Christians.[41] Drawing upon the complex literary inheritance of the Rabbis, one of his primary purposes was to demonstrate that the love God had demonstrated for biblical Israel remained without blemish, and that despite Israel's backsliding, God remained her beloved protector and would be her ultimate savior.

Let us recall that Rashi, who lived in Troyes and studied in the Rhineland centers of Mainz and Worms, lived through the era of the crusades. He would have been acutely aware, as both Baer and Grossman have illustrated, of what happened to his colleagues and teachers during the summer of 1096.[42] He would have almost a decade before his death in 1105 to ruminate on the tragedy of those communities. From the testimony of his grandson, Rabbi Samuel b. Meir, we know that Rashi continuously revised his biblical commentaries.[43] However, as Grossman has recently demonstrated, there was a consistent negative attitude toward the Christian faith that existed long before the tragedies of 1096.[44] Therefore, even if we were to argue that Rashi recasts the vast literature of the Talmuds and Midrash into a coherent narrative without attention to the recent eruptions of violence, we would still be able to assert that the non-Jewish cultural environment sharpened his perspective. He would have been re-narrating the Jewish story of God's love for Israel within the specific context of a Christian environment which, in contrast to the Jewish intellectual climate under Islamic culture, required continued attention to the words, laws, and narratives of the Hebrew Bible which Christians claimed as their own.[45]

In the commentary on Psalms we have the opportunity to observe Rashi creating specific arguments in refuting Christian interpretations.[46] His locution is "*teshuvah leminim*," the standard formula in the Middle Ages for answering Christian interpretations. The Psalter was, of course, the liturgical compendium of the Church. Its recitation on a daily basis by monastic houses and cathedral chapters since antiquity had evoked a rich tradition of Christian exegesis.[47] The contemplation of the Psalms as prophecies of Christ, therefore, evoked a sharp response from Rashi. What is remarkable is that aside from Rashi there was so little exegesis specifically written for this book during the period of our study.[48]

Rashi responded directly to Christian assertions that certain verses referred to Jesus. It is also significant that on some occasions he framed his refutation by creating a Jewish counternarrative that took into account both the grounding of the psalmodic verses in a specific biblical historical event and the eschatological interpretation of the psalm within a Jewish context.[49] The best illustration of this technique is the second Psalm, "Why do the nations rage." Rashi begins his exposition of the Psalm with the following introduction.

> Our rabbis expounded the subject of this psalm as king/messiah. However, according to its context in the narrative of Scripture [mashma'o] and as a refutation to the Christians it would seem correct to explain it about David himself in accordance with the subject stated in Scripture [2 Sam. 5:27]: The Philistines heard that the Israelites had anointed David as a king over them, and the Philistines gathered their legions and they fell into his hand. It is with respect to them that he [David] said, "Why do the nations assemble?"

Rashi embeds this poem in the narrative about David's coronation which is presented in 2 Sam. 5:27. This enables him to place succeeding verses of the Psalm within the historical occasion when the enemies of the biblical David rose up against him. Therefore, even when the Psalmist indicates, "The Lord said to me" (Ps. 2:7), Rashi indicates that God's words to David were delivered by Nathan, Gad, and Samuel—and were not a direct statement of God to a human being. A delicate task remained for the exegete to resolve. How could one maintain that a poem written for the occasion of the Philistine rebellion would have a message for later generations? Rashi responds to this challenge by utilizing a gap in the sequence of psalm verses at verse 10, where the psalm turns from the direct address of God to an address to "Kings":

> *Therefore O kings.* The prophets of Israel are men of mercy who adjure the nations of the world to turn aside from their evil ways. For the Holy One Blessed be He puts forth his hand toward the evil and the good.

The final verses of the psalm (2:10–12) turn outward to the gentile nations. It is the prophets of Israel who reach out with the message that God will accept them if they turn from their evil. They will join those who are "happy in their trust in God." The psalm thus becomes both a narrative of Israel's deliverance through David in the past and—ultimately—the message of Israel's prophets reaching out to the gentile nations.

It is also significant to note Rashi's division of the psalm into three narrative units: of the Philistines and David; of God's message to David through the Prophets; and the mercy of Israel's prophets to the nations. This question corresponds directly to the division of the Psalm offered by the classical Christian commentator on Psalms, Cassiodorus, who proposed a three-fold division of the Psalm into: Christ as a prophet (vv. 1–5); Christ himself (6–9); and Christ or a prophet in the manner of an apostle.[50] Not only is Rashi's three-fold division of the Psalm an innovation in Jewish commentary on this Psalm. It also proposes a refutation of the Christological explanation, and a complete narrative which stretches from biblical Israel into the eschatological moment of God's ultimate judgment on those who act against the divine will and bring harm to Israel.

Rashi developed another pivotal counternarrative in his introduction to the Song of Songs. The interpretation of this biblical book reveals a lengthy history of opposing interpretations by both Jews and Christians, who understood the message of Solomon's song to be focused on them.[51] Rabbinic interpretation in mystical, midrashic, and targumic versions all read the Canticle in light of God's history of love and caring for Israel. Alternatively, patristic and medieval Christian authors understood this book in terms of the love that God had for his bride, the Church.[52] The realities of Jewish existence during the eleventh century called out for an overarching theme which would indicate that God's love song for Israel could still make sense when the scroll was read on Passover. On each Passover it became clearer that Israel was not yet redeemed. Rashi offered the following resolution:

> I claim that Solomon understood by means of the Holy Spirit that the Israelites were destined to endure one exile after another and one destruction after another. They would mourn in their current exile over their earlier position of honor, and remember His initial affection and that they were the unique people among all peoples, saying, "I will return to my first husband because it was better for me than now"

(Hosea 2:9), and they would remember God's steadfast love and their transgressions, and the rewards which God promised them at the end of days. He structured this book by means of the Holy Spirit about a woman abandoned by her husband without a bill of divorcement (2 Sam. 20:3) who was clinging to her beloved, remembering her youthful love for him. Her beloved also took pity upon her sorrow and recalls the love of her youth and her beauty and the aptness of her deeds which bound him to her in powerful love. He does this to acknowledge to her that she has not left his heart and that her divorce is not final, because she remains his wife and he remains her husband.[53]

This introduction provided a hermeneutical key for reading the Canticle. Solomon's book was prophetic and Israelites would read it in their exile. What makes the narrative cohere are two allusions to other biblical books which refer to various states of relationship between husband and wife. The quotation from Hosea 2:9 would remind Jewish readers that God would ultimately return to them in the same manner that Hosea's wife sought him out after abandoning him. Love denied and betrayed could and would again be love fulfilled. The other image is derived from a most unusual biblical locution in 2 Sam. 20:3, which literally means a "living widow," a woman who had been abandoned by her husband without a bill of divorce. This state of suspension of relations is fulfilled by reading the book of the Canticle which recalls Israel's earlier period of direct relationship with God. She remains a fit object of God's love who has never left his heart. Ultimately, like the bond between Hosea and his wife, God will return to Israel. Rashi's introduction to the Canticle allows for the less than ideal status of Israel. She is in exile. She feels abandoned. However, the Canticle reminds her that despite her sense of being abandoned she is still bound to God, and will be returned to her former status. The use of the marriage/divorce tension aptly frames the commentary on a biblical book which encompasses the history of God's relationship with Israel from the Creation to the final redemption.

The psalms and Canticle provided Rashi with opportunities to expound books of Scripture which were in the third section of the Jewish canon, the Ketuvim. The prophetic books, the second section of the canon, also provided him with opportunities to demonstrate the ultimate justification of Israel at the end of history.[54]

What about the Pentateuch, that portion of Hebrew Scripture that rabbinic theology declared revealed to Moses on Mt. Sinai, and that Christian scholars acknowledged as the books of Moses? We are aware that for the Christian community, "The Law" had constituted a hermeneutical and theological problem from its earliest days. Two principal resolutions to the problem of "The Law" are offered within the canon of Christian Scripture. In chapter 3 of the Epistle to the Galatians, Paul characterized the Mosaic law as an appropriate device for the education of Israel before the incarnation.[55] The law was a "pedagogue" (3:23–26) which was fulfilled and transformed by the incarnation. A more elaborate hermeneutical relationship is suggested in the Epistle to the Hebrews. Hebrews suggests that the law is a shadow or prefiguration of things to come. The key to the interpretation of the Old Testament is Christ, who transcends Moses and whose priesthood is greater than Aaron's. The mutability of the Law or its transformation since the incarnation became one of the cornerstones of the Christian theological interpretation of the Hebrew Bible.[56] I propose that Rashi provides a consistent series of interpretations which provide a narrative context for each of the five books of the Pentateuch. In the first few sentences of his commentaries on Genesis, Exodus, Leviticus, Numbers, and Deuteronomy, he offers arguments that cumulatively assert that God's law and love for Israel are one and the same.[57] Both the content and form of the argument reveal his artistry as a biblical exegete and an apologist for the constancy of God's love for Israel.

The commentary on Genesis begins with a statement about the narrative framework of the Pentateuch.

Rabbi Isaac said, "The Torah should really have started with the words from Exodus 12:2, 'This shall be the first of months for you,' because this is the first commandment given to Israel in the Torah." What is the reason that Torah opens with the [narrative] of *Bereshit*? It is because [of the words in Psalm 111:6], 'He revealed His powerful works to His people to give them the inheritance of the nations.' For if the nations of the world should say to Israel, 'You are thieves because you captured the lands of the seven [Canaanite] nations,' They [Israel] should respond, 'All the earth ['*Aretz*] belongs to the Holy One Blessed Be He. God has created it and given it to those who are upright in his eyes. By

God's will He gave it to them, and by the divine will He took it from them and gave it to us.'[58]

Baer has called attention to the focus on the interchange between Israel and the nations of the world in this passage as an apologetic motif reflecting the period of the Crusades in the late eleventh century.[59] It is Israel, the Jewish people, to whom the land of Israel has been entrusted. The divine will has the power to bestow gifts of grace to those "who are upright in his eyes." Closer attention to this remarkable statement by Rashi, however, reveals a broader apologetic motif: the connection between the people Israel and its God, and how this bond is reflected in the unfolding chapters of the book of Genesis. The proposal that the Torah begin with Exodus 12:2 would mean that God's revelation had been limited exclusively to Law and commandment.

The limitation of Jewish revelation to a particularized law has characterized Christian perceptions of Judaism from Paul of Tarsus to the modern period. In the Latin apologetic literature of the eleventh and twelfth centuries, questions about the validity and permanence of the commandments are a standard trope.[60] Gilbert Crispin's Dialogue, written at the end of the eleventh century, commences with a question about the nature of the law.[61] Therefore, Rashi juxtaposes the commandment for celebrating the Passover—an example of law commemorating an act of divine grace—with the narration of Genesis. The question of Paschal commandment and Genesis is resolved by the verse from Psalm 111:6. God tells or relates His mighty acts to His People. The creation story, therefore, is an indication that even the creation of the universe is joined to the narrative of Israel. Its telling provides an occasion for Israel to remember that the creation of the ʾAretz or earth foretold that they would have an inheritance—a land—among the nations of the world. No competent Hebrew reader would have missed the multiple meanings of the word ʾAretz, which meant "the earth" but also "the land of Israel." The allusion to the rabbinic idea that the earth was created from the Temple mount in Jerusalem could also be part of the larger field of associations with Rashi's apologetic motif.

Turning back to the text of Rashi's commentary, we observe that Psalm 111 opens up further apologetic dimensions in his introductory statement on Genesis.[62] Psalm 111:4 states that God has won renown for His wonders, and that the Lord is gracious and compassionate. Rashi elucidates this theme by noting that God's renown and mercy are proclaimed because "he has set Sabbaths and festivals and commandments for Israel." In verse 5 the Psalm tells us that "God is ever mindful of his covenant," which Rashi conjoins with Deuteronomy 5:15, "You shall remember that you were slaves in the Land of Egypt," because God is merciful and gracious to his children and wants to make them righteous [to justify them] through his commandments. In the conjunction of these two verses Rashi demonstrates that God's laws and the Jewish calendar are part of the grace which God has bestowed upon Israel. The motif that the commandments are given by God to make Israel righteous and constitute a sign of the eternal validity of the covenant casts light on Rashi's opening comment on Genesis. In the Psalm commentary on verse 6 Rashi provides an explicit statement of his more artful and oblique comment on Genesis:

> Midrash Tanhuma wrote that God composed the story of creation for Israel to make them know that the land is His, and it is in His power to uproot these nations and bring other nations to dwell there.

Read as a diptych, the comment at the beginning of Genesis and the commentary on Psalm 111 complement one another. They indicate that law and creation are reciprocal signs of divine grace. Precisely in the observance of the commandments, Israel becomes righteous in God's eyes. God keeps Israel eternally in mind with thoughts of mercy.

Two further sentences in Rashi's introduction to Genesis recapitulate the initial themes. Rashi focuses upon the unusual Hebrew construction *Bereshit Bara.*

> This [scriptural] locution cannot be explained without homiletical interpretation in the manner that our Rabbis explained it [in Genesis Rabbah 1:2]. [The letter *bet* means that God created] for the sake of Torah which is called 'The beginning of God's way' and for the sake of Israel who are called 'The first fruits of God's harvest.'

The initial words of the Pentateuch express God's preference for the Jewish people. Torah as commandment guides God's very act of creation.

All of the works of creation ultimately point toward God's chosen and beloved people.

The theme of God's love and caring for Israel provides the introductory theme for Rashi's comment on the book of Exodus. He raises the question of the narrative link between God's love and those ancestors who left the land of Israel for Egypt. Could the sin of Jacob's sons, who had sold their brother and left the land of Israel, have brought about a change in the divine affection?

> *Ve'eleh Shemot [These are the names]* Although God enumerated the names of the tribes while they were yet alive [Gen. 46:8–26], God returns to enumerate them after their death to make divine affection known to them, for they were compared to the stars whom God brings out and causes to go in [to set], as Scripture states [Isa. 40:26], 'He who sends out their hosts by count, who calls them each by name, because of His great might and vast power not one of them fails to appear.'[63]

Rashi recasts earlier sources from the Midrash Tanhuma and Pesikta Rabbati, which emphasize that enumerating the names of the Israelites as an indication of the unchanging character of divine love.[64] The supercommentaries on Rashi point out various contradictions between the quotation from Isaiah and the claim that God causes Israel to come in and go out in the same manner as the stars rise and set. Yet as the editors of the new *Rashi HaShalem* on Exodus correctly point out, the most significant dimension of this introductory comment is the conjoining of the Genesis and Exodus narratives.[65] By use of the comparison with stars, Rashi provides a key symbol of the divine promise to the Patriarchs that Israel will multiply like the stars in the heavens. The stars seem to disappear when they set. However, they reappear. Those whom God brought down to Egypt, even though they enter a period of hardship and slavery, will emerge as beneficiaries of God's might in their Exodus.

We know that the next book in the Pentateuch, Leviticus, was understood as a primary source of Israel's purity for the ancient Rabbis. Rashi introduces an openly apologetic motif in his initial comment on this book, which begins with the words "And God called Moses."

> All of God's words, statements and commandments were preceded by "calling." This "call" is an expression of affection, for this is the way the

ministering angels express themselves in Scripture [Isa. 6:3], "They called to one another." However, God spoke to the nations of the world in an episodic manner or in the language of impurity, as Scripture explains, *Vayiqr 'el Bil'am*, "He called Balaam." [Num. 23:4][66]

The contrast between the spelling of qr' ("call") in Leviticus 1:1 with an aleph and in Numbers 23:4 without an aleph is a recasting of earlier Rabbinic texts.[67] Israel is compared to the ministering angels, which continues Rashi's motif in both Genesis and Exodus that Israel has a unique status comparable to the creations in the superterrestrial world. The choice of Numbers 23:4, of God's call to Balaam, was pointed toward disparaging Christianity, since Balaam was often utilized by the Rabbis as a cipher for Jesus.[68] A correlative reading of Rashi's comment on Numbers 23:4 sharpens the negative contrast: The defective spelling is an indication of the impurity of seminal emission, harshness, and utter contempt. God would not have appeared to Balaam in daylight—a sign of clear revelation—except to demonstrate affection for Israel. The multiplicity of divine legislation in Leviticus is preceded by God's vocation of Moses from the Tent of Meeting in order to express divine affection. However, the nations of the world, a cipher for Christians, have a vocation grounded in impurity.

In the introductory comment on the book of Numbers, Rashi creates a coherent narrative linking the incidents at the end of Exodus with the census which commences this book. The problem of God's constancy in light of Israel's sin and backsliding is important here.

> *God spoke . . . in the desert of Sinai* God enumerates them at every moment out of affection. When they left Egypt God counted them [Ex. 32:23]; when they fell at [the incident of] the golden calf [Ex. 32:26] God counted them to know the number of those who remained alive; and when God came to bring the divine presence to dwell among them, they were counted again: on the first day of the month of Nisan the tabernacle was established [Ex. 40:17], and on the first day of the month of 'Iyyar, God counted them.[69]

Once more Rashi turns to Midrash Tanhuma to focus on the activity of census as an expression of divine affection. Even the sin of the Golden Calf did not shift God's affection for Israel. They were enumerated to determine how many remained alive. As the conclusive proof that God still loved her, Israel was counted once again immediately after the divine presence descended upon the altar in the desert tabernacle.

The book of Deuteronomy with its recapitulation of Israel's history was filled with passages recounting Israel's rebellious nature and God's rebuke for those who failed to be loyal to the covenant. One might suppose, and there are indications that Christian exegetes proposed as early as Acts 7:37, that the book of Deuteronomy indicated God's threats against a people who had been stubborn and would continue to defy Him. Rashi provided his Jewish readers with an antidote to a reading of the final book of the Pentateuch that might diminish Israel's status with God.

> *These are the words* Since these are words of rebuke and Moses recounts here all the places where Israel angered God, he speaks indirectly and mentions them with an allusion for the sake of Israel's honor [*mipne kevodan shel yisrael*].[70]

Rashi indicates that the first verse of the book of Deuteronomy utilizes euphemisms for the Israelite desert encampments in order to preserve her honor. He explicates each of the allusions by providing the appropriate verse in earlier books of the Pentateuch:

> *In the wilderness* . . . in the plains of Moab (Num. 36:13). *In the plain* . . . that they had sinned through Baal Peor at Shittim in the plains of Moab (Num. 36:13). *Over against Suph* . . . they had shown themselves rebellious at the Red Sea (Ex. 14:11). *and Hazeroth* . . . at the insurrection of Korah (Num. 16). *and Di Zahab* . . . on account of the golden calf (Ex. 32).

Rashi presses beyond a counternarrative here. The language of Scripture is deliberately oblique and allusive at the beginning of Deuteronomy because God is concerned with Israel's *kavod*, her honor. No matter how many times the Israelites might rebel and evoke the divine wrath, God's concern for them never wavered.

Each of these comments on the books of the Pentateuch creates a powerful narrative of God's unchanging love for Israel. The world is created for the sake of giving her the Land of Israel. The Israelites' departure from the Land into Egypt continued to evoke God's affection. The legal intricacies of Leviticus are prefaced by a call to Moses which indicates God's love. Even the sin of Israel at the Golden Calf did not diminish God's concern to enumerate each one of them. Ultimately God would even have Moses' final address begin with allusions to Israel's acts of rebellion rather than diminish her honor. The Pentateuch commentary, like commentaries on other books of the Hebrew canon, reveals Rashi's consummate artistry in creating a complete and coherent narrative of the relationship between God and Israel. It recasts earlier rabbinic traditions and brings them to bear on the immediate problem of Israel's continued existence in the Christian diaspora. God's affection was unchanging. Through obedience to the divine commandment and understanding her unique story, Israel would ultimately be released from her status of living widow and rejoice in the eschatological reconciliation.

The new emphasis on biblical studies by Jews and Christians in twelfth-century Europe was far more than elementary pedagogy. The Bible was the foundational document for both Jews and Christians. Both communities viewed themselves as direct inheritors of a rich tradition of biblical exposition. Weaving a web of interpretation which tied them back to their ancestors and yet provided for a life in full community was the task of biblical interpreters. At a crucial moment in this development, the end of the eleventh and beginning of the twelfth century, we can look to the biblical commentaries written by Rabbi Solomon ben Isaac of Troyes as a successful example of negotiating this complex task.

Notes

1. On liturgy and liturgical expression in Medieval Europe, compare Ismar Elbogen, *Jewish Liturgy: A Comprehensive History*, trans. Raymond P. Scheindlin (Philadelphia and New York, 1993), pp. 16–18; Stefana C. Reif, *Judaism and Hebrew Prayer: New Perspectives on Jewish Liturgical History* (Cambridge, 1993), pp. 166–180. The classical formulation of the relationship between Jewish suffering and liturgical creativity is to be found in Leopold Zunz, *Die synagogale Poesie des Mittelalters* (Frankfurt am Main, 1920; reprint, Hildesheim, 1967), "Leiden," pp. 9–58.

2. It is difficult to discern the impact of Christian art and architecture on the Jewish community during the Middle Ages. From the narrative of Hermannus we learn that he was initially shocked at the sight of art inside the Church, and thought that he was seeing an idol. See Hermannus quondam Iudaeus, *Opusculum de conversione sua*, ed. G. Niemeier, MGH, supp. 4 (Weimar, 1963), p. 75. In addition, Ruth Mellinkoff, *Outcasts: Signs of Otherness in Northern European Art of the Late Middle Ages*, 2 vol. (Berkeley and Los Angeles, 1981), provides examples of reactions to and by Jews, as does Mark Epstein, *Dreams of Subversion in Medieval Jewish Art and Literature* (University Park, Pa., 1997).

3. Robert Chazan, *European Jewry and the First Crusade* (Berkeley and Los Angeles, 1987), summarizes the important debates about the impact of the Crusades on the intellectual life of Ashkenazi Jewry.

4. Gavin Langmuir, "Doubt in Christendom" and "Peter the Venerable: Defense against Doubts," in *Toward a Definition of Antisemitism* (Berkeley and Los Angeles, 1990), pp. 100–134 and 197–208. Anna Sapir Abulafia, *Christians and Jews in the Twelfth-Century Renaissance* (London and New York: 1995), pp. 4–7. The studies by John Van Engen, Jan Ziolkowski, and Jonathan Elukin in the present volume extend the discussion on "doubt" or "anxiety" as a significant factor in the historiography of twelfth-century relations between Jews and Christians.

5. The text and translation of the poem composed by David b. Meshullam of Speyer may be found in *The Penguin Book of Hebrew Verse*, ed. and trans. T. Carmi (New York, 1981), pp. 374–375. The genre of "lament" is discussed by Zunz, *Die synagogale Poesie*, and by Chazan, *European Jewry*. Yosef Hayim Yerushalmi emphasizes the use of liturgy rather than chronicle or memoir writing by medieval Ashkenazi Jews in *Zakhor: Jewish History and Jewish Memory* (Seattle, 1982); and see also Robert Bonfil, "How Golden Was the Age of the Renaissance in Jewish Historiography?" *History and Theory* 27 (1988): 78–88.

6. "The Chronicle of Solomon bar Simson," in *The Jews and the Crusaders: The Hebrew Chronicles of the First and Second Crusades*, ed. and trans. Shlomo Eidelberg (Madison, Wisc., 1977), pp. 47–49, concludes the section on the Mainz persecutions with a liturgical formulation that is filled with curses and violent imprecations against the Crusaders.

7. Israel J. Yuval, "Vengeance and Damnation, Blood and Defamation: From Jewish Martyrdom to Blood Libel Accusations" [Hebrew], *Zion* 58 (1993): 33–90, and his forthcoming book *Two Nations Are in Your Womb*.

8. Jacob Katz, *Exclusiveness and Tolerance: Jewish-Gentile Relations in Medieval and Modern Times* (New York, 1962), pp. 67–81; and the discussion of recent research on this question by Michael Toch in *Die Juden im Mittel-*

alterlichen Reich, Enzyklopädie deutscher Geschichte, vol. 44 (Munich, 1998), pp. 123–125.

9. Jacob Katz, "Even Though He Sinned, He Remains an Israelite" [Hebrew], *Tarbitz* (1958): 203–217. A. Grossman, *The Early Sages of Ashkenaz: Their Lives, Leadership and Works* [Hebrew] (Jerusalem, 1988) pp. 122–127; and also his book *The Early Sages of France: Their Lives, Leadership and Works* [Hebrew] (Jerusalem, 1995), pp. 152–155. I. Agus, *Urban Civilization in Pre-Crusade Europe*, 2 vols. (New York, 1965), presents a translation of selected *responsa* which focus on problems that apostates caused within the life of Jewish communities.

10. Rabbi Joseph HaMeqqaneh, *Sefer Josef HaMeqqaneh*, ed. Judah Rosenthal (Jerusalem, 1970), p. 79.

11. On Rabbi Joseph of Orléans, see G. Walter, *Joseph Bekhor Shor* (Breslau, 1890); N. Porges, *Joseph Bekhor Shor* (Leipzig, 1908); S. A. Poznanski, *Introduction to the Commentary of Eliezar of Beaugency* (Warsaw, 1923), pp. lv–lxxv [Hebrew]; E. E. Urbach, *The Tosafists* [Hebrew] (Jerusalem, 1980), and A. Grossman, *The Early Sages of France*, pp. 302–320, 473–492.

12. *The Commentaries of Rabbi Joseph Bekhor Shor on the Pentateuch*, a critical edition with notes and commentary by J. Nevo (Jerusalem, 1994). See pp. 9–10 of Nevo's introduction for the anti-Christian polemical passages.

13. B. Blumenkranz, "Juden und Jüdische in christlichen Wundererzälungen. Ein unbekanntes Gebiet religiöser Polemik," *Theologische Zeitschrift* 10 (1954): 417–446, and "Juden und christliche Konvertiten im jüdisch-christlichen Religionsgepräch des Mittelalters," *Miscellanea Mediaevalia* 4 (1966): 264–282. Both have been reprinted in *Juifs et chrétiens: Patristique et Moyen Age* (London, 1977).

14. This is precisely the formulation of Rabbi Joseph Kimhi, who composed one of the first treatises refuting Christian claims about Hebrew Scripture ca. 1140–50. See Joseph Kimhi, *The Book of the Covenant*, ed. and trans. Frank Talmage (Toronto, 1972), p. 27. Jacob b. Reuben, his contemporary in Gascony, compiled a disputation manual with the same stated purpose. See Jacob b. Reuben, *The Wars of the Lord*, ed. J. Rosenthal (Jerusalem, 1963). Jewish authors in Ashkenaz did not compose polemical manuals during the period from 1050 to 1200, but included their refutations in commentaries on the Bible and religious poetry [*Piyyutim*], and Chronicles. See Abraham Grossman, "Jewish-Christian Polemic and Jewish Biblical Exegesis in France during the Twelfth Century," *Zion* (1986): 29–60.

15. There is an immense literature on Rashi and his cultural milieu. Two recent conference volumes illustrate the scope of these investigations: *Rashi et la culture juive en France du Nord au moyen âge*, ed. G. Dahan (Louvain: Peeters,

1997); and *Rashi 1040–1990: Hommage à Ephraim E. Urbach: Congrès Européen des Etudes Juives*, ed. Gabrielle Sed-Rajna (Paris, 1993). For a survey of Rashi's exegetical writings on Scripture, see Moshe Greenberg, *Jewish Biblical Exegesis: An Introduction* (Jerusalem, 1983), pp. 70–75, and M. A. Signer, "How the Bible Is Read in the Jewish Tradition," in *New Interpreters' Bible* (Nashville, Tenn., 1994), 1: 42–73.

16. A. Grossman, *The Early Sages of France*, pp. 209–210, citing the research by J. Florsheim, *Rashi on the Bible in the Talmud*, 3 vols. (Jerusalem, 1987–89). J. Fraenkel, *Rashi's Methodology in His Exegesis of the Babylonian Talmud* (Jerusalem, 1980).

17. On the "northern French school of biblical exegesis," see M. Greenberg, *Jewish Biblical Exegesis: Introduction*, pp. 72–85; S. Poznanski, *Introduction*, pp. 44–83. A discerning analysis of the problem of "peshat" is found in Sara Kamin, *Rashi's Approach to Peshat and Derash* (Jerusalem, 1986), and B. J. Gelles, *Peshat and Derash in the Exegesis of Rashi* (Leiden, 1981).

18. M. Banitt, "The La'azim of Rashi and the French Biblical Glossaries," *World History of the Jewish People: The Dark Ages*, ed. by C. Roth (Jerusalem, 1964), 1:291–296, and "Les Poterim," *Revue des Etudes Juives* 125 (1966): 21–33.

19. Sara Kamin, *Rashi*, especially her concluding chapter, pp. 263–264. She also wrote a number of essays focusing on "plain meaning" and culture in twelfth-century biblical exegesis which were collected in *Between Jews and Christians in Biblical Exegesis* (Jerusalem, 1991). E. A. Touitou, "The Historical Background of Rashi's Commentary on Genesis," in *Rashi: Investigations of His Works*, ed. M. Steinfeld (Ramat Gan, 1993), pp. 211–242.

20. M. Signer, "King Messiah: Rashi's Exegesis of Psalms 2," *Prooftexts: A Journal of Jewish Literary History* 3 (1983): 273–284: "*Peshat, Sensus Litteralis,* and Sequential Narrative: Jewish Exegesis and the School of St. Victor in the Twelfth Century," in B. Walfish [ed.], *The Frank Talmage Memorial Volume* (Haifa, 1993), 1:203–216; "Rashi as Narrator," in *Rashi et la culture juive en France*, ed. G. Dahan, pp. 104–110.

21. I introduced the term "sequential narrative" in my study of the construction of the land of Israel in Jewish biblical exegesis of the Middle Ages, "The Land of Israel in Medieval Jewish Exegetical and Polemical Literature," in L. Hoffman, *The Land of Israel: Jewish Perspectives* (Notre Dame, Ind., 1986), pp. 210–233. For the affinities between Christianity and the development of communal narrative, see Hans Frei, *The Eclipse of Biblical Narrative* (New Haven, 1974), and "The 'Literal Reading' of Biblical Narrative in the Christian Tradition: Does It Stretch or Will It Break?" in *The Bible and the Narrative Tradition*, ed. F. McConnell (Oxford, 1986), pp. 36–77, and Paul Ricouer, *Interpretation Theory: Discourse and the Surplus of Meaning* (Fort Worth, Tex., 1976).

22. Beryl Smalley, *The Study of the Bible in the Middle Ages* (Oxford, 1986), emphasized the affinity between the search for the literal sense and new cultural horizons. Henri de Lubac, *Exégèse Medievale* (Paris, 1959–1964), vol. 2, part 1, pp. 99–301, demonstrates the continuity between scholars in the twelfth century and the Patristic authors. G. R. Evans, *The Language and Logic of the Bible* (Oxford, 1984), and R. W. Southern, *Scholastic Humanism and the Unification of Europe* (Oxford, 1995), describe the use of liberal arts to develop a coherent view of the diverse traditions of Christian theology.

23. Abulafia, *Christians and Jews in the Twelfth-Century Renaissance,* especially pp. 34–47 ("The Christianization of Reason") and pp. 77–99 ("Christianized Reason at Work"), where she demonstrates the influence of Anselm on Gilbert Crispin, pseudo-William of Champeaux, Guibert of Nogent, and Hildebert of Lavardin.

24. Richard W. Southern, *Saint Anselm: A Portrait in a Landscape* (Cambridge, 1990), pp. 195–227, describes the position of Jews as the "unbelievers" in the *Cur Deus Homo* and the broader structure of the argument in that treatise. See also Anna Sapir Abulafia, "Christians Disputing Disbelief: St. Anselm, Gilbert Crispin, and Pseudo-Anselm," in B. Lewis and F. Niewöhner, *Religionsgespräch im Mittelalter* (Wiesbaden, 1992), pp. 131–148; and "St. Anselm and Those Outside the Church," in D. Loades and K. Walsh, *Faith and Identity: Christian Political Experience,* Studies in Church and History, Subsidia 6 (Oxford, 1990), pp. 11–37.

25. For a survey of Rupert's biography and theological themes within the context of twelfth-century thought, see John H. Van Engen, *Rupert of Deutz* (Berkeley and Los Angeles, 1983). Anna Sapir Abulafia has examined Rupert's thought about the Jews in "The Ideology of Reform and Changing Ideas Concerning Jews in the Works of Rupert of Deutz and Hermannus quondam Iudeus," *Jewish History* 7 (1993): 43–63. Rupert also wrote a dialogue about Jews called *Anulus sive Dialogus inter christianum et Iudaeum,* which was edited by R. Haacke in Maria Lodovica Arduini, *Ruperto di Deutz e la controversia tra cristiani ed ebrei nel secolo XII* (Rome, 1979), pp. 183–242.

26. *De sancta trinitate et operibus eius,* ed. R. Haacke, CCCM, vols. 21–24. Van Engen, *Rupert of Deutz,* 242–248, examines the relationship of this work to Rupert's thinking about the Jews in the *Anulus.*

27. Beryl Smalley, *Study of the Bible,* pp. 83–106, called attention to the innovations of Hugh of St. Victor in the investigation of the literal sense scriptural exegesis and his contacts with Jews. The most comprehensive studies of Hugh's biblical exegesis and thought were written by J. Chatillon and reprinted in *Le Mouvement Canonial au Moyen Age: Réforme de L'Eglise, Spiritualité et Culture,* ed. P. Sicard, Biblioteca Victorina 3 (Turnhout, 1992), pp. 327–418. On the role of the literal sense in Hugh's development of biblical narrative, see

Grover Zinn, "*Historia Fundamentum est:* The Role of History in the Contemplative Life According to Hugh of St. Victor," in *Contemporary Reflections on the Medieval Christian Tradition: Essays in Honor of Ray Petry*, ed. G. H. Shriver (Durham, 1974), pp. 135–138. See also Rebecca Moore, *Jews and Christians in the Life and Thought of Hugh of St. Victor* (Atlanta, 1998).

28. Hugh presents the most extensive discussion of the literal sense in *Didascalicon seu de studio legendi* Book 6, which is available in J. Taylor's translation, *The Didascalicon of Hugh of St. Victor: A Medieval Guide to the Arts* (New York and London, 1968), pp. 131–154. There are slightly different formulations in his *De Scripturis et scriptoribus sacris praenotatiunculae* (PL 195:9–28) and in the preface to the *De Sacramentis christianae fidei* (PL 196:173–175).

29. *De arca Noe morali*, PL 196:617–680; *De arca Noe mystica*, PL 196:681–712. P. Sicard, *Diagrammes médiévaux et exégèse visuelle: Le libellus de formatione arche de Hugues de Saint-Victor*, Bibliotheca Victorina 4 (Turnhout, 1993), and *Hugues de Saint-Victor et son Ecole* (Turnhout, 1991).

30. *De sacramentis christianiae fidei*, PL 176:173–618.

31. *Liber Exceptionum*, ed. J. Chatillon (Paris, 1958). J. Chatillon points to the popularity of this work, which summarized the biblical narratives and provided the correspondences between the literal text of the Hebrew Scriptures and the New Testament.

32. Smalley describes the use of Peter Comestor's work as a "textbook" for the first courses in theology at the medieval university, *Study of the Bible*, pp. 196–263. There has been some controversy about whether or not Comestor utilized Hebrew sources. See G. Dahan, *Les intellectuels chrétiens et les juifs au moyen âge* (Paris, 1990), pp. 298–299, who cites the study by E. Shereshevsky, "Hebrew Traditions in Peter Comestor's Historia Scholastica," *Jewish Quarterly Review* (1968–69): 268–289, which has been criticized by S. T. Lachs, "The Source of Hebrew Traditions in the Historia Scholastica," *Harvard Theological Review* (1973): 385–396; and also H. Merchavia, *The Church versus Talmudic and Midrashic Literature* (Jerusalem, 1970), pp. 167–193.

33. E. Randolph Daniel, *Abbot Joachim of Fiore: Liber de concordia novi ac veteris testamenti* (Philadelphia, 1983), surveys this work. The relationship between historical writing and biblical narrative has been explored by Amos Funkenstein, *Heilsplan und natürliche Entwicklung: Formen der Gegenwartsbestimmung im Geschichtsdenken des hohen Mittelalters* (Munich, 1965), and Wilhelm Kamlah, *Apokalypse und Geschichtstheologie: Die mittelalterliche Auslegung der Apokalypse vor Joachim von Fiore* (reprint, Vaduz, 1965). The relationship between Joachim and Judaism has been discussed by B. Hirsch-Reich, "Joachim von Fiore und das Judentum," in *Judentum im Mittelalter. Beiträge zum christlich-jüdischen Gespräch*, ed. P. Wilpert and W. P. Eckert (Berlin, 1966),

pp. 228–263. See also Joachim of Fiore, *Adversus Judaeos*, ed. A. Frugoni (Rome, 1957).

34. *De emanuele: libri duo*, PL 196:601–666, which has been discussed by Smalley, *Study of the Bible*, pp. 110–111, and by Rainer Berndt, *André de St. Victor: Exégète et Théologien*, Bibliotheca Victorina 1 (Turnhout, 1991), pp. 294–301.

35. For perceptions of historical writing among the Rabbis, see Yerushalmi, *Zakhor*, and Amos Funkenstein, *Perceptions of Jewish History* (Berkeley and Los Angeles, 1993).

36. There is an extensive literature on this question. See J. Maier, *Jesus von Nazareth in der talmüdischen Überlieferung* (Darmstad, 1978) and *Jüdische Auseinandersetzung mit Christentum in der Antike* (Darmstadt, 1982), and M. Simon, *Verus Israel: A Study of Relationships between Christians and Jews in the Roman Empire* (New York, 1986). An accessible summary is found in Stephen G. Wilson, *Related Strangers: Jews and Christians 70–170 C.E.* (Minneapolis, 1995), pp. 169–194.

37. Beyond the discussions by J. Maier in *Jesus von Nazareth* and *Jüdische Auseinandersetzung*, many of the texts have been assembled and translated in R. Travers Herford, *Christianity in Talmud and Midrash* (New York, 1966), and Samuel Krauss, *Das Leben Jesu nach Jüdischen Quellen* (Hildesheim, 1977).

38. Yosef Hayim Yerushalmi, *Haggadah and History* (Philadelphia, 1975), surveys use of the Passover rite as a mirror of Jewish historical memory. For a Passover Haggadah with historical commentary, see *The Passover Haggadah*, ed. N. Glatzer (New York, 1989).

39. Israel J. Yuval, "Passover and Easter as Early Jewish-Christian Dialogue," in *Passover and Easter: Origin and History to Modern Times*, ed. Lawrence A. Hoffman and Paul F. Bradshaw (Notre Dame, Ind., 1999), and his article in Hebrew, "Those Who Jump between Two Branches: Jewish Pesach and Christian Pascha," *Tarbitz* 45 (1996): 5–25.

40. Yuval, "Vengeance and Damnation, Blood and Defamation: From Jewish Martyrdom to Blood Libel Accusations," and "The Lord will Take Vengeance, Vengeance for His Temple—Historia sine Ira et Studio" [Hebrew], *Zion* 59 (1994): 351–414; Grossman, "Jewish-Christian Polemic and Jewish Biblical Exegesis in the Twelfth Century," and "Exile and Redemption in Rashi's Works," in *From Slavery to Redemption*, ed. J. Berukhi, H. Halperin, and Y. Milo (Jerusalem, 1996), pp. 239–266 [Hebrew].

41. See preceding note, and especially my study, "Rashi as Narrator," in *Rashi et la culture juive en France*, ed. G. Dahan, pp. 103–110.

42. Y. Baer, "Rashi and the Historical Reality of His Time," *Tarbitz* 20 (1949): 320–332; and "The Persecutions of 1096," in *Assaf Festschrift*, ed.

M. Cassuto (Jerusalem, 1953), pp. 126–140. A. Grossman, *The Early Sages of France*, pp. 122–146, 250–254.

43. The *locus classicus* for these revisions in the commentary to Genesis 37:2 may be found in Martin Lockshin, *Rabbi Samuel b. Meir's Commentary on Genesis: An Annotated Translation* (Lewiston, N.Y., 1988), pp. 240–242. On Rabbi Samuel b. Meier see D. Rosin, *Rabbi Samuel b. Meir als Schrifterklärer* (Breslau, 1880); S. Poznanski, *Introduction*, pp. xxix–l; S. Kamin, "Rashbam's Conception of the Creation in Light of the Intellectual Currents of His Time," in *Jews and Christians Interpret the Bible* (Jerusalem, 1991), pp. 27*–68*, which focuses on parallels between Rashbam and Christian exegesis of the creation narrative. M. Berger, *The Torah Commentary of Rabbi Samuel ben Meir* (diss., Harvard University, 1982), focuses on exegetical technique.

44. A. Grossman, "Rashi's Commentary on Psalms and the Jewish-Christian Debate," in *Studies in Bible and Education: Festschrift Moshe Arend*, ed. Dov Rapel (Jerusalem, 1996), pp. 59–74 [Hebrew].

45. The contrast between life under Islamic rule and Christian sovereignty in Ashkenaz focuses on the greater interpenetration of Islamic thought and Arabic language into Jewish literature. At times this has led modern scholars to describe a "Jewish-Arab" symbiosis in contrast to a more separate and "pure" rabbinic culture in Ashkenaz. See S. D. Goitein, *Jews and Arabs, Their Contacts through the Ages* (New York, 1955), who describes the symbiotic relationship, and Mark R. Cohen, *Under the Crescent and the Cross: The Jews in the Middle Ages* (Princeton, 1994), who provides a more sober analysis of the varieties of experience under both Islamic and Christian rulers.

46. See Grossman, "Rashi's Commentary on Psalms." A critical edition of Rashi's commentary on Psalms was compiled by Isaac Maarsen, *Parshandata* (reprint, Jerusalem, 1972), vol. 3. An edition and super-commentary based on Maarsen's text has been written by Haim Pardes, *The Book of Psalms with Rashi's Commentary* (Jerusalem, 1998), and an English translation with a new edition of the Hebrew text by Mayer I. Gruber, *Rashi's Commentary on Psalms 1–89 with Translation, Introduction, and Notes* (Atlanta, Ga., 1998).

47. For an explanation of the Psalms in Christian liturgical life, see Jacques Dubois, "Comment les moines du Moyen Ages chantaient et goûtaient les Saintes Ecritures," in *Le Moyen Age et la Bible*, ed. Pierre Riché and Guy Lobrichon (Paris, 1984), pp. 261–304. For the development of Psalms exegesis in the twelfth century, see Marcia L. Colish, *Peter Lombard* (Leiden, 1994), 1:155–188; and Theresa Gross-Diaz, *The Psalms Commentary of Gilbert of Poitiers: From Lectio Divina to Lecture Room* (Leiden, 1996).

48. Commentary on individual verses from Psalms appears in polemical works such as the *Sefer Yosef HaMeqqanneh* or in commentaries on religious poetry [*piyyut*] such as R. Abraham b. Azriel, *Sefer Arugat HaBosem*, ed. E. E.

Urbach (Jerusalem, 1963), 4 vols., or in liturgical compendia such as Simhah of Vitry's *Mahzor Vitry*, ed. S. Hurvitz (reprint, Jerusalem, 1988). For a survey of commentary on religious poetry in Ashkenaz, see A. Grossman, *The Early Sages of France*, pp. 457–538. More systematic commentaries were written in Spain, Provence, or other lands under Islamic cultural influence. See Uriel Simon, *Four Approaches to the Book of Psalms: From Saadia Gaon to Abraham ibn Ezra* (Binghamton, N.Y., 1991).

49. The following argument is a summary of my article "King/Messiah: Rashi's Exegesis of Psalm 2," *Prooftexts: A Journal of Jewish Literary History* 3 (1983): 273–284. All translations included in the present article are my own.

50. Cassiodorus's commentary was transmitted to the Middle Ages by the Glossa Ordinaria, which has been the object of intense study. See Margaret Gibson and Karlfried Froehlich, "Introduction," in *Biblia Latina cum Glossa Ordinaria: A Facsimile Reprint of the Editio Princeps Adolph Rusch of Strassburg 1480/81* (Turnhout, 1992), 1:vii–xxi. For the Glossa Ordinaria as a source for the transmission of medieval anti-Judaism, see Michael Signer, "The *Glossa ordinaria* and the Transmission of Medieval Anti-Judaism," in *A Distinct Voice: Medieval Studies in Honor of Leonard E. Boyle*, ed. Jacqueline Brown and William P. Stoneman (Notre Dame, Ind., 1997), pp. 591–605.

51. A survey of the history of Jewish and Christian exegesis on Song of Songs with extensive bibliography is found in *Song of Songs: A New Translation with Commentary and Notes*, Anchor Bible, vol. 7c (New York, 1977).

52. A full history of Jewish interpretation of the Canticle remains a desideratum. Robert Gordis, *The Song of Songs: Study, Translation, and Modern Commentary* (New York, 1967), provides some details. For patristic and medieval Christian interpretation, see E. Ann Matter, *The Voice of My Beloved: The Song of Songs in Medieval Western Christianity* (Philadelphia, 1990).

53. A critical edition of the Hebrew text was compiled by J. Rosenthal, "Rashi's Commentary to Song of Songs," in *Samuel K. Mirsky Jubilee Volume*, ed. S. Bernstein and G. Churgin (New York, 1958), pp. 130–188. My translation for this essay is part of a forthcoming translation of the entire commentary.

54. Ivan G. Marcus, "Rashi's Historiosophy in the Introductions to His Biblical Commentaries," *Revue des Etudes Juives* 157 (January–June 1998): 47–55, has analyzed Rashi's introductions to Song of Songs and Zachariah in light of the classical rabbinic notions of the fate of Israel until the final redemption. He concludes that these two introductions as well as Rashi's introduction to Genesis "express a metahistorical or historiosophical statement about the deeper meaning of—or lack of real—change over time as it relates to God and the nations."

55. There is an enormous literature on the relationship of Galatians to the history of Jewish-Christian relations in the ancient and modern period, with

relatively little about medieval interpretation. See James D. G. Dunn, *Jesus, Paul and the Law: Studies in Mark and Galatians* (Louisville, Ky., 1990), and *Jews and Christians: The Parting of the Ways*, A.D. 70–135 (Tubingen, 1992).

56. Harold Attridge, *The Epistle to the Hebrews: A Commentary* (Philadelphia, 1989), discusses the major themes of Hebrews. Stephen G. Wilson, *Related Strangers*, devotes an entire chapter to a discussion of Hebrews and the Epistle of Barnabas, pp. 110–142, and the relevant literature cited in his extensive notes, pp. 341–351.

57. The rabbinic literary tradition did not produce a formal introduction comparable to the classical "accessus ad auctores." However, the "accessus" literature which has been surveyed by A. G. Minnis, *Medieval Theory of Authorship: Scholastic Literary Attitudes in the Later Middle Ages* (Aldershot, 1988) provides suggestive material. Jewish authors who wrote under the influence of Islamic culture did produce highly stylized formal introductions which followed the classical form. In the commentaries of Rashi we have what appear to be separate compositions written with the intention of providing a broad framework for the reader. In the following section of this essay, I suggest that the initial lines of each book of the Pentateuch were composed to provide the framework for reading it. I hope to provide further documentation for these introductory compositions in future studies.

58. The Hebrew text is based on *The Pentateuch with Rashi HaShalem* (Jerusalem, 1986), 1:2. Translation is my own.

59. Y. Baer, "Rashi and the Historical Reality of His Time" and "The Persecutions of 1096" (note 42).

60. G. Dahan, *Les intellectuels chrétiens*, pp. 473–508, and Daniel J. Lasker, *Jewish Philosophical Polemics against Christianity in the Middle Ages* (New York, 1977).

61. Gilbert Crispin, Abbot of Westminster, *The Works of Gilbert Crispin*, ed. A. S. Abulafia and G. R. Evans (London, 1986).

62. *Rashi's Commentary on Psalms*, ed. Pardes, pp. 337–338.

63. *The Pentateuch with Rashi HaShalem* (Jerusalem, 1992), 4:2–4.

64. *Midrash Tanhuma HaQadum vehaYashan*, 2, ed. Solomon Buber (reprint Jerusalem, 1977), p. 25; and the translation by John T. Townsend (Hoboken, N.J., 1989), vol. 2, p. 120; and *Midrash Pesikta Rabbati*, 10, ed. Rivka Kern-Ulmer (Atlanta, 1997), p. 145; and the translation by William G. Braude (New Haven, 1968), p. 160.

65. The discussion is found in *Pentateuch with Rashi HaShalem*, 4:4–5, nn. 3–4.

66. The Hebrew text of Rashi here is based on the edition of H. D. Chavel and appears in the compendium of medieval biblical commentaries on the Pentateuch, *Torat Hayyim* (Jerusalem, 1990), Leviticus 1:1, p. 1.

67. *Midrash VaYiqrah Rabbah,* ed. M. Margaliot (reprint, Jerusalem, 1993), 1.1, pp. :–9.

68. On Balaam as a problematic figure in rabbinic literature, see Judith Baskin, *Pharoah's Counsellors: Job, Jethro, and Balaam in Rabbinic and Patristic Literature* (Chico, Calif., 1983).

69. Rashi in *Torat Hayyim* (Jerusalem, 1991), Numbers 1:1, p. 1.

70. Rashi in *Torat Hayyim* (Jerusalem, 1993), Deuteronomy 1:1, p. 1.

n 1 n e

Ralph of Flaix: The Book of Leviticus Interpreted as Christian Community

JOHN VAN ENGEN

About the year 1140, a Benedictine named Ralph gathered with fellow monks at St. Germer in Flaix, an abbey sixty miles north of Paris, to argue about Jewish claims to interpret Scripture. Their group included, almost certainly, a Jewish refugee from the murderous riots of 1096 in Rouen, a man later baptized and consecrated a monk. Ralph watched carefully the faces of his confreres, and perceived their souls to waver (*fluctuare*) with the winds of argument, especially those less learned among them (*minus se eruditorum se status habet*). While none dared say it aloud, their faces betrayed uncertainty about which side to follow and a readiness to give the nod first to Jewish positions and then to Christian. Had they not been predisposed (*praeiudicium*) by the church's teaching imbibed with their mother's milk, Ralph observed, they might well have sided with the Jewish positions. This shocked him. He realized that most Christians, even monks, might take "the truth of our profession" as a given (*multis communis sit*), but held to it mainly on the say of the many (*multitudinis auctoritate confisus*). Only a few had any real grasp (*intelligentia*) of the truth; indeed most knew little Scripture and had no understanding of what they believed. Deeply upset by his dawning realization (*Ingemuimus re uera et dolore coepimus retractare*),[1] Ralph launched upon the largest and most original commentary on Leviticus written by a Christian in a thousand years.

He resolved to confront head-on any supposed Jewish reading of Torah, and so undertook a detailed commentary on Leviticus, the book with which Jewish boys began their study. Ralph of Flaix produced twenty books in four hundred folio columns, completed in about six years' time during the 1140s. The work enjoyed enormous success. Widely copied despite its length, his commentary made it onto the Paris stationer's list in 1275–86, and dominated Christian exegesis until works by university masters gradually displaced it. Thirty years ago Beryl Smalley surveyed the purposes, methods, and sources of this commentary in a learned article, and culled out some of its pithier observations on contemporary issues. She perceived "a clear purpose [running] through the twenty books . . . Ralph aimed first and foremost at refuting Jewish arguments. . . ." Smalley, focused on approaches to the literal sense, concluded a little indignantly that "Ralph has made a system out of the search for absurdities [in the biblical text] and consequent rejection of the letter. . . ." Over against her beloved Victorine exegetes, she saw in him a cloistered scholar, removed from the schools and urban interaction, producing a work of learning that became largely an end in itself. Her essay told one part of the story, but it neglected Ralph at his best, as Smalley herself conceded.[2] More, in historical terms, it failed to account for the enormous readership Ralph achieved.

Ralph touched a nerve in the Christian community, however improbably, with a dense commentary on Leviticus. Christian commentators since Origen and Jerome had found this book especially difficult, usually limiting their interpretation to selected christocentric renderings, enriched by moral accounts of sin, priestly ministry, or a sacrificial self. In the ninth century Rhabanus Maurus summarized this tradition and passed it on to Ralph, who used it sparingly—and found it inadequate. To understand how or why he took a new approach, and to grasp his sensitivity to the task and audience at hand, requires that historians consider four matters, all revolving around the basic question: Why Leviticus?

1. What notions of "law" did medieval Christians bring to a book like Leviticus?
2. If Jewish positions ostensibly occasioned this commentary, to what degree did Jews represent a real alternative, a threat in any sense, even real people?

3. Which Christians found this work so compelling and bothered to copy such an enormous biblical commentary?
4. What, finally, were the Christian themes that Ralph elicited from the heart of Jewish law?

Medieval Christian peoples understood themselves as subject to law, indeed, a variety of laws: social and political customs in their region, church law dictated by priests and bishops, and ultimately God's law inscribed in sacred books. Practice was the heart of religion, and religious practice was widely regarded as obligatory and communal. The term "law" consequently acquired an additional meaning. In twelfth-century Europe the word (*lex*) also stood comprehensively for the rites, practices, and customs that defined the solidarities of an entire religious community. Latin Christians reached for this word especially, it seems, when they confronted other groups. An epitaph for Pope Urban II (d. 1099) invoked this term to celebrate recent Christian conquests: "Through him the holy city is open, our law triumphs, pagan peoples were conquered, and the faith expands throughout the world."[3] What triumphed in Jerusalem during Urban's reign—"our law"—was the community spearheaded by crusaders: Latin Christians and their practices. This usage went back at least to Carolingian times, and may have rested on a Pauline expression (*lex Christi*: Gal. 6:2). During the twelfth century, as the baptized grew more aware of communities with a distinct *lex*, the term circulated more widely, also in the vernacular, as a common way to denote personal and communal religious allegiance. In 1169 Pope Alexander III instructed the archbishop of Reims to "treat humanly and kindly those who are converted from Judaism to our law" (*postposito Judaismo ad legem nostram conuertuntur*).[4]

Jews claimed, as Ralph heard it, to keep faith with and submit themselves to biblical law (see note 15 below). That resonated for him in a double sense: it was an assertion both that they rightly understood and kept levitical law, and that they enjoyed God's unique sanction for their "law," their community practices. The Jewish convert baptized as Petrus Alfonsi employed exactly this language at the opening of his pamphlet about the year 1110. Its purpose, he declared, was to defend his conclusion that Christian law excelled over all others (*christianam legem omnibus praestantiorem esse conclusi*). He introduced himself as a man who had accepted the "law and faith of Christians" (*legem et fidem accepissem Christianorum*), whence Jews accused him of "showing contempt for God and law" (*Deum et legem contempseram*), of improperly understanding the words of the prophets and the law, and of seeking only worldly honor once he saw that the people of the Christians were now dominant over others.[5] "Faith" was certainly at stake in such conversions or confrontations, that is, distinct beliefs personally or communally held. But so was "law," meaning rather a way of life, a pattern of practice and obligation that defined people in community.

In the year 1111 Guibert of Nogent felt compelled to instruct Count John of Soissons about Christian law. This was a man, in Guibert's acid portrait, who called himself a Christian, attended church, received communion, venerated the passion, gave alms, and yet looked on intrigued at Jewish ceremonies, defended some of their ways (*instituta*), and evinced hostility to Christian practices (*in leges odium christianas exerceat*). Guibert labeled him a "neuter," for he neither followed the [Jewish] laws he praised (*ea quae laudat iura*) nor praised the Christian laws he seemed to follow (*quae uidetur prosequi christiani studii iura non laudat*).[6] This portrait of a "judaizing" count may represent, in part, a nasty literary smear.[7] Yet the situation that elicited Guibert's pamphlet seems altogether intelligible. Contact between Jews and Christians—in neighborhood streets, in marketplaces, at princely and episcopal courts—could provoke questions, even doubts, about which "law" was right.

This same language entered the story of the Jewish-born man who joined Ralph's Benedictine house in rural Flaix. Guibert of Nogent (d. 1124) spent nearly forty years at St. Germer (ca. 1066–1104), the gestation period for his "memoirs" and his moral exegesis of the minor prophets. Among the monks there, as Guibert recounts it, was this man rescued as a child from the massacre at Rouen in 1096. The rescuer's noble mother asked the boy if he wished to apply himself now to Christian ways (*utrum christianis uellet legibus applicari*). This adolescent, who reportedly had begun to learn Hebrew, agreed and was baptized, then entrusted to a monastic teacher of grammar to learn "our law" (*nouo illi homunculo necessariam nostrae legis notitiam*). Later—a mark of the suspicion that prevailed—the man was placed at St. Germer to distance him from his birth community. Guibert then sent him, as a learning aide, the instructions he had written for Count John.[8]

"Law," in short, even in a religious context, did not first call to mind heavy theological questions about law and grace, prominent as those were in the New Testament and in subsequent Christian teachers, especially Augustine. It referred rather to the defining marks and divinely sanctioned practices of a religious community. The question Jews continuously raised, the one that most troubled Christians, bound together conceptions of God and of community/law: Was it thinkable that God had changed, that he had commanded one "law" at one time, and then abandoned it for another? Was the Christian God unreliable? Rupert of Deutz, in his Leviticus commentary of about 1113–14, posed this issue and offered a face-saving solution. He proposed to recognize a literal law issued by Moses, but deemed this as "perpetual law" only where it proved consistent also with the prophets—thus, he concluded, "perpetual not with respect to the veil of the letter but the charity of spiritual intelligence."[9] This "spiritualized" perpetual law became manifest, moreover, in the sacraments of the church (baptism, eucharist, forms of penance), in the priesthood and its mediating functions, and in Jesus as the ultimate priest and sacrifice. Rupert wrote at the height of the so-called Gregorian Reform. Though more than usually sensitive to this Jewish charge, he aimed his barbs in fact mostly at negligent churchmen who besmirched their priestly duties.

Who, then, were these Jews that troubled Christians? Scholars argue about "historical" and "hermeneutic" Jews, that is, about the real or figurative character of the Jewish *persona* found in Christian commentaries and dialogues. Medieval Christian writers frequently made no apparent mental distinction between the figure of a Jew construed from ancient biblical texts and the person of a Jew encountered in contemporary European communities. Beyond imagined fantasies, the Jewish *persona* in literary creations was made to work, all too easily, as a foil for Christian assertions. As the only non-Christian alternative within medieval kingdoms, Jews could serve as ciphers for the repudiated "other." And yet, scholars must not so emphasize the rhetoric of texts as to overlook the reality of human contact, the possibility that these texts recreated, however distantly, real persons representing real alternatives. Thus, about 1090 Gilbert Crispin became friendly with a Jew who came to him first on business, then simply to visit (*me uidendi gratia*). Each time they talked through religious differences, keeping a friendly spirit (*amico animo*). Gilbert Crispin's written acount, however construed to Christian advantage, was born of social interaction and recognized, as did Ralph, that Jewish arguments might seem compelling.[10] Likewise, when a contemporary chronicler set out to praise Rudolph of St. Trond's excellence as abbot of St. Pantaleon (1121–23) in Cologne, he noted his hospitality, how he reached out to high churchmen and to humble workers and to Jews: "With the Jews he frequently had easy conversation, not arguing with them or reproaching them but softening the hardness of their hearts with whatever touch and stroking was necessary; for which reason he was so loved by them that even their women went to see him and talk with him."[11] Whatever the exaggeration here, historians must allow for such informal relations. And they must grasp the danger these relations appeared to pose for both sides. For a few, at least, they held out an allure, an alternate way to worship and obey God or to understand Scripture.

This same Abbot Rudolph asked the most learned Christian writer in Cologne, Rupert of Deutz, to compose an exemplary dispute. The instructions, as Rupert recounted them, were to set up a "full-fledged duel in which the Christian invites the Jew to adopt the Gospel faith and the Jew strikes back with whatever he can from the letter of the law and his own thought (*sensus*)." Rupert proposed to make the work attractive, a real "spectacle," a "festive combat," the better to draw in "Christian boys" (*pueris fidelibus*). Rudolph judged such a work necessary, not perhaps, he said, for experienced monks (*veteranis*) but for "our beginners" (*nostris tirunculis*)—that is, novices and younger monks beginning to think for themselves about scriptural law. Rupert conceded, too, the need for one "fortified place" where inexperienced Christians could find all the arms required to withstand Jewish objections to Christian beliefs, practices, and scriptural interpretations.[12]

Informal contact posed no danger for those utterly convinced of the rightness of their own community, especially learned churchmen or rabbis and—at the other end of the spectrum—the mass of people blinded by ignorance of, prejudice toward, or hatred for the other community. The risk lay with middling groups: Jewish merchant travelers who interacted with Christians, Christian clerics or princes open enough to become intrigued by Jewish claims or practices. Either might glimpse possibilities in the other's "law." In Laon, then a major center for student-clerics, an adolescent cleric (*puerulus*) witnessed a remarkable exchange. Inside someone's house, he listened to an argument between a Jew and a cleric. He observed that the cleric was unable to stand up to the "windy words" of the Jew, and therefore resorted to a trial by ordeal (of hot iron).[13] Indeed, most of the Christian converts to Judaism—to judge from known accounts, and in keeping with this angle on social interaction—were middling clerics, and most of the voluntary Jewish converts to Christianity were traveling merchants.

How much Ralph had talked and debated with Jews is unclear. He knew that Jews would grow angry with him if he suggested that their Torah represented only a shadow of God's real intentions.[14] So he mustered texts from their own prophets. Even a cursory reading in them, he asserted, revealed an array of signs whose import lay in their meaning, not in the literal words or matters as such. The reader had to get at what God intended to communicate (*tradere intendit*). Probably with Jewish interlocutors in mind, Ralph nonetheless conceded a key point. While the miracles of martyrs and the manifest victory of the faith (the world first opposed and now subject) should suffice as proof, the faith stood uniquely (*singulare firmamentum*) upon Scripture—in our times, he added, clearly fulfilled. Given such a scriptural foundation, Ralph stated his purpose:

> Weighing therefore all these things, since we wish to be armed against the whisperings of the Jews, we have focused our mind on the treatment of the Law, to which they wish to seem subject themselves but whose purpose (*intentionem*) they in no way understand. For they do not look into the brightness of the face of Moses—which can easily be proved from their own books.[15]

Whether the "whispered" interchanges were real or imagined, Ralph perceived it as a vital contest of interpretation.

The Jewish *persona*, that is, real and figurative, offered a perceptible challenge. So it was in the work Rupert of Deutz wrote for Rudolph. Whatever personal experiences may have informed this work of 1125, Rupert promised "diligently to furnish the Jew with every possible objection." His *persona* took hard-hitting positions, powerful enough to unsettle any Christian reflecting seriously on Scripture. His Jew introduced himself at the outset with an objection: We are the people of circumcision with whom God first made covenant; how can Christians make God so changeable as to alter or abandon this mandated covenantal practice? Why call such rites merely a sign? Or is God forgetful? By denying that covenant, the Jew objects, you wish to wipe out the memory of our people, to meld them uncircumcised, undifferentiated, into all other peoples. Later, he went on: If your baptism forgives sin and overcomes death, why are you still dying? Such hard questions continue. Later still, in an exceptionally long paragraph, the Jewish *persona* objected to Jesus as the Messiah: Why then is Jerusalem not exalted, Zion not prosperous? He rejects, similarly, the Christian's arbitary reading of the law: Was not all of it ordered by Almighty God? What about the ban on images? What about the sabbath?[16] Twelfth-century Christians able to understand and reproduce such questions were anxious to arm younger monks and clerics against them. Their efforts betrayed unsettling worry about the Jewish presence, in person or as a perceived religious alternative.

Ralph stated his own interpretive stance in a bold rhetorical question, prominent in the preface he added upon completion: "Who cannot see that in these precepts Moses enunciated not righteousness itself but only the image of righteousness?" His negative subjunctive (*quis non uideat*) deserves note. Smalley took it as callous triumphalism, a position so obvious only fools would miss it—and it may indeed hint at overconfidence. But in context Ralph's question also sounded an anxious appeal. At the end of this preface Ralph returned to it pointedly: Those in our time who doubt Jewish blindness—these, thus, are the people who worried him, who did not "see" it as obvious—either have not read Holy Scripture or cannot understand it. How could they imagine God to lie, to issue one set of divine commands and then take them back? Ralph then turned on the Jews themselves: God warned sinful Jews that they might be deprived of knowing him. If today they are deprived of king, prince, and sacrifice (as we see!), why not then of God too?[17] This was nasty, but concrete. In an argument over exegesis and theology, the social state of Ashkenazi Jewry, as so often for medieval Christians, was invoked to offer visible proof for the truth of the Christian position.

Ralph explained Leviticus to his confreres first in oral colloquies, then wrote his interpretation down lest it be forgotten.[18] Beyond his fellow monks, who did this monk imagine as readers, as the audience for a detailed commentary on Leviticus? A very brief preface, using the *accessus* model, indicates how he began, setting out the author, title, and "material" of the book—then proceeding with the verbal contents. In this exposition the teacher emerges everywhere, whatever his models or his own education, both unknown. Thus he often stopped to explain figures of speech, referred to chapters elsewhere for fuller discussions, and in later prefaces (Books XIV–XVII) explained the kinds of writing found in Scripture, forms of interpretation, and so on. Most importantly, and no doubt the key to its later success, Ralph divided his commentary into books that followed topically the prescriptions of the biblical book: the forms of sacrifice, clean and unclean foods, kinds of leprosy, sexual relations, and so on. (In Paris the Victorines would also approach Leviticus thematically at roughly the same time.) Most unusual for a commentary, Ralph also divided these books into chapters with titles that referred to Levitical items, the "showbread," the types of unclean food, the prescriptions for leprosy. He then completed his major preface, and his work, by setting out a systematic table of contents identifying in detail the "matters" of this biblical book.

If Ralph imagined Jewish adversaries, he wrote for Christian readers, particularly the "semi-literate" who had seemed the most unsettled by alternative Jewish readings. These people—monks, clerics, some informed laypeople, their numbers steadily increasing in this era—confronted the text as such and sought to make sense of a book often judged bewildering. For monks or clerics reading this book word by word for themselves, to focus only on selected passages or to retreat hastily into christocentric allegory no longer satisfied. Christians had to give a plausible account of the "plain meaning" or "letter" in this biblical text, as Jews apparently did. Ralph's task was to devise such an exposition without conceding the "letter" to the Jews, one that saved the divine status of Leviticus as containing God's own words, and also addressed meaningfully the lives of Christians. Those newly taken with the letter of the text, especially ever more literate clerics, had to learn how to read texts that were designed in fact, as Ralph saw it, to point beyond the letter. On occasion Ralph addressed these new word-for-word readers directly. After, for instance, laying out seemingly contrary prescriptions about offering leavened or unleavened bread (Lev. 7:11 ff.), Ralph declaimed: "Let the enthusiasts of the letter (*sectatores litere*) see how they get past this one, for if we stick to the letter, the law sanctions contrary things. Inner contradictions drive us to the spiritual sense."[19] From this example he drew an apodictic lesson: Rather than arguing about words, we must pass over to arguing out "mysteries," those inner meanings suitable for *advancing learners*.[20] This is the audience (*proficientibus discipulis*) Ralph had in mind, the same crucial "endangered" group for whom Abbot Rudolph, Rupert, and others thought that a handy, forceful response to Jewish positions was needed.

Ralph appealed to an audience that found the Levitical prescriptions often foreign and sometimes unintelligible. He dismissed, thus, any literal meaning for the prohibition against touching the unclean or the dead (Lev. 5:2) with a rhetorical question: For what vice can it be, I ask you, to have touched the dead or even to have buried them? His question worked only for an audience with no taboos concerning corpses, one indeed that venerated relics. Moses must have meant something else, Ralph pointed out to Christian enthusiasts of the letter. In this instance, the dead (and all things unclean) referred to sin. Touch was the self's orientation toward it, the personal consent to the deadly vice of another.[21]

Ralph's clerical audience was not about to convert to Judaism, though suspicion lingered. Too many became fascinated and troubled by a close reading of the biblical text. Whatever the role and presence of known Jews, then, the hermeneutic Jew, the figure of a Jewish interpretation, required attention. For the "less learned" or the newly learned enthusiasts, Ralph had a double task, to account for and to debunk the letter. Smalley fixed on the second, and perhaps presumed the first. But Ralph had to do both explicitly for potentially every word of the text, hence the length and the detail. Nothing in the law, Ralph asserted "most firmly," lacked a rationale or use—precisely that which the true interpreter must uncover (*illius dandi ratio sive utilitas*). Yet a plain reading would not do. Take, for instance, Leviticus 10:9, a ban on wine-drinking issued to Aaron and his sons when they entered the tabernacle. This ban, absurd in itself and unworthy of a divine writer, as Ralph saw it, obviously pointed toward a "*mystica profunditas*." The biblical text says that the proscription was meant to preserve a priest's capacity to discern the clean from the unclean, the sacred from the profane. But the hermeneutical hinge is to grasp "wine" "*allegorice*" by studying its meaning in the prophets, namely, that which overturns the self and ruins discerning judgement: thus not a mug of wine but the inebriating and confusing forces of desire that overturn a moral, sacrificing self.[22]

In some cases there could be a plain-sense referent for Christians, but not as obligation. Thus prescriptions about the uncleanness of new mothers, Ralph noted, appeared to make them guilty for giving birth— which is unacceptable.[23] Yet, he conceded, Christian women absented themselves from church for forty days after childbirth, but in their case to honor the example of the Virgin Mary, who had voluntarily (*sponte*) subjected herself to this Levitical law.[24] This precept, he explained, pointed in reality to spiritual rebirth, the renewing of mind and conscience amidst the uncleanness of the human condition. "Advancing learners," in sum, those Christians (mostly, but not exclusively, younger monks and clerics) reading this biblical text carefully had to learn the proper technique for getting beyond the complexities, even the sheer nonsense, of the words and prescriptions as they appeared. They had to claim a superior exegetical technique, derived from reading the Bible as it was intended, for the practice and beliefs of their community.

In this era nearly all who took up the challenge to answer Jews— Gilbert Crispin, Odo, Guibert, Rupert, Ralph, Peter the Venerable, even Abelard—were Benedictine monks, not bishops or secular clerics, and not adherents to a new order. Black Monks (traditional Benedictines) occupied a unique social and religious space: they lived in contact with the world (too much so, according to reformers), often in or near towns, and as learned clerics were not yet overtaken by university schoolmen. Though contemplatives, they saw and interacted with their world. Thus Ralph regarded it as self-evident that there be a place for laity who "lived according to divine laws" while enjoying the sweetness of the temporal world (*temporali iocunditate fruitur*), embracing their spouses, producing children, and procuring possessions for themselves and their heirs.[25] Yet they too had to keep the divine law entire: He knew foolish laypeople who gave alms, thinking thereby to appease God, while acting unfaithfully toward spouses, cruelly taking plunder from neighbors, and contemptuously swearing falsely in God's name.[26] Beyond lords, whose society he knew all too well, he critiqued learned clerics who gave up the world in the name of study only to become proudly inflated with knowledge.[27] Though a monk writing for monks,

Ralph kept at least three additional audiences in mind: all Christians expected to live by Gospel law, newly learned clerics with hard questions about the biblical text, and Jews in northern France who claimed to keep the letter of biblical law.

With the fervor of church reform a generation in the past, the queries of literate readers on the rise, and a "Jewish" reading strangely unsettling, Ralph adopted an interpretive stance at once traditional and original. He owed little to earlier commentaries on Leviticus—Smalley also found this—but much to a deep reading of Gregory on Job, still the most influential commentary on the interior spiritual life (*moralia*). Ralph's interpretive approach may be illustrated, appropriately enough, by his treatment of sacrifice. Christian exegetical tradition had already identified the "head" in the sacrificial victim (Lev. 1:12) with the moral disposition of a person, Jerome locating it in the heart (*sensus in corde est*), Gregory in that which rules the body (*sensu nostro quo omne corpus regitur*), the interlinear Ordinary Gloss in the "mind" (*principale mentis et intelligentie*), and Rupert in "intention" (*Caput intentio est, quam cuncta totius operis membra sequuntur*).[28] Ralph too identified this sacrificed "head" as standing for a person's "inner orientation" (*interior intentio*), a point he then elaborated upon. In the biblical account of the sacrificial victim, the stripping away of its skin meant the external superficialities of human life, and the offering up of its innards the person's spiritual interior. The Levitical sacrifice signified the subordination of a whole human person to the divine will, that is, to gospel law.[29]

Ralph saw the human person, however, even at the depths of spiritual intention, as acting in community. The two came together in his experience and in his reading of Leviticus. Therefore, at the very outset of his commentary, explaining the two forms of sacrifice prescribed, he proposed to "refer them to us and to consider what they signify mystically in the church." This double-sided central theme guided his reading or rereading of Leviticus. Thus the "holocaust" or burnt offering signified those who offered themselves up entirely on the altar, such as professed religious; the "peace offerings" those who offered what they could while maintaining a lay married life free of criminal offense.[30] Ralph insisted that the sacrifices prescribed in Leviticus not be read as detailing any finite handling (*localis*) of offerings or of blood, but rather as pointing to human moral acts, good or ill. Like the smoke of sacrifices, such acts transcended their finite place and time to penetrate the skies and come into the presence of God.[31] According to Ralph's understanding, where Jews sought to locate the unchanging character of eternal God in his prescription of ritual acts, Christians, with their transformed reading of Leviticus, understood it to reside in unchanging commands to love God and neighbor, to do justice, and so on, that is, moral acts of which the laws must be seen as intentional "signs."[32] Such a reading would unlock the biblical book's real intention.

To read the intended "mystery" of Leviticus, then, was to probe into the whole "faithful" people and into each moral person. For this Ralph had no precise precedent. But in the early twelfth century others had begun to think of Leviticus as a guide to Christian community. Rupert, too, in one of his earliest commentaries (1113–14), had categorized the various sacrifices for the reader, and applied "sacrifice," for him meaning worship, to each Christian estate, in his view the received scheme of prelates, contemplatives, and the married laity. Ralph, however, considered the Christian community he saw and experienced all around him, and was not at all satisfied with received forms. He brought to his reading of Leviticus a perception of most Christians as mired in hypocrisy, carried along by uninformed and unmotivated practice. We see far too many, he commented, who spend their lives intent upon eating, sleeping, and talking; just because they hold themselves back from theft, plunder, and murder, they consider themselves most religious. Such Christians, in his view, merely conformed to the herd: they kept to appearances without ever exercising individual powers of discernment (*deliberationis proprie iudicio*). Their apparent ethical "innocence" was worthless apart from real devotion and love.[33] Levitical sacrifice must arise from love and desire, the thoughts of the heart, not the forms of words.[34] Most people in fact, as he saw it, neglected the worship of God and their own salvation (*Multa hominum erga Dei cultum et suam salutem negligentia*).[35]

Ralph's call for discernment and intentionality was subtle. In the very opening chapter of his commentary, where he noted the two "life-forms" representing the sacrificing faithful (see note 30 above), Ralph introduced the internal optic through which he read all forms of "offering," lay and religious. Sacrifice must not be a manipulative exchange but something "voluntary" (*uoluntarie Deo sacrificandum sit*), an act aimed at pleasing God and not other humans.[36] Thus, reading and study, though inner acts and often considered the work of churchmen, too easily served the false ends of gaining human renown.[37] People who possessed material power and goods, on the other hand, might gain eternal merit if they did not expend their assets to pursue proud or lusty ends but generously to achieve fit purposes. Indeed, even when they appeared publicly on horse in glorious array, they might, while exalting themselves outwardly, humble themselves inwardly (*se etiam dum foris eleuant, intus abiiciunt*).[38]

For Ralph, getting beyond appearances, in both the letter of the biblical book and in the practice of religious life, came as linked actions: this was the heart of his contribution. For the careful reader of his book, the inner meaning of sacrifice and ceremonial law pointed beyond letter to mystery, beyond actions to intentions, beyond conformity to self-examination. Truly to read the *intentio* or inner purpose of this biblical book was at the same time to move toward bringing the *intentio* or inner purpose of a Christian person into focus. Not to "take away the salt of the covenant" (Lev. 2:13), for instance, was not to remove the salt of both scriptural testaments from your personal sacrifice. Ralph then rendered this positively: We must order all of our inward parts to the rule of the divine precepts in Leviticus (*omnia interiora nostra ad divinorum preceptorum regulam componamus*).[39] While it was true that elements in the ancient law deserved keeping as containing the form of true righteousness (*Tenebant itaque in illa sua religione formam perfecte iustitie*),[40] and the "terror" of the law also usefully curbed some evil humans, the righteous, he insisted, were not strictly "under law" but "with law," justice thereby becoming part of their own will (*Non enim sub lege sed cum lege est, hoc habens in uoluntate quod illa in preceptione*).[41] The true end of religion comes into focus when a person begins to know himself (*sibi innotescat*) as abandoned and despoiled, and calls out from the depths of his inner being.[42] In sum: To show a half-learned, half-indifferent, sometimes troubled Christian majority that meaningless, customary practice would not do as their biblical sacrifice—this was to reveal the "mystical" import of the book.

An encounter with Jews, real and imagined, drove Christians back upon their own resources, to rethink and reargue their positions, and to reread holy law for themselves, however begrudgingly or polemically.

Ralph set out from the position that Levitical law was fully coherent and divine but full of "mystery," always to be interpreted according to its "*intentio*."[43] This meant that sometimes, even often, the "shadowy letter" could not be rendered noncontradictory or coherent in its plain sense; it had to be rendered intelligible by its intended "mystery," its teaching for Christian people.[44] And this meant the close examination and right ordering of the inner moral person, an action parallel to that of reclaiming the inner sense of the text. Thus the redemptions associated with the year of jubilee, the texts with which Ralph was struggling in these last two quotations, point finally to the redemption of lost virtues and the renewal of the inner self.[45] This is what God meant to teach in holy law, not the bewildering letter that newly learned Christians found so fascinating or disturbing, nor the religious practice that Jews lived and "whispered" to Christians. Ralph went beyond his predecessors, consciously so, to derive from Leviticus a kind of moral thinking that turned sacrifice into a trope for the inner disposition of believers. Ralph did not reduce sacrifice and observance to so many christocentric symbols, but rather rendered them as human belief and action, especially as the inner intention and innermost desire which were to enliven a blind Christian conformity.

Wavering monks provoked Ralph's massive commentary. Semi-learned schoolmen made it a success. Both had similar needs. Increased literacy meant that more people were reading the biblical text word by word for its supposed plain meaning, even as towns and social mobility brought greater interaction with Jews. In response to both perceived challenges, Ralph read Leviticus with new eyes and found a full moral program of interior religion, one that cut across the distinction between clergy and laity: each was engaged in offering sacrifice, and each had to do so properly, that is, with their inner parts, their *intentio*, in order. Ralph's repudiation of any presumed Jewish reading of Leviticus—there is no evidence that he had access to Jewish teaching on this book— reflexively projected a contrasting image of Jews as a certain type of social body and interpretive community. During this era Christians palpably grew increasingly frustrated when Jews, despite arguments and exchanges, clung to their readings and communities. Guibert noted explicitly that conversions were rare (*insolitam nostro tempori*).[46] Christians could also become irritated that a handful of Jews could stir such doubt and rethinking in the majority community, and annoyed that Jews resisted renewed Christian argument.

Intellectuals detected in Jews a vice they knew better as their own, an arrogant holding to and promotion of their own "*sensus*" over against the knowledge of God passed down through the church. What they saw in the stubborn or proud contentiousness of their own colleagues or rivals, they thought they recognized in Jews who refused to yield to their arguments and interpretations. Not just iconoclastic types like Peter Abelard, but a monk like Rupert of Deutz had to fight charges all his life that he arrogantly innovated in his reading of Scripture. The Latin word *sensus* is complex in meaning, suggesting "thought" but also "perception" or "understanding." In the prefatory letter to his Jewish-Christian dialogue, Rupert opened with a tormented personal response to charges of promoting his *sensus* over against the received fathers—only to turn the same charge against his Jewish *persona*![47] What Jews clung to, Christians could render or perceive only as their stubbornly idiosyncratic "sense" of Scripture. This led to charges, in extremities, that Jews were not only "fleshly" rather than "spiritual" but also "thick," something less than fully or sensibly rational.[48] Such animus, expressed in ever stronger language, sprang in part from the worrying and puzzling strength of Jewish objections. An independent *sensus* was a dangerous and wrongheaded force in society—more so when let loose among an audience of semi-learned clerics and independent laypeople.

Within the Christian community, the amazing influence and attractiveness of Ralph's commentary arose directly from its ability to give compelling meaning to a difficult book, and that for an audience of the newly learned or half-learned genuinely puzzled about its meaning and the kind of God it revealed. Ralph provided a new class of Christian reader, enthusiasts of the letter, with a reading meant to satisfy those troubled by Scripture's puzzles and by any "Jewish" solution—even if the actual social and religious act of crossing over from one community to the other remained exceedingly rare. By calling for interiority and intentionality, this Black Monk moved in mental rhythm with the spiritual aspirations of new monks like Bernard and the ethical reflections of new schoolmen like Peter Abelard. But he also intuited sensitively the rhythms of the larger Christian community. The confusion and wavering that Ralph saw in the faces of his fellow monks revealed the empty

conformity of Christian belief and practice and the alluring reality of a
Jewish alternative. Jews offered a reading of this text and its law and
forced hard questions about how God could have changed his mind
after issuing this first "law."[49] Ralph turned this challenge, at once intellectual and social, into a fresh reading of the biblical book and of his
own majority community, taking as his Archimedean point the principle of sacrificial religion—that which God intended to mandate—as
resident in inner intention and innermost desire.

NOTES

1. The author told this story in a lengthy preface written after he had
completed the entire commentary, thus, several years later. Ralph, *Super Leviticum*, Prefatio. For this essay, I have used the edition in the *Maxima bibliotheca
veterum patrum* 17 (Lyons, 1677), 47–246.

2. The only significant study remains that of Beryl Smalley, "Ralph of
Flaix on Leviticus," *Recherches de théologie ancienne et médiévale* 35 (1968):
35–82, here 52, 65, 67.

3. "Ecce per hunc urbs sancta patet, lex nostra triumphat,/Gentes sunt
uicte, crescit in orbe fides." This poem, here two lines out of sixteen, was
recorded by Ordericus Vitalis, *Historia Ecclesiastica* 10.1, ed. Marjorie Chibnall
(Oxford, 1975), 5:194.

4. Shlomo Simonsohn, *The Apostolic See and the Jews*, vol. 1 (Toronto,
1988), 52.

5. Petrus Alfonsi, *Dialogi*, Praefatio, PL 157, 538.

6. Guibert, *Tractatus de incarnatione contra Iudaeos* 1.1, PL 156, 489–91.

7. Guibert, *Autobiographie*, ed. Edmond-René Labande, Les classiques de
l'histoire de France au moyen âge 34 (Paris, 1981), 252, 422–28. Compare Jan
Ziolkowski's paper in this volume.

8. Guibert, *Autobiographie* II.5, 246–52.

9. Rupert, *In Leviticum* II.3, 39; ed. Rhabanus Haacke (CCCM 22,
804–5, 854). Compare my *Rupert of Deutz* (Berkeley, 1983), 263–65.

10. "Plurimum mihi familiaris sepe ad me ueniebat, tum negotii sui causa,
tum me uidendi gratia, quoniam in aliquibus illi multum necessarius eram; et
quotiens conueniebamus, mox de scripturis ac de fide nostra sermonem amico
animo habebamus." Gilbert Crispin, *Disputation Iudei et Christiani* 4 (part of his
introductory letter to Anselm), ed. Anna Sapir Abulafia and G. R. Evans, *The
Works of Gilbert Crispin Abbot of Westminster* (London, 1986), 9.

11. "Cum Iudeis frequenter lene habebat colloquium, neque disceptando neque reprobando, sed duritiam cordis eorum palpatu et fricatione qua opus erat emolliendo; quam ob rem ita amatur ab eis, ut etiam mulieres eorum irent uidere eum et alloqui." *Gesta abbatum Trudonensium* 11.16, ed. R. Koepke, MGH Scriptores 10 (Hannover, 1852), 304.

12. Rupert, *Anulus siue dialogus inter Christianum et Iudaeum*, Prologus, in Maria Ludovica Arduini, *Ruperto di Deutz e la controversia tra Cristiani ed Ebrei nel secolo XII*, Studi storici 119–121 (Rome, 1979), 184.

13. "Erat, ut testatur, Lauduni; et in quadam domo quemdam cum Judaeo aliquo clericum disceptantem adhuc puerulus audiebat. Cumque clericus perfidi illius resistere uentositati non posset. . . ." Guibert, *De incarnatione* 3.11, PL 156, 528.

14. "Quid igitur succenset mihi Iudaeus, si dicam Mosaicas traditiones umbraticas esse et solam ueritatis imaginem continere . . .?" Ralph, *Super Leviticum*, 49.

15. "Hoc igitur perpendentes, cum aduersus Iudeaeorum subsannationes armari uellemus, ad sacrae legis considerationem apposuimus animu, cui subditi ipsi uideri uolunt, sed eius intentionem nequaquam intelligenut. Non enim intuentur claritatem uultus Moysi, quod ex eorum libris facile probari potest." Ralph, *Super Leviticum*, 48.

16. For the text, edited by Rhabanus Haacke, see Arduini, *Ruperto di Deutz*, 183–242. For interpretation, see the contrasting view in my *Rupert of Deutz* (Berkeley, 1983), 229–41.

17. " . . . quis non uideat quod in preceptis illis non ipsam iustitie bonitatem, sed iustitie solam dicat esse imaginem? . . . De caecitate uero Iudeorum temporibus nostris quicumque dubitat, scripturas sacras aut non legit aut legens nequaquam intelligit. Ut enim omnis humana cesset disceptatio, quomodo fieri potest ut mentiatur Deus, qui per legem, per prophetas, hoc eis minatus est, quod sua cognitione priuandi esset, et sicut sine rege, sine principe, sine sacrificio—quod manifeste uidemus impletum—sic et sine Deo uero futuri?" Ralph, *Super Leviticum*, 48, 49.

18. Thus a part of his preface recovered by Smalley, "Ralph of Flaix," 82, from a twelfth-century manuscript from St. Victor in Paris: "Deinde monuerunt nos ut quod familiari fuerat sermone tractatum stilo traderetur et paginis ne de memoria laberetur."

19. "Videant litere sectatores qualiter hunc locum transeant. Si enim litere haereamus, lex hic sibi contraria sancit. . . . Quid est igitur quod panes fermentati in hoc loco precipiuntur offerri? Ipsa litere repugnantia nos ad spiritualem sensum compellit." Ralph, *Super Leviticum*, 91.

20. "In his ergo doctrinam non iam primam que fidei simplicita re contenta est, sed eam potius intelligimus que ad mysteriorum disputationem transit,

et interna scripturarum proficientibus discipulis tradit." Ralph, *Super Leviticum*,
91–92.

21. Ralph, *Super Leviticum*, 74.

22. "Ridiculum est hoc et a sapientia tanti scriptoris prorsus alienum.
Querenda est igitur loci huius mystica profunditas, et primo sciendum allegorice
uinum in diuersa posse transferri. . . .Vinum quippe reprobrum est omnis peruersa
cupiditas que mentem inebriat et euertit, sicut est auaritia, luxuria, superbia,
immoderata iracundia. Qualibet namque harum mens grauata et consopita
fuerit, acumen discretionis amittit, ut aut discernere non possit quid sequi debeat, aut si diiudicare iustum ab iniusto potuerit, tamen sequi contemnat."
Ralph, *Super Leviticum*, 116.

23. "Nihil in lege esse quod aut utilitate careat aut ratione, firmissime
tenendum est. . . . In hac tamen sanctione si literam solam sequamur, que ratio
esse poterit cum partum hominis culpae legislator ascribat?" Ralph, *Super
Leviticum*, 127.

24. "Siquidem iuxta literam traditio hec ab ecclesia eius non obseruatur.
Solummodo namque mulieres nostre ob uenerationem imitationemque beate
uirginis Marie, que legi nichil debens sponte in hac parte legi se subdidit, ab
ecclesie introitu quadraginta continent diebus. . . . Mysterium itaque constitu-
tionis huius inuestigandum est, qualiter scilicet ecclesia spiritualiter impleat
quod lex carnaliter iubebat." Ralph, *Super Leviticum*, 127.

25. Ralph, *Super Leviticum*, 295.

26. Ralph, *Super Leviticum*, 231.

27. Ralph, *Super Leviticum*, 76.

28. Jerome, *Epistola* 64.1, ed. Hilberg, CSEL 54, 587; Gregory, as transmitted through Paterius on Lev. 1:17, PL 79, 755–56; *Biblia latina cum glossa ordinaria* (1480–81, reprint, Turnhout, 1992), 211; Rupert, *In Levit.* 1.5, ed. Haacke,
CCCM 22,807.

29. "Caput enim hostie nostre interior intentio est, que in omni opere nostro principatum tenet. Hec igitur in primis super ligna ordinanda est, euangelicis
scilicet preceptis coaptanda ut iuxta Domini mandatum simplex et munda sit, ne
forte per illius deprauationem totius laboris nostri reprobatio sebsequatur. . . .
Adipes igitur hostie nostre affectus nostri sunt, congrua ad succedendum mater-
ies. . . . Sunt enim nonnulli qui carnales iam voluptates abiiciunt, nec tamen
feruore debito ad spiritualia desideria consurgunt. . . . Nos itaque super lignorum
compositionem adipes nostros ordinare debemus, ut affectuum uarium discur-
sum ad diuine uoluntatis regulam reuocare conemur. . . . Altare in quo omnis
quam supra descripsimus composito fit, lignorum scilicet cesorumque membro-
rum, cor nostrum est. . . ." Ralph, *Super Leviticum*, 53.

30. "Sed quia iuxta Apostolum (1 Cor. 10:6) omnia hec figuraliter fiebant
in illis, ad nos eadem referamus, et quid mystice in ecclesia signent discutiamus.

Duo quippe hec sunt conuersationis genera. Quicumque ergo ex fidelium numero seculo huic renunciantes, ex integro diuinis se mancipant obsequiis, holocaustum se Deo exhibent, quia uinculis coniugalibus liberi et carnis uoluptatibus emancipati, omnes affectus suos ad celestia querenda conuertunt. Hostias uero pacificas offerunt qui ad culmen perfectionis minus idionei, quamquam celsiora uirtutum merita minime assequantur, per mediocrem tamen conuersationem pacem cum Deo faciunt, pro uiribus precauentes ne odium illius per criminalem offensam incurrant. Hi, licet omnia sua non deserant, de his tamen que possident fideliter Domino ministrant." Ralph, *Super Leviticum*, 52.

31. Ralph, *Super Leviticum*, 67.

32. Ralph, *Super Leviticum*, 114.

33. "Videmus namque quamplurimos qui dormiendo, comedendo, uanis sermocinationibus intendendo, uitam consumentes; quia tamen a furtis, rapinis, homicidiis manus continent, religiosissimos se arbitrantur. . . . Multi huiusmodi et in uita seculari et in continentium conuersatione inueniuntur, qui tamen bonis corporaliter admixti quasi oues gregem sequentes pene absque deliberationis proprie iudicio, absque remunerationis aeterne intuitu, formam uiuendi, quam ab aliis sumunt multitudinis auctoritate tracti, specietenus custodiunt. Isti ergo deuotionis adipem non habent, quia innocenter uiuendo, non ut deo placeant sed ut hominibus conformentur inuigilant. Horum innocentia inutilis est, quia quicquid fecerit homo, nisi ex caritate hoc fecerit, nihil ei prodest." Ralph, *Super Leviticum*, 64.

34. " . . . non nisi amantium uirtus orationis est. Amor nempe desiderium parit, desiderium orantes facit. Vera namque postulatio non in oris est uocibus sed in cogitationibus cordis." Ralph, *Super Leviticum*, 56.

35. Ralph, *Super Leviticum*, 75.

36. Ralph, *Super Leviticum*, 52.

37. Ralph, *Super Leviticum*, 55.

38. Ralph, *Super Leviticum*, 123.

39. Ralph, *Super Leviticum*, 61.

40. Ralph, *Super Leviticum*, 169.

41. Ralph, *Super Leviticum*, 184.

42. Ralph, *Super Leviticum* XVI, Prefatio, 197.

43. "Sacre tamen legis in loquendo tanta est diligentia, nimirum que tota mysteriis incumbit et spiritum semper respicit, ut eorum que aut facta recolit aut tradit facienda, ea quidem proferens que mysticis legibus seruiant, his que ab hac sua deuiant intentione supersedeat, et suo etiam silentio multa nos doceat." Ralph, *Super Leviticum* XIX, Prefatio, 226.

44. "Nos tamen de litera tunc securius dubitamus aut forte nonnumquam secus quam debeat aliquid pronunciamus cum mysterium non impedit, seu quod dubie profertur seu quod incautius forsitan definitur. . . . Quomodocumque igitur

se habeat hec umbratica legis traditio, manifestum est quod nobis seruiat, et nostre libertatis—que aut singulis nobis post mortem confertur aut omnibus pariter in fine seruatur—typum gerat." Ralph, *Super Leviticum*, 232.

45. "Hic tempus est ut reuouetur interior homo noster, et uirtutes aut nouas acquirat aut certe reformet quas habitas ante perdiderat." Ralph, *Super Leviticum*, 227.

46. Guibert, *Autobiographie* II.5, 252.

47. "Nimirum sensum uerborum huiusmodi experimento [visionary experience] melius addidici quam lectione addiscere potuerim, et hinc est quod et ego nunc usque locutus sum et loquar in lingua mea fronte hactenus dura facie quasi adamantina. . . . Iudaeo quantumcumque potest ex littera legis et ex sensu suo repercutiente Christianum. . . ." Later Rupert actually stages such a confrontation, with the Jew objecting: "Tu scripturas tuo sensu tractare consueuisti et ducis ac reducis, ut iam dixi, qualem in partem uis." To which the Christian responds: "Non ego sensu meo scripturas inuoluo sed hoc tibi ostendere cupio, quia . . . scriptura euangelica, quam tu non accipis, stat fundata in manfesta auctoritate ueteris scripturae. . . ." Arduini, *Ruperto di Deutz*, 184, 227.

48. This, as an unfortunate biproduct of the so-called "twelfth-century renaissance," has been argued more extensively by Anna Sapir Abulafia, *Christians and Jews in the Twelfth-Century Renaissance* (London, 1995).

49. "Dicat igitur mihi Iudaeus, cur in hoc loco constitutio illa soluatur, cur quod generaliter decretum est non ubique seruetur?" Ralph, *Super Leviticum*, 205.

Martyrdom, Eroticism, and Asceticism in Twelfth-Century Ashkenazi Piety

ELLIOT R. WOLFSON

"For is the experience of language (or, rather before any discourse, the experience of the mark, the re-mark or the margin) not precisely what makes the *articulation* possible and necessary? Is that not what *gives rise* to this articulation between transcendental or ontological universality, and the exemplary or testimonial singularity of *martyred* existence? While evoking apparently abstract notions of the mark or the re-mark here, we are also thinking of scars. Terror is practiced at the expense of wounds inscribed on the body."
—Jacques Derrida, *Monolingualism of the Other, or, The Prosthesis of Origin*

FIRST CRUSADE AND GERMAN-JEWISH PIETISM: THE UNSPOKEN AS A FACTOR IN HISTORICAL CAUSALITY

In this study, I will explore the nexus of martyrdom, asceticism, and eroticism in the Rhineland Jewish piety of the twelfth century, although to some extent texts from the thirteenth century will be utilized in the effort to reconstruct earlier patterns of belief and behavior. My focus will be on works written by authors who belonged to one of the major circles of Jewish pietists active in the Rhineland towns of Mainz, Speyer, Regensburg, and Worms, the Hasidei Ashkenaz. To state my thesis at

the outset: The intensified emphasis on asceticism in the pietistic material must be seen in tandem with an augmented prominence attributed to an erotic theosophy, which in part was shaped in response to or
as a result of the ideal of martyrdom that developed in the wake of the
First Crusade in 1096. In brief, my hypothesis is that the link between
death, eros, and vision—a theme surely not uncommon in the history of
mysticism—in the Ashkenazi conception of the martyr inspired the
model of the ascetic visionary in Rhineland Jewish pietism.

In order to avoid potential misunderstanding, let me state clearly
that my hypothesis concerning the impact of the Crusades on the formation of Ashkenazi piety does not preclude the possible influences of
much older sources, both Jewish and non-Jewish. I am not arguing that
either the ascetic practices or the theosophical doctrines of Hasidei
Ashkenaz should be viewed solely as a direct response to the antecedent
historical event of the Crusades. On the contrary, as Gershom Scholem
long ago noted, it would be a mistake to assume that the impact of the
Crusades upon the Jewish religious consciousness of the Ashkenazi rabbinic leadership was the source of an entirely novel mystical disposition.
The textual evidence indicates convincingly that with respect to ascetic
esotericism, the German-Jewish pietists drew their inspiration from earlier mystical traditions that were most likely transmitted to Ashkenaz
through southern Italy.[1] It is true that Scholem also suggested that the
pietists' interest in eschatological matters as well as their ascetic tendency betrayed the influence of the events of 1096,[2] but he was reluctant to assume that the specific connection between these events would
rule out all other possible explanations to account for the formation of
Ashkenazi pietism in the twelfth and thirteenth centuries.[3] More recent
scholarship has confirmed Scholem's surmise that some of the traditions
developed by the medieval Ashkenazi pietists originated in ancient
Palestinian pietistic groups,[4] most likely responsible for the cultivation
of the theurgical practices reflected in Hekhalot literature.[5] Moreover,
the act of martyrdom as a fulfillment of the obligation to sanctify the
name not only has older roots in Ashkenazi culture,[6] but it is affirmed in
passages from the classical rabbinic corpus wherein the willingness to
die is presented as the ultimate expression of the love of God.[7] The
point is exemplified in the narrative about the demise of the heroic
R. Akiva,[8] who is portrayed therein as the historical embodiment of the

pietistic ideal disclosed through the concealment of the midrashic reading of the scriptural command, "You shall love YHWH your God with
all your soul" (Deut. 6:5)—"even if he takes your soul away."[9] The limit
of love for God—to be tested in the case of both the individual Jew and
the people of Israel collectively—is the laying of one's life on the line,
the suffering of eros unto death, a point that is exegetically linked as
well in some of the relevant rabbinic sources with Psalm 44:23 ("For you
we die every day, we are considered like sheep to the slaughter") and
Song of Songs 1:3 ("thus the maidens love you," *'al ken 'alamot 'ahevukha*,
which is read as "thus they loved you unto death," *'al ken 'al mawet
'ahevukha*).[10] Notwithstanding the obvious textual precedent, one
should not ignore the novel element that emerged as a consequence of
the crisis of the late eleventh century, which clashed overtly with prior
halakhic norms regarding the passive obligation of sanctifying the
name.[11] Why presume that the hermeneutical conditioning gleaned
from the past precludes the novelty of the moment?

   The link between the persecution of 1096 and the emerging Rhineland pietism has been challenged by a number of scholars on the grounds
that there are very few references to the Crusades in the works of
Hasidei Ashkenaz.[12] This is sufficient reason, in the mind of these scholars, to question the claim that the pietistic ideal of ascetic renunciation
is based on the experience of martyrdom in the First Crusade.[13] Even if
it is reasonable to presume that the relatively pessimistic attitude toward
history and the material world found in pietistic sources reflects the persecutions of the Rhineland Jewish communities, the lack of a more
focused recollection of the details of the massacres in the writings
produced by Hasidei Ashkenaz suggests that in the cultural memory of
this segment of twelfth-century Ashkenazi Jewry, the calamity of the
First Crusade did not occupy a watershed of a theological or sociopolitical
nature.[14]

   The relative silence of subsequent Ashkenazi sources on this matter
is certainly an important factor that would justify the warning not to exaggerate the impact of this event on the formation of the pietistic disposition. I must say, however, that the logic implied in this form of
argument is somewhat suspect. The lack of explicit reference to an event
does not necessarily mean that the event has left no imprint. On the
contrary, an equally plausible argument can be made to the effect that

precisely the most important factor is the one that is not mentioned overtly, that is, the unspoken, which overwhelmingly preoccupies one's attention and informs one's behavior. By the unspoken I do not mean the mere absence of speech due to the incommunicability of what is thought, but that which is withheld from speaking because it provides the ground for that which is spoken. In writing about history, historians generally do not heed the unspoken as a category of historical inquiry—understandably so, because it is not spoken. Yet, what is unspoken often speaks more loudly than what is spoken.[15]

In the particular case of the relationship of the First Crusade and the Rhineland Jewish pietism of the twelfth century, I propose that the former provides the tacit framework within which the latter evolved, although I again emphasize that this should not be construed as if I were arguing that German-Jewish pietism in all of its complexities can be explained in terms of a linear historical causality. Specifically, the area of influence lies in the fact that the eschatological perception of God's glory occasioned by acts of martyrdom, which were understood primarily as expressions of a liturgical pathos,[16] gave way to the cultivation of ascetic and mystical practices that facilitated the imaginal seeing of the glory marked by a similar convergence of death and eros.[17] We should not expect this connection to be mentioned explicitly since it is the unspoken, that is, the condition necessary for the phenomenon to appear as it did on the stage of history, a condition that we may call in the most general sense the historical facticity that semiotically marks the fate of an epoch, which is subject before, during, and after its manifestation to diverse interpretations.

My claim, then, is that the First Crusade (or, at the very least, its narrative retelling)[18] served as a catalyst to bring to the surface latent or only partially expressed tendencies in a manner that crystallized into a comprehensive, albeit not necessarily systematic, worldview.[19] The almost sensual pleasure of the self-abnegation essential to the life of the martyr was transposed into the erotic asceticism underlying the pietistic comportment in the world. Just as it has been argued that the emphasis on the excessive demand of the divine will, which is one of the innovative doctrines in the pietistic religious philosophy, can be traced to patterns of behavior in 1096,[20] I contend that the correlation of seeing the divine presence and ascetic self-abrogation (related especially, as we shall see, to the control of sexual desire) resonates with the idealized portrait of the martyr. Both the negating of one's own will through an act of self-sacrifice and the unconditional submission to the will of the infinite in daily religious praxis represent an expansion of—albeit not necessarily deviation from—the halakhic norm, which has been tagged as a key element of the pietistic sensibility: The full potential of the Jew is not realized merely by strict compliance to traditional laws and customs, but by the acceptance of a path that carries one beyond the limit of legalism, a trespassing of boundary that helps one attain the greater goal of complete devotion.[21]

In a measure, a comparable position was already stated by Scholem, whose profound insights into the intellectual and cultural world of the Rhineland Jewish pietists have lamentably been obscured by far inferior conceptions peddled more recently in the marketplace of ideas. I have already noted in passing that Scholem was well aware of the older sources that influenced Hasidei Ashkenaz. Precisely on account of these sources he considered it mistaken to view the whole movement in a reductionist manner as a response to the suffering of the Jewish population at the hand of the missionizing Christians.[22] However, Scholem suggested that the Crusades did have an instrumental role in shaping the eschatological attitude of this pietism. It is worthwhile citing his words verbatim:

But in spite of the innate conservatism of German Judaism, the novel circumstances in the end called forth a new response. It will always remain a remarkable fact that the great catastrophe of the Crusades, the incessant waves of persecution which now broke over the Jews of Germany, failed to introduce an apocalyptic element into the religious tenets of German Jewry. Not a single apocalypse was written during that period. . . . It is true that the chroniclers of the persecutions and the writers of the new school of religious poetry . . . sought consolation in eschatological hopes, but they laid far more stress on the blessed state of the martyrs and the transcendent splendor of the coming Redemption than on the terrors of the end and the vision of the Last Judgment. . . . But for all the lack of apocalyptic elements in the Messianic conception of Hasidism it would be a mistake to overlook its eschatological character. . . . If it is true that their religious interest does

not center on the Messianic promise in the strict sense, it is no less true
that the imagination of these writers is powerfully affected by everything which concerns the eschatology of the soul. . . . Eschatological
ideas concerning the nature of the state of bliss in Paradise, the dawn of
Redemption, the nature of Resurrection, the beatific vision of the just,
their bodies and garments, the problem of reward and punishment, etc.,
were of real importance to a man like Jehudah the Hasid. These notions . . . belong to the very heart and core of the religious faith of these
men which manifested itself in so many different ways. . . . For Jehudah
the Hasid, mysticism represents something like an anticipation of a
knowledge which, strictly speaking, belongs to Messianic times. There
are secrets which are revealed in the upper world and which are preserved there for "the time to come." Only the mystics and the alle-
gorists of this world "absorb something of the odor of these secrets and
mysteries."[23]

My own research basically confirms Scholem's insight: The pietism
of the Kalonymide circle is not so much anti-eschatological as it is a
mystical interpretation of the eschatological aspirations expressed in the
narrative accounts of the persecutions of the Rhineland Jews at the end
of the eleventh century. Just as the martyrs attained the state of eschatological felicity through sacrificial death, the pietists attain the state of
ecstatic bliss through ascetic piety. The otherworldly condition is experienced by the pietist in his comprehension of the ancient secrets en-
coded as allusions (*remazim*) in the text of Scripture. The mysteries are
revealed to him in accord with his intellectual acumen and exegetical
prowess.[24] But this state is ultimately attainable only by the one who
adopts the ascetic lifestyle, which is itself a form of self-sacrifice related
to the renunciation of the physical world. It is true that in general martyrdom and asceticism are not necessarily identical,[25] but in the particular case of the Rhineland Jewish pietists the ascetic ideal is portrayed in
some of the critical images used to depict acts of martyrdom. In this
study, I shall focus on what is perhaps one of the most important of these
literary tropes: The nobility of the martyr's death and the discipline of
the ascetic's life both involve a weakening of carnal sex and a concomitant affirmation of a spiritualized eros.

To be more precise, the ascetic ideal is not what one finds in the
standard devotional literature produced by Hasidei Ashkenaz. Indeed,

as I shall argue, there is a discrepancy between the ascetic dimension as
it is portrayed in the more overtly popular pietistic treatises, such as
Sefer Hasidim of Judah ben Samuel of Regensburg, and in the esoteric
works, such as *Sodei Razayya'* of Eleazar ben Judah of Worms. I do not
mean to suggest, however, that one can distinguish exoteric and esoteric
compositions in an absolute fashion; on the contrary, there is a significant amount of overlap between the two literary forms, for in the exoteric texts we find allusions to the esoteric doctrines, just as in the
esoteric works there are references to motifs that figure more prominently in the exoteric presentations.[26] Indeed, the preservation of the
relevant texts makes it nearly impossible to separate out the esoteric and
the exoteric strands in any clear-cut manner; the textual warp and woof
is far more complex than what may be accounted for by utilizing such a
typological classification. Moreover, I am inclined to agree with the
view that even a work like *Sefer Hasidim* has only a tentative relationship to any existing social phenomenon;[27] the exempla contained in the
different recensions of this anthology reflect an elitist approach rather
than a widespread pietism.[28] From that vantage point as well, I do not
see any justification to consider the ideas presented in *Sefer Hasidim* as
any less esoteric than what is found in the more ostensibly arcane compositions like *Sodei Razayya'*. Nor am I persuaded that we can distinguish neatly between the social-communal approach to pietistic ethics
of Judah and the individualistic-mystical approach of Eleazar.[29] A closer
examination of all the relevant texts indicates that this taxonomy cannot be consistently upheld. Nevertheless, with respect to some of the
critical theological and anthropological issues, it is possible to discern a
different orientation as they are treated respectively in the exoteric and
esoteric works. The topic of asceticism provides an interesting illustration of this larger hermeneutical point, for only in the more esoteric texts
do we find unambiguous evidence of an ascetic piety that is a symbolic
equivalent to martyrdom based on the link between death and eros.

Martyrdom as Realized Eschatology

The Hebrew narrative accounts of the First Crusade present the ultimate reward for the act of martyrdom in eschatological imagery.[30] For
instance, according to a passage in the short narrative known as the

Mainz Anonymous, some of those preparing to offer themselves as sacrifices before God express their expectation of seeing the "great light" as a reward for their sanctification of the name.[31] In a second passage from this version of the text, the martyred souls are described as returning to the "great light in paradise" wherein they were eternally "bound up in the bond of life."[32] In a third passage, it is reported that the martyrs approached their death by sword at the hands of the Christian enemies by steadfastly proclaiming that they would nevertheless "remain alive," for their souls would gain repose in paradise, basking eternally "in the radiance of the great light."[33] Finally, in a fourth passage from this work, David ben Nathaniel reportedly said to the band of crusaders who had gathered to force him to convert, "If you kill me, my soul will repose in paradise, in the light of life."[34]

The angelification of the soul and the consequent vision of the divine glory, which are related already in classical rabbinic sources to the eschaton,[35] are applied in the Crusade chronicles to the martyrs. The justification for this appropriation of images is obvious: Those who gave their life as a sacrificial act for the sake of sanctifying the divine name attain thereby the status of the righteous in the world-to-come. In the longer chronicle erroneously attributed to Solomon bar Simson, it is written that the martyrs of Mainz "were set apart in holiness and purity and were sanctified to ascend to God all together."[36] The souls of martyrs rise to the celestial paradise, the "light of life," and are transformed into angelic beings who sit or stroll with the righteous, basking in the luminous glow of the divine glory.[37] Typical of this sentiment is the following passage in the longer chronicle, which has an almost verbatim parallel in the Mainz Anonymous:[38]

> Blessed are all those who are killed and slaughtered and die for the unity of his name. They are destined for the world to come and shall sit in the circle of the righteous, R. Akiba and his associates, "the pillars of the universe," who were killed for his name. What is more a world of darkness will be exchanged for a world of light, a world of pain for a world of happiness, a transitory world for a world that is eternal and everlasting.[39]

The assurance that martyrdom leads to eternal life renders the physical dying itself irrelevant. The material world of darkness and pain is overcome by the spiritual world of light and bliss.[40] Martyrdom is a form of realized eschatology, expressed particularly by the desire of the pious ones to die and thereby join the circle of the saints who glow in the "great light" before the throne of glory.[41] Rather than being saved by enemies, the righteous Isaac ben David allowed himself to be consumed by fire so that his soul might be "hidden in the portion of the saintly in paradise."[42] The saintly who were slaughtered for the sanctification of the name are destined "for the life of the world-to-come. Their souls will reside in paradise, bound up in the bond of life."[43] Echoing this motif, Ephraim of Bonn remarks in his account of the Second Crusade in Sefer ha-Zekhirah that the martyrs of Würzburg shall "abide in the Garden of Eden, arrayed in a circle, standing there in a ring, transcending temporal life, in eternal existence, constant ascent, abounding in strength and exultation."[44] Toward the conclusion of his chronicle, Ephraim describes more generally the fate of all the saintly Jews who were slain bearing witness to the oneness of the name in eschatological images applied in rabbinic homiletical midrashim to the righteous in Paradise: Each martyr is said to possess eight vestments like the high priest and two crowns. The garbing of the martyr signifies the preparation that is necessary for him to dwell in the presence of the divine effulgence, a posture that is attained by sacrificing oneself as a sin-offering, for in accomplishing this task one surpasses even the high priest, who merely offers animals as sacrifices before God.[45] It is likely that this motif is reflected in a passage in Sefer Hasidim wherein the souls of the righteous in general (and not only righteous martyrs) are portrayed as the burnt-offerings sacrificed by Michael.[46] Combined in this remark are two distinct traditions that occur sequentially in one talmudic passage: According to the first, Michael, who is called the "great archon" (sar ha-gadol), offers sacrifices on the heavenly altar, and, according to the second, the sages engaged in the study of Torah are considered as if they themselves offered sacrifices.[47] The author of the passage from Sefer Hasidim blended together the two rabbinic traditions: the sacrifices offered by Michael are identified as the very souls of the righteous. We may surmise that the reinterpretation of the aggadic dicta along these lines betrays the impact of the cultural understanding of the act of martyrdom as that which promotes the attainment of a state of proximity to the divine. For the pious visionary, the intimate cleaving to God also occurs as a consequence of an ecstatic translation to the celestial abode through rapturous prayer.[48]

It is precisely this aspect of dwelling in the immediate presence of God's glory that underlies Gerson Cohen's attempt to view the Hebrew Crusade chronicles as part of the genre of Ashkenazic liturgical commentary, for prayer itself was understood primarily as the means to stand in close proximity to God.[49] The chronicles reflect this literary genre because their authors wished to convey the idea that the martyrs occupied a place in the inner sanctum of the heavenly palace before the throne of glory, which is achieved by the pious as a result of ecstatic worship. Consider the description of the angelic transfiguration of martyred souls in the long recension of the Hebrew Chronicle:

> Let us offer ourselves up as a sacrifice to the Lord, "like a whole burnt offering" (1 Sam. 7:9) to the Most High offered on the altar of the Lord. We shall exist in a world that is entirely daylight, in paradise, in the shining light. We shall see him eye to eye, in his glory and in his majesty. Each one shall receive a golden crown on his head, in which are set precious stones and pearls. We shall be seated there among "the pillars of the universe" and shall eat as part of the society of the saintly in paradise. We shall be part of the company of R. Akiba and his associates. We shall be seated on a golden throne under the Tree of Life. Each of us shall point to him by finger and say: "This is our God; we trusted in him [and he delivered us. This is the Lord, in whom we trusted]; let us rejoice and exult in his deliverance" (Ps. 25:9).[50]

The coronation of the Jewish martyrs, one of the main signs that points to the drama of angelification, figures prominently in the addition of Eleazar of Worms to the dirge composed by his father, Kalonymous ben Judah of Mainz, *mi yitten ro'shi mayim*, which recounts the catastrophic experience of the First Crusade:[51] *kelulei keter 'al ro'sham le'atterah we-'al 'addirei qehal maggensa' ha-hadurah*, "their heads are crowned and encircled with a diadem / upon the nobles of the glorious community of Mainz."[52] In Eleazar's own writings, as in the compositions of other pietists of the Rhineland Jewish communities, the description of coronation is applied specifically to the visionary experience that results from the utterance of prayer. Here I will provide but one example from the early pietistic *Shir ha-Kavod*, "Hymn of the Glory," which in all probability was composed in the twelfth century:

> Abode of righteousness,
> house of his splendor,
> shall he raise above his joyous head.
> His treasured possession shall be a crown in his hand,
> a royal diadem, glorious beauty.
> He uplifted the ones who have been supported,
> He bound them with a crown.
> Because they were precious in his eyes,
> He honored them.
> His glory is upon me and my glory is upon him,
> and he is near me when I call to him.[53]

In this web of skillfully crafted biblical images, the author of *Shir ha-Kavod* has alluded to one of the basic mythic ideas later expressed in the more fully developed theosophic treatises composed by Hasidei Ashkenaz, namely, the reciprocal coronation of God and the Jewish people. The context wherein this correlative crowning occurs is liturgical in nature, for God is crowned by Israel's prayers and Israel by the divine effulgence that radiates as a consequence of the glory being crowned.[54] In some of the pietistic sources, the splendor of God, which is the object of liturgical contemplation, is referred to as the "great light," the very term utilized in the Crusade chronicles to denote the eschatological recompense bestowed upon the martyred souls.[55] The theosophic implications underlying the ritual act are underscored by the fact that the crown on God's head is identified further as Jerusalem (the "abode of righteousness," *neweh ha-sedeq*),[56] the Temple (the "house of his splendor," *beit tif'arto*),[57] and the collectivity of the people of Israel ("his treasured possession," *segullato*).[58] It is reasonable to propose, moreover, that the crowns refer to the phylacteries worn by God and the Jewish male.[59] This is implied in the statement, *pe'ero 'alay u-fe'eri 'alaw*, "His glory is upon me and my glory is upon him," for the word *pe'er* is interpreted in rabbinic sources as a reference to the phylacteries, connected exegetically to the verse *pe'erkha havosh 'alekha*, "put on your turban" (Ezek. 24:17).[60] The donning of the phylacteries serves as a catalyst for the mutual crowning of God by Israel and Israel by God, which results in the vision of the divine glory.[61]

In the writings of the Rhineland pietists, the beatific vision of the glory on the part of the righteous ensues from contemplation of the Tetragrammaton, which is identified further as the mystical essence of both the crown and the phylacteries.[62] The vision of the name occasions the crowning of the righteous in divine splendor. A structural similarity is thus established between the crowning of God by the prayers of the righteous and the crowning of the righteous by the vision of the presence. Just as the angelic adjuration of the name lifts the crown to the head of the enthroned glory, so the utterance of the name causes the righteous to be crowned in glory. The pietists, like the kabbalists, removed the image of coronation from its eschatological context as it appears both in Jewish apocalypses and talmudic-midrashic literature, and understood it as a symbolic depiction of a mystical state of communion with the glory or divine presence.[63] Alternatively expressed, the pietists combined the image of the eschatological crown with that of the crown worn by the glory, an older motif rooted in ancient merkavah mysticism. According to that tradition, the crown is made of the prayers of Israel and is placed on the head of the glory by one of the highest angels, identified in some textual units as Metatron and in others as Sandalphon.[64] In the esoteric theosophy cultivated by the Rhineland pietists, the liturgical crown is treated hypostatically as a divine emanation, in some passages identified as the *kavod* or *Shekhinah* and in other passages as Akatriel.[65]

The motif of coronation provides a key example to support the claim that the pietism that evolved in the Rhineland communities in the twelfth century in the wake of the Crusades must be viewed in part as an application of eschatological motifs to an ecstatic experience occasioned by intense forms of liturgical worship.[66] I note, in passing, that the thematic connection between the martyrological experience and mystical ascent may explain the literary contextualization of a version of the dirge describing the fate of the ten second-century martyrs, *'asarah harugei malkhut*,[67] in the manuscript recensions of *Hekhalot Rabbati*.[68] I surmise that the Ashkenazi scribes were responsible for appending a version of the lament to this text, and the justification for doing so lies in the homology that they assumed pertained to the eschatological trans-

formation of the martyr into a heavenly being and the mystical experience of the *yored merkavah*, the one who enters before the chariot.[69]

MARTYRDOM AND THE EROTICISM OF ASCETIC SELF-DENIAL

The link between martyrdom and the ascetic ideal is made by Samuel
the Pious in a passage in *Sefer ha-Yirʾah*, which is included in the Parma
recension of *Sefer Hasidim*:

> If the evil inclination overpowers you to transgress or to do [a sinful ac-
> tion], consider as if you were in the time of the religious persecution
> (*bi-sheʿat ha-shemad*), you would have experienced suffering or death for
> the sake of the blessed holy One. "Therefore do maidens love you"
> (Song of Songs 1:3), to the point of death they love you. If they wanted
> to murder you or to torture you until death was chosen rather than life,
> you would have endured it. All the more so regarding this matter,
> which is not so great, and your desire overcomes you, but you receive a
> great reward, for it is better for a person to control his desire more than
> fulfilling one hundred commandments.[70]

As I remarked above, the connection between the ideal of asceticism and the experience of the Crusades has been both duly noted and
challenged by prior scholarship. What has not been appreciated, however, is the erotic dimension of the martyrological ideal and its impact
on the eroticized form of asceticism cultivated by the Rhineland pietists.
At the outset, the reader must be reminded of a simple philological
point: The Hebrew word for martyrdom is *qiddush ha-shem*, "sanctification of the name," but the pluralized form of the Hebrew word for
"sanctification," *qiddushin*, has the connotation of "betrothal." An
examination of the Hebrew chronicles, and particularly the longer
version, supports the contention that the ritualized self-sacrifice was
understood as an act of betrothal of the soul and the divine. Thus, when
it is stated that certain martyrs accepted for themselves the judgments of
heaven with love and affection,[71] this is more than a rhetorical flourish.
Willingness to die on behalf of God's glory is the decisive expression of
love on the part of the martyr. This ideal is articulated in the above

citation from *Sefer ha-Yir'ah* on the basis of the midrashic reading of the
verse *'al ken 'alamot 'ahevukha*, "Therefore do maidens love you," as *'al
mawet 'ahevukha*, "they love you unto death."[72]

The nexus of martyrdom and love of God, as I have already pointed
out, is implied in the rabbinic exegesis (attributed in some contexts to
Akiba) of "You should love the Lord your God with all your heart"
(Deut. 6:5), "even if he takes your life." It comes as no surprise that this
traditional model of piety served as the basis for the form of behavior attributed to the martyrs. Repeatedly in the chronicles, the righteous who
are willing to die for the sanctification of the name are compared to
Akiba, who expressed his love of God by allowing his life to be taken.[73]
In one passage, the chronicler explicitly reworks the rabbinic reading
of Song of Songs 1:3 to which I have alluded.[74] The midrashic interpretation of the verse conveys the idea that the love of God must extend
to the point of death, which is applied more specifically by the writers
of the Crusade narrative to the act of self-sacrifice on behalf of the divine unity. In one passage, the verse "Like a groom coming forth from the
chamber, like a hero eager to run his course" (Ps. 19:6) is applied to the
faithful as they joyfully accept the fate of a martyr's death.[75] The didactic purpose of citing this particular verse is surely to underscore the
erotic nature of martyrdom. According to another passage, the example
of David ben Isaac underscores the fact that loving God to the point of
death on occasion entailed the weakening of physical vitality brought
about by afflicting oneself with excessive fasting.[76] To be sure, the ultimate act that facilitated the realization of the mandate to love God
even to the point of death was the willingness to be slaughtered, but in
preparation for that act some of the martyrs deliberately diminished
their bodily strength so that their souls would be pure when they returned to God. The discipline of ascetic denial prepares one for the decree of sacrificial death. The death of eros climaxes in the eros of death.

The eros of martyrdom is also related in some passages to the unwavering love of a couple who proclaim their everlasting commitment
to one another by accepting the fate of death together. In one particularly chilling narrative, Judah ben Abraham of Cologne is described as
killing Sarit, the woman who was destined to wed his son, Abraham, so
that she would not flee and marry someone else. The concurrence of
eros and thanatos is here established by the fact that the bond of love
between Abraham and Sarit was to be secured by their mutual death:

He seized her and held her outside the window and kissed her on the mouth and raised his voice in weeping along with the lass. He cried out loudly and very bitterly and said to all those standing there: "Behold, all of you. This is the bridal canopy of my daughter, my bride, that I make this day." They all wept with great weeping and wailing and "mourning and moaning." The pious Judah said to her: "My daughter, come and lie in the bosom of Abraham our ancestor. For in one moment you shall acquire your future and shall enter the circle of the saintly and pious." He took her and placed her in the bosom of his son Abraham, her betrothed, and cut her with his sharp sword into two pieces. Subsequently he also slaughtered his son.[77]

In contrast to other passages in the chronicles, the narration of this episode affirms that martyrdom as the ultimate expression of love for God is intertwined with love in the human plane between man and woman. The very ground upon which Sarit and her betrothed Abraham were murdered by Judah the pious is imaginatively and symbolically transformed into the bridal canopy. The sacrificial death is thus eroticized not only on account of the love the martyrs express for God in their willingness to die, but also because the love of man and woman is fully consummated in their shared death.[78] Their love is sealed with the sacrificial blood of their lives, which have been taken for the sake of affirming the basic tenets of the Jewish faith, belief in one God and in the everlasting truth of Torah.

The eroticization of death is similarly implied in the remark of Kalonymous ben Judah of Mainz in one of his laments describing the martyrdom in the Rhineland communities: "Together fathers and sons, bridegrooms and brides / rush to slaughter as in their wedding canopy."[79] The rhetorical image is obviously suggested by the reference to the bridegrooms and brides, but beyond the rhetoric it is necessary to perceive that the intent of the poet is to convey that the death of lovers epitomizes the sacrificial ideal. Hence, in the continuation of the dirge, the poet implores God, "See these sacrifices that have been bound / beloved in their lives and in their death they have not parted[80] / they were assiduous in sanctifying the unity of your name / be mindful of their righteous affection when they are united."[81] Unification is utterly achieved when the couple die together in sanctifying the name—only then do they become a "holy couple" (*zug qodesh*).[82] Thus the very place where the dying occurs is transformed symbolically into a bridal chamber.

The nexus between love and death has its parallel in the pietistic sources wherein the erotic bond of the adept and God, which is presented as the peak religious experience, is connected specifically with the nullification of the individual's will through the passionate love of God in an effort to fulfill the divine will.[83] As one might expect, inasmuch as the abjuration of the will is depicted metaphorically as a form of death, the all-consuming love is related to the ideal of martyrdom.[84] Thus, in a passage from *Sefer Hasidim* we read:

> The yearning for children and wives, the jesting with friends, excursions, and the innovation of useless things cause one to neglect the words of Torah. Thus, [it is written] "with all your heart and all your soul" (Deut. 6:4) with respect to the love and worship [of God], so that one might abandon them on behalf of the blessed holy One. He should worship and love the blessed holy One, "in all your ways know him" (Prov. 3:6), "to love the Lord" (Deut. 11:13), for the soul is filled with love, and it is bound in joy, and that joy drives away from his heart the pleasures of the body and the delight of the world. That joy is so strong and augmented in his heart that even if a young man who has not had intercourse with his wife for many days, and he has a great desire, and when he ejaculates his semen like an arrow he has pleasure, this is nothing in comparison to the strength and the vigor of the joy of the love of the Lord. All the love of the joyance of the heart of the one who loves the Lord with all his heart and all of his thoughts are on how to execute the will of the Creator, to exonerate the masses, to fulfill the sanctification of the Lord, and to offer himself in the love of the Creator . . . and the love should be like Phinehas who offered himself for the sake of the Creator,[85] and Abraham our father who feared the Lord, as it says, "I swear to the Lord, God Most High, Creator of heaven and earth, I will not take so much as a thread or a sandal strap" (Gen. 14:22–23),[86] and Elisha who did not want to take from Naaman.[87] That love prevents a person from abrogating the words of Torah on account of joking and toying around with his children, or on account of the love of seeing women and [engaging in idle] speech, and it also enables him to abandon excursions, and it causes him to sing sweet songs in

order to fill his heart in the joy of the love of the Lord, and he toils and labors in the path that is the will of the Creator.[88]

What is particularly noteworthy is the analogy that is made between the love of God and the love that one has for the woman whom he constantly craves. In spite of, or perhaps on account of, the concordance between the love of God and carnal desire, the pious man must curtail his pursuit of sensual gratification—including playing with his children, going for recreational walks even with his wife,[89] looking at women, and participating in idle chatter—so that he may passionately fulfill the will of God. The paradigms of pietistic behavior are Abraham, Phinehas, and Elisha, each of whom expressed their love for God with unqualified zeal and devotion. Following the rabbinic ideal, the Rhineland Jewish pietists affirmed that the ardent love of God demands the sacrifice of the soul, *mesirat ha-nefesh.*

The abnegation of self linked to the fervent passion of the pious soul yearning for God is formulated vividly by Eleazar of Worms in his *shoresh ha-ʾahavah,* "the principle of love," which is part of the principles of pietism that he appended to his major halakhic work, *Sefer ha-Roqeah:*

> The soul is full of love of God and it is bound with ropes of love in joy and the goodness of the heart. He is not like one who serves his master against his will; rather, even if there were those who tried to hinder him, the love burns within his heart to worship and he is glad to fulfill the will of his Creator. . . . He does not worship for the sake of his benefit or for his glory. He says: What am I? Despised and helpless, here today and tomorrow in the grave, beaten by transgression, I am filled with excrement, yet I have been chosen and I have been created to be a servant of the glorious king. . . . The lover thinks not about the pleasure of this world, and he is not concerned about the excursions of his wife, nor about his sons and daughters, and everything is as nothing for him apart from fulfilling the will of his Creator, to render others meritorious, to sanctify his name, and to give himself in the love of him as Abraham, "I swear [to the Lord, God Most High, Creator of heaven and earth], I will not take so much as a thread or a sandal strap" (Gen. 14:22–23), and as Phinehas who gave of himself when he killed Zimri (Num. 25:14). They do not elevate themselves, speak trivial words,

look at the faces of women, and they listen to their reproach but do not respond, and all of their thoughts are with their Creator, and they sing sweet songs to their Creator, and all the designs of their thoughts burn from the fire of his love.[90]

There is little doubt that the nature of the love of God articulated by Eleazar reflects the ideal of the martyr described in the literary accounts of the Crusade massacre, even if Eleazar does not make that association explicitly. In passing, it is worth recalling that Abraham Habermann began his collection of documents related to the Christian atrocities committed against the German and French Jewish communities in the Crusade period, *Sefer Gezerot 'Ashkenaz we-Sarfat*, with this passage from Eleazar.[91] I assume that his selection of this text indicates that in his own mind Eleazar's depiction of the mystical love of God is indebted to the phenomenon of martyrdom. More importantly, in Eleazar's admonition that the lover of God must be not only indifferent to worldly pleasure but also apathetic to the plight of his own family, one can perhaps detect an allusion to an emotional struggle that ensued from his own circumstance. In his written account of the slaughter of his wife and two daughters at the hands of Christians in 1197, Eleazar extols the saintly virtue of the afflicted in language that betrays enormous love, sentimentality, and respect. Yet, even in that context, Eleazar exonerates God from all wrongdoing, concluding his lament by confirming the need to acclaim divine righteousness over and against human iniquity, even to the point of identifying his own transgressions as the ultimate cause of his suffering.[92] His exhortation to love God so completely that even the love of one's family must be put aside is not an empty elocution; on the contrary, when viewed against his existential situation, it becomes clear that Eleazar well understood the psychological gravity that this ideal imposed upon a person, for he spoke of it from the depths of personal experience.

The devout love of God, therefore, demands an unequivocal turning away from mundane affairs and especially the pursuit of physical pleasure. As Eleazar concisely puts it, "the pleasure of the world is vanity and deceit."[93] Or, according to the formulation of another passage, "Thus the righteous despised this world because it is entirely vain."[94] Pious devotion demands an unwavering commitment to God that ren-

ders all concern with mundane matters trivial. Again, to cite Eleazar of
Worms, "Whoever fears the word of the Lord is not anxious about the
love of his wife or the delight of his children, but only with the darts of
fire of the heavenly flame.[95] . . . and every man who has the spirit of wisdom and understanding is not concerned with the pleasures of the
world . . . and he does not speak of idle things."[96] To be sure, as several
scholars have pointed out, the Ashkenazi pietists did not advocate a life
of absolute celibacy on a par with medieval Christian monasticism.
Indeed, in *Sefer Hasidim,* an extreme ascetic denial of physical pleasure
is not presented as the most desirable way of religious life. On the contrary, a sexually active life (limited, of course, to one's spouse) is embraced as a viable, indeed necessary, path for the faithful.[97] I would
argue, however, that the attenuated asceticism is part of their more
popular teaching, but does not accurately reflect the truly esoteric dimension of Rhineland Jewish pietism, which is predicated on a more
stringent ascesis rooted in an essentially negative view about the physical world,[98] which may reflect older pietistic elements in Judaism as well
as the contemporary medieval Christian milieu.[99] Indeed, their understanding of the love of God, which is described in intensely erotic terms,
entails the renunciation of carnal passion. One must substitute the sear-
ing flames of sensual lust[100] for the purifying blaze of the heavenly fire.
The inordinate form of asceticism is found in other sources, some of
them reflecting the earlier stages of the pietistic orientation as it evolved
in the twelfth century. For the purposes of this study I will focus on se-
lect passages where the ascetic quality is related to the transmission or
recitation of the divine name and/or vision of the glory. The link between recitation of the name and the weakening of the physical status of
the individual is emphasized in the following comment in the *Sefer
Gimatri'ot* of Judah the Pious: "When is [the name] mentioned? On Yom
Kippur, ten times corresponding to his ten essences (*hawwayotaw*), with
empty entrails. 'When the nations gather together, the kingdoms, to
serve the Lord' (Ps. 102:23). And it is written afterward 'He drained my
strength' (ibid., 24), mortification also weakens the strength of man.
Therefore, they would utter the explicit name on Yom Kippur."[101] The
name can be mentioned only on Yom Kippur when the physical potency
of man is diminished by the fast, a point that is made as well by Eleazar
of Worms in a number of his own compositions.[102] Given the fact that

rabbinic law forbids sexual intercourse on that day, we may presume that
the weakening of the strength of man to which Judah refers also relates
to the abrogation (albeit temporary) of carnal desire. Only in such a
state of depletion could the high priest vocalize the Tetragrammaton ten
times corresponding to the ten essences, *hawwayot*,[103] which are contained within the name, a point to which I will return.

A more specific connection between transmission of the name and
eradication of carnal eros is found in a passage in a pietistic text that is
preserved in manuscript: "This is [the meaning of the verse] *shemi
le-ʿolam*, 'This shall be My name forever' (Exod. 3:15), [the word *shemi*
signifies] *shem yod* [i.e., the name that begins with *yod*, the Tetragram-
maton], it is written *le-ʿolam*, for [the name is transmitted] to the one
who in the world (*ʿolam*) is pure of all transgression. . . . *Shemi le-ʿolam*,
the unique name (*shem ha-meyuhad*) is only revealed to one who has ab-
rogated the desire for women from his heart."[104] According to this
source, the transmission of the Tetragrammaton, which is the main
praxis to bring about the vision of the glory, is linked to the nullification
of sexual desire. The name can only be promulgated to one who has ex-
tirpated erotic yearning from his heart. Eleazar of Worms expresses the
same idea in *Sefer ha-Shem*, unquestionably the most recondite of his
writings: "The unique name is only revealed to one who has nullified
the desire for women and to one whose heart is anxious."[105] The causal
relation between control of sexual lust and the dwelling of the divine
glory is underscored in a second passage from this work: "[God] chose
the small *yod* for his name [YHWH], for there is no place devoid of him,
as it says, 'for I fill both heaven and earth' (Jer. 23:24), and he constricts
his presence on that which is small, on the Ark and on the covering.
[He dwells a distance of] ten handbreadths above the Ark to indicate
that the *Shekhinah* dwells on the one who subjugates his impulse (*kofef
yisro*)."[106] In this passage, Eleazar reworks the older midrashic motif that
God constricted his presence (*mesamsem ʾet shekhinato*) between the two
poles of the Ark, an exegetical strategy employed by some rabbinic figures to explain the biblical claim that God, who is ubiquitous, spoke to
Moses from between the two cherubim that were on top of the Ark of
Testimony stationed within the spatial confines of the Tabernacle
(Exod. 25:22; Num. 7:89).[107] For Eleazar, the moralistic implication of
the rabbinic dictum that God delimits his omnipresence to a place that

is small is that God dwells upon the soul that diminishes the power of the impulse, *yeser*, which here relates in a more restrictive way to sexual lust. Heeding the idiom of the text in its original resonance, *kofef yisro*,[108] we may say the pietistic ideal of humility, typified by Moses,[109] involves the subduing of sexual desire, a bending of wanton impulse into orderly obedience, an overturning by turning over, harnessing the erotic energy and lifting it up as a crown in the service of God.

It must be noted, however, that even in *Sefer Hasidim* one can find vestiges of the more esoteric position based on the nexus of eros and vision. For example, consider the following passage: "The hair of a woman is a lewd matter, as it says, 'your hair is like a flock of goats' (Song of Songs 4:1). [He who looks at the hair of a woman] will not merit [to see] 'the hair of His head that is like lamb's wool' (Dan. 7:9). If he is careful not to look at a woman he will see the glory, as it says, 'When your eyes behold the king in his beauty' (Isa. 33:17)."[110] Building on the statement attributed to R. Sheshet, "a woman's hair is a lewd matter,"[111] the author of this passage in *Sefer Hasidim* notes that the punishment for looking at a woman's hair is being denied a vision of the hair of the glory related in the verse from Daniel. The correlation of seeing the *Shekhinah*, the divine presence, and abstaining from looking at women is enunciated in a second passage from *Sefer Hasidim*:

> The essential strength of pietism is that, even though [people] insult him, he does not abandon his piety, and his intention is directed to God and he does not look at women whereas others apart from him do look. Thus he merits the abundant goodness that is hidden and his eyes will be satiated by the splendor of the presence (*ziw ha-shekhinah*), "when your eyes behold a king in his beauty" (Isa. 33:17), [that is] whoever does not look at women in their nakedness or at a virgin, as it says, "[I have covenanted with my eyes] not to gaze on a maiden" (Job 31:1). . . . Every one whose [sexual] impulse does not derive pleasure from lewdness will merit to see the splendor of the presence in the future.[112]

The imperative not to gaze at women is based on earlier rabbinic statements[113] and is also reflected in an Aramaic adjuration, which is preserved in the ostensibly older visionary tracts known in scholarly parlance as the Hekhalot literature, that contains a litany of conditions necessary for one who aspires to encounter the divine presence.[114] Notwithstanding the earlier textual sources available to explain the literary genesis of the idea, the very essence of the pietistic lifestyle is here linked to the overcoming of visual temptation.[115] In the language of the following section from *Sefer Hasidim:* "Whoever separates from prostitution and adultery, and closes his eyes from seeing what is lewd, will merit to see 'that you, O Lord, appear to every eye' (Num. 14:14), 'for every eye shall behold' (Isa. 52:8), and he will not conceal his eyes from him, for his eyes will see the glory, and he will find favor in the eyes of God and humanity."[116] The link established in this passage between the eschatological vision of the *Shekhinah* and refraining from looking at a woman's nakedness is not merely a homiletical device, but rather it reflects a mythical conception of the glory that imputes gender (in intensely erotic terms) to the divine. To attain the beatific vision, therefore, it is necessary to control one's sexual impulses, and especially the casting of the eyes upon something that would excite the libidinous energy. As we read in another passage from *Sefer Hasidim:*

> "Thus it is good for a man to distance himself from every desire, and to give his heart to love and to fear the Creator with all his heart and with all his might, and to abhor the life of vanity, for we cannot lower ourselves and conquer our inclinations, which drive us from the land of the living, except by subjugating our hearts to return to our Creator in a complete repentance, to worship him and to fulfill his will with a undivided heart. The sages said, "You should eat a morsel of bread with salt and you should drink a small measure of water,"[117] and you should be careful not to look at women for they remove a man from this world,[118] and he should love human beings,[119] and he should judge every person in the scale of merit[120] . . . and he should be humble before everyone.[121]

An austere lifestyle, intended to procure the subduing of sensual desires, is recommended for the one who repents fully and returns back to God. The life of piety is predicated on loving God with all the depths of one's thoughts,[122] a contemplative state that fosters ecstatic rapture and the consequent turning away from the pursuits and affairs of the

world.[123] The point is reiterated by Eleazar in the laws of penitence included in *Sefer ha-Roqeah:*

> This is the instruction for one who repents with all his heart and all his
> soul, and he comes to cleave to his Creator. Each person should con-
> sider in his heart [the verse] "and I am sanctified in the midst of the
> children of Israel" (Lev. 22:32). If it were a time of decree, he must be
> killed and he must subject his soul to suffer difficult tribulations on ac-
> count of his Creator. He must say to his heart: I should not restrain my
> spirit for the sake of my Creator for even a short while, and I should not
> take pleasure for even a short while in matters of adultery and impurity.
> I must accustom my eyes not to look at the face of a woman for she is
> fire. . . . Everyone looks at the face of women, but he does not, and this
> is the worship of the Creator in truth. One must avoid all physical plea-
> sure with women, seeing them, touching them, sitting with them, see-
> ing their lovely garments, hearing their voices in speech or song,
> speaking with them, whether married or single, with the exception of
> his wife. He should delight in her with all the desire of his heart when
> she is pure. . . . Therefore, he should hasten and hurry from having
> thoughts about women except for the wife of his bosom. He should de-
> light and enjoy her with love at any time that he desires, for she guards
> him from sin.[124]

In this passage, Eleazar makes explicit the connection between martyrdom and ascetic renunciation, two acts that are linked together in his
mind on account of the fact that both presumably help one fulfill the in-
junction to sanctify the name of God. Just as in a time of persecution
one must suffer even to the point of death on behalf of the divine glory,
so in general one must be willing to nullify one's physical appetites in
the service of God, a nullification that may be viewed as a form of simu-
lated death. Eleazar enumerates several activities that ought to be
avoided if one is to attain the highest level of pietistic devotion, but the
particular gesture that is signaled out above all the others is withstand-
ing the temptation to look at women; indeed, the true worship of God is
identified specifically with abstaining from gazing at the face of women
and risking the chance of being sexually aroused.[125] To be sure, in the
above passage, Eleazar condones man's seeking gratification of his desires

from his wife, and thus there seems to be credible grounds to argue that
Eleazar did not advocate, either practically or theoretically, an unconditional ascetic abrogation. However, it is patently clear that the promotion of physical sex between husband and wife is merely a concession on
Eleazar's part to the weaknesses of the flesh. That is, satisfaction of the
couple's sexual needs—and particularly those of the husband—within
the marriage is viewed by Eleazar (along with other pietists) as the best
way to curb man's potentially unruly libido.[126] In the final analysis,
Eleazar affirms a purely instrumentalist view of a woman, for the wife is
objectified as the means by which the male can satisfy his sexual appetite
and thereby avoid the temptation of falling into illicit relationships with
other women.[127] Ideally, however, it is best for one to overcome even
this state of controlled gratification with one's spouse and to annul carnal desire even more comprehensively so that one's (phallic) gaze is
fixed exclusively upon the mental image of the divine glory that is con-
jured through meditation on the image that takes shape in one's heart.

The link between the visual manifestation of the *Shekhinah* and the
abrogation of sexual desire parallels the connection made in pietistic
sources between transmission of the divine name and sexual abstinence:
Just as only one who is sexually abstinent can receive the name, a reception that involves esoteric gnosis and mystical praxis, so only one who
has mastered the sexual passions is capable of visually contemplating the
Shekhinah. Eleazar of Worms applies this pietistic ideal to explain the
phenomenological contours of the Sinaitic theophany: By virtue of abstaining from sexual intercourse for three days (Exod. 19:15), the male
Israelites became holy like the ministering angels, who lack any impulse,
including that of the libido, and as a consequence they were worthy to
experience the revelation of the glory.[128] Inasmuch as the world-to-
come is described (on the basis of a talmudic dictum attributed to the
third-century Rav)[129] as a state in which the righteous partake of the beatific vision of the glory, having abolished the basic physical activities
(eating, drinking, and sexual intercourse), it may be said that the
pietists proleptically attain this state of eschatological angelification as a
result of their asceticism.[130] Consider, for example, Eleazar's description of
the visionary ascent of the righteous soul through the liturgical utterance:

> The soul has no body, and it sees like an angel when it goes out from
> the body, and it has no shadow. Even the soul of the righteous sees

through prophecy and in a vision since it contemplates all day long like Jacob, [of whom it says] "he had a dream, and behold there was a ladder" (Gen. 28:12). The [word] *sullam* ["ladder"] is numerically equivalent [to the expression] *zeh kisse' ha-kavod* ["this is the throne of glory"].[131] . . . The [word] *sullam* is numerically equivalent to [the word] *qol* ["voice"], for by means of the voice of prayer the angels ascend, and similarly the souls of the righteous rise in the voice of praise that is heard. . . . With respect to the matter of this world [it says] "When your eyes behold the king in his beauty" (Isa. 33:17), but in the future the righteous man shall see from all his sides like the supernal ones before and behind him. . . . The soul of the righteous is bound beneath the throne of glory,[132] and it delights in the vision of the glory from all the pleasures of the garden.[133]

The visionary ascent of the righteous mimics the ascent of the angels inasmuch as the means for the ascension is the liturgical utterance. The angelification of the righteous, which is clearly a reference to the pietists themselves, is a prolepsis of what occurs to the righteous after the death of the body when the soul is restored to the celestial paradise. In this corporeal existence, the righteous soul is capable of becoming angelic by subjugating the physical passions. The vision of the divine presence bestowed upon the pietist is thus in direct correlation to the ascetic practices that assist the soul in attaining the eschatological state prior to the final demise of the body.

Precisely such a motif underlies the connection between the rite of circumcision and the vision of the *Shekhinah* that one finds in pietistic literature,[134] a theme expressed in older midrashic texts and further developed in kabbalistic works.[135] To appreciate the particular appropriation of this theme in the pietistic context, it is necessary to bear in mind that, in line with other medieval rabbinic commentators,[136] Hasidei Ashkenaz understood the act of cutting the foreskin as a symbolic excision of sexual desire. The rite of circumcision, therefore, was interpreted symbolically in the pietistic writings as a reference to the ascetic neutralization of erotic craving. The point is expressed succinctly in the following comment in Judah's *Sefer Gimatri'ot:* "[The word] *'arel* [un-circumcised] is numerically equivalent to [the word] *yeser* [impulse].[137] Therefore, it is written, 'You shall circumcise the flesh of your foreskin' (Gen. 17:11), for you are like the ministering angels since there is no desire for women amongst you."[138] The circumcision of the flesh signals the abrogation of carnal lust, which is localized in the foreskin, and as a consequence of this act the Jewish male is transformed into an angelic being. The angelification is occasioned by ascetic denial, for only as a consequence of this ontological transformation is one capable of apprehending the epiphany of the divine glory. In the continuation of Judah's *Sefer Gimatri'ot*, Esau, who is described as removing the sign of his covenant (literally, pulling on his foreskin, which is the rabbinic idiom for epispasm),[139] rebelling against God, and having intercourse with a woman engaged to another man (*na'arah me'orasah*),[140] is set in contrast to the Jews who attain the higher spiritual state through circumcision. The defiant behavior, which is manifest principally in the rejection of circumcision, is linked to Esau's forfeiting his birthright (Gen. 25:32).[141]

I note, in passing, that this text must be seen as a rather strident polemic against Christianity, which is represented typologically by Esau; the standard claim to the spiritual superiority of Christianity over Judaism, which in great measure is based on the Pauline argument regarding the overcoming of the circumcision of the flesh by baptism or the circumcision of the spirit,[142] is here turned on its head.[143] The inferior spiritual status of Christianity is signified by the fact that Esau relinquished his privileged position by repudiating the covenant of circumcision.[144] By contrast, Israel maintains the superior position by preserving circumcision of the flesh according to the literalness of the law: "Thus, Adam was born circumcised,[145] as it says, 'Now that Adam has become like one of us' (Gen. 3:22), like Abraham,[146] for it took twenty generations for him to return to the days of youth.[147] Thus, the nation that is circumcised is compared to a infant that is born."[148] The anti-Christian dimension is accentuated by the fact that the blessing of the first-born is linked to the offering of sacrifices.[149] Since it is forbidden for one who is uncircumcised to enter the sanctuary, he obviously is not ritually fit to offer sacrifices.[150] Not only is Israel superior to Esau on account of the bodily circumcision, but this supremacy is related as well to their preservation (at least from the ideal halakhic perspective developed by the rabbis from the formative period) of the sacrificial cult. If we further appreciate that the Rhineland Jewish pietists, like other medieval rabbinic commentators, transferred the liturgical efficacy of sacrifices to the words of prayer, then we can say, according to the passage in Judah's *Sefer Gimatri'ot,* that the genuine means of atonement still lies in the voice of Jacob, not in the hands of Esau. For these medieval pietists, the clash between Esau and Jacob, the Church and the Synagogue, could also be cast in psychosexual terms as the torment of the one being tempted and lured to trespass the line to the other side. The males within the house of Jacob are seduced by the females in the flock of Esau, but those very males are inscripted with the sign that empowers them apotropaically to withstand the temptation; indeed, the mark of circumcision affords the elite of these males the opportunity to adopt a life of ascetic restraint and control over sexual desire. The spiritual in-tent of circumcision, therefore, does not clash with the literal perfor-mance of the ritual, although the latter is significantly transformed in light of the former.

The angelic rank of the Jewish people is tied specifically to the diminution of the sexual urge, which is effected by cutting the foreskin. The special standing of Israel is related in the image of the nation that is compared to an infant, which in the original Hebrew is *qatan,* literally, the small one. To grasp the connotation of the word *qatan* when applied to Israel, one would do well to recall the statement of Eleazar cited above to the effect that God "constricts his presence on that which is small (*qatan*) . . . to indicate that the *Shekhinah* dwells on the one who subdues his lust."[151] The sense of smallness (*qatnut*) signifies the angelic transformation that ensues from the ascetic overcoming of the body,[152] the point that Judah wished to convey as well by the claim that cir-cumcision is given to the nation that is comparable to the small child. From a closer look at the fuller context of Eleazar's remark, we propose that the constriction of the *Shekhinah* in a demarcated place is repre-sented semiotically by the letter *yod,* for the *yod* is the smallest of all the letters, and it is thus the most appropriate to represent the mystery of the contraction of the divine. At the same time, however, the *yod* is also the first letter of the sacred name, YHWH. According to the tradition that Eleazar reports in several passages in his writings,[153] the *yod* symbol-ically alludes to the ten essences (*hawwayot*), which are also associated with the ten names of God that cannot be erased,[154] the ten *sefirot* mentioned in *Sefer Yesirah,* the ten utterances (*ma'amarot*) by means of which the world was created,[155] and the ten commandments revealed at Sinai that comprise within themselves all 613 commandments of the Torah.[156] The ten potencies are contained within the one name, a point that is represented orthographically by decomposing YHWH into *yod hawah*.[157] The *yod*, therefore, concomitantly signifies diminishing and expansion, depletion and fullness, the mystery of the constriction (*simsum*) of the *Shekhinah*. The ontological claim about the nature of the divine glory is reflected in the ethical demand imposed upon the individual, for the presence dwells only upon the righteous one who has emulated the ways of God by making himself small through acts of humility and contrition, which involve the dissolution of sensual desire.[158]

The semiotic representation of the diminishing of the *hasid* through the ascetic domestication of the erotic impulse is the letter *yod*, the sign of the covenant that is inscribed on the circumcised phallus. Simply put, the name that begins with *yod* can only be transmitted to one who has become the *yod*, but to become the *yod* one must eradicate the erotic impulse. This, I surmise, is the implication of Eleazar's remark in *Sefer ha-Shem* that the name is only transmitted to the modest (*senu'in*).[159] Obviously, this term has a wider range of meaning in the lexicon of the Hasidei Ashkenaz, as is attested by the fact that Eleazar himself immediately glosses the expression *senu'in* as "those who do not get angry." Following this sequence of thinking, it may be most appropriate to render the term *senu'in* in this passage as "meek." However, it is reasonable to assume that in this context, as we find elsewhere in the pietistic corpus, the term *senu'in* also has the connotation of those who are chaste. The implication of Eleazar's remark, therefore, would be that esoteric gnosis of the name is transmitted only to one who is sexually pure, a point that he affirms explicitly in other passages, as we have seen.[160]

Ascetic restraint results in the humbling of oneself, which enables one to become the chariot upon which the gravity of the glory comes to rest. The attainment of a state of humility occasions a dying to this world and a concomitant attainment of the world-to-come, which is understood as an enriched state of spiritual sustenance. Reworking an older talmudic statement,[161] Eleazar writes: "The world-to-come was created by the *yod*, for those who attain the world-to-come are few just like the *yod*, which is smaller than the [letters] associated with it, and the *yod* is like a humble man whose posture is bent over."[162] The rabbinic tradition that the world-to-come was created by means of the *yod*, in contrast to this world, which was created by the letter *he*ʾ, is explained not only in terms of the fact that quantitatively those who inhabit this spiritual world are few in number, but also in terms of the fact that qualitatively they are bowed in humility in the manner of the crooked *yod*. Even more relevant to the view of Hasidei Ashkenaz, especially as it is formulated by Eleazar, is the statement in one of the older esoteric works, *Massekhet Hekhalot*: "Why did the blessed holy One create the world-to-come with a *yod*? For any one who diminishes himself (*ha-maqtin ʿasmo*) in this world merits and inherits the world-to-come, which was created by a *yod*."[163] A similar point is related in one of the recensions of the semi-mystical treatise, ʾ*Otiyyot de-Rabbi ʿAqivaʾ*: "Why is the *yod* the smallest of all the letters? For whoever diminishes himself (*maqtin ʿasmo*) in this world, and he has no arrogance, merits and inherits the life of the world-to-come, which was created with a *yod*. . . . Why was the world-to-come created by a *yod*? Because those who are in the world-to-come are small in number."[164]

Eleazar appropriated this older theme by interpreting the act of self-diminution specifically in terms of abrogating the sexual appetite. To inherit the world-to-come, which signifies the angelic transformation occasioned by the separation of the divine soul from the animal body, one must become small like the *yod* by overcoming carnal desire. By becoming small, however, one is enlarged,[165] for one is conjoined to the infinite force of the name manifest in the ten luminous and inscrutable essences (*hawwayot*) or measures (*middot*) of the divine. As Eleazar puts the matter in *Sefer ha-Shem*, the Tetragrammaton begins with a *yod*, the smallest of the Hebrew letters, because "God is above and he fills everything, and he is great in his will, but he constricts his presence (*mesamsem shekhinato*) by his will in between the cherubim, for he is in accord with his essences. . . . God is 'exalted and sublime,' but he is with the 'humble and contrite'[166] who diminishes himself."[167]

The notion that the exalted God dwells with the low in spirit is well attested in biblical and rabbinic sources.[168] What is distinctive about the pietistic perspective, reflected in the words of Eleazar, is that contrition is tied exclusively to the quelling of eros, a constraint that facilitates conjunction with the divine glory, itself portrayed in the poetic image of jouissance (*shaʿashuʿa*).[169] The mystery of faith, the unity of God and

his name, is predicated on the claim that the limitless God willfully delimits his presence in the ten unknowable measures that are contained
within his name. These measures are beyond the reach of human understanding. Reflecting on the description of the *sefirot* in *Sefer Yesirah*,
"their measure is ten that have no end," Eleazar writes: "There is no sage
who can know and understand how to find the ten *sefirot*, for if the sage
inquires to find them, he cannot. '[All this I tested in wisdom;] I said, I
will comprehend it, but she is far from me' (Eccles. 7:23), for man cannot find what he toils to find but cannot. . . . there is no man who can
fathom these matters."[170] Eleazar's skepticism with regard to the possibility of metaphysical certitude is another key feature of the notion of
humility that colors the path of his thinking. Thus he commends to
those who seek positive knowledge of the ten potencies that make up the
essence of the name the example of the holy beasts who bear the throne:
Whenever the beasts want to rise in an erect posture, they are pushed
back down by the fear of the *Shekhinah*, and they return to worshipping
him. Similarly, the one who inquires about the unknowable must bend
down and bear the burden of being that which bears the burden, that is,
he must humble himself before the presence, deplete himself of all but
the sense of being depleted. To bear that burden one must become the
yod of the name YHWH, which points to the ten essences that cannot
be comprehended by human beings.[171]

The humbling of oneself is an expression of the soul's passionate
embrace of the divine, which ensues from the subjugation of the sexual
impulse. In one passage in *Sefer ha-Shem*,[172] the ideal of erotic asceticism
is linked by Eleazar to the verse "Your name is like fine oil; thus the
maidens do love you" (Song of Songs 1:3). The first part of the verse relates to the liturgical utterance of the Tetragrammaton in the Temple,
for the original Hebrew *shemen turaq shemekha*, "Your name is like fine
oil," has the same numerical value as the expression *'arba'ah 'otiyyot
shemekha*, "four letters of your name," i.e., both equal 1456. The articulation of the name results in the divine emanation, which is compared
to the fine oil that overflows.[173] The second part of the verse indicates
the conditions that serve as a catalyst to set the process in motion:
"'Thus the maidens (*'alamot*), for they know the concealed name (*ha-
shem ha-ne'elam*), 'do love you' (*'ahevukha*) in this world and in the
world-to-come. . . . 'The Lord is far from the wicked' (Prov. 15:29) and

'far from their thoughts' (Jer. 12:2), but [concerning] the righteous [it says] 'The Lord is near to all those who call him' (Ps. 145:18), 'The Lord is close to the brokenhearted' (Ps. 34:19), for his essences are near the humble."[174] The righteous are compared to maidens, ʿalamot, for they have knowledge of the name that is hidden, shem ha-neʿelam. Implied in this play on words is a gender transformation, for the attainment of the esoteric gnosis comes about by the humbling of oneself through the overcoming of sexual desire. The feminization of the meek expedites the erotic communion with the divine, which is portrayed in the allegorical representation of the name as the fine oil with which the soul is anointed. Tellingly, the same verse that yields the exegetical basis for the insight that the terminus of the love of God is the willingness to die also yields the basis for the view that the righteous who humble themselves by conquering their sexual impulse are transformed into the female vessels that receive the overflow from the divine.

By way of summary, then, it may be said that the mystical love of God cultivated by the Rhineland Jewish pietists was a form of erotic union occasioned by the ascetic negation of eros. The triangular relationship of death, eros, and vision, which informed the theological reflections on the nature of martyrdom, was transposed into a mystical ideal in the pietistic spirituality that evolved in the Rhineland in the twelfth and thirteenth centuries. Ascetic renunciation as it is expressed in the thought of the pietists functions in a manner similar to the martyrological ideal set forth in the Hebrew chronicles. And just as the death of the martyrs is portrayed as an erotic experience for the soul vis-à-vis the glory, so too the sexual abstinence adopted by the pietist is depicted as an expression of the passionate love of God.

NOTES

1. See G. Scholem, Major Trends in Jewish Mysticism (New York, 1956), pp. 84–85. On the nexus between southern Italy and the Rhineland, see also R. Bonfil, "Between Eretz Israel and Babylonia," Shalem 5 (1987): 1–30 (in Hebrew); idem, "Myth, Rhetoric, History: A Study in the Chronicle of Ahimaʿaz," in Culture and Society in Medieval Jewry: Studies Dedicated to the Memory of Haim Hillel Ben-Sasson, ed. M. Ben-Sasson, R. Bonfil, and J. R.

Hacker (Jerusalem, 1989), pp. 99–135 (in Hebrew). Also relevant to this dis-cussion is E. R. Wolfson, "The Theosophy of Shabbetai Donnolo, with Special Emphasis on the Doctrine of *Sefirot* in *Sefer Hakhmoni*," *Jewish History* 6 (1992): 281–316.

2. Scholem, *Major Trends*, pp. 80, 104–105. See the rather dogmatic as-sertion of G. Scholem, *On the Possibility of Jewish Mysticism in Our Time and Other Essays*, ed. and with an introduction by A. Shapira, trans. J. Chipman (Philadelphia and Jerusalem, 1997), p. 132: "Mysticism appeared in an entirely new form among the circles of Ashkenazic Hasidim, even though they at-tempted to preserve the earlier heritage. There is hardly any doubt that the movement arose in response to the tremendous shocks brought about during the period of the Crusades and the related persecutions of Jewish society." In this context, Scholem follows the approach of Y. Baer, "The Socioreligious Orientation of 'Sefer Hasidim,'" in *Binah: Studies in Jewish History, Thought, and Culture*, vol. 2, ed. J. Dan (New York, 1989), pp. 59–60 (the original Hebrew version of this study appeared in 1938).

3. The point is missed by I. Marcus, *Piety and Society: The Jewish Pietists of Medieval Germany* (Leiden, 1981), p. 150 n. 57, who only presents one side of Scholem's argument that assumes a causal nexus between the Crusades and German-Jewish pietism.

4. See Y. Baer, *Israel Amongst the Nations* (Jerusalem, 1955), pp. 36–39, 48 (in Hebrew); idem, *Studies and Essays on the History of the Jewish People* (Jerusalem, 1986), 1:151–152 (in Hebrew); I. Marcus, "History, Story, and Collective Memory: Narrativity in Early Ashkenazic Culture," in *The Midrashic Imagination: Jewish Exegesis, Thought, and History*, ed. M. Fishbane (Albany, 1993), p. 275 n. 45.

5. See P. Schäfer, "The Ideal of Piety of the Ashkenazi Hasidim and Its Roots in Jewish Tradition," *Jewish History* 4 (1990): 199–211. On the literary activity of Hasidei Ashkenaz with respect to the Hekhalot Corpus, see E. R. Wolfson, *Through a Speculum That Shines: Vision and Imagination in Medieval Jewish Mysticism* (Princeton, 1994), p. 80, and reference to the work of I. Gruenwald, I. Ta-Shema, A. Farber, and P. Schäfer cited in n. 35 ad loc. The development of older esoteric themes in the writings of the Hasidei Ashkenaz has been discussed by a number of scholars, of whom I offer a representative list-ing: A. Farber, "The Concept of the Merkabah in Thirteenth-Century Jewish Esotericism: Sod ha-ʾEgoz and Its Development" (Ph.D. thesis, Hebrew University, 1986, in Hebrew); E. R. Wolfson, "The Image of Jacob Engraved Upon the Throne: Further Speculation on the Esoteric Doctrine of the German Pietism," in *Massuʾot Studies in Kabbalistic Literature and Jewish Philosophy in Memory of Prof. Ephraim Gottlieb*, ed. M. Oron and A. Goldreich (Jerusalem, 1994), pp. 131–185 (in Hebrew; expanded English version in E. R. Wolfson,

Along the Path: Studies in Kabbalistic Myth, Symbolism, and Hermeneutics [Albany, 1995], pp. 1–62 and notes on pp. 111–187); idem, "Metatron and Shi'ur Qomah in the Writings of Haside Ashkenaz," in *Mysticism, Magic, and Kabbalah in Ashkenazi Judaism*, ed. K. Grözinger and J. Dan (Tübingen, 1995), pp. 60–92; A. Kuyt, "Traces of a Mutual Influence of the Haside Ashkenaz and the Hekhalot Literature," *From Narbonne to Regensburg: Studies in Medieval Hebrew Texts*, ed. N. A. van Uchelen and I. E. Zwiep (Amsterdam, 1993), pp. 62–86; D. Abrams, "The Boundaries of Divine Ontology: The Inclusion and Exclusion of Metatron in the Godhead," *Harvard Theological Review* 87 (1994): 291–321; idem, "From Divine Shape to Angelic Being: The Career of Akatriel in Jewish Literature," *Journal of Religion* 76 (1996): 43–63; idem, "Special Angelic Figures: The Career of the Beasts of the Throne World in Hekhalot Literature, German Pietism, and Kabbalistic Literature," *Revue des études juives* 155 (1996): 287–310; idem, *Sexual Symbolism and Merkavah Speculation in Medieval Germany* (Tübingen, 1997). A separate, although certainly a related, issue is the relationship of the ideational and the practical content of the teachings of Hasidei Ashkenaz and the Provençal and Spanish kabbalists of the same period. This, too, is a subject discussed by a variety of scholars, notably, G. Scholem, J. Dan, M. Idel, A. Farber, E. Wolfson, and D. Abrams.

6. See A. Grossman, "The Roots of Sanctification of the Name in the Older Ashkenaz," in *Sanctity of Life and Martyrdom: Studies in Memory of Amir Yekutiel*, ed. I. M. Gafni and A. Ravitzky (Jerusalem, 1992), pp. 99–130 (in Hebrew).

7. See D. Boyarin, *Intertextuality and the Reading of Midrash* (Bloomington and Indianapolis, 1990), pp. 122–126; idem, "Interpretation and Fact—On the Historical Investigation of Rabbinic Literature," in *Saul Lieberman Memorial Volume*, ed. S. Friedman (New York and Jerusalem, 1993), pp. 105–117, esp. 110–116 (in Hebrew). My own reading resonates with some of the hermeneutical strategies mapped by Boyarin. Also relevant is the discussion on the sanctification of God in love in M. Fishbane, *The Kiss of God: Spiritual and Mystical Death in Judaism* (Seattle and London, 1994), pp. 51–86, esp. 66–71.

8. Palestinian Talmud, Berakhot 9:5, 13b; Sotah 5:7, 20c; Babylonian Talmud, Berakhot 61b.

9. Mishnah, Berakhot 9:5; *Sifre on Deuteronomy*, ed. L. Finkelstein (New York, 1969), § 32, p. 55. A similar exegesis of Deuteronomy 6:5 is transmitted in a number of sources in the name of R. Eliezer. See Babylonian Talmud, Pesahim 25a, Yoma 82a, Sanhedrin 74a.

10. *Mekhilta' de-Rabbi Ishmael*, ed. H. S. Horowitz and I. A. Rabin (Jerusalem, 1970), Shirah, ch. 3, p. 127; *Sifre on Deuteronomy*, § 32, p. 55; *Midrash Tehilim*, ed. S. Buber (Vilna, 1891), 9:17, p. 91.

11. See H. Soloveitchik, "Religious Law and Change: The Medieval Ashkenazi Example," *AJS Review* 12 (1987): 205–221. R. Chazan, *European*

Jewry and the First Crusade (Berkeley, 1987), pp. 144–145, has argued that in the wake of the Crusade the more radical responses were mitigated and the cultural memory of martyrdom was such that martyrdom was understood as consistent with the viewpoints articulated in classical rabbinic literature. But in a sense, this only calls attention to the fact that the self-sacrifice occasioned by the massacre of 1096 was indeed a departure from the strictures of traditional Jewish law. The view that in rabbinic sources the sanctification of the name is only passive has been recently confirmed by a close intertextual reading of a particularly important talmudic discussion (Babylonian Talmud, Sanhedrin 74a–75b) in A. Cohen, "Towards an Erotics of Martyrdom," *Journal of Jewish Thought and Philosophy* 7 (1998): 227–256.

12. J. Dan, *The Esoteric Theology of Ashkenazi Hasidism* (Jerusalem, 1968), pp. 32–33 (in Hebrew); idem, "The Problem of Sanctification of the Name in the Teaching of the German Pietists," in *Milhemet Qodesh u-Matirologiah be-Toledot Yisra'el u-ve-Toledot ha-ʿAmim* (Jerusalem, 1968), pp. 122, 126–127; Marcus, *Piety and Society*, p. 151 n. 57; Chazan, *European Jewry*, pp. 143–144; idem, *In the Year 1096: The First Crusade and the Jews* (Philadelphia, 1996), pp. 109–111.

13. Dan, "Problem of Sanctification of the Name," pp. 121, 127–129, and the reservation expressed by Marcus, *Piety and Society*, pp. 150–151 n. 57. On the Hasidic conception of sanctification of the name and the persecutions of 1096, see Baer, "Socioreligious Orientation," p. 68.

14. See Chazan, *European Jewry*, pp. 197–210; S. Schwarzfuchs, "The Place of the Crusades in Jewish History," in *Culture and Society in Medieval Jewry*, pp. 251–267. The claim that 1096 did not represent a watershed in Ashkenazi religious and cultural history has been challenged by a number of scholars. See Grossman, "Roots of Sanctification of the Name," pp. 101–105; S. Zfatman, *The Jewish Tale in the Middle Ages: Between Ashkenaz and Sepharad* (Jerusalem, 1993), p. 91 n. 48 (in Hebrew).

15. In this matter, I am particularly influenced by the notion of the unspoken in Heidegger's thought. Consider, for instance, M. Heidegger, *On the Way to Language*, trans. P. D. Hertz (San Francisco, 1971), p. 120: "Everything spoken stems in a variety of ways from the unspoken, whether this be something not yet spoken, or whether it be what must remain unspoken in the sense that it is beyond the reach of speaking. Thus, that which is spoken in various ways begins to appear as if it were cut off from speaking and the speakers, and did not belong to them, while in fact it alone offers to speaking and to the speakers whatever it is they attend to, no matter in what way they stay within what is spoken of the unspoken." For analysis of this Heideggerian motif, see W. J. Richardson, S.J., *Heidegger through Phenomenology to Thought*, 3d ed. (The

Hague, 1974), pp. 21–22, 221–223, 609–610, 638; D. A. White, *Heidegger and the Language of Poetry* (Lincoln and London, 1978), pp. 43–49, 70–71.

16. See the study by G. D. Cohen cited below, n. 49.

17. The connection between the martyrological ideal and the ascetic renunciation of the world is noted by Dan, *Esoteric Theology*, pp. 32–33, although he minimizes the issue of historical causality. The impact of the martyrological ideal on the pietistic virtue of sanctifying the name (principally through fulfillment of the traditional commandments) is affirmed more recently by idem, *On Sanctity: Religion, Ethics, and Mysticism in Judaism and Other Religions* (Jerusalem, 1998), pp. 272, 345–346, 407–409 (in Hebrew).

18. The recent debate regarding the question of how to evaluate the historical facticity of these literary documents is of no consequence to the main thrust of this analysis. See Chazan, *European Jewry*, pp. 38–49, and the critique by I. Marcus in his review of Chazan's book in *Speculum* 64 (1989): 685–688. The response of Chazan to Marcus appeared as "The Facticity of Medieval Narrative: A Case Study of the Hebrew First Crusade Narratives," *AJS Review* 16 (1991): 31–56. See also idem, "Representation of Events in the Middle Ages," *History and Theory* 27 (1988): 40–55; and idem, "The Timebound and the Timeless: Medieval Jewish Narration of Events," *History and Memory* 6 (1994): 5–34. For yet another view, see J. Cohen, "The 'Persecutions of 1096'—From Martyrdom to Martyrology: The Sociocultural Context of the Hebrew Crusade Chronicles," *Zion* 59 (1994): 169–208 (in Hebrew). Closest to the mark is the insight of Fishbane, *Kiss of God*, pp. 71–72, which is based on the anthropological/literary orientation adopted by Marcus, especially in his review of Chazan, p. 686, and developed more fully in "History, Story, and Collective Memory": "The literary shaping of martyrological events serves a double purpose: it instructs the culture in models of spiritual resistance and provides dramatic examples of sanctification whereby these acts could be inscribed in cultural memory. Indeed, the historicity of these examples (in the strict sense) is less important than the tradition of pious behavior transmitted. The rhetoric of literary models thus invokes a mythic moment, foundational for religious memory; just as the recitation of this content (in study or prayer) has a liturgical dimension that exalts the martyrs . . . and idealizes the merit of their deeds" (*Kiss of God*, pp. 71–72). In my judgment, the question of the historical veracity of the Crusade chronicles has to be examined from the wider perspective of the relationship between presumed historical facticity and the narratological imagination expressed in earlier rabbinic sources. Particularly instructive in this regard is J. Neusner, "Beyond Historicism, After Structuralism: Story as History in Ancient Judaism," *The 1980 Harry Spindel Memorial Lecture*, Bowdoin College, Brunswick, Maine. Also relevant here is the insight of M. R. Niehoff, "The Phoenix in Rabbinic Literature,"

Harvard Theological Review 89 (1996): 249, that in rabbinic literature myth be-comes a "natural and intimate part of history and of everyday life." The implica-tion of this approach is that there is no reason to assume that the rabbinic figures distinguished sharply between myth and history, the symbolic and the literal, the imaginative and the real. The dispute among historians of the Jewish Middle Ages regarding the factual merit of literary sources such as the Crusade chroni-cles betrays a naive historicism that has neglected the philosophical insight that the narrative structure of temporality and the temporal structure of narrativity provide the hermeneutical circle that accounts for the inseparability of history and story. The phenomenological construction of the historical event involves a subtle and complex interplay between experience and interpretation, which ren-ders suspect any attempt to distinguish fact from fiction in a dichotomous fash-ion. See J. H. Nopta, S.J., *Phenomenology and History* (Chicago, 1967); G. Funke, "Phenomenology and History," in *Phenomenology and the Social Sciences*, vol. 2, ed. M. Natanson (Evanston, 1973), pp. 3–101; also in Natanson's volume, D. M. Lowe, "Intentionality and the Method of History," pp. 103–130; P. Ricoeur, *Time and Narrative*, 3 vols., trans. K. McLaughlin and D. Pellauer (Chicago, 1984–1988); D. Carr, *Time, Narrative, and History* (Bloomington, 1991); G. Warnke, *Gadamer: Hermeneutics, Tradition, and Reason* (Stanford, 1987), pp. 5–41. I would apply the same philosophic insight to the debate regarding the question of the historical facticity underlying the pietistic works. Regarding this issue, see I. G. Marcus, "The Historical Meaning of *Hasidei Ashkenaz*: Fact, Fiction, or Cultural Self-Image?" in *Gershom Scholem's Major Trends in Jewish Mysticism 50 Years After: Proceedings of the Sixth International Conference on the History of Jewish Mysticism*, ed. P. Schäfer and J. Dan (Tübingen, 1993), pp. 103–114. For further references related to this topic, see below, n. 27.

19. In principle, the logic of my argument is similar to Marcus, "History, Story, and Collective Memory," p. 265: "Parts of the pietist ideal were ancient and consisted of several intersecting features that cannot be reduced to an anti-Tosafist ideology. Nevertheless, the medieval historical stimuli which helped precipitate the pietistic ideal in written form may be related to other anti-French polemical trends we find among the German pietists." I agree with the need to strike a balance between older traditions and more contemporary stim-uli that may have triggered the specific response of the medieval pietists. (I note, parenthetically, that the need to strike such a balance is plainly evident in the pioneering study of Baer, "Socioreligious Orientation.") A sustained analy-sis of the evolution of a particular motif in medieval Ashkenazi culture that ex-emplifies this methodological approach can be found in I. Marcus, *Rituals of Childhood: Jewish Acculturation in Medieval Europe* (New Haven and London, 1996). Curiously, with respect to the question of the impact of the First Crusade

on Hasidei Ashkenaz, Marcus does not adopt such an approach. See Marcus, *Piety and Society*, p. 151 n. 57.

20. Chazan, *European Jewry*, pp. 215–216. See also R. Chazan, "The Early Development of Hasidut Ashkenaz," *Jewish Quarterly Review* 75 (1985): 199–211.

21. See Marcus, *Piety and Society*, pp. 13, 26, 65–66.

22. Scholem, *Major Trends*, p. 84.

23. Ibid., pp. 87–90.

24. See Marcus, *Piety and Society*, pp. 26, 65–71.

25. As noted by Marcus, *Piety and Society*, p. 151 n. 57.

26. For discussion of this matter, see Wolfson, *Through a Speculum That Shines*, pp. 189–190.

27. See J. Dan, "Review of Ivan Marcus, *Piety and Society*," *Tarbiz* 51 (1981–82): 324–325 (in Hebrew); idem, "On the Historical Personality of R. Judah Hasid," in *Culture and Society*, pp. 389–398 (in Hebrew); idem, "Ashkenazi Hasidim, 1941–1991," in *Gershom Scholem's Major Trends in Jewish Mysticism 50 Years After*, pp. 96–100. The question of the historical facticity of Hasidei Ashkenaz is examined from another perspective by M. Beit-Arié, "Ideal Versus Reality: Scribal Prescriptions in *Sefer Hasidim* and Contemporary Scribal Practices in Franco-German Manuscripts," in *Rashi 1040–1990: Hommage à Ephraïm E. Urbach*, ed. G. Sed-Rajna (Paris, 1993), pp. 559–566.

28. See H. Soloveitchik, "Three Themes in *Sefer Hasidim*," *AJS Review* 1 (1976): 311–357, esp. 350 n. 126; idem, "Concerning the Date of *Sefer Hasidim*," in *Culture and Society in Medieval Jewry*, pp. 383–388 (in Hebrew).

29. As suggested by Marcus, *Piety and Society*, pp. 109–120.

30. An earlier source for the depiction of martyrdom in eschatological imagery, particularly the motif of being restored to the "great light" (*'or gadol*), is *Sefer Josippon*. The relevant passage is cited by Grossman, "Roots of Sanctification of the Name," pp. 118–119. For discussion of this expression in *Sefer Josippon*, see Wolfson, "Theosophy of Shabbetai Donnolo," pp. 295–296. I note, finally, that the biblical origin of the expression *'or gadol* is Isa. 9:1, a context that has an eschatological implication.

31. Chazan, *European Jewry*, p. 231. For the purposes of this study I have availed myself of Chazan's translations of the Crusade chronicles, although I have examined the original Hebrew documents published in A. M. Haberman, *Sefer Gezerot 'Ashkenaz we-Sarfat* (Jerusalem, 1946).

32. Chazan, *European Jewry*, p. 232. On the application of the eschatological image of being bound to the bond of life, which is derived from 1 Sam. 25:29, to the martyred souls, see the poem *'elohim 'al dami le-dami* by David ben Meshullam, in Haberman, *Sefer Gezerot*, p. 70. Consider as well the words used

by Eleazar of Worms, *Sefer Gezerot*, p. 166, in describing the status of his own wife, who was slaughtered as a martyr by the Christians in 1197: "Her soul is bound in the bond of life in order to have delight / grant her the fruits of her hands in paradise, *tesorar nafshah bi-seror ha-hayyim lehit'adden / tenu lah mi-peri yadeha be-gan 'eden*. See ibid., p. 167, where Eleazar utilizes the same eschatological image to depict the souls of his two daughters, who were murdered as well.

33. Chazan, *European Jewry*, p. 237. For a parallel in the longer chronicle, see ibid., p. 254.

34. Ibid., p. 241.

35. The *locus classicus* for this view is the description of the world-to-come attributed to Rav in the Babylonian Talmud, Berakhot 17a. For a wide-ranging discussion of the background of this dictum, see I. Chernus, *Mysticism in Rabbinic Judaism: Studies in the History of Midrash* (Berlin, 1982), pp. 74–87.

36. Chazan, *European Jewry*, p. 252.

37. See ibid., pp. 276, 286.

38. Ibid., p. 237.

39. Ibid., p. 254.

40. Ibid., p. 291.

41. Ibid., p. 263.

42. Ibid., p. 264.

43. Ibid., p. 268. See also pp. 271, 283.

44. S. Eidelberg, *The Jews and the Crusaders* (Madison, 1977), p. 128.

45. Ibid., p. 132. See also pp. 281–282. On the use of the image of the sacrificial blood of the martyrs rising before the throne of glory as a means of atonement, see the particularly poignant passage from the long chronicle in Chazan, *European Jewry*, p. 264. Compare the analogy of the sacrifice on the part of the martyrs to the binding of Isaac on p. 273 (and analysis of this motif on pp. 158–159, 164).

46. *Sefer Hasidim*, ed. J. Wistinetzki and J. Freimann (Frankfurt am Main, 1924), § 511, p. 146. Unless otherwise noted, references to *Sefer Hasidism* in the notes correspond to this edition, which is based on the Parma manuscript. On the use of the motif of Michael offering the pure souls of the righteous martyrs as sacrifices, see the dirge for the martyrs of Blois in *The Liturgical Poems of Rabbenu Barukh bar Samuel of Mainz*, ed. A. M. Haberman (Jerusalem, 1945), p. 136 (in Hebrew). The same image is used by this author in another poem, p. 146.

47. Babylonian Talmud, Menahot 110a.

48. The mystical ideal of prayer proffered by Hasidei Ashkenaz is captured compactly by Eleazar in his *Sod Ma'aseh Bere'shit*, in *Sefer Razi'el* (Amsterdam, 1701), 8b, and in the more recent edition, *Sode Razayya'*, ed. S. Weiss (Jerusalem, 1991), p. 8: "The principle of prayer: the rapture of the heart in the

love of the blessed holy One, as it is written, 'let all who seek the Lord rejoice' (1 Chron. 16:10). Thus David played an instrument."

49. G. D. Cohen, "The Hebrew Crusade Chronicles and the Ashkenazic Tradition," in *Minhah le-Nahum: Biblical and Other Studies Presented to Nahum M. Sarna in Honour of His Seventieth Birthday*, ed. M. Brettler and M. Fishbane (Sheffield, 1993), pp. 36–53. Another dimension of this homology is related to the fact that the very act of composing the lament is a form of liturgical worship by means of which one comes close to the divine. See, for instance, the concluding couplet of the dirge composed by Eleazar of Worms, in *Sefer Gezerot*, p. 167: "I bless thee with every poetic measure that I pronounce / to thee I bow down and worship," *lekha ʾavarekh be-khol middah shir ʾahawweh / lekha ʾekhraʿ we-ʾeshtahaweh*.

50. Chazan, *European Jewry*, p. 281.

51. The poem, together with the addition of Eleazar, is published in Haberman, *Sefer Gezerot*, pp. 66–68.

52. *Shirat ha-Rokeah: The Poems of Rabbi Eleazar ben Yehudah of Worms*, ed. I. Meiseles (Jerusalem, 1993), p. 269 (in Hebrew).

53. I have translated from the version of the poem in A. M. Haberman, *Shirei ha-Yihud we-ha-Kavod* (Jerusalem, 1948), p. 49. For discussion of this liturgical poem, with special reference to the motif of divine coronation, see A. Green, *Keter: The Crown of God in Early Jewish Mysticism* (Princeton, 1997), pp. 106–120.

54. This older mystical motif is attested in a passage from the long chronicle translated in Chazan, *European Jewry*, pp. 278–279: "His prayer ascended to the heavens, to the chair [of the glory], sweetness for the eternal. It became a crown and a diadem for the head of the almighty God, the King of all kings, the Holy One blessed be he." In this context, however, the utilization of the older mythical theme is meant to underscore the deplorable condition of Jews during the time of the Crusade, when not even prayer could alter the heavenly edict.

55. See the Ashkenazi text in MS New York, Jewish Theological Seminary of America Mic. 1878, fol. 108b, cited and analyzed in Wolfson, *Through a Speculum That Shines*, p. 202; H. Liss, *Elʿazar Ben Yehuda von Worms: Hilkhot ha-Kavod. Die Lehrsätze von der Herrlichkeit Gottes: Edition, Übersetzung, Kommentar* (Tübingen, 1997), pp. 124–125, and in the Hebrew section pp. 21 (§ 21), 22 (§ 23), and 40 (§ 44).

56. Jer. 31:22.

57. Isa. 60:7.

58. Ps. 135:4.

59. See M. Bar-Ilan, "The Idea of Crowning God in Hekhalot Mysticism and Karaitic Polemic," *Jerusalem Studies in Jewish Thought* 6, 1–2 (1987): 221–233 (in Hebrew).

60. Palestinian Talmud, Mo'ed Qatan 3:5 (ed. Venice, 82d); Babylonian Talmud, Berakhot 11a, 16b; Sukkah 25b; Mo'ed Qatan 15a. See Targum to Ezek. 24:17, and the commentary of Rashi ad loc., as well as the latter's commentary to Babylonian Talmud, Ta'anit 16a, s.v. *pe'er tahat 'efer*.

61. See Wolfson, *Along the Path*, pp. 37–39, 158–159 n. 234, 161–163 nn. 246–248; idem, "Sacred Space and Mental Iconography: *Imago Templi* and Contemplation in Rhineland Jewish Pietism," in *Ki Baruch Hu: Ancient Near Eastern, Biblical, and Judaic Studies in Honor of Baruch A. Levine*, ed. R. Chazan, W. Hallo, and L. H. Schiffman (Winona Lake, 1999), pp. 587–628, esp. 610–614. On the identification of the crown and the divine name in older esoteric works, see G. Scholem, *Jewish Gnosticism, Merkabah Mysticism, and Talmudic Tradition* (New York, 1965), pp. 54–55.

62. Wolfson, *Through a Speculum That Shines*, pp. 264–265.

63. To provide one example that I have not cited previously in my published work, see Liss, *El'azar Ben Yehuda von Worms: Hilkhot ha-Kavod*, p. 86, and in the Hebrew section, p. 58 (§ 58): "When Israel make the blessing, the glory is expanded. 'Your pious ones will bless you. They shall speak of the glory of your kingship, to make his mighty acts known among men, and the majestic glory of his kingship' (Ps. 145:10–12). For the glory of the splendor expands, and the diadem of blessings is glorified as one blesses with the love of the heart, in joy and in fear combined, and they make a crown until the righteous departs from the world, and they shall restore it to him, 'the Lord of Hosts shall become a crown of beauty and a diadem of glory' (Isa. 28:5)."

64. See P. Schäfer, *The Hidden and Manifest God: Some Major Themes in Early Jewish Mysticism* (Albany, 1992), pp. 104–106.

65. Wolfson, *Along the Path*, pp. 40–41. On the theurgical role of Akatriel as the angel who places the crown woven from the prayers of Israel on the head of the glory, and the identification on the part of some figures of Akatriel and God, see *Sefer Gematriot of R. Judah the Pious, Facsimile Edition of a Unique Manuscript*, introduced by D. Abrams and I. Ta-Shema (Los Angeles, 1998), pp. 40–41 (in Hebrew). Regarding the angelic versus the divine status of Akatriel, see the sources discussed in Wolfson, *Through a Speculum That Shines*, p. 262 nn. 314–315; and Abrams, "From Divine Shape to Angelic Being," pp. 52–55.

66. An illustration of the use of eschatological images to describe the mystical state of the pietists is found in *Sefer ha-Yir'ah*, included in *Sefer Hasidim*, § 15, p. 17: "There are righteous individuals (*saddiqim*) who merit to be near the *Shekhinah*, as it says, 'The Lord will shine upon you' (Isa. 60:2), and it is written, 'the soul of my lord will be bound up in the bundle of life of the Lord, your God' (1 Sam. 25:29), and it is written, 'and the Lord will be a light for you everlastingly' (Isa. 60:19)." A careful contextual reading of the passage indicates that

these verses are interpreted as a reference to the condition of the righteous individual while he is still alive in a bodily state in this world.

67. For a synoptic edition and translation of several recensions of this legend, see G. Reeg, *Die Geschichte von den Zehn Märtyrern* (Tübingen, 1985).

68. See A. Goldberger, "Eine Bemerkungen zu den Quellen und den redaktionellen Einheiten der Grossen Hekhalot," *Frankfurter Judaistische Beiträge* 1 (1973): 1–49; J. Dan, "Hekhalot Rabbati and the Legend of the Ten Martyrs," ʾ*Eshel Beʾer Shevaʿ* 1 (1980): 63–80 (in Hebrew).

69. For a different approach to this question, see I. Marcus, "The Sanctification of the Name in Ashkenaz and the Story about R. Amnon of Mainz," in *Sanctity of Life and Martyrdom*, pp. 131–147 (in Hebrew).

70. *Sefer Hasidim*, § 2, pp. 4–5. A fuller depiction of the love of God together with the fear of God occurs in § 13, pp. 11–12, and § 15, p. 17.

71. Chazan, *European Jewry*, pp. 254, 283, 285, 287.

72. See Babylonian Talmud, ʿAvodah Zarah 35b.

73. Chazan, *European Jewry*, pp. 119–121, 163, 221, 242, 254, 267. See also Fishbane, *Kiss of God*, pp. 72–73.

74. Chazan, *European Jewry*, p. 281. Curiously, the verse is attributed to King David even though the Song of Songs is traditionally ascribed to Solomon.

75. Ibid., p. 282; see p. 286.

76. Ibid., pp. 279–280.

77. Ibid., p. 279.

78. It is of interest to consider the narrative about the slaughter of Gedaliah and Yehiel ben Samuel in Chazan, *European Society*, pp. 276–277. The love of the two young men is described in terms of the love between Saul and his son Jonathan depicted in 2 Sam. 1:23, "beloved and cherished, never parted in life or in death." No explicit connection is made to the love of God, but it is possible that the emphasis on their love must be understood in this light.

79. *Sefer Gezerot*, p. 65.

80. 2 Sam. 1:23. Significantly, in the biblical context, the reference is the love of Saul and Jonathan.

81. *Sefer Gezerot*, p. 65.

82. Eliezer ben Natan, a leading Ashkenazi rabbinic figure of the eleventh century, uses this expression in one of the laments he includes in his chronicle of the First Crusade. See *Sefer Gezerot*, p. 73.

83. Scholem, *Major Trends*, pp. 95–96; G. Vajda, *L'Amour de dieu dans la théologie juive du moyen âge* (Paris, 1957), pp. 149–162; M. Harris, "The Concept of Love in Sepher Hassidim," *Jewish Quarterly Review* 50 (1959): 13–44; Marcus, *Piety and Society*, pp. 35–36; J. Dan, *Hebrew Ethical and Homiletical Literature* (Jerusalem, 1975), pp. 134–136 (in Hebrew); idem, "A

Re-evaluation of the 'Ashkenazi Kabbalah'," *Jerusalem Studies in Jewish Thought*
6:3–4 (1987): 136–137 (in Hebrew).

84. Interestingly enough, in the passage from *Sefer Hasidim*, § 53, p. 45,
the lust that a man has for a married woman is expressed in terms of the biblical
image, "For love is as potent as death" (Song of Songs 8:6). Just as the love of
God must be tested to the point of death, licit desire is as powerful as death.
The connection between love of God and martyrdom is noted by Dan, *Hebrew
Ethical and Homiletical Literature*, p. 136.

85. The reference most likely is to Num. 25:11–14, which recounts the
zealousness of Phinehas on behalf of God. In the biblical narrative, Phinehas
does not express this enthusiasm by sacrificing his own life, but by taking the
life of another who desecrated the name.

86. The citation of these verses in this context is rendered more transpar-
ent by a remark in *Perush ha-Roqeah ʿal ha-Torah*, ed. C. Konyevsky (Benei
Beraq, 1986), 1:140 (ad Gen. 14:23). The author of this text, who was part of
Eleazar's circle, connects the oath of Abraham with the state of a religious persecution on account of the statement in the Babylonian Talmud, Sanhedrin
74b, wherein the example used to illustrate the "light commandment" (*miswah
qalah*) that cannot be transgressed in the time of crisis is the demand to change
the straps of the sandal. Plainly, this exegesis underlies the inclusion of these
verses in the passage from *Sefer Hasidim*. That is, Abraham stands as an example of someone who sanctified God's name by refusing to change a custom
that would blur the distinction between Jew and non-Jew.

87. 2 Kings 5:15–16.

88. *Sefer Hasidim*, § 815, p. 206. An abbreviated, but almost verbatim,
version of this passage is found in Eleazar of Worms, *Sod Maʿaseh Bereʾshit*,
which is the first part of *Sode Razayyaʾ*, printed in *Sefer Raziʾel*, 9a (*Sode
Razayyaʾ*, pp. 9–10). For a slightly different version of this text, see *Sefer
Hasidim*, ed. R. Margaliot (Jerusalem, 1957), § 14, pp. 64–65, and § 300, p. 240
(this recension is based on the *editio princeps* of *Sefer Hasidim*, Bologna, 1538).
In the continuation of the former passage, the passionate love that one must
have for God is described in terms borrowed from Maimonides' account in the
Mishneh Torah, Hilkhot Teshuvah 10:2–3, which must be seen as a later addition to the base text, as noted by Dan, *Hebrew Ethical and Homiletical Literature*,
p. 126.

89. The original Hebrew is *tiyyulim*. The expression most likely has a sexual connotation. In Eleazar's *Sod Maʿaseh Bereʾshit* (see reference in the previous
note) as well as in his *Sefer ha-Roqeah* (see following note), the reading is *tiyyulei
ʾishto*, "excursions with his wife." See the use of the expression *halakh*, "to
walk," in the exemplum regarding the man who withstood the temptation of

committing adultery in *Sefer Hasidim*, § 53, p. 45, translated and discussed in D. Biale, *Eros and the Jews: From Biblical Israel to Contemporary America* (New York, 1972), pp. 72–73.

90. *Sefer ha-Roqeah* (Jerusalem, 1967), pp. 5–6. See reference to the passage from Eleazar's *Sod Maʿaseh Bereʾshit* cited above, n. 88.

91. *Sefer Gezerot*, p. xiii.

92. Ibid., pp. 164–167.

93. *Perushei Siddur ha-Tefillah la-Roqeah*, ed. M. Hershler and Y. A. Hershler (Jerusalem, 1992), p. 98.

94. Ibid., p. 704.

95. Based on Song of Songs 8:6.

96. *Perushei Siddur ha-Tefillah la-Roqeah*, p. 451.

97. Scholem, *Major Trends*, p. 106; H. Ben-Arzi, "Asceticism in Sefer Hasidim," *Daʿat* 11 (1983): 39–45 (in Hebrew). On the pietistic attitude toward sexuality, see also Marcus, *Piety and Society*, pp. 42–43, 46–47, 79; Biale, *Eros and the Jews*, pp. 72–82; E. Kanarfogel, "Rabbinic Attitudes towards Nonobservance in the Medieval Period," in *Jewish Tradition and the Nontraditional Jew*, ed J. J. Schachter (Northvale, N.J., 1992), pp. 3–35, esp. 17–26.

98. Marcus, *Piety and Society*, pp. 11 and 34, correctly notes that the asceticism advocated by Hasidei Ashkenaz is grounded in the soteriological principle that an increase of suffering in this world maximizes the reward in the spiritual hereafter. See also Dan, *Hebrew Ethical and Homiletical Literature*, pp. 137 and 144.

99. See Baer, "Socioreligious Orientation," pp. 64, 73, 85; Scholem, *Major Trends*, p. 92; Dan, *Esoteric Theology*, pp. 36–37.

100. See the description of the woman as fire in the passage from Eleazar cited below at n. 124.

101. *Sefer Gematriot*, p. 27.

102. *Sefer ha-Shem*, MS London, British Museum 737, fol. 171a; *Perushei Siddur ha-Tefillah la-Roqeah*, pp. 464–465.

103. A number of scholars have discussed this key term in the theosophical writings of Hasidei Ashkenaz. For references, see E. R. Wolfson, "The Doctrine of Sefirot in the Prophetic Kabbalah of Abraham Abulafia," *Jewish Studies Quarterly* 3 (1996): 64–65 n. 162, to which may now be added Liss, *Elʿazar Ben Yehuda von Worms: Hilkhot ha-Kavod*, pp. 180–185. Another important literary attestation to the notion of God's *hawwayot* in a relatively early Ashkenazi source is the poem for the circumcision ritual by Judah the Pious, published in Abraham bar Azriel, *Sefer ʿArugat ha-Bosem*, ed. E. E. Urbach (Jerusalem, 1963), 4:190.

104. MS Oxford, Bodleian Library 1566, fol. 38a. I have previously cited or referred to this source and the ones mentioned in the following two notes. See *Through a Speculum That Shines*, p. 239 n. 202; *Along the Path*, pp. 113–114 n. 20.

105. MS London, British Museum 737, fol. 213a.

106. Ibid., fol. 310b.

107. *Midrash Tanhuma'* (Jerusalem, 1972), Wayyaqhel, 7. On God constricting his presence to the Ark, see also *Bere'shit Rabbah*, ed. J. Theodor and C. Albeck (Jerusalem, 1965), 4:4, pp. 27–28.

108. Consider the liturgical formula preserved in the Babylonian Talmud, Berakhot 60b, "overturn my impulse to worship you," *we-khof 'et yisri lehishtta'bed lakh*. And the description of Abraham in *Bemidbar Rabbah* 14:11, "he subdued his inclination (*she-kafaf 'et yisro*) and he withstood the ten trials."

109. Two themes related to Moses are combined here: his distinctive modesty, which is mentioned explicitly in Numbers 12:3, and his sexual abstinence, which is derived exegetically from a number of verses, including most prominently Numbers 12:8 and Deuteronomy 5:27–28. See *'Avot de-Rabbi Natan*, ed. S. Schechter (Vienna, 1887), ch. 2, p. 10; Babylonian Talmud, Shabbat 87a, Yevamot 62a; *Sifre on Numbers*, ed. H. S. Horowitz (Jerusalem, 1966), sec. 103, p. 101; *Shemot Rabbah* 46:3.

110. *Sefer Hasidim*, § 59, p. 47. I have previously discussed the prohibition of looking at women in some of the relevant sources of Hasidei Ashkenaz in "The Face of Jacob in the Moon: Mystical Transformations of an Aggadic Myth," in *The Seduction of Myth in Judaism: Challenge and Response*, ed. S. Daniel Breslauer (Albany, 1997), pp. 243–244, and again in "Sacred Space and Mental Iconography," pp. 627–628.

111. Babylonian Talmud, Berakhot 24b.

112. *Sefer Hasidim*, § 978, pp. 241–242.

113. Babylonian Talmud, 'Eruvin 18b; Nedarim 20a; 'Avodah Zarah 20a-b; Zevahim 118b.

114. *Synopse zur Hekhalot-Literatur*, ed. P. Schäfer with M. Schlüter and H. G. von Mutius (Tübingen, 1981), § 314. The requirement to curtail conversation with women is found in ibid., §§ 507 and 623. See also *Geniza-Fragmente zur Hekhalot-Literatur*, ed. P. Schäfer (Tübingen, 1984), G 19, p. 165, where the recommendation is not to look at men or women, indeed not even an infant. Regarding these sources, see R. Lesses, "Speaking with Angels: Jewish and Greco-Egyptian Revelatory Adjurations," *Harvard Theological Review* 89 (1996): 57 n. 80.

115. On the contrast between the pietist (*hasid*) who does not gaze upon the face of women and a non-pietist who does, see *Sefer Hasidim*, § 1940, p. 469.

On the problematic role assigned to the feminine in the pietistic literature, see J. R. Baskin, "From Separation to Displacement: The Problem of Women in *Sefer Hasidim*," *AJS Review* 19 (1994): 1–18.

116. *Sefer Hasidim*, § 978, p. 241.

117. Mishnah, 'Avot 6:4.

118. Ibid., 4:21. The precise language of that passage, which is attributed to Eliezer ha-Qappar, is, "Jealousy, desire, and glory remove a man from the world."

119. Ibid., 1:12.

120. Ibid., 1:6.

121. *Sefer Hasidim*, § 31, pp. 94–95 (Margaliot edition); see ibid., § 35, pp. 97–98.

122. *Sefer Hasidim*, § 991, p. 245.

123. The model for the pietist is the description of the prophet given in *Sefer Hasidim*, § 425, p. 126 (a better reading in this case is preserved in the Bologna edition, § 773): When his soul was bound to God with a powerful love, it was as if he were no longer in this world.

124. *Sefer ha-Roqeah*, p. 30. On the prohibition of gazing at women or at their jewelry, see ibid., p. 26.

125. Eleazar emphasizes the importance of not looking at the face of women in *Hokhmat ha-Nefesh* (Safed, 1913), 13d. In that context as well, this is presented as a necessary condition for the attainment of a visionary experience in the afterlife. On the requirement not to sin with the eyes, which are associated particularly with the cherubim, see *Sode Razayya'*, p. 152.

126. See Biale, *Eros and the Jews*, pp. 78–80. Biale insightfully gives the title "sexual pleasure as prophylactic against temptation" to his discussion of the pietists' advocacy of sex with one's wife as a means of diminishing the erotic impulse.

127. See *Sefer ha-Roqeah*, p. 27. The voyeuristic portrayal of the woman as essentially a sexual object that arouses man's desire is also suggested by *Sefer Hasidim*, § 1084, p. 275. In that context, the verse "Your wife should be as a fruitful vine within your house" (Ps. 128:3) is interpreted didactically as providing the model for sexual modesty: A man should engage in sexual relations with his wife only within the confines of his house and not in a spot that would be open to public view so that others might desire her. It would be of interest to compare the pietistic application of this verse to the kabbalistic interpretation. Regarding the latter, especially in zoharic literature, see E. R. Wolfson, "Occultation of the Feminine and the Body of Secrecy in Medieval Kabbalah," in *Rending the Veil: Concealment and Secrecy in the History of Religions*, ed. E. R. Wolfson (New York, 1999), pp. 139–141.

128. *Perushei Siddur ha-Tefillah la-Roqeah*, p. 674, previously cited in Wolfson, "Sacred Space and Mental Iconography," pp. 626–627.

129. Babylonian Talmud, Berakhot 17a.

130. See *Perushei Siddur ha-Tefillah la-Roqeah*, p. 433. According to a much older motif, which is appropriated by Hasidei Ashkenaz, on Yom Kippur as well the people of Israel attain the status of angels. See ibid., p. 694.

131. That is, both expressions, *sullam* and *zeh kisse' ha-kavod*, equal 130.

132. Babylonian Talmud, Shabbat 152b.

133. *Hokhmat ha-Nefesh*, 13b-c.

134. The nexus between vision of the glory and circumcision is stated explicitly in the pietistic text transcribed by J. Dan, *Studies in Ashkenazi-Hasidic Literature* (Ramat-Gan, 1975), pp. 186–187 (in Hebrew). See also the German pietistic sources mentioned in *Through a Speculum That Shines*, pp. 249 n. 251 and 343 n. 53.

135. See E. R. Wolfson, "Circumcision, Vision of God, and Textual Interpretation: From Midrashic Trope to Mystical Symbol," *History of Religions* 27 (1987): 189–215, revised version in idem, *Circle in the Square: Studies in the Use of Gender in Kabbalistic Symbolism* (Albany, 1995), pp. 29–48, and notes on pp. 140–155.

136. See references to Judah Halevi and Maimonides cited in Wolfson, *Circle in the Square*, p. 145 n. 32. See also Biale, *Eros and the Jews*, pp. 91–92.

137. That is, both words equal 300.

138. *Sefer Gematriot*, p. 105. On occasion in the writings of Hasidei Ashkenaz, following remarks made in earlier rabbinic sources, the Jewish males below are rendered superior to the angels above insofar as the former subdue their evil inclinations whereas the latter have no evil inclinations. See, for instance, *Perushei Siddur ha-Tefillah la-Roqeah*, p. 429.

139. *Midrash Tanhuma'*, ed. S. Buber (Vilna, 1885), 1:127.

140. The biblical basis for this transgression is Deuteronomy 22:23–27, and it is applied exegetically to Esau in earlier aggadic sources. See *Pesiqta' de-Rav Kahana*, ed. B. Mandelbaum (New York, 1962), 3:1, p. 37.

141. This exegetical connection is already implied in the earlier midrashic sources. See reference in previous note, and the statement transmitted by R. Levi in the name of R. Hama bar Haninah in *Bere'shit Rabbah* 63:13, p. 698.

142. See J. J. Collins, "A Symbol of Otherness: Circumcision and Salvation in the First Century," in *"To See Ourselves As Others See Us": Christians, Jews, "Others" in Late Antiquity*, ed. J. Neusner and E. S. Frerichs (Chico, Calif., 1985), pp. 163–186; A. Segal, *Paul the Convert: The Apostolate and Apostasy of Saul the Pharisee* (New Haven, 1990), pp. 187–223; and D. Boyarin, *A Radical Jew: Paul and the Politics of Identity* (Berkeley, 1994), pp. 25–27, 36–38, 106–135.

143. On the possibility that the rabbinic legend about Esau's rejection of circumcision was originally meant to be anti-Christian in nature, see L. Ginzberg, *The Legends of the Jews* (Philadelphia, 1968), 5:273 n. 25.

144. The Ashkenazi polemic with Christianity over the issue of circumcision is evident in Ephraim ben Simson, *Perush ʿal ha-Torah*, ed. E. Korach, Z. Leitner, and C. Konyevsky (Jerusalem, 1992), p. 54. In his commentary to the verse, "At the age of eight days every male among you you shall be circumcised," *u-ven shemonat yamim yimmol lakhem kol zakhar* (Gen. 17:12), he writes: "*u-ven shemonat yamim*, the first letters spell *yeshu* [Jesus]. This alludes to the fact that in the future he would perform the circumcision and he would remove it. There is an allusion at the end of the verse 'from every one who is a stranger' (*mi-kol ben nekhar*) that his actions were alienating to his father in heaven. 'Who is not from your seed,' that is, the birth of Jesus was not from a legitimate seed, for his mother was impregnated through fornication." The passage was cited by M. Leahman, "Allusions to 'That Man' and to Mohammed in the Commentaries of Hasidei Ashkenaz," *Sinai* (1980): 39 (in Hebrew).

145. This, too, is an older rabbinic theme. See *ʾAvot de-Rabbi Natan*, ch. 2, p. 12; *Midrash Tanhumaʾ*, Bereʾshit 11, Noah 5.

146. On the homology between Adam and Abraham, which is related more specifically to the divine image, see *Perushei Siddur ha-Tefillah la-Roqeah*, pp. 704–705. See also *Sode Razayyaʾ*, p. 145: "He commanded circumcision in order to declare that there is no matter of the foreskin above, and that one should not marry the uncircumcised amongst those who worship their other gods, and they should preserve the 248 positive [commandments] *bi-selem ʾelohim* ('in the image of God'), which is allusion to *ʾavraham*." That is, the name for Abraham in Hebrew equals 248, which is the numerical equivalent of the expression "in the image of God," as well as the number of positive commandments. The connection between Adam, Abraham, and the divine image in the esoteric teaching of Hasidei Ashkenaz bears resemblance to a symbolic complex evident in a passage from *Sefer ha-Bahir* and developed by later kabbalists. See *The Book Bahir: An Edition Based on the Earliest Manuscripts*, ed. D. Abrams (Los Angeles, 1994), § 6, p. 121 (in Hebrew); and discussion in Wolfson, *Along the Path*, p. 210 n. 91.

147. See Eleazar's remark in *Sefer Raziʾel*, 8b (*Sode Razayyaʾ*, p. 6): "Moreover, the *yod* corresponds to Abraham, for the *yod* [when spelled out as *yod-waw-dalet*] equals twenty, and there were twenty generations from Adam until Abraham." If we may assume that the *yod* also relates to the sign of circumcision first given to Abraham, then it seems that implicit in this passage is the idea that through circumcision the perfection of Adam is realized.

148. *Sefer Gematriot*, p. 105. See also pp. 33–35.

149. A similar presentation is offered by Eleazar of Worms, *Perushei Siddur ha-Tefillah la-Roqeah*, pp. 723–724.

150. Eleazar of Worms, *Perushei Siddur ha-Tefillah la-Roqeah*, p. 723, cites Ezek. 44:9 as the prooftext to support the contention that Esau, the uncircumcised one, was not worthy to offer sacrifices and thus he was compelled to give up the birthright to Jacob. See discussion of this exegetical point in Babylonian Talmud, Zevahim 18b and 22b. On the tannaitic exclusion of one who is uncircumcised from the sacrificial rite, see Mishnah, Zevahim 2:1.

151. See Ms London, British Museum 737, fol. 310b.

152. Particularly relevant is the angelic form of the cherub, which is associated in rabbinic literature with either the small visage or an infant (Babylonian Talmud, Hagigah 13b). Consider, for example, Eleazar, *Hokhmat ha-Nefesh*, 13c, where the word *keruv* ("cherub") is said to be numerically equal to the expression *ke-yeled qatan* ("like a small child"). In fact, the word *keruv* equals 228 and the expression *ke-yeled qatan* equals 223. It is possible that the text should be emended so that the latter expression is *ke-yeled ha-qatan*, which equals 228; I have not, however, found an extant version of this text to support this surmise. On the use of the adjective *qatan* to designate the cherub, and especially the association of this symbolism with Jacob, see Wolfson, *Along the Path*, pp. 14–15, 32–36, 43, 121–122 n. 66, 155–156 n. 224, 156 n. 226. When I wrote the study on the image of Jacob engraved on the throne (October–November 1989), I was of the opinion that the locution *qatan* when applied to the cherub signified the feminization of a lower glory in relation to the masculine nature of the upper glory. I did not, however, pay attention to the possibility that this terminology might also suggest an ascetic dimension when applied to the earthly Jacob. In the final analysis, these two explanations may be viewed as two sides of the same coin, for ascetic renunciation on the part of the male can be viewed as a form of emasculation.

153. See *Sefer ha-Shem*, MS London, British Museum 737, fols. 166b, 169a, 302a. See below, n. 157. On the confluence of these different symbolic images, see Eleazar's observation in his *Perush Sefer Yesirah*, 1d, on the first passage of that work wherein ten names of God are delineated: "Thus he mentioned ten names . . . and you find that the ten commandments that the blessed holy One made audible to our forefathers before Mount Sinai correspond to the ten sayings until the point that there did not remain any commandment, for every one was comprised under the ten commandments."

154. For the distinction between the names that can be erased and those that cannot, see Babylonian Talmud, Shavu'ot 35a.

155. Mishnah, 'Avot 5:1.

156. Regarding this older midrashic motif, see E. R. Wolfson, "Mystical Rationalization of the Commandments in Sefer ha-Rimmon," *Hebrew Union*

College Annual 59 (1988): 224 n. 42. See Moses ben Eleazar ha-Darshan, *Sefer ha-Qomah*, MS Rome-Angelica 46, fol. 12a: "YHWH [signifies the] ten commandments (*yod dibberot*). He who denies the name, even if he fulfills all of the ten commandments, is a complete heretic (*goy gamur*), and it is as if he denies the entire Torah. Since the *yod* is the smallest of all the letters, it merited to stand at the head of the name, and the *yod* governs the world-to-come."

157. See, for example, *Sefer ha-Shem*, MS London, British Museum 737, fol. 166b; and the text of Eleazar published by Dan, *Studies in Ashkenazi-Hasidic Literature*, p. 88, wherein YHWH is glossed as *ʿeser hawwayot*, the "ten essences," which are identified as the ten depths mentioned in *Sefer Yesirah* as an explanation of the *sefirot*.

158. It is important to recall that Eleazar added an epithet to his own name, the "one who is small," *ha-qatan*, in order to qualify the ostensible pride of mentioning his own name as the author of a particular work with a sense of humility. See, for example, *Perushei Siddur ha-Tefillah la-Roqeah*, p. 228, previously cited by a number of scholars, for instance, Dan, *Esoteric Theology*, p. 15. Regarding this scribal practice of Eleazar, see Marcus, *Piety and Society*, p. 113. It is plausible that this self-referential term was meant to convey in a more technical sense Eleazar's ascetic practices. Indeed, for Eleazar, this is the true meaning of docility, for to be humble one must conquer bodily temptation.

159. *Sefer ha-Shem*, MS London, British Museum 737, fol. 165b. On the esoteric transmission of secrets to those who are chaste and meek, see *Sefer Hasidim* § 796, and discussion of this passage in Marcus, *Piety and Society*, p. 67.

160. In *Perushei Siddur ha-Tefillah la-Roqeah*, p. 708, Eleazar alludes to the secret of the divided throne, which is only revealed to the "humble of the generation" (*sanuʿa ba-dor*). On the sexual, and presumably phallic, connotation of this mystery, see Wolfson, *Along the Path*, p. 159 n. 234.

161. Babylonian Talmud, Menahot 29b.

162. *Sefer Raziʾel*, 8b (*Sode Razayyaʾ*, p. 6).

163. K. Herrmann, *Massekhet Hekhalot Traktat von den himmlischen Palästen, Edition, Übersetzung, Kommentar* (Tübingen, 1994), pp. 182, 310–311, and in the Hebrew section p. 78 (§ 26, 4).

164. *Battei Midrashot*, ed. S. Wertheimer (Jerusalem, 1980), 2:406.

165. The pietistic ideal of enlargement through diminution is reminiscent of a passage in *Zohar* 1:122b (parallel in 3:168a), "Praiseworthy is the man who belittles himself in this world. How great and exalted he shall be in that world! . . . Whoever is small will be great; whoever is great will be small."

166. Based on Isa. 57:15.

167. MS London, British Museum 737, fol. 168b. For a parallel to this passage, see Liss, *Elʿazar Ben Yehuda von Worms: Hilkhot ha-Kavod*, pp. 27, 93–94, and in the Hebrew section p. 4 (§ 2).

168. *Wayyiqra° Rabbah*, ed. M. Margulies (New York and Jerusalem, 1993), 7:2, p. 152; *Midrash Tehilim*, 4:3, p. 43; *Midrash °Otiyyot de-Rabbi °Aqiva°*, in *Battei Midrashot*, pp. 369–370.

169. See, for instance, Eleazar of Worms, *Sode Razayya°*, ed. I. Kamelhar (Bilgoraj, 1936), p. 6.

170. Eleazar of Worms, *Perush Sefer Yesirah* (Przemysl, 1883), 2c–d.

171. *Sefer ha-Shem*, MS London, British Museum 737, fols. 167a–b; and parallel in *Perush Sefer Yesirah*, 3a.

172. *Sefer ha-Shem*, MS London, British Museum 737, fol. 169a.

173. For a more detailed discussion of this passage, see Wolfson, *Through a Speculum That Shines*, p. 246.

174. *Sefer ha-Shem*, MS London, British Museum 737, fol. 169a.

Signs of Romance:
Hebrew Prose and the
Twelfth-Century Renaissance

SUSAN EINBINDER

At the turn from the eleventh to the twelfth century, a new Hebrew prose genre vividly portrayed the effects of the crusades and of subsequent persecutions on the Jewish communities of Ashkenaz and northern France. While the historical events have understandably captured the attention of scholars, this new turn to prose also commands attention. It is all the more intriguing because it occurred nearly simultaneously with the appearance of vernacular romance. This essay will explore the connections between these two phenomena, with particular attention to those narrative techniques that allowed an exploration of inner conflict and motive, hence a new sense of self.

Certain attitudes and interests associated with twelfth-century romance appear in our Hebrew prose texts, where romance techniques are employed to express human stances. Moreover, as romance evolved, so did, in an analogous shift, the Hebrew prose. To show this, this essay will compare, first, vernacular romance and Hebrew prose texts, and then compare earlier Hebrew prose to later works, namely, the 1096 chronicles to the works of Ephraim of Bonn. Piyyut, left for future examination, proved largely resistant to narrative and to the techniques under discussion.

Of all the vernacular genres to which Jews, especially northern French Jews, might have been exposed, romance, like Hebrew prose, was the newest. The metrical, rhymed narratives of Chrétien de Troyes appeared in Champagne in the mid-twelfth century. The romance form was preeminently suited to explore inner life together with issues of psychological conflict and growth, concerns important for the Hebrew texts. The romance, moreover, was written. While vernacular hagiography and religious drama are attested in writing only from the thirteenth century onward, despite earlier oral circulation, the great religious and military epics known as chansons de geste took written form in the twelfth century. They counterpoint romance concerns and deserve a separate study. Romance writing, like the Hebrew, captures certain attitudinal trends. The genre did not cause these changes but rather reflected their presence in the culture, even as it reinforced and disseminated these new modes of representation and self-perception.

An attention to detail and realia, to shifting points of view and individual motive, to inner conflict and self-awareness, to private desire over against public demands, and to love as a source of ennoblement or degradation—all these are early romance characteristics that convey a new sense of self. So, too, is the new literary visibility of women. As the romance hero is tested in love, his inner growth is reflected in the types of women who surround him; women embody the best and worst of the protagonist's private impulses and public obligations. Their presence documents as well greater attention to the domestic sphere and to emotional life. The following examples examine narrative techniques, such as the monologue, that express inner conflict and doubt; techniques which create pathos through images of women and children; and use of the narrative doublet. The adoption of similar techniques in Hebrew prose attests to its participation in the intellectual concerns and cultural spirit that characterized the romance world. Hebrew prose, likewise, evolved over the twelfth century. In part that evolution parallels trends in the romance, which becomes more pessimistic, salvific, and misogynist in the thirteenth century. In part this development points toward interests particular to the Jewish writers and their audience, including a returned emphasis on the communal and conventional that moves toward a historiographical prose.

The monologue, with roots in Ovid,[1] is a major tool of romance writers and has been widely discussed by scholars.[2] It evolved from "painful self-confrontation" inspired by love to an anatomy of inner moral and intellectual conflict.[3] The early *Roman d'Éneas* uses monologue,[4] and the technique is fully developed in Chrétien's "Erec and Énide" in the series of internal debates that mark Énide's maturation as a heroine.[5] In our Hebrew texts, monologue figures in Solomon b. Samson's depiction of the tormented R. Isaac the Parnas.[6] As Jeremy Cohen noted, this is the longest story devoted to a single martyr in the chronicle. Its contradictions revolve around issues of public and private apostasy, and Isaac's monologue pointedly captures his shame, confusion, and contradictory rationalizations.[7] Having survived the Crusader attack by submitting to baptism, Isaac returns to the cellar of his house, saying to himself:

> Of what good is all this money to me now, since the enemy fulfilled its purposes . . . to distance me from the Lord and to cause me to rebel against the Torah of our holy God. . . .[8]

Slowly, Isaac arrives at the decision that he must atone for his error by death. God knows, he nonetheless rationalizes, that he only converted in order to save his small children, who are so young they "cannot distinguish between good and evil."[9] As Cohen observes, this argument is contradicted later, when Isaac asks his children's assent to their sacrifice.[10] Isaac, who has already burned his mother in her bed, slaughters his children in the sanctuary in the name of "the sublime and exalted God, who commanded us . . . to cleave to his holy Torah" (*ledabbeq betorato*). Setting fire to the sanctuary, he ignores the Christians who hold out a beam (*vayoshitu lo toren*) for him to grasp.[11] The monologue presents all the confusion and contradiction of Isaac's decision, and the narrative parallels them in polarized images of light and fire (*'ur* and *'or*), *Torah* and *toren*.

Isaac's monologue explores his motives by allowing us to follow his unfolding thoughts and compare them to other details supplied in the narrative. The monologue dramatizes the process of conflict and resolution. In our next example, motive is also a chief concern, but the internal struggle of the protagonist is not explicitly revealed. Motive is rather to be inferred from the split-second decisions of characters in crisis, and their consequences. This is the story of R. Amnon of Mainz, attributed in the *Or Zarua* to Ephraim of Bonn.[12] Although Ivan Marcus has discussed this small text in detail, let me emphasize its literary finish. The vividness, hysteria, and confusion that mark the 1096 story of Isaac the Parnas stand in sharp contrast to the studied symmetry and minimalism of the later story, which owes much to martyrological conventions.[13] The treatment of Isaac the Parnas followed his doubts and terrors to the horror of their final resolution. In contrast, Ephraim's R. Amnon appears only through an externalized series of oppositions, set first in the bishop's court and then symmetrically resolved in the synagogue. At the story's core, his name, Amnon, signals his faith (*emunah*) and counterpoints his refusal (*me'un*) to convert. The actions in the story are stylized and iconographic; they focus attention on the "sin" of Amnon's doubt.

Such a price for an infinitesimal hesitation! Marcus has observed that no other Ashkenaz tale of martyrdom centers on the protagonist's doubt, or punishes wavering with such extremity.[14] But there is a romance analogue in Chrétien's "Knight of the Cart,"[15] where a moment's wavering has long and painful consequences. When Lancelot, unarmed and unhorsed, pursues the kidnapped Guinevere, he encounters a dwarf with a horse-driven cart used to draw convicted criminals through the town. Hesitating briefly, he climbs in. After a series of perilous escapades, he succeeds in rescuing the queen. To his horror and humiliation, however, she refuses to speak to him. Much later, she will explain:

> Did you not hesitate for shame to mount the cart? . . . That is the reason why I would neither address nor look at you.[16]

In her eyes, his brief hesitation mars the purity of his love. Penance is exacted on the tourney field where, at the Queen's signal—and to public abuse—the best knight in the world must deliberately joust poorly and lose. The magnified flaw and punishment reflect the extreme ideal of service to the beloved. In the story of R. Amnon, who failed *his* Beloved in a second of doubt, the Hebrew prose text provides a religious analogue.

Human love in the Hebrew chronicles tends to be familial rather than romantic. In clear contrast to the romance's emphasis on adulterous love, to the chanson de geste's emphasis on political marriage, and to vernacular hagiography's emphasis on celibacy, much of the pathos of Jewish martyrology is evoked in family scenes. This conforms to Kenneth Stow's observation that the increasing importance of the monogamous family unit was reflected in martyrdom as a "demonstration of family solidarity," an interpenetration of "Jewish familial and spiritual ideals."[17] Even so, the great detail, liveliness, and narrative sympathy with which scenes of pathos are related owe much to romance style. The gruesome story of Rachel and her four children stresses the 1096 narrative's concern with details that convey Jewish resolve amidst chaos.[18] The mother cries and wails, then slays one boy; the two girls offer their necks to the knife; and the fourth child must be dragged out, shrieking, from under a chest. In general, the women of 1096 exemplify the courage of their community; here, the mother's action reinforces our sense of its singlemindedness. The two daughters old enough to understand willingly offer themselves to be killed.

Compare the scene in "Amis et Amiloun" (or "Amis et Amile"), whose oldest version, by Rodulfus Tortarius, dates to about 1090.[19] The story found wide circulation on the continent and in Britain in different genres, including chanson de geste, romance, and a saint's vita. Amis is told in a divinely inspired dream that his friend Amile may be cured of leprosy by bathing in the blood of Amis' two children. At night, Amis enters the children's room, where the two children gently sleep in their bed. Overcome with sorrow, he hesitates, then steels himself to the task. In the French chanson de geste, the elder boy awakens:

> Biax tres douz peres, dist l'anfes erramment,
> Quant vos compains avra garissement
> Se do nos sans a sor soi lavement
> Nos sommez vostre, de vostre engenrement,
> Faire en poez del tout a vo talent.
> Or noz copex les chies isnellement. . . . (3000–3005).

> Li cuens Amiles vint vers le lit esrant,
> Hauce l'espee, li fiuls le col estent,
> Or est merveilles se li cuers ne li ment.
> La teste cope li peres son anfant
> Le sans recuit el cler bacin d'argent
> A poi ne chiet a terre. (3018–3023)[20]

"Dear sweet father," said the boy right away, "If your companion can be healed with the blood of our bodies, do with us as you will; you gave us life, and we are your flesh. Cut off our heads quickly. . . . Count Amile stepped up to the bed and, as he raised the sword, his son stretched forth his neck. It's a wonder his heart didn't fail him—but the father brought the blade down on his child and collected the blood in the shining silver bowl. He could hardly keep from fainting away.

And in the Middle English romance,

> No lenger stint he no stode,
> Bot hent his kniif with dreri mode
> & tok his children tho;
> For he nold nought spille her blode,
> Ouer a bacine fair & gode
> Her throtes he schar atvo.
> & when he hadde hem bothe slain,
> He laid hem in her bed ogain. (2305–2315) [21]

When Amis' wife rises in the morning and seeks to go into the nursery, he explains to her what he has done. Her response affirms the primacy of the friendship over the parental relation:

> "O lef liif," sche seyd tho,
> God may sende ous childer mo,
> Of hem haue thou no care. . . . (2390–2392)

Both Rachel and Amis are depicted in intimate settings. Their thoughts, dialogue, and actions are rendered with vivid realism. Yet the differences are also obvious: Amis' wife is not present at her children's slaughter. In the English version, the children do not awaken to consent to their slaughter, and in neither version is the mother's approval sought before the deed. In all versions, God heals the leprous Amile and restores the boys to life as well—this is the 'miracle.'

Solomon b. Samson's story of Sarit, the young fiancee among the Cologne martyrs, also illustrates the new narrative interest in women and pathos.[22] The scene is portrayed with vivid confusion—the "beautiful and comely" young woman trying to flee, her father-in-law seizing her and holding her up to the window, then seating her in her betrothed's lap and hewing her in two. The narrator ensures that the bride's death takes place before witnesses, as would have her marriage; the symbolism of slaughter and sexual consummation converge in her graphic dismemberment. This story exposes a curious ambivalence. Its biblical echoes go back to Amnon and Tamar, and to Lot and his daughters. The event fluctuates on a spatial border unclearly established between inside and out (the window) and on a typological border dangerously blurred (between "the bosom of Abraham your father" and Abraham the son, Sarit's betrothed; between the father-in-law and the proxy consummation with Sarit he shares with his son). Sarit's martyrdom is cast ambivalently. But the energy and breathlessness with which the characters are depicted, the urgency and emotion of the father's dialogue, the girl's panic and iconic death, owe much to romance style. Sarit's martyrdom, too, is exemplary; it integrates her into an ideal as it immortalizes her struggle. Her story still reinforces the moral emphasis of the narrative, ambivalences and all.

By the late twelfth century, however, at least one Jewish author shows signs of a shift in interest and convention. Ephraim's *Sefer Zekhirah* (1177) describes a young scholar, Shimon bar Yitzhaq of Wurzburg, who was brutally wounded in an attack precipitated by a blood libel.[23] Despite his twenty wounds, he survived a year (1.133). His sister was dragged into the church to be baptized, but she spat on the cross and was beaten:[24]

> They beat her with stone and fist, as they would not bring swords into the house of impurity. But she did not die, but fell to the ground among them. So she pretended to be dead, and they wounded her with their hands and blows, and burned her burn upon burn to see if she was dead or not. They laid her upon a marble stone, from [Ramreaux?], but she did not stir or move or budge her arms or legs. Thus she deceived them until nightfall, until a Christian laundress came and carried her to her home and hid her and saved her. The rest of the Jews found refuge among their neighbors. . . . (135–44)

In comparison to the stories of 1096, the woman's passivity is striking. The biblical references to Exodus 21:18,25 create an uneasy and powerful subtext of justice denied, of excess without compensation. Symmetrically, the girl's behavior inverts an earlier event: the incident begins with a libel accusation in which the corpse "made signs" (i.e., as if it were alive), and concludes with the just-cited description of the live girl playing dead. Once she has spat on the cross, her actions are either negative or passive: she "didn't die," "didn't stir," "didn't move or budge." The result is that "she deceived them." The truly energetic female in the story is the laundrywoman, who "carried her," "hid her," and "saved her," in rapid verbal sequence. In contrast, the sister's de-animation functions to illustrate other behavior. Like her brother, she survives, auguring the fate of the remaining Jews, who find refuge among Christian neighbors.

In sum, the Wurzburg sister's depiction is very different from what we have seen in the prose narratives of 1096. It lacks any interest in interior motive or thought process, it emphasizes her passivity and negative action, and it situates her in a context that stresses a failure of legal justice and reciprocity. Ephraim actually "forgets" to finish her story,[25] an accusation hardly suitable to the case of Sarit. The scene is drawn with great detail and yet reinforces thematically the averted disaster that drives the overarching narrative. But a different convention is at work. Taken with the other women in the *Sefer Zekhirah*, the sister's story suggests a more subdued role for women in Ephraim's scheme of things, and an increasing tendency to devalue them as autonomous agents. The Jewish women of the *Sefer Zekhirah* still reinforce male values and actions. Close inspection of Ephraim's addendum, however, completed about 1196, confirms that even this convention gives way. The only woman's martyrdom described in the later text, that of the mother buried alive in Neuss, concludes with an all-male list of martyrs and the rescue of the Jews. Her death is not only marginalized, it runs counter to the direction of the overall narrative.

Another standard characteristic of romance narrative is its reliance on doublets, either in the form of doubled figures or plots. Often two women dramatize an internal conflict for the hero torn between different values or options, as he struggles toward some new identity.[26] Sometimes they represent the ideal versus the available—Lancelot is torn between Guinevere and Elaine, Tristan between the two Iseults. In other cases, two knights embark on separate paths to the same goal. In "The Knight of the Cart," Lancelot, inspired by love, takes the Sword Bridge and Gawain, moved by reason, the water bridge, both to rescue Guinevere.

The narratives of 1096 display doubling in the use of iconographic polarities and conflated imagery (the earthly and eternal, the holy and profane, the Jewish and Christian), which characterize many individual stories. Narrative doublets are not part of this repertoire, but are a common feature in the work of Ephraim of Bonn. Sequential doubling structures the highly symmetrical narrative of R. Amnon, as it does the inverted imagery of the "live" corpse and "dead" sister in the Wurzburg story. The *Sefer Zekhirah* provides still other examples. The story of Shimon of Triers, who is beheaded, is followed by the story of Mina, whose ears and hands are cut off.[27] Two Jewish boys are murdered, when "they were impelled by their youthful spirit" (*vatesiyam yaldutam*) to leave their village and come up (*la'alot*) to see the Jews in Wolkenburg;[28] soon after, three Worms moneylenders are killed when "they were impelled by the king's decree (*vatesiyam gezerat hamelekh*) to go down (*laredet*) the hill, to meet with disaster as well.[29] In Ephraim's addendum to the *Sefer Zekhirah*, composed some twenty years later, this feature becomes even more startling. As Chazan has observed, the entire appended text is organized in a chronological loop. First it depicts five disastrous incidents between the years 1171 and 1196, then six covering the same period in which intervention by secular authorities saved the Jewish communities from destruction.[30] But the larger double narrative is echoed in many miniature examples. The two opening stories bring us high-ranking and powerful women, one Jewish and two Christian, all implicated problematically in the fate of the Jews. Complementing these incidents, two stories have lower-class Christian women incite Christians against Jews, once in the market and once in the church. In two stories, female corpses provoke violence against the Jews. The mother in Neuss is buried alive following the story of the dead Jewish daughter, in Cologne, whom the Christians exhume.

Ephraim, in my view, has adapted a romance technique to convey his sense of history as driven by political forces, and not by individual moral conflicts. His vision of history is one which guarantees retributive justice and sees Jewish safety linked to monarchical protection and power. Just as vernacular romance is turning sharply inward, Ephraim signals a movement away from the personal and back toward a more collective historical view. In this, he both diverges from and converges with thirteenth-century trends. As exemplified in the Grail romances, the prose romance moves away from the twelfth-century quest for glory, adventure, and love, and toward a knightly preoccupation with "the salvation of the soul." Characteristic of the increasing "discord and fragmentation" of thirteenth-century courtly literature, too, is a more ambivalent portrayal of women. Spiritually suspect and morally weak, she is potentially destructive to the knight's salvation.[31] Both the greater misogynism and the ambivalence about female types are recognizable in Ephraim's work. Jewish women he marginalizes and silences; his Christian women are outspoken and destructive. The most positive portrayal of a woman martyr in the 1196 text, the mother of Neuss, occurs in a narrative where the chief conclusion is that disaster was averted, thus undermining her martyrdom.

Certain trends in twelfth- and thirteenth-century hagiography may also be reflected in Ephraim's later writing,[32] including the suppression of "independent female piety"[33] as well as the popularity of the genre known as hagiographical romance, which employed romance techniques in the portrayal of holy women and men. Most striking, however, is the shift away from the vivid portraiture that characterized the 1096 texts. Whether this movement is generic or idiosyncratic requires further study, but it is curious. One century after Hebrew prose narrative bursts upon the scene, it has become a highly conventionalized and stylized narration of events, far from the agony and immediacy of its prose beginnings.

In sum, romance techniques and interests, particularly as related to the expression of interiority and inner conflict, are visible in twelfth-century Hebrew prose. Their use was mediated through Jewish communal and textual institutions and preexisting conventions of Hebrew writing. The narratives of 1096, at one end of the century, like the writings of Ephraim of Bonn at the other, testify to a comparably significant degree of literary innovation.

NOTES

1. Robert Hanning, *The Individual in Twelfth-Century Romance* (New Haven, 1977), 69.

2. Cesare Segre, "What Bakhtin Left Unsaid: The Case of the Medieval Romance," in *Romance: Generic Transformation from Chrètien de Troyes to Cervantes*, ed. Kevin and Marina Brownlee (Hanover, N.H., 1985), 29.

3. Hanning, *The Individual*, 58.

4. Christopher Baswell, "Men in the Roman d'Eneas: the Construction of Empire," in *Medieval Masculinities: Regarding Men in the Middle Ages*, ed. Clare Lees, Thelma Fenster, and JoAnn McNamara, Medieval Culture Series 7 (Minneapolis, 1994), 163–164.

5. Chrétien de Troyes, *Erec et Énide*, ed. and trans. (bilingual Old and modern French) Jean-Marie Fritz (Paris, 1992); English translation by W. Comfort, "Erec and Enide," in *Arthurian Romances* (New York, 1976).

6. A. Habermann, *Sefer gezerot ashkenaz vetsarefat* (Jerusalem, 1946), 36; Adolph Neubauer and Moritz Stern, *Hebräische Berichte über die Juden-verfolgungen während der Kreuzzuge* (Berlin, 1892), 13–14 (henceforth Neubauer and Stern); English translation by Robert Chazan, in *European Jewry and the First Crusade* (Berkeley, 1996), 243–297, at 262–264. The passage is treated at great length by Jeremy Cohen in "The 1096 Persecutions—Events and Narratives: Martyrological Stories in Socio-cultural Context" [Hebrew], *Tsion* 59 (1994): 169–208.

7. Cohen, "1096 Persecutions," 185, esp. 185–189; 193.

8. Neubauer and Stern, 11; English translation in Chazan, *European Jewry*, 263.

9. Ibid.

10. Cohen, "1096 Persecutions," 186–187 (ll.18 and 29) and discussion on p. 190; see Chazan, *European Jewry*, 264; Neubauer and Stern, 11.

11. Ibid. As Cohen notes, "1096 Persecutions," 787 (l.41) and compare the discussion on p. 194, the symmetric polarization extends to the imagery of fire and light as well. Isaac plans his suicide as a way of joining his comrades en route "to their circle, to the great light" (*'or*). The Christians scream to him to leave the burning building by telling him to "go out from the fire" (*'ur*).

12. Ivan Marcus, "Ashkenaz Martyrdom and the Story of Rabbi Amnon of Mainz" [Hebrew], in *Qedushat hahayyim vekheruf hanefesh*, ed. I. Gafni and A. Ravitzky (Jerusalem, 1993), 131–147; see also S. Eidelberg, "The Historical Background to the Tale of R. Amnon and the Prayer *Unetaneh toqef*" [Hebrew], *Hadoar* 53 (1974): 645–646.

13. See Charles Altman, "Two Types of Opposition and the Structure of Latin Saints' Lives," *Medievalia et Humanistica* 6 (1975): 2.

14. Marcus, "Ashkenaz Martyrdom." In Jacobus de Voragine's version of the life of St. Francis, the devil tempts St. Francis by telling him that "if someone kills himself with excessive penances, he will not obtain mercy forever."

St. Francis does inflict extreme penances upon himself for seemingly insignificant lapses. None, however, is a lapse of doubt or an instance of hesitation. See Jacobus de Voragine, *Legenda Aurea*, ed. T. Graesse, 3d ed. (1890; reprint, Osnabrück, 1965), 666. English translation by William Granger Ryan, *The Golden Legend: Readings on the Saints*, 2 vols. (Princeton, 1993), 2:223.

15. Chrétien de Troyes, *Le Chévalier de la Charrette, ou, Le Roman de Lancelot*, ed. Charles Mela (Paris, 1992); English translation by Comfort in *Arthurian Romances*, 270–359.

16. Comfort, *Arthurian Romances*, 327; Mela, *Le Chévalier*, 4484–85 and 4488–89.

17. Kenneth R. Stow, *Alienated Minority: The Jews of Medieval Latin Europe* (Cambridge, Mass., 1992), 93, 117, 197; 117.

18. Habermann, *Sefer gezerot*, 34; Neubauer & Stern, 11–12; Chazan, *European Jewry*, 258–259.

19. The oldest version is prose. The oldest vita dates to the first half of the twelfth century, and the chanson de geste version to c. 1200. According to J. Bedier, the versions are essentially the same and derive from a French chanson de geste "which combined feudal and Christian elements," in "Les Chansons de Geste et les Routes d'Italie," *Romania* 36 (1885): 343, cited by MacEdward Leach, ed., *Amis and Amiloun*, Early English Text Society, orig. ser. 203 (London, 1937), xix.

20. Peter Dembowski, ed., *Ami et Amile: Chanson de geste* (Paris, 1969), 96, laisse 154; English translation by Samuel Danon and Samuel Rosenberg, *Ami and Amile* (York, S.C., 1981), 116.

21. Leach, *Amis and Amiloun*.

22. Habermann, *Sefer gezerot*, 47; Neubauer & Stern, 20; Chazan, *European Jewry*, 279.

23. Ephraim of Bonn, *Sefer Zekhirah*, ed. A. M. Habermann (Jerusalem, 1970), 22–23 (lines 124–144), my translation.

24. Spitting on the cross would appear to be another recurring motif, as it appears also in a piyyut describing the martyrs of Erfurt (1221) by R. Eliezer bar Yehuda. I am compiling a list of such motifs.

25. He does this also, however, in the story of Pucelina of Blois.

26. Joan Ferrante, *Woman as Image in Medieval Literature: From the Twelfth Century to Dante* (New York, 1975), 75.

27. Habermann, *Sefer Zekhirah*, 18–19.

28. Ibid., 20, ll.75–84.

29. Ibid., 21, ll. 94–102.

30. Robert Chazan, "Ephraim Ben Jacob's Compilation of Twelfth-Century Persecutions," *Jewish Quarterly Review* 84.4 (April 1994): 397–416.

31. Ferrante, *Woman as Image*, 120; 99.

32. For the hagiographical trends, see Peter Dembowski, "Literary Problems of Hagiography in Old French," *Medievalia et Humanistica* 7 (1976): 117–130.

33. See, e.g., John Coakley, "Friars, Sanctity and Gender: Mendicant Encounters with Saints: 1250–1325," in *Medieval Masculinities*, 91–110, esp. 91; Michael Goodich, "The Contours of Female Piety in Later Medieval Hagiography," *Church History* 50 (1981): 20–32, esp. 21; JoAnn McNamara, "The *Herrenfrage:* The Restructuring of the Gender System, 1050–1150," in *Medieval Masculinities*, 3–29; André Vauchez, *La Sainteté en occident aux derniers siècles du moyen âge* (Rome, 1981), 219.

Anti-Jewish Attitudes in Twelfth-Century French Literature

MAUREEN BOULTON

The twelfth century in France, as elsewhere in Latin Europe, was a period of revival and expansion in social, cultural, and economic domains. French Jews in this period participated in this prosperity, and thrived as a community. At the same time, however, it is impossible to overlook the threatening signs which anticipate the deterioration of their situation in the next century. Both the development and the decline of the Jewish community in France have been examined by a number of eminent historians.[1] While the general role of Christian intellectuals in contributing to this change of status has been explored by these and other scholars over the last quarter-century,[2] the effect of contemporary vernacular literature on public opinion toward the Jews of France has received rather less attention. My object in this essay is to examine the attitudes toward Jews in general expressed by writers of vernacular works of the twelfth century and to establish whether and how they changed.

Some attempts have already been made to discern attitudes toward the Jews in the literature in Old French,[3] but only Gilbert Dahan, in studying dramatic literature, has made any attempt to trace changes in attitudes over time, especially in the earlier part of the period. Dahan found that until the thirteenth century, "nous n'avons guère relevé de portraits injurieux à l'égard des Juifs, ni de propos diffamatoires à leur endroit."[4] What emerges from my own examination of narrative texts composed toward the end of the twelfth century, however, is a clear, if unsurprising, hardening of anti-Jewish sentiments, culminating in violent denunciation in the early thirteenth century. These lines from one of Gautier de Coinci's *Miracles* (composed before 1230) will serve as an example of such sentiments:

> Mout les haï et je si fas.
> Et Diex les het et je les has
> Et toz li mons des doit haïr (209–11)
> Jez bruïroie toz ensanble. (316)[5]

> Greatly have I hated them, and so I do.
> And God hates them, and I hate them
> And everyone must hate them . . .
> I would burn them all together.

A progressive hardening of attitudes may be followed through four works written in the period 1181–1200: a biblical poem by Herman de Valenciennes, a passage from Chrétien de Troyes' *Conte du Graal*, an anonymous epic called the *Venjance Nostre Seigneur*, and Robert de Boron's *Joseph d'Arimathie*. Two of these (Herman de Valenciennes' poem and the *Venjance*) are vernacular versions of New Testament apocrypha that grew rapidly in this period. These texts actually add little to anti-Jewish views found in Latin works. As texts in the vernacular, however, with a much wider distribution among the laity, they had a greater influence on those people who were to perpetrate the increasingly frequent and serious outrages against the Jewish community in the later twelfth and the thirteenth centuries. In examining the attitudes toward Jews in vernacular texts, which both reflected and molded popular opinion, this essay highlights ways in which hostility towards the Jews of France was also promoted by the clerical elite in the final decades of the twelfth century.

Herman de Valenciennes, in his *Roman de Dieu et de sa mère*, made the first attempt (c. 1188–95) to produce anything like a complete vernacular Bible in a Romance dialect.[6] His work does indeed imitate the bipartite structure of the Christian Bible, but the Old Testament history is reduced to a series of anecdotes about notable individuals. In a similar fashion, the section referred to as the New Testament substitutes for the canonical collection of Epistles and Gospels a single versified life of Christ. From the canonical Gospels his so-called New Testament

borrows the Nativity, a selection of stories from the life of Christ, and
the Passion,[7] but includes in addition extensive apocryphal sections devoted to the life of the Virgin and concludes in many manuscripts with
an Assumption narrative. Clearly, Herman's poem was not based directly on the Bible; his source was the set of readings and lessons included in the Missal and Breviary.[8]

Before turning to representations of Jews in the *Roman de Dieu*, we
should note its form and style, which are significant in gauging its impact.
Herman adopted the monorhymed alexandrine laisses of the epic chanson de geste, and in the fashion of epics, he made frequent addresses to
his intended audience: "Signor, or entendez ice que vos dirai" (Lords,
listen to what I shall tell you [4161]); "Signor, que Dex vos doint sa grant
beneïçon! / Se vos bien m'escoutez, si orrez bon sermon" (Lords, may God
give you his great blessing / If you listen well, you will hear a good speech
[4280–81]); "Signor, icel miracle m'avez oï conter. / Ja en orroiz .i. autre
sel volez escouter (Lords, you have heard me recount this miracle. / Now
you will hear another if you wish to listen [4533–34]); "Or entendez,
signor, .i. pou si m'escoutez! (Now hear, lords, and listen to me a little
[4669]).[9] Herman thus establishes, and maintains by frequent repetition,
an immediate relationship between narrator and audience. His narrative
style is lively, and he has a good ear for dialogue. In addition to his es-
thetic claim on his audience, he maintains that his tale is true and composed at the request of no less a personage than the Blessed Virgin herself,
who is his patron. The fact that his poem is preserved in thirty-seven
manuscripts attests to his success in attracting an audience of lay noblemen to a collection of what amounts to Bible stories.

One might well expect to find positive representations of Jews in
the first portion of Herman's poem, and this is indeed the case. The portraits of Abraham, Isaac, Jacob, Joseph, Moses, Samuel, David, and
Solomon are all favorable.[10] What is striking, however, is how infre-
quent are the references to their Jewishness. Abraham is, indeed, acknowledged as the father of the Jewish people:

> Partriache en fist Diex si com trovons escrit;
> Des qu'il ot .xiiii. anz ainc a Dieu ne mentit,
> Ne ne le correça ne en fet ne en dit;
> Les commanz son signor volentiers aamplit.

Signor, vos le savez et bien l'avez oït
Que la genz des Gïus de cel saint home issit. (474–79)

God made him patriarch, as we find written;
From the age of fourteen, he was never false to God,
Nor angered him either in deed or word.
He willingly fulfilled the commands of his Lord.
Lords, you know, and have indeed heard it,
That the Jewish people issued from this holy man.

At Abraham's death Herman remarks: "Puis fu morz Abrehanz, pere a la bone gent" (Then Abraham died, who was the father of the good people [606]). Nevertheless, from this point in the poem until the account of the Exodus (some 1400 lines later), there is no indication that the actions and exploits recounted were performed by Jews. Even when the descendants of Abraham are distinguished from the Egyptians, Herman does not call them Jews but "the people of Joseph."[11] It is only during the account of their wanderings in the desert that they are identified as Jews. It is also notable that as references to the Jews increase in the next section of the work, so do the negative observations made about them. When they reproach Moses, Herman notes: "Li Gïu s'en tornerent a grant seducïon" (The Jews turned towards great seduction [2168]). The golden calf is made, he says, by "icele averse gent" (this perverse people [2183]). A little later in his account he asserts without explanation: "Signor, icil Gïu si furent molt felon" (Lords, these Jews were very treacherous [2273]).

   In fact, Herman de Valenciennes systematically suppressed the fact that these patriarchs were Jews. Furthermore, he appropriated them to his own (Christian) purposes. His text calls Abraham "nostre peres" (467, 500: our father),[12] and speaks of receiving reparation through him.[13] Likewise it attributes to David a prophecy of the virgin birth:

Cil David, icil rois, de Deu profetiza
Et de som bon linage dont la virge naistra,
De cui ventre Diex hom en terre devendra. (2497–99)[14]

This David, this king, prophesied about God
And of his lineage from whom the virgin will come,
In whose womb God will become man on earth.

In Herman de Valenciennes' account, then, the Jewish patriarchs become ancestors of the Christians,[15] and Jews are for the most part only mentioned as such when they are turning away from their God. These ideas were traditional in patristic literature;[16] Herman's innovation was to transmit clerical opinion to a lay audience.

If the appropriation of Jewish history to Christian purposes is at first implicit in the *Roman de Dieu*, Herman makes it explicit as he shifts his attention to the time of Christ.[17] The so-called New Testament portion of the poem actually contains four summaries of Jewish history, each inserted at a crucial point in the Christian narrative. The first, invoking the "linage Davi," prefaces the introduction of Joachim and Anne, the apocryphal parents of the Virgin.[18] The second passage associates the account of the birth of Mary with prophetical tradition (2993–3039), and includes a denunciation of Jewish unbelief in the Virgin from the mouth of Isaiah himself:

> Au profete Yssac [=Isaiah] .i. pou me tornerai.
> Or dites, bons profetes et je l'escouterai.
> "Par foi, dist Ysaïes, as Gïus parlerai.
> Qant lor dis l'aventure molt felons les trovai,
> La verge ele est florïe, dont je a aus parlai." (3012–16).

> I shall turn for a bit to the prophet Isaiah,
> Now speak, good prophet, and I will listen.
> By faith, says Isaiah, I will speak to the Jews.
> When I told them the tale, I found them very treacherous,
> The rod has flowered which I told them about.

The third summary forms a preface to the account of the Passion (5036–5086). The refusal of Jesus' contemporaries to be convinced by his miracles is set in the context of a long history of unbelief:

> Bien savez que la Bible escristrent ancessor,
> Icist livre fu faiz dou tens ancïenor.
> Ainz que Jhesus fust nez mil anz enqui entor
> Ama Diex les Gïus et mostra grant amor. . . .
> Or oez des Gïus, com furent deputaire.
> Ancontre lor escrit—si com il m'est viaire—

> Ce que dist lor escriz com il furent contraire
> Que d'aus naistra Cristus et rois et emperaire
> Et naistra de la virge. . . . (5036–39; 5077–81)

> You know well that the ancestors wrote the Bible,
> This book was made in ancient times.
> Before Jesus was born, for more than a thousand years,
> God loved the Jews and showed great love. . . .
> Now hear about the Jews, how they are of a bad race.
> Against their scripture—such is my opinion—
> They were opposed to what their scriptures told them,
> That from them would be born Christ, king and emperor,
> And he would be born of the virgin. . . .

The fourth passage, set immediately before the section describing the plans to arrest Jesus, underscores the theme of the Jews' ingratitude (5338–5448):

> Molt par furent toz jors et cuvert et felon.
> Qant furent delivré de la chaitivison,
> Faraons fu noiez dedanz mare Rubrun
> Et sa granz oz o lui a grant perdition,
> Et donnee lor fu dou ciel la garison. . . . (5350–54)

> They were always very miserable and treacherous.
> When they were delivered from slavery,
> Pharaoah was drowned in the Red Sea
> And his great host with him, to perdition,
> They were given sustenance from heaven. . . .

The account continues, showing them unsatisfied each time they received what they asked of God. Despite the fact, complains Herman, that they have had prophecies to warn them, the Jews refuse to recognize the arrival of the Messiah:

> Il troevent en lor livres,—ice n'est mie fable—
> Par la bouche au profete, qui dist parole estable,
> Que, qant icil naistroit qui feroit le miracle,
> Ja puis ne seroit jorz lor ointure durable. . . . (5406–09)

They find in their books—this is not a fable—
From the mouth of the prophets, who speak reliable words,
That, when he was born who would perform the miracle,
Their law would no longer be lasting.

Herman presents this persistent refusal to believe as the crowning ingratitude of Jewish history:

> Li sires ert venuz entr'ax por aus sauver,
> Grant amistié lor mostre, il nel voelent amer.
> Il les siut, il le fuient, nel voelent ancontrer.
> A soi les voet atraire, il le voelent damner. . . .
> Li felon molt deüssent itel signor amer. (5438–41; 5445)

The Lord came among them to save them,
He shows them great friendship, they do not wish to love him.
He follows them, they flee from him, they do not wish to meet him.
He wishes to attract them to him, they wish to condemn him. . . .
The traitors ought to have loved such a lord.

Furthermore, Herman cites in this passage a series of Jewish witnesses—
Symeon, Herod, and the crowd at the Palm Sunday entrance to Jerusalem—who did recognize Jesus.

    The reader is struck not only by the biased version of Jewish history
presented in these passages, but also by the repeated derogatory references to the Jews, who are relatively seldom simply "li Gïus," but are
usually characterized pejoratively: "felon" (treacherous), "chaitif" (mis-
erable), "dervé" (mad), "cuvert" (vile).[19] It is significant that in other
contexts the adjective "cuvert" is used to describe both Goliath and the
devil.[20] At one point there is a whole passage of insult:

> Molt par furent felon et de molt povre sens
> Molt servoient deables, pas n'en estoient lent,
> Plus erent venimex que n'en est .i. serpanz,
> Molt orent male entente, molt orent mal porpens. (5326–29)

They were very treacherous and of little sense
They served the devil well, and were not reluctant,

They were more poisonous than a serpent
They had most wicked intentions, they had most wicked aims.

The account of the Passion itself is remarkable for its tendency to excuse Roman participation in the execution and to place most of the blame on the Jews. For instance, when Pilate first appears, Herman says of him "molt ert sages hom" (he was a very wise man [6236]); this in sharp contrast to the Jewish accusers, whom Pilate refers to as "icil cu-vert felon" (those base traitors [6262]). Nevertheless, unlike some later French authors, Herman *does* attribute to the Romans the responsibility for the flagellation and crowning with thorns. However, it is not clear who—Romans or Jews—actually performed the crucifixion in Herman's narrative. Pilate turns Jesus over to the "sergenz" (6503), called "cel omecide" (those murderers) in the next line, and "cil felon bacheler" (those treacherous youths [6596]) somewhat later, and all three refer-ences could perfectly well refer to Roman soldiers. On the other hand, the citizens of Jerusalem,[21] in a marked departure from the gospel ac-counts, show sympathy for the crucified Jesus and declare that the "gïue genz" (the Jewish people [6674]) have brought destruction on the city by this act. After Jesus' death, Herman shows Roman officers in a rather positive light: Longinus pierces Jesus' side with a lance because "Ne voloit de ses os qu'il fussent entamé" (he did not want his bones to be broken); [22] and either he or another centurion is moved to an act of faith at the sight of the crucified body.[23] In another departure from the gospel accounts, it is Jews who arm themselves to guard the body, lest it be stolen by the disciples of Jesus.[24]

Herman de Valenciennes confines his hostility to Jews living in the time of Christ. He draws no explicit conclusions about Jews in his own society, and certainly does not exhort his listeners to attack them. This may seem a feeble virtue, but it is worth noting. On the other hand, the distinction between Jews of ancient and contemporary times seems to have been too subtle for the average twelfth-century layman, and Herman de Valenciennes is certainly responsible for promulgating a hostile attitude toward the former group.

There is evidence of this hostility in the last of the extremely influ-ential romances of Chrétien de Troyes (d. 1189/90), who was an older contemporary of Herman de Valenciennes. In Chrétien's *Contes du*

Graal, a group of penitent noblemen reproach the hero Perceval for not observing Good Friday.[25] When he asks what is special about the day, they respond with a brief account of the Crucifixion and Resurrection (6266–91) which is striking for its final lines:

> Li faus juïf par lor envie,
> C'on devroit tüer come chiens,
> Firent als mal et nos grans biens,
> Quant il en la crois le leverent;
> Als perdirent et nos salverent. (6292–96)

> The wicked Jews,
> whom we should kill like dogs,
> brought harm to themselves
> and did us great good when in their malice
> they raised him on the cross:
> They damned themselves and saved us.[26]

It is the second line of this passage that shocks, in its almost casual violence. This line has been cited as an example of the anti-Jewish sentiment of Chrétien himself, but in fact it is unsafe to attribute any passage in direct discourse to him, for he maintains an ironic detachment from most of the attitudes of his characters.[27] What the passage does illustrate, as it is meant to, is the common attitude of the nobility towards Jews in the final years of the twelfth century—an attitude which, in the light of the policies of the new king Philippe Auguste,[28] is less surprising than shocking.

The scriptural interpretation (and revisions) popularized by Herman de Valenciennes might seem sufficient to provoke such hostility, but it is still a leap to hold descendants guilty of a wrong committed more than a millennium earlier. Two other French texts, the epic *Venjance Nostre Seigneur* and the hagiographic romance *Joseph d'Arimathie*, bridge that gap and help to explain the virulent anti-Jewish hostility that emerges in the thirteenth century.

The anonymous *Venjance Nostre Seigneur*, composed in the latter part of the twelfth century, recounts in some 2,300 lines how the emperor Vespasian was miraculously cured of leprosy when he gazed upon the image of the face of Christ imprinted on Veronica's veil.[29] In gratitude for the cure, he decides to punish those responsible for the death of such a marvelous healer, including Pontius Pilate as well as the Jews. The sources of the poem, which include the *Cura sanitatis Tiberii*, the *Mors Pilati*, the *Vindicata Salvatoris*, as well as a Latin translation of Josephus's *History of the Jewish War*, were all used with considerable freedom, and the combination itself is original.[30]

The author has cast his poem in the same epic form as Herman, and clearly aimed at a similar audience. If the opening stanza is addressed to "baron, chevalier, et serjant / [Et li] home et les fames, li petit et li g[r]ant" (Barons, knights, and men-at-arms / And men and women, little and great [1–2]), elsewhere the author calls for the attention of "Seignor" (Lords).[31] In keeping with such an audience, the *Venjance* is military in character: fully a third of its stanzas deal with the attack and siege of Jerusalem by a Roman army (alternatively described as both pagan and Saracen) under the leadership of Vespasian and Titus. Although this poem itself probably had a relatively restricted circulation—it survives in only four manuscripts in its oldest form, and five others represent later verse redactions—still later prose versions are preserved in nearly fifty manuscripts, suggesting a wide readership.[32] Here again, even if the specific anti-Jewish attitudes found in the poem are traceable to older Latin sources, the author of the *Venjance* was responsible for circulating these attitudes among a wide audience of lay people.

A striking feature of the epic is the strong portrayal of good Jews, particularly Jacob (the father of Mary Magdalen) and a certain Josephus (who is intended to represent the historian). The author, however, had precisely one criterion for goodness in Jews: belief in Christ. Jacob is first presented to the audience with this attribute. He is:

> A un riche Juïf [qui] bone creance [a].
> Mout aime le sepulcre ou Dex resuscita
> Il i vait chascun jor, mout grant fiance i a
> Par lo mien escient bon loier en avra,
> S'arme iert en paradis si que ja ni faudra. (153–57)[33]

> A rich Jew who has good belief.
> Greatly does he love the tomb where God rose.
> He goes there each day and has great confidence,
> In my opinion he will have a good reward,
> His soul will be in paradise. . . .

His credentials established, Jacob is elsewhere referred to simply as "li bons Juÿs" (the good Jew [266, 366]). Jew though he is, he shares Christian and Roman opinion about those Jews implicated in the death of Jesus:

> Malement sont bailli nostre Judeu fellon
> Qui Jhesum travaillerent, en tort, en traïson (1180–81).

> Badly are our treacherous Jews rewarded
> Who tormented Jesus wrongly, by treason.

and he has no qualms about advising Vespasian on how best to lay siege to Jerusalem (1190–1203).

The portrait of Josephus is somewhat different, for he is clearly a scholar:

> Illuec est Josephus li prouz, li enseignez,
> Li hardis et li sages, li cortois, li proisiez,
> Ainz ne fu miaudres clers des noviax ne des viez . . .
> Li gentils clers, li larges, li cortois, li sachanz
> Mout par iert grant la joie quant en Deu ert creanz
> Car mout sot bien escrivre et latin et romanz.
> Ceste estoire escrira, s'en sera voir disanz,
> De ce qu'il vit as iaux por quoi seroit mente[n]z? (1246–48; 1371–75)

> There is Josephus the brave, the learned,
> The bold, the wise, the courtly, the esteemed,
> Never was there a better clerk, whether young or old . . .
> The noble clerk, generous, courtly, knowing
> There was great joy when he believed in God
> For he could write well in Latin and Romance.
> He wrote this story (and it is truthful),
> About what he saw with his eyes, why would he lie?

Unlike the other "good Jews," Josephus is caught in the siege of Jerusalem and wounded in one of the assaults. When he is ransomed by the Romans, he informs Vespasian about the state of the city (1536–38), and his description of the misery of the inhabitants moves Jacob to tears of pity. Nevertheless, the Josephus of this poem is also a believer in Jesus, who regrets that his fellow citizens have been misled by Pilate.[34]

It emerges clearly in this poem that there is no excuse for Jewish unbelief. Even participation in the execution of Jesus might be absolved by repentance and acceptance of his message,[35] but stubborn refusal to believe merits only one response, and that is punishment of the most extreme sort:

> Cil de Jafes lo voient . . .
> Volunters se rendissent por lor vie alonger,
> Mais Vaspasianus nel preïst nul denier
> Car toz les vorra prendre et vendre et essiller,
> Car i firent Judeu lor Seignor travailler.(736–40)
> Titus les prist a force, et il et si donzel
> Les Judex ont toz morz, mout en font grant moncel;
> Toz les ont destranchés. . . . (765–67)

> Those of Haifa see him . . .
> Willingly would they surrender to prolong their lives,
> But Vespasian would accept no ransom
> For he wished to take them all, sell them and exile them,
> For the Jews tormented their lord.
> Titus took them by force, he and his men
> Killed all the Jews, and made a great heap of them;
> They cut them all apart. . . .

When Pilate convinces the citizens of Jerusalem to surrender in the hope of ransoming themselves, Vespasian refuses their terms and sells them all into slavery at the insulting price of thirty slaves for ".i. denier" (a single piece of silver [2076]), because Jesus himself had been bought for thirty "deniers." Furthermore, the poet clearly considers Vespasian as the deputy of Jesus Christ himself: "Que ainsi prist venjance li poissanz Rois de Gloiri" (So the powerful King of Glory took his vengence [2349]). It is perhaps small comfort that a special punishment is reserved for Pilate. Vespasian orders "Que il le facent vivre longement en morant" (that they make him live a long time in dying [2288]). Pilate is locked in a well for two years; when he is brought out, he is put into an empty house that is promptly swallowed up by the earth and taken to hell (2324–2337).

Some of the distortions of history may be amusing to modern readers, but the overall message of the text—that Jews who refuse Christian belief deserve the most extreme punishments—can only appall. In the late twelfth century, in a society surrounding Jews with threats for a variety of other reasons, the audience of such a text might easily have considered their Jewish neighbors guilty of the same sort of refusal to believe, and hence felt justified in taking whatever vengeance was convenient.

Robert de Boron's poem on the Joseph of Arimathea legend is entitled, in the only manuscript that preserves it, *Le Roman de l'Estoire dou Graal*.[36] He composed it some years after Chrétien's *Conte du Graal* (1191–1202) with the intention of resolving some of the questions not answered by that unfinished romance, particularly about the nature of the Grail. Its survival in a single manuscript suggests that the original poem had but little success; however, Robert's poem was soon rendered into prose in a version that achieved a much wider popularity and is preserved in eighteen manuscripts.[37] Somewhat later still, the prose version was reworked into the *Estoire del saint Graal*, a belated prologue to the enormously successful Vulgate Cycle of Arthurian romances, and is thus likely to have exercised a very wide influence in the thirteenth and fourteenth centuries.

Although the Grail passages have most interested scholars to date, Robert's poem is significant in the current context because it illustrates the mechanism of the reception of the Passion narrative by means of repeated accounts of its main events. The cumulative effect of these narratives is to focus the guilt of the Crucifixion exclusively on the Jews, even to the point of exonerating Pilate.[38] The work opens with an account of the Passion and Resurrection that is comparatively neutral in tone (209–706). The condemnation of Jesus and Pilate's attempt to dissociate himself from it are recounted, but the actual crucifixion is not, because at the crucial point the author shifts his attention to Joseph's attempts to claim the crucified body for burial. The identity of the executioners, however, is not clearly specified in this original account. In this opening sequence, there is one insulting reference to the Jews which occurs in the passage introducing the protagonist of the romance. Joseph of Arimathea—described in Matthew's gospel as "a certain rich man from Arimathea . . ., who also himself was a disciple of Jesus," and by Luke as "a counsellor, a good and just man . . . [who] had not consented to their counsel and doings"[39]—is presented here as one of Pilate's soldiers who hid his love of Jesus because he feared the Jews, "la gent de pute aire" (the base-born people [206]).[40] With this exception, however, the remaining references to "Li Juïf" occur without modifiers.[41]

The original account of the events leading up to Jesus' death is summarized five more times in the poem, and with each new narrator it receives different emphasis and interpretation. On the first occasion, the imprisoned Joseph sees a vision of Christ, who explains to him the importance and significance of the Grail, here identified as the chalice of the last supper (707–960; esp. 779–90). Trying to be sure of the identity of his vision, Joseph asks if he is indeed Jesus:

> Cil que Judas trente deniers
> Vendi as Juïs pautonniers
> Et qu'il fusterent et batirent
> Et puis en la crouiz le pendirent? (783–787)

> The one whom Judas sold for thirty pieces of silver
> To the Jewish scoundrels
> And whom they struck and beat
> And then hung on the cross?

The Jesus of Joseph's vision accepts this rather biased account of the passion: "Je sui icil tout vraiement" (Truly I am that one [791]), and later in their conversation contributes his own description of "mauveis Juïs mescreanz" (wicked misbelieving Jews [846]).

The remaining summaries of the Passion narrative are inserted into the section of the poem dealing with the vengeance taken against the Jews. Two of these are associated with the pilgrim who carries the tale of Jesus' miraculous cures and disgraceful death to Rome, where the emperor's son Vespasian suffers from leprosy. First the author provides a rapid summary of the miracles witnessed by this pilgrim (971–80), and then he asserts that Jesus was crucified by the Jews for refusing to obey their commandments and for seducing the populace (981–86). Upon his arrival in Rome, the pilgrim recounts these events to his innkeeper (1047–62), attributing to the Jews all the violence done to Jesus and making no mention of Roman participation. When news of his tale reaches the emperor, the pilgrim is questioned and then invited to retell the story to the imperial council. In this version (1149–62), the pilgrim's account of the miracles is summarized, but he assures the emperor that Christ would certainly have cured his son, and refers him to Pilate for corroboration.

The emperor, seeking to verify this story, sends messengers to Palestine to investigate. In an effort to avoid implication in the death of Jesus, Pilate gives his own version of the events (the fourth in the poem) to the imperial investigators. In his own interest, Pilate emphasizes the Jews' hatred and abuse of Jesus, and their envy of his miracles. When he comes to the arrest, he stresses his reluctance, and claims that it was the Jews who gave him no choice:

> Quant virent que nou vous jugier,
> Si se prisent a couroucier,
> Qu'il estoient genz mout puissant,
> De richesces comble et mennant;
> Et il distrent qu'il l'ocirroient,
> Que ja pour ce nou leisseroient. (1315–20)

> When they saw that I did not wish to judge him,
> They became angry,
> For they were very powerful people,
> Endowed with wealth and rich;
> And they said that they would kill him
> And would not leave him alone.

Indeed, not only (according to Pilate) did the Jews claim responsibility for the execution (1329–32), but they also carried it out:

> Il le pristrent et l'em menerent
> Et le batirent et fraperent,
> Et en l'estache fu loiez
> Et en la crouiz crucefiez
> Et ce que vous avez oï
> Avant que vous venissiez ci. (1333–37)

> They took him and led him
> And beat him and struck him,

> And he was bound to a stake
> And crucified on the cross
> Which you heard
> Before you came here.

Pilate ends his account with a reminder that he had publicly dissociated himself from the whole affair by "washing his hands of it" (1339–50).

Pilate's self-serving narrative succeeds in its object and convinces the emperor's deputies of his innocence.[42] The investigators turn next to the Jewish leaders, who, misled as to the nature of the inquiry (1417–30), unwittingly corroborate his account of the events. In a fifth version of the story, they highlight Pilate's reluctance to execute a culprit who wished to make himself king, and in so doing confirm Pilate's claim to innocence even as they admit their own guilt.[43] The investigation continues as the messengers inquire about Jesus' belongings, and Veronica is brought to them, with her veil that bears the imprint of his face. Both she and the veil are brought to Rome, where the sight of the relic cures Vespasian's leprosy. Rejoicing in his new-found health, Vespasian seeks to express his gratitude in a tangible way, and asks his father the emperor that he be allowed to avenge the death of Jesus, his "seigneur droiturier" (rightful lord) at the hands of "cil larrun puant Juïs" (those theiving, stinking Jews [1736–37]). In Palestine, after concluding his investigations, Vespasian announces:

> Je vueil touz ces Juïs destruire,
> N'en i avra nul qui ne muire;
> Bien s'unt seü tout descouvrir
> Pour quoi il doivent tout morir. (1887–90)

> I wish to destroy all these Jews
> And don't want there to be one who does not die;
> They have indeed revealed everything
> For which they ought all to die.

At the end of this speech, the emperor peremptorily kills thirty Jews. This section concludes a long conversation between Joseph of Arimathea and Vespasian, who is converted to Christianity; the remainder of his vengeance is summarized in two lines: "Vespasÿens a un seul mot / Fist des Juïs ce que lui plot" (Vespasian, by a single word, / did as he pleased with the Jews [2285–86]). In the final section of the poem, Joseph sails with his family and the Grail to England, preparing the groundwork for Arthur's knights.

The slippage in the attitude toward the Jews evident in Herman's account has here reached its culmination. The Romans escape any implication of guilt, which falls wholly on the Jews, and become the righteous avengers of the man executed as a criminal under Roman law. Even Joseph of Arimathea, one of the "good Jews" of the Gospel accounts, is transformed into a Roman soldier. If the actual scenes of violence against Jews are reduced in Robert's poem, the impact of Vespasian's summary executions is all the stronger. The editor of Robert de Boron's poem has described him as "a sorry poet. . . . But what he lacks in graceful expression and elegant poetic turn of phrase is made up for by a magnificent vision of universal history centered on the Holy Grail."[44] Unfortunately, there was no room for Jews in this immensely influential vision of history.

In this group of late twelfth-century French texts, all of which enjoyed considerable popularity and diffusion, there is a striking range of anti-Jewish sentiment—from verbal abuse to extreme physical violence directed against first-century Jews. As the only exoneration for a Jew was belief in Jesus, or conversion, the continued existence of a separate Jewish community clearly constituted persistent refusal to believe. With the spread of texts portraying the punishment and destruction of unbelievers of Jesus' day, it was not a great step to mete out the same treatment to contemporaries.[45]

NOTES

1. Robert Chazan, *Medieval Jewry in Northern France: A Political and Social History* (Baltimore, 1973), 49; Emily Taitz, *The Jews of Medieval France: The Community of Champagne* (Westport, Conn., 1994); Gérard Nahon, "Condition fiscale et économique des juifs," *Cahiers de Fanjeaux* 12 (1977): 37–43; William Chester Jordan, *The French Monarchy and the Jews: From Philip Augustus to the Last Capetians* (Philadelphia, 1989).

2. Gilbert Dahan, *Les Intellectuels chrétiens et les Juifs au moyen âge* (Paris, 1990), 23.

3. Manya Lifschitz-Goldin, *Les Juifs dans la littérature française du moyen âge, Mystères, miracles, chroniques* (New York, 1935; reprint, Geneva, 1977); Gerald Herman, "A Note on Medieval Anti-Judaism as Reflected in the *Chansons de Geste,*" *Annuale Mediaevale* 14 (1973): 63–73; Gilbert Dahan, "Le *Iudeus* du *Jeu de saint Nicolas* dit de "Fleury": Contribution à l'étude de l'image du Juif dans la littérature médiévale," *Cahiers de Civilisation médiévale* 16 (1973): 221–26; idem, "Les Juifs dans les Miracles de Gautier de Coincy," *Archives Juives* 16 (1980): 41–49, 59–68; idem, "Les Juifs dans le théâtre religieux en France du XIIe au XIVe siècles," *Archives Juives* 13 (1977): 1–10; Bernard Guidot, "L'Image du Juif dans la Geste de Guillaume d'Orange," *Revue des études juives* 137 (1978): 3–25; Udo Schöning, "Die Juden in der Chanson d'Antioche," *Zeitschrift für romanische Philologie* 102 (1986): 40–52. See also n. 27 below.

4. Dahan, "Le *Iudeus,*" 221. Similarly Bernard Guidot, in "L'Image du Juif," notes "Le *Moniage Rainouart* (c. 1190–1200) est la seule chanson de la Geste de Guillaume . . . qui, non seulement rende le peuple juif responsable de la Crucifixion, mais l'accuse de faits qui, objectivement, sont à mettre au mains des Romains" (11).

5. *Les Miracles de Nostre Dame par Gautier de Coinci,* ed. V. F. Koenig (Geneva and Paris, 1961), vol. 2.

6. Ina Spiele, *Li Romanz de Dieu et de sa mère d'Herman de Valenciennes,* Publications romanes de l'Université de Leyde 21 (Leiden, 1975). The problems of dating the text were reviewed by André de Mandach, "A Quand remonte la Bible de Herman de Valenciennes," *Mémoires du Cercle archéologique et historique de Valenciennes* 9 (1976): 53–69, who proposed the period 1188–95 as the probable date of composition.

7. In her description, Spiele, *Li Romanz de Dieu,* separates the Passion (laisses 528–688) from the rest of the New Testament section; her edition does not contain the end of the Passion, however, because the scribe of the manuscript she edited (Paris, B.N., fr. 20039) replaced the remaining laisses with an extract from the prose *Roman du Graal* by Robert de Boron, which she prints in the notes to her edition (389–91). In order to read the end of Herman's text, one must consult laisses 694–98 (his laisse 693 is Spiele's 688) of the edition by Ernst Martin, *La Bible von Herman de Valenciennes,* part 5, *Von Christi Einzug in Jerusalem bis zur Himmelfahrt* (Greifswald, 1914), 93–104.

8. Spiele, *Li Romanz de Dieu,* 40–45.

9. "Signor," 4230, 4305, 4417, 4433, 4581, etc.

10. "Abrehans fu prodom et plains de grant bonté, / Molt mena sainte vie puis qu'il vint en aé; / Onques n'ama mançonge, ainz ama verité, / Ne fu luxuriex, ainz ama chasteé" (331–34); "Molt fu prex Yssac et de grant vasselage" (610); "Or s'en va danz Jacob o sa beneïçon; / Son oncle va querant icil saintismes

hom" (957–58); "Or oez de Joseph, le beneoit anfant" (1252); [Moses] "Il estoit sages hom, molt s'est bien porpansez" (2099); "Et Moÿses, li sages" (2156); "Donc fu nez Samuel, que Diex molt honora" (2280); "Or en mainnent David, cel beneoit anfant" (2402); "Li rois David fu prex si mena grant ponee" (2471); "David fu molt bons rois et longuement regna" (2493); [Solomon] "Merveilles i fist faire, merveilles i ovra. / Nus ne le porroit faire, ce dist qui veü l'a / S'il n'avoi itel sens comme Diex li dona. Que il fu primes rois et enaprés rainna, / Ses jugemenz assist, garder les commenda" (2534–38); "Onques hom fors Adam n'en ot si grant savoir, / Ne en cest mortel siecle n'ot onques tant avoir; / Molt par fu redoutez et fu de grant pooir" (2623–26). The anonymous twelfth-century poem L'Estoire Joseph, ed. Ernst Sass, Gesellschaft für romanische Literatur 12 (Dresden, 1906), contains similarly favorable portraits of the patriarchs.

11. "La gent Joseph" (2028); "Li linages Joseph" (2035).

12. Cf. 516–17: "Or entendez a moi trestuit communement / Que Diex par Abrehan nos doint amendement."

13. "Que Dieux par Abrehan nos doint amendement" (517).

14. Spiele, Li Romanz de Dieu, 24, does not indicate any source for this attribution.

15. Cf. Yosef Hayim Yerushalmi, "Medieval Jewry from Within and Without," in Aspects of Jewish Culture in the Middle Ages, ed. Paul Szarmach (Albany, N.Y., 1979), 1–26, at 2–3.

16. Cf. Rosemary Radford Ruether, "The Adversus Judaeos Tradition in the Church Fathers: The Exegesis of Christian Anti-Judaism," in Aspects of Jewish Culture, ed. Szarmach, 27–50, at 31.

17. The author of the Estoire Joseph accomplishes the appropriation of Jewish history by means of a gloss: "L'estoire avez öie, / Oez que senefie. / Joseph dont nos lison / Senefie Jheson" (1587–90).

18. Spiele, Li Romanz de Dieu, 2692–2715.

19. Neutral references: 5039, 5114, 5121, 5131, 5138, 5249, 5273, 5300, 5306, 5319, 5338, etc; instances of "felon," 3031, 5064, 5110, 5159, 5165, 5350, 5362, 5366, 5398, 5445, etc.; "Chaitif," e.g., 5391; "Deputaire," e.g., 5077, 5086; "Dervez," e.g., 5196, 5413; "Cuvert," e.g., 5350, 5362.

20. See 5357 (Goulias); 4112, 4116, 4147.

21. "La genz de la cité," 6649, 6652, 6665; "La genz de Jurzalem," 6663.

22. Martin, La Bible, 6798.

23. "Centurions et autre qui che ont esgardé / Ont dit tot vraiement que chist est le fix dé" (Martin, La Bible, 6810–11).

24. Martin, La Bible, 6812.

25. Chrétien de Troyes, Le Roman de Perceval ou Le Conte du Graal, 2d ed., ed. William Roach, Textes Littéraires Français 71 (Geneva and Paris, 1959).

Another reference to Jews occurs in the instructions of Perceval's mother (577–94), but there it is a question only of those involved in the crucifixion; she makes no reference to contemporary Jews.

26. Chrétien de Troyes, *Arthurian Romances*, trans. William W. Kibler ("Erec and Enide," trans. Carleton W. Carroll) (London, 1991), 458.

27. Indeed, Chrétien's *Perceval* can be seen as deeply influenced by Jewish traditions. See Eugene J. Weinraub, *Chrétien's Jewish Grail: A New Investigation of the Imagery and Significance of Chrétien de Troyes's Grail Episode based upon Medieval Hebraic Sources*, North Carolina Studies in Romance Languages and Literatures (Chapel Hill, N.C., 1976); Leslie A. Fiedler, "Why Is the Grail Knight Jewish?" *Aspects of Jewish Culture*, ed. Szarmach, 151–70.

28. Chazan, *Medieval Jewry*, 64–69.

29. L. A. T. Gryting, *The Oldest Version of the Twelfth Century Poem, 'La Venjance Nostre Seigneur,'* University of Michigan Contributions in Modern Philology 19 (Ann Arbor, Mich., 1952). On the basis of linguistic evidence, Gryting says that the poem was written "c. 1200, certainly not long after and more probably a few years before," 31.

30. The sources of the poem have been examined in detail by Walther Suchier, "Ueber das altfranzösische Gedicht von der Zerstörung Jerusalems (La Venjance nostre seigneur)," *Zeitschrift für romanische Philologie* 25 (1901): 94–100.

31. 687, 942, 1381, 1405; cf. "Baron,": 18. 2136–38 invoke a wider audience: "Seignor, ceste chançon doit mout bien estre oïe / D'evesques et d'abés et de tote clergie, / De rois, de dus, de contes qui terre ot en baillie."

32. See Gryting, 2–4, on the verse manuscripts; for the later prose versions see Alvin E. Ford, *La Vengeance de Nostre Seigneur: The Old and Middle French Prose Versions*, Studies and Texts 63, 115 (Toronto, 1984, 1993).

33. Later in the poem he is described by means of a declaration of belief: "Je cuit en vostre terre ne n'a mellor baron / Bien croit en la prophete qui soffri passion" (452–53). According to Richard Heinzel, *Über die französischen Gralromane*, Denkschriften der Kaiserlichen Akademie der Wissenschaften in Wien: Philosophisch-Historische Classe 40 (Wien, 1891), 106, this Jacob is to be identified with James the Less.

34. "Amis, dist Josephus, je crei ben et aor / Ici com je doi faire Jhesum le Creator" (1561–62); "Pilate nos a mors, li cuvers soudoiamz" (1593).

35. Cf. Longinus: "Et Longis lo feri de la lance a bandon / Puis l'encria merci et il l'en fist pardon" (569–70).

36. The older edition, Robert de Boron, *Le Roman de l'Esoire dou Graal*, ed. William A. Nitze (Paris, 1927), has now been replaced by Richard O'Gorman, *Robert de Boron, Joseph d'Arimathie: A Critical Edition of the Verse*

and Prose Versions, Studies and Texts 120 (Toronto, 1994), which contains an extensive bibliography. See Rupert T. Pickens, "Histoire et commentaire chez Chrétien de Troyes et Robert de Boron: Robert de Boron et le livre de Philippe de Flandre," *The Legacy of Chrétien de Troyes*, ed. Lorris J. Lacy, Douglas Kelly, and Keith Busby, Faux Titre 37 (Amsterdam, 1988), vol. 2, 17–39, at 18–20 and n. 3. See also idem, "Robert de Boron," *Medieval France: An Encyclopedia*, ed. William W. Kibler and Grover A. Zinn (New York, 1995), which gives the date; and Pierre Le Gentil, "The Work of Robert de Boron and the *Didot Perceval*," *Arthurian Literature in the Middle Ages: A Collaborative History*, ed. Roger Sherman Loomis (Oxford, 1959), 251–62.

37. On these manuscripts, see O'Gorman, *Robert de Boron*, 6–12.

38. See ibid., 351, n. 423.

39. Matthew 27:57; Luke 23:50–51 (Douay Rheims translation); see also Mark 15:42–43 and John 19:38.

40. "La terre de Judee estoit / Souz Romme et a li repondoit, / Non toute, meis une partie / Ou Pilates avoit baillie. / A lui servoit uns soudoiers / Qui souz lui eut cinc chevaliers; / Jhesucrist vit, et en sen cuer / L'aama mout . . ." (195–202). The reasons for this transformation of Joseph's status are unclear. Jean Frappier, "Le Graal et la chevalerie," *Romania* 75 (1954): 165–210, at 188, suggested that Robert wished to glorify knighthood. For other explanations, see O'Gorman, *Robert de Boron*, 344, n. 200. For further discussion of Joseph, see Richard O'Gorman, "The Legend of Joseph of Arimathea and the Old French Epic *Huon de Bordeaux*," *Zeitschrift für romanische Philologie* 80 (1964): 35–42; and Valerie M. Lagorio, "Joseph of Arimathea: The Vita of a Grail Saint," *Zeitschrift für romanische Philologie* 91 (1975): 54–68.

41. "Li Juïf," 214, 606, 623, 649; "Uns Juïs," 397; "Li Juïs," 433.

42. "Quant li message unt ce escouté, / N'unt pas en Pilate trouvé / Si grant tort cum trouver quidoient" (1375–77); the messengers in turn convince the emperor, who observes: "Pylates si grant tort pas n'a / Cum nous jugïuns par de ça" (1639–40).

43. This interchange, including another manipulative ploy by Pilate, is repeated before Vespasian (1768–84).

44. Richard F. O'Gorman, "Robert de Boron," *The Arthurian Encyclopedia*, ed. Norris J. Lacy (New York, 1986).

45. Cf. Léon Poliakov, *The History of Anti-Semitism*, vol. 1, *From the Time of Christ to the Court Jews*, trans. Richard Howard (New York, 1974), 123.

Baptised Jews in German Lands during the Twelfth Century

ALFRED HAVERKAMP

Our topic will focus upon a central and deep rift in the diverse network of Jewish-Christian relations.[1] At the same time, however, it could also lead to overlooking the links between the two sides. It is important to stress from the outset that this essay does not intend to add to the continuing discussions that seek to pinpoint the precise time of the turning point in Jewish-Christian relations.[2] It would appear to me that these arguments do not always maintain sufficient distance from an organic and hence teleological model, or, in other words, that they are influenced by the assumption of an underlying movement toward a certain goal. In any case, it seems more pressing to grasp sufficiently the multifaceted nature of this network of relationships and its geographical and social demarcations. This is why I have restricted myself geographically, while hoping not to restrict the field of vision.

Despite the limitations put on the temporal and geographic scope, the horizons of this topic are still much too broad for us to elucidate them completely in this essay. The events and context of 1096 are only briefly touched on here because there are those at this and other conferences who have dealt with this subject recently.[3] The fact that the events of 1096 affected baptised Jews far into the twelfth century, and even beyond, remains unchanged by this omission.

The *Regnum Teutonicum* stood at the center in the aftermath of 1096. This is reason enough for concentrating geographically on the Roman Empire of Germany,[4] with its own particular conditions for Jewish life. Among these, the Jewish settlements themselves provided

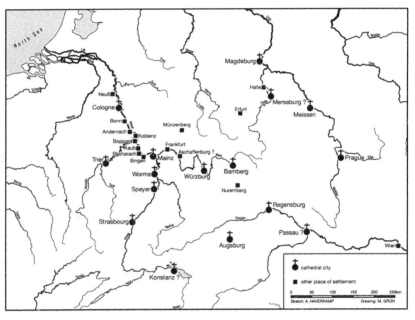

Jewish Settlements in the "Regnum teutonicum," c. 1200

the essential basis (see section I). Further reasons for focusing the field
of vision are found in the specific conditions for mission work and,
hence, for baptism. These include the norms and ideas of Christians toward baptism, the Jewish perceptions, and the problem of voluntary versus coerced baptism. I hope to offer an approach toward how baptised
Jews were valued by both Christians and Jews, and what position they
held in society in general (section II). I will not dwell for long on the
unrealistic question as to how many of the Jews did accept their baptism
and become Christians for good. However, based on a source which has
remained largely unheeded so far, it should be possible to shed more
light on the particular case of those young Jewish women who became
Christian owing more or less to intimate relationships with clerics (section III). The exceptional source material from Cologne allows for a
closer look at Jewish converts in the Rhenish metropolis (section IV).
These findings draw our attention to that especially informative type of
Jew who became baptised after long contact with the court of a bishop
or who was exposed to missionary attempts there. In this context, we

must also briefly mention the history of Hermannus quondam Judaeus from Cologne, which has aroused considerable attention in recent research, but it seems to me that other narrative material deserves more attention than it has received to date (section V). I want to look more closely at a tradition from the north Holland monastery, Egmond, remote even in the *Regnum Teutonicum*—the peculiar tale about a baptised Jewish martyr in Regensburg, one of the outstanding centers in the empire with an equally outstanding Jewish community (section VI). This Christian narrative from a region where Jews were only known from stories gives an occasion for a few concluding remarks (section VII).

I

Jewish communities suffered serious losses in 1096 and persecution in 1146/47 in connection with the Second Crusade. Despite these events, existing communities grew and Jewish settlements spread into new urban centers during the twelfth century, especially in the central *Regnum Teutonicum*, settled at an early date. During a phase of massive urbanisation, the cathedral cities—those outstanding centers of Christian cult which became so intimately bound up with the history of salvation and which contained an enormous number of clerics and a diversity of religious congregations[5]—remained the home of large Jewish communities.[6] In the course of the whole twelfth century, these communities were growing rapidly again. Only in Metz, the prosperous center of Lorraine, in many ways the equivalent of Cologne on the Lower Rhine,[7] did the pogrom of 1096 seem to have caused the end of a Jewish community.[8] On the other hand, besides those cathedral cities with surviving Jewries—such as Cologne, Mainz, Trier, Speyer, Worms, Regensburg, Magdeburg, Merseburg, and Prague—a number of others first attest to Jewish settlements during the twelfth century. These certainly included Strasbourg,[9] Würzburg, and Bamberg, and probably also Meißen, Augsburg,[10] and Passau.[11]

For the first time, we also have reliable evidence of permanent Jewish settlements in centers that were generally much younger and had much less in the way of urban life. These were amassed on the lower and middle Rhine and included Bonn, Andernach, Boppard, Bacharach,

Kaub, and Bingen.[12] In addition, there were the palatinate town of Frankfurt am Main and Münzenberg, which was the principal borough of the Staufen emperors' chamberlains.[13] Further away, there was Nuremberg, another Staufen palatinate town, Erfurt, the important center for the church of Mainz in Thuringia, and Halle, a trading center in the archbishopric of Magdeburg.[14]

Among these more recent settlements, apart from the cathedral towns, of which in total there were about half a dozen, the proportion of settlements under the control of the Staufer imperial rule was very high. Besides Frankfurt, Münzenberg, and Nuremberg, these included Boppard, Bacharach, Kaub, and Andernach (which in 1167 was placed under the control of the archbishop of Cologne). The few remaining towns were, without exception, under the authority of the archbishops of Cologne, Trier, or Mainz.[15] At Halle, the influence of the archbishop of Magdeburg certainly outweighed that of the king or emperor. Cathedral cities with larger Jewish communities—like Worms, Speyer, and also to some degree Strasbourg—were located in the center or vicinity of the Salian-Staufen imperial holdings. Alternatively, and this applies to Cologne, Mainz, Trier, and also Magdeburg, they were placed under the authority of the archbishops, who were, throughout the twelfth century and especially during the reign of Frederick I, closely linked to the imperial rule,[16] despite the various conflicts caused above all by territorial policies. Regensburg deviated from this rule, since it was an old center of the Bavarian dukedom, but the dukes, including Henry the Lion, did not exert a dominating influence there. After the fall of the Welf, Frederick I could even further strengthen his imperial position in the metropolis on the Danube.[17] In 1182, probably only a few months after Philip II Augustus had exiled Jews from the lands of the French crown,[18] this found expression in the imperial guarantee of rights for *Iudaei nostri Ratisponenses*, based on pro-Jewish principles, which basically counted Jews among the imperial *fideles*.[19] Only in Prague were the Bohemian dukes or kings the decisive power, although their bishops entertained close relations with the Staufer imperial court for some time.[20]

The bishops' network of relations[21] held even greater weight for Jews in the *Regnum Teutonicum* because the *kehillot* resident in the diocesan centers also had a crucial impact on Jewish settlements outside the cathedral towns in terms of Jewish cult and law.[22] This preeminence already had its roots in the fact that the majority of the newer Jewish settlements did not have conditions suitable for maintaining a cultic community and, therefore, were unable to develop further forms of communal organisation.

At the same time, the bishops based around cathedral towns in the old settlement areas of the *Regnum* were more closely involved with the work of the government than in any other kingdom. Only here did the bishops, along with the king, whose position was uniquely linked to theirs, hold considerable rights of lordship even over the Jews.[23]

Perhaps in no other kingdom where Jews lived in large communities in the twelfth century (and that excludes, for example, the towns in the *Regnum Italiae*[24] and in Flanders[25]) did Christian town communes gain greater scope for action along with, and partly against, the bishops. This could not but affect their relationships with the Jews living within their walls.[26] Nevertheless, the bishops—that is, the highest representatives of the Church in the empire—were by far the most important persons with whom almost all the large Jewish communities had close relationships. These by no means stood in conflict with intensive contacts between Jews and members of the municipal leadership, among whom, especially in the cathedral cities, economically active *ministeriales* played an essential role. Such relations with influential municipal groups as well as with the bishop's court were firmly based on the Jews' continuous trading activities,[27] often connected with moneylending, that framed their day-to-day dealings with Christians in whose midst they lived.[28] Moreover the bishops, thus placed at the center of Jewish networks, in various ways provided the most important link between the crown and the Jews.

As a consequence of this concentration of Jewish communities in the Salian-Staufen imperial holdings and in cathedral cities, the crown was able to influence, both directly and via the bishops, the position of Jews in the *Regnum Teutonicum* much more directly than that of groups within the Christian community.[29] Even the imperial *ministeriales* lived predominantly in a more 'diffuse' proximity to the crown.[30] On the other hand, emperors and kings carried out their duty on the move throughout the wide-ranging empire with its peculiar structure of lordship. In clear contrast to all other west European kings, they had no fixed center and were far removed from anything like a central administration. For relations with the Jews, they had to rely above all on the cooperation of the bishops and also of the Christian communities in places where Jews resided.

This basic situation is only a reflection of the manifold ties Jews had with powers who were not only dependent on each other but who were also in competition. This could entail acute threats to the Jews' existence, but it also offered the guarantee that neither individual kings nor bishops nor communities alone could make decisions about them in essential matters. It was even less likely that a united plan to convert Jews would emerge from this conglomeration of interests. Kings were least interested in that.

This network secured the effectiveness of kings and emperors in their function as holders of legitimate authority over and for the Jews. We need only look at the basic privileges, issued in 1090 by Henry IV, an emperor deposed by the Gregorian Pope, for the Jewish communities of Worms and Speyer in the Salian heartlands.[31] The long-term consequences and general spread of these documents, drawn up at the request of the Jews and largely framed on their wishes,[32] is evident, at the latest, from 1236. In that year, we have the first explicit evidence for the diplomas of Henry IV and that of Frederick I of 1157 being 'extended' to all Jews of the empire by the latter's grandson, Frederick II. Their impact lasted long afterwards and beyond the limits of the empire.[33] The effect was considerably aided by the outstanding position of the *ShU"M* communities (Speyer, Worms, and Mainz) within Ashkenazic Jewry as well as by that of their cities in the empire's structure.[34] The Middle Rhine region formed the "maxima vis regni," in the words of Otto of Freising.[35]

II

We must remember that the Roman Empire in Germany—lying on the edge of Christendom since its formation—was, during the twelfth century, a center of and point of departure for missions to the pagans, much more than any other western Latin dominion in which Jews lived. Mission was, even before the crusade of 1146/47, in part characterised by crusading motivations.[36] Bernard of Clairvaux found an extreme expression of these motives in the alternative of 'death or baptism', to be presented to the heathen Slavs east of the Elbe and the Saale, even at the expense of canonical tradition. In the Wendian Crusade the influential Cistercian abbot had little success with his summons; rather, he met with passive resistance from secular and spiritual princes and also with disapproval from groups of differing religious motivation.[37]

Bernard took up a battle cry which had been put into practice, principally by crusaders, a half century earlier against the Jews in the Empire's large urban centers,[38] while the alternative 'exile or baptism' was apparently being promoted only very rarely.[39] In no other land was the ground so ripe for combining violent missionary crusades with similarly violent action against the Jews as it was in wide areas of the *Regnum Teutonicum*. These deeply rooted attitudes and form of behaviour were rekindled in 1146 by the monk Radulf against the Jews. The crusading mood had been stirred up by the Cistercian abbot himself in the cathedral cities and other places in the Rhineland, and Radulf brought it to the extreme of murdering Jews. The atmosphere of pogrom he caused, which apparently led to uprisings in some towns, led Jews in a few cases to be offered the alternative 'baptism or death' according to the witness of Ephraim bar Jacob.[40] The Annals of Würzburg, whose contemporary author clearly criticises the Second Crusade and the crusaders' motives in general, placed much stronger emphasis on the fact that baptism or murder of Jews was the crusaders' motto.[41] Bernard of Clairvaux tried too late, but—as the Jewish side certified—not without success, to counteract these misinterpretations of his teaching, which were by no means far-fetched, just as his teaching was not without anti-Jewish elements.[42]

In any case, the events of 1146/47 which were linked with the missionary crusades strongly contributed to the coerced baptism of Jews, often carried out under threat of death. In the *Regnum Teutonicum*, where the pogroms of 1096 had already been concentrated, this occurred to a greater extent than in any other land of Roman Christendom prior to the mid-twelfth century.[43] In the second half of the same century, coerced baptisms were only on a few occasions carried out in the German areas of earlier settlement. For example, at Neuß in 1197, according to the testimony of Ephraim bar Jacob, the mother and uncle of a mad Jewish murderer chose death rather than baptism offered to them under threat. Similarly, another woman in Neuß was forced into baptism along with her three daughters, but they were able to return to their faith after only a few days.[44] According to the same source, in 1179 Jews in Boppard who were prosecuted for the alleged murder of a Christian girl refused to be baptised and were therefore drowned in the Rhine.[45] The chronicle does not record any coerced baptisms of adult Jews in France during the same period.[46]

For the reasons given above, the public return to their ancestral faith by Jews baptised in this manner was most widespread in the *Regnum Teutonicum*, at least until the middle of that century. From the Christian point of view, this was equal to the accumulation of apostasy insofar as coerced baptism was viewed as irrevocable.[47] On the other hand, apparently a few Jews forced into baptism, both after 1096 and after 1146/47,[48] remained Christian. Thus, the Ashkenazic Jews too were confronted with apostasy from their Jewish roots. For these Jews, coerced baptism was therefore followed by some sort of 'voluntary' decision to let that baptism stand as it was. This meant that differences between the two types of conversions were reduced, if not blurred—an effect which was heightened when the Jews concerned had agreed to coerced baptism in the hope that this act would later be undone. These links are picked out as the central theme in two exempla in the *Sefer Hassidim* of Judah the Pious.[49] When descendants of Jewish scholars who had advised their flock to accept coerced baptism later underwent baptism voluntarily, this was considered to be divine punishment for what was perceived as the sinful course of their forefathers who had encouraged baptism rather than death.[50]

The percentage of children and young women among those who, having been forcibly baptised, remained part of Christianity must have been much higher than that of men. In any case, persecutors of Jews during the pogroms of the Crusades and later during other periods of violent action against Jews were more likely prepared to remove children and women from the slaughter and coerce them to accept baptism.[51] This group of people had fewer chances of returning to their former faith because they were so socially dependent, given that their close relatives or a large part of the Jewish community had been murdered in the pogroms.

Basic regulations created as part of the imperial privileges dealt with the coerced baptism of Jewish children and other Jews. They stipulated that even Jews coming 'voluntarily' to the font must wait a period of three days until the rites could be performed. During this time, a third party was supposed to examine whether they wanted to be converted because of their own convictions or because of an ill inflicted on them.[52] Moreover, by accepting conversion they lost all legal claim to their inheritance. It would remain among members of their family and therefore within the Jewish community, which was responsible for services to Christian authorities.[53] The emperor himself followed the legal norms fixed in this way, after the intervention of a Jew from Speyer, Moshe ben Jektuiel,[54] immediately upon returning from his long stay in Italy. Despite the extremely weak political position of Henry IV and the weakness equally of bishops who were hampered by the 'investiture contest', the imperial orders caused—or at least contributed to—the fact that in 1097 the large majority of Jews who had undergone baptism under coercion were again practising their faith openly. This, of course, was contrary to canonical norms and went in the face of express protests from the 'imperial' pope. But while several religious authors expressly regretted it,[55] there was apparently no significant resistance from the local Christian communities—not even from those urban groups which less than a year before had actively participated in the persecution of Jews by insisting on the alternative of death or baptism. A similar thing happened in 1147, as it seems, without special measures from the royal court. On this, the witnesses of the *Annales Herbipolenses*[56] and of Ephraim bar Jacob[57] are in general agreement.

The return to Jewish faith was possible without serious resistance because it was based on the canonical authorities' long-standing internal paradox. These authorities did indeed disapprove of coerced baptism on one hand,[58] but on the other, they considered such an act irreversible once it had been completed. This paradox must have strengthened willingness, both among the canonically unschooled or indifferent population and among some of the higher clergy, to at least tolerate the return of Jews to their faith, above all in such cases of coerced baptism which stood in spectacular contrast to the traditional baptismal rites[59] which had been found in liturgical books for centuries.[60] Such tendencies could rely on the marked conservatism of the sacramentaries and missals, expressed, for example, in keeping the Easter night service 'a place of prime importance for the administration of baptism' and the linking of baptism with communion and confirmation.[61]

Thus, Berthold of Regensburg criticised the tradition 'that pupils and young men would jokingly shove Jewish children and old people into water in order to baptise them against their will'.[62] The Franciscan popular preacher[63] was condemning as improper anti-Jewish harrass-ment a custom which closely corresponded to the way that some one and a half centuries earlier—in 1096—the Jews in Regensburg had been baptised against their will under the leadership of crusaders.[64]

Such practices of coerced baptism also stood in sharp contradiction to the canonical norms which continued to dominate far into the twelfth century, and which were handed down by Burchard of Worms above all. This can principally be seen in the regulation which was still upheld by Gratian that Jews needed a seven-months' period of prepara-tion before baptism. Ivo of Chartres and also Gratian further demanded a forty-day fast.[65]

In a letter of 1201, Pope Innocent III sought to reduce the contra-dictions between, on one hand, the prohibition of coerced baptism and, on the other, the impossibility of revoking such a baptism.[66] He declared that the rites were null and void if those who had undergone them had never agreed to baptism and had refused it completely. However, bap-tism would remain valid for those who had been forced to accept it and had faked their conversion for fear of violence.[67] Thus, the pope and lawyer still allowed for the possibility of declaring coerced baptisms void. As a matter of fact, opinions among theologians concerning the legitimacy of coerced baptism and its effectiveness remained divided even later.[68] The loopholes had apparently been used to a large extent during the twelfth century by Christians with regard to Jews who had been forced into baptism.

Solomon bar Simson's statement at the end of his report on the pogrom of 1096 regarding his 'praise' for those forced into baptism also corresponds to this: 'Even the gentiles (ha-Goyim = the non-Jews) themselves knew that the conversions were not from upright hearts but from fear of the errant ones. They knew that they did not follow their religion and remained more devoted to the fear of God, keeping a firm hold on the highest God.' This was the case even though those forced into baptism—as Solomon further relates—at times faked their accep-tance of Christianity.[69]

To all appearances, the return to the practice of Judaism by the vast majority of Jews who had been coerced into baptism reinforced tradi-tional reservations among religious circles regarding the faithfulness of

Jewish converts to Christianity, even against those Jews who had become Christians without any direct force. In the papal schism these prejudices were exploited for political gain by Innocent II and his followers against the Pierleoni pope Anaclete II, the great-grandson of the Jew Baruch who had been christened in the name of Benedictus Christianus. One of Innocent's followers was Bernard of Clairvaux, who showed his support in a letter to Emperor Lothar III about 1136.[70] His abuse peaked in the anti-Semitic reproach that the negative characteristics which Jews were assumed to have were still imprinted on Christians several generations after the conversion of their Jewish ancestors.[71] These polemics must also have spread into the *Regnum Teutonicum*, which was crucial in this schism. At any rate, they would have served to strengthen the prejudices which were in existence anyway. Admittedly, such attitudes and effects should not be generalized in any way. Churchmen and members of religious orders were probably most susceptible to them, but even among this group there is no evidence of a general consensus.

One of their voices is recorded in the *Gesta Treverorum*, written by a collegiate priest in Trier around 1132, that is, shortly after the outbreak of the papal schism. He is the same author who described in detail the coerced baptism of Jews in Trier during the 1096 pogrom. He also reported that all the baptised had become apostate in 1097, except for one *legis* doctor, Micheas.[72] In this context, he tells of the conversion of the Jew Josua, whom he praised highly as a scholar—above all in the *scientia totius iudaismi*—and who served the influential Trier archbishop, Bruno (1102–1124) as one of his *medici*. The archbishop treasured this man more than others—that is, more even than important Christians in the court—even before the Jew had accepted baptism (under the name of Bruno).[73] The archbishop subsequently provided for the material wellbeing of the convert and probably wrote him a letter of recommendation.[74] Despite his very positive description of the convert, who even as a Jew was said to lead a chivalrous lifestyle (*militaris habitus*), the author explained this care by the archbishop with the fact, apparently taken for granted, that *genus illud hominum multum est in fide instabile*. As a further negative characteristic not erased by baptism, he stated that the Jewish *genus* always *desiderat in vitae necessariis habundare*, that is to say, Jews were greedy.[75] Cosmas, a leading cleric from Prague, had said much worse a short time earlier when referring to the baptised Jew, Iacobus, who had been raised to the *vicedominus* for the Duke. Even before his return to Judaism, Iacobus seemed to Cosmas to be the embodiment of Satan.[76]

Christian mistrust of those Jewish converts who did remain faithful could become even more acute because their baptism was 'not recognised in any way' by Jewish law. Therefore, the apostate 'did not discard his Judaism by changing his religion' according to 'Jewish authorities who were learned in the Law', even though he did lose certain rights. Likewise, children of a female apostate could be accepted into the Jewish community without hesitation.[77]

In the twelfth century, as a result of the polemic against Anaclete II mentioned above, these basic convictions, frequently attested by great scholars of the Ashkenazic communities, became a focus of attention at the highest level in the complex network of relationships between Jews and Christians, especially in those centres which were equally Jewish and Christian within the German Roman Empire. It is impossible to say what role the Ashkenazic legend of the Jewish Pope Elchanan played in this. The legend probably antedates the confrontation, and some of its features were taken over from the Jewish myth regarding the first pope, Simon Peter. The legend, extant in several versions, tells of the son of Rabbi Shimeon of Mainz, abducted as a child and brought up as a Christian. The 'moral' of the tale is that despite baptism, years of Christian upbringing, ordination into the priesthood, and a rapid rise in the Church, he could only suppress the positive imprint of his high Jewish background but never lose it. At his father's advice, he atoned for his transgressions against Judaism committed as a Christian and as pope by publicly declaring his faith and—according to one version—by a fatal fall from a tower when priests threatened to kill him.[78] In this 'atonement', clear reference can be found to accounts of events in Mainz in 1096[79] and thus to the practice of *Kiddush ha-Shem* which had spread since that time.[80] At about the same time, Rome as a center of Christendom was contrasted with the 'holy community of Mainz, treasured as gold', which, according to other contemporary witnesses, was considered as the heir to Jerusalem.[81]

Christians showed disdain toward the Christian faith of baptised Jews, a view widespread among a large number of clerics. Together with ideas about the negative characteristics, continuing beyond baptism, of the 'Jewish race', this disdain expressed a basic stance that in no way lent itself to defending a policy of coerced baptism.[82] Rather, such a stance would have appeared justified by the resistance of numerous Jews, women not least among them, during the pogroms, and especially by the practice of *Kiddush ha-Shem*. It was further justified by the 'apostasy' of the great majority of those who survived as victims of coerced baptism. They constituted another extremely unfavourable point of departure for a systematic mission to the Jews. The consensus in recent research is that in the twelfth century, there can be no question of such a mission.[83]

III

The dearth of evidence regarding baptised Jews in twelfth-century sources within our sphere of study—and beyond—prevents us from establishing even a rough estimate as to the number of converts who permanently became Christian.[84] Therefore, the only viable approach is to discuss those isolated cases which we do have, in order to see if they suggest common situations which could provide a common rule. In order to do this, it is of course necessary to distinguish between the sexes.

The most significant record of a baptised Jewish woman is presented in a source which has until now generally been neglected in this particular aspect. It is dated around 1190 and mentions a woman baptised under the name of Anna. The document twice accords her the title of *domina*. She had—as the abbot of the Cistercian monastery in Neuburg near Hagenau in Alsace relates, in a charter dealing with a transfer of possessions—converted (*pervenit*) *de iudaismo ad fidem catholicam*, due to the will of God as well as to the *consilium* of a dominus Burchardus, *vicedominus* of the church in Strasbourg.[85] Her counsellor was no doubt one of the most interesting characters in the wider circle around the court of Frederick I. He was none other than that long-standing administrator to the bishops of Strasbourg, principally entrusted with secular tasks. He was a *frater*, no doubt a member of the collegiate church of St Thomas in Strasbourg, which was closely linked to the Staufen emperors.[86] Burchard must have had extraordinary abilities, or else it would scarcely be possible to explain how in 1175, under orders from the Staufen emperor, he led an embassy to the court of Sultan Saladin which brought him as far as Egypt and Syria.[87] For this task, he must also have had a position of trust in the Staufer court, as can be taken for granted in the case of imperial chaplains. As a matter of fact, there is evidence for an imperial chaplain and public notary named Burchard, fairly continuously present at the imperial chancery between late 1174 and the autumn of 1179. However, evidence is conspicuously absent—or at least unclear—for the period between April 1175 and the end of July 1176, that is, the probable date for the journey to the East by Burchardus (*vicedominus*).[88]

As can be gathered from his report, during this journey (which included a trip to Jerusalem) Burchard keenly observed how Muslims, Jews, and Christians were living together in Egyptian and Syrian cities, and he did so without expressing any aversion to the Jews.[89] In the Staufer imperial court, Burchard may also have met prominent Jews such as Rabbi Kalonymos ben Meir, who was 'among the courtiers' close to the emperor and served him 'with loans and in many other ways'. At the same time, Kalonymos was head of his home community at Speyer.[90] Burchard probably also had close contacts with Hugh of Honau, palatinate deacon to the emperor and scholasticus of the chapter at Honau, near Strasbourg. Probably at Paris, Hugh had studied under Gilbert of Poitiers, who was accused of heresy, mainly by Bernard of Clairvaux and his secretary (from 1145), Geoffrey of Auxerre. Hugh was on several occasions employed in imperial missions to Byzantium, was a friend of Peter of Vienna, and entertained scholarly exchanges with Burgundio of Pisa and with Hugo Etherianus, also from Pisa, who had worked at the Byzantine imperial court for a long time.[91]

Burchard, the highly regarded canon with experience of the world, was also the generous patron of the convert, *domina* Anna. For 64 pounds of no doubt Strasbourg coins, he bought estates in Donnenheim,[92] which lay about a day's journey to the northwest of Strasbourg. He gave these to the Cistercian monastery in Neuburg,[93] which was also closely linked to the Staufer dynasty, on condition that the monastery would annually deliver to Strasbourg for him 50 *quartalia* of winter grain which must have been about the value equivalent of 2,500 liters of wine.[94] After Burchard's death, this arrangement was to be continued for the benefit of *domina* Anna. Burchard further insisted that, in return for this good deed, both he and *domina* Anna would become full members of the memorial brotherhood of the prime Cistercian house in Alsace.[95]

From these stipulations, we can conclude that Burchard and Anna lived in the same household in Strasbourg.[96] In any case, they had a close personal relationship and nothing suggests the convert had been forced to change her religion. Therefore, the relationship may have existed before her conversion and may even have been the reason for her to become baptised. Considering the Vicedominus's many travels, it is impossible to say where the Jewish woman came from and where her baptism occurred. Just as little can be determined about the question of the convert's high social prestige within Christian society. It is uncertain whether this position was due to the influence of the priest, who made her his equal in material and spiritual well-being, or to her origins in a respected Jewish family. Should the latter be true, this would surely imply that her family were known in Alsace and therefore most likely lived in the upper Rhine cathedral city of Strasbourg.

Conversions of Jewish women which started in this way were clearly not uncommon. This is confirmed by the Cistercian, Caesarius of Heisterbach from Cologne. He construed an *exemplum* along similar lines but admittedly subordinated it to his didactic views regarding the glory of Christianity and the corresponding *confusio* of Judaism.[97] The tale was told him by a 'certain' abbot of his order, but a basic version of it was certainly also known in the remote Benedictine monastery of Egmond.[98] Caesarius moves the story to a 'certain' English town. The couple was composed of a very beautiful *puella, secundum genus suum satis speciosa,* and a young cathedral canon, who was related to the bishop. The clerical youth from (as the monk saw it) excessive love became enslaved to the girl, who was also deeply loved by her father. Sexual intercourse took place on the night following Good Friday at the invitation of the *puella.*[99] In the early hours of Saturday, the father discovered the clerical lover and reproached him for his serious transgression against the Christian faith. However, out of fear of the bishop, he abandoned his intention to kill the man whom he had caught in the act. Instead, the father went to the church together with many other Jews, in order to demand, publicly before the bishop, justice against the *iuvenis* for his transgressions. This was to be done at mass, which the sinner was to help celebrate. The lover, however, repented in the face of this threat. As a result, the Christian God miraculously prevented the Jews from issuing their complaint by striking them dumb. After mass, the canon confessed his guilt to the bishop, who persuaded his young relative to marry the *puella deflorata* after baptism, and to renounce his Church career. Afterwards—the time is vague—the *clericus* and, at his instigation, the convert, became lay members of the Cistercian order.[100]

Obviously, the Cistercian created his stories of Jewish girls or women and clerics from a narrative which was widespread among clerics. A Benedictine monk from Egmond in Holland, writing between 1170 and 1180, placed one version into his chronological presentation of the *Annales Egmundenses,* covering the years 1112 to 1168.[101] The case corresponds in basic plot to the *exemplum* presented by the Cistercian monk. While the Rhinelander, Caesarius, set the events in some English cathedral town in some uncertain time, the monk from Egmond moved it to the time of Frederick I's reign. The setting in which the compassion and love of God toward the *populus christiane religionis* were to be shown was an unnamed cathedral city on the Rhine, a region which—according to the monk—had an abundance of *synagogae Iudeorum*.[102] In the foreground stands the 'unchaste' love of a cathedral cleric toward a very beautiful Jewish woman, who is however characterised by the monk as *deformis et iniocunda* because of her heretical faith and her malicious cunning. The deacon's (or 'Levite's') courting was only successful after a long time, when the *puella* arranged intercourse on Good Friday at the advice of her father and his close confidants. In contrast to Caesarius, the Benedictine described the father of the Jewish girl as the man behind the Jewish machinations. Their intention was to publicly expose the sinful cleric and then throw into confusion the Christian religion during High Mass at Easter, where—again as with Caesarius—the deacon was to read the Gospel before the bishop. This plan failed because of the intervention of the Almighty God. The deacon repented and confessed even before his reading, and the Jews could not make their accusation. After the Gospel reading, the bishop called the Jews to him and asked them why they were present. They answered, revealing to the bishop and those Christians present the incident and its cause. In this manner was 'the name of Christ glorified by Christians and Jews together'.[103] The future fate of the Jewish woman and the cleric disappear behind this narrative aim.

Caesarius, in a second story about the sexual relations of a *iuvenis quidam clericus* with, again, the comely daughter of a Jew (allegedly from Worms), writes without specifying the social environment, but with much greater anti-Jewish emphasis. This time, the main purpose was to mock the Jewish belief in a future Messiah, even at the expense of including a baptism of the Jewish girl.[104] Then again in the following story, Caesarius condemned the bishop of Liège for endeavoring to undo the baptism of an under-age Jewish girl, supposedly because her father had given him money. The tale includes specific details of the events, which even went as far as the intervention of the Pope. The chaplain of the Duke of Brabant is said to have induced the girl to Christianity during conversations he had in her father's house. He had encouraged her to run away and then baptised her before she was placed in a Cistercian convent.[105]

Caesarius rounded off this sequence on Jewish women with a tale of the daughter of a Jew from Linz on the Rhine (between Bonn and Koblenz). The girl was apparently ready to be baptised of her own free will and was handed over by a woman, in whom the girl had confided, to a young *miles* who was to offer her *consilium, auxilium, vel temporale subsidium*. This man also protected her for three days after baptism since there was a danger that her father, should he see her, could undo the baptism in this period—in accordance with the imperial privileges of 1090 and 1157.[106] The *miles*, who was successful in this but still young and by no means rich, cared for the baptised virgin as he would for his own daughter and aimed either to have her married or placed in a convent.[107]

The marriage of a baptised Jewish woman and a Christian of a lower social background leads us from the level of Benedictine and Cistercian didactics to cases recorded in other types of documentation. One such case can be found in the archival records of the Cologne parish of St Lawrence, which included the city's Jewish quarter. Not long after the middle of the twelfth century, *Theodericus de B . . ., homo advocati, et uxor eius Sophia, filia Vivi Iudei*, renounced the whole inheritance from the Jew, Vivus, to which his wife and unnamed descendants had claim. They did so in court, making it legally binding, before the municipal authorities of the community of St Lawrence and before the aforementioned advocate, who was now known as Gerhard and was master of Theoderich. With this renouncement, they swore not to raise further complaints in this matter.[108] By all appearances, the Christian husband was a vassal of the *advocatus*, who was certainly a member of the town council and perhaps even identical with the highly influential Gerhard Unmaze.[109] Theoderich therefore was no doubt from a ministerial background or one of the lower nobility. Sophia was not clearly said to have been baptised. Even her name is no unambiguous sign of a conversion. It is otherwise only used for Christian women in the records from the chests at Cologne, but non-Jewish names were relatively common among Jews, especially Jewish women.[110] The wife apparently had already had a long relationship with Theoderich, to judge from the mention of descendants who were not listed by name and were therefore probably still under age.

Had the imperial rights of Jews been indisputably valid in the community of St Lawrence at Cologne, then the claim for inheritance by the Jewish daughter would not even have reached court nor would the couple have had to expressly renounce further proceedings, provided Sophia had been baptised in the meantime. Precisely this premise does not seem to apply to Cologne around the middle of the twelfth century. Thus, the Jew Moyses and his wife, Guda sold to Iosep, *qui nunc (factus Cristianus) Petrus vocatur,* and his sons that half of a house and estate which had belonged to his father, Nathan.[111] The fact that the baptised Jew, whose Christian name suggests an influence on the part of leading clerics in his conversion,[112] sold part of his father's house was no doubt principally because he no longer lived among the Jews. Regarding the religious denomination of Sophia, therefore, the conclusion is that she was baptised and did not live in a 'mixed marriage.'[113]

The documentary evidence about Anna and Sophia suggests some of the conditions of life for baptised Jewish women in varying but, in both cases, higher social environments. They were situated in a transitional position between domestic and marital relations with Christians. This is emphasised and qualified in the *exempla* by Caesarius of Heisterbach. This 'narrative' source supports the thesis that Jewish women also lived in convents after baptism. The chances of finding evidence for this in other types of sources are considerably less, especially as there is much less recorded evidence from convents than from monasteries.[114] As Caesarius explains in one of his episodes, there was an existential need for 'advice, help, and material support' among young female Jewish converts. Therefore, the alternatives of marriage or a convent were basically the only ones remaining.[115] Marriage or a similarly close relationship in the house of a man presented themselves sooner to 'voluntarily' baptised Jewish women, especially given that relationships between the sexes could already act as a basis for baptism. However, because of the lack of evidence it is completely impossible to say whether more than just a few of the forcibly baptised, or even voluntarily converted, women spent any time or even their whole lives in a convent. In marriage, as in the convent, their return to their ancestral faith was made extremely difficult, if the desire to do so remained at all. Furthermore, we must conclude that neither the 'narrative' nor the 'documentary' sources offer any proof of a mission specifically aimed at Jewish women. Rather, many of those conversions which did not involve any manifest force occurred because of close if not intimate relationships between Christian men and Jewish women or as a consequence of religious conversation between a cleric and a Jewish family in their home.

IV

Excepting Hermannus quondam Judaeus, who later became a Premonstratensian, Jewish converts' membership in monasteries or collegiate churches during the twelfth century can only be ascertained from the use of a first name with the addition *Iudeus*. In the wider region of the Rhineland and Westphalia, three such canons and even a provost—the latter named *Israelita*—are known in this way.[116] However, it is impossible to prove that any of the people thus characterised, some of whom were equated with Hermannus quondam Judaeus in earlier research,[117] were actually converted Jews. Rather, the added *Iudeus* would appear to indicate an epithet which was perhaps already used in some cases to describe a whole family.[118] It is impossible to give a general answer to the question (discussed later in other contexts) whether such families can be traced back to a baptised Jew.[119]

Wholly extraordinary is a note of c. 1187 about the commendation of one Henry *Iudeus* for an annual tax of five *denarii*, to be paid by a layman and laid on the altar of St Nicholas—that is, the main altar—at the Augustinian chapter of Klosterneuburg.[120] There is a lot to suggest that this concerned a baptised Jew who was using a widespread legal procedure to become a *censualis* in return for a customary tax amount, and so to receive the protection of the monastery, which was closely linked with the Babenberger dukes. This status involved a protective relationship between the monastery and the man who was 'handed over', but left the *censualis* with freedom of movement and independent economic activity.[121]

Obviously, the chances of promotion were greater for Jewish converts in the urban world and within the legal sphere of town rulers and municipalities. As I have already said, the Cologne community of St Lawrence which was so closely linked even physically with the Jewish community—and also perhaps the whole municipality of the Rhineland center—maintained baptised Jews' entitlement to their inheritance, although this was contrary to the letter of the imperial privileges. However, to my knowledge this is yet to be proven for other towns, though decisions were taken at the Third Lateran Council of 1179 against loss of property and the disinheriting of baptised Jews.[122]

The unusual evidence for the rise of converts in this city's Christian society could be based on this fact. Thus, *Everhardus ex Iudeo christianus* and his brother Walter held high prestige among Cologne *burgenses* at the time of the Second Crusade.[123] Openly mentioning his Jewish background was not held against him, which, in this urban context, is only conceivable where influential Christians had a generally positive view toward Jews.

At about the same time, perhaps a bit earlier, *Ekkebret, qui judeus fuit,* was one of the two *magistri vicinorum,* that is, the leaders of the Cologne community of St Lawrence.[124] In previous research, this evidence about Egebreth-Ekkebret served as the key element in a theory about the character of Christian-Jewish relations in the Rhineland center during the first half of the twelfth century. In an essay of 1886 which laid the foundations for this idea, Robert Hoeniger considered it a 'natural assumption', although 'for the time being impossible to prove with sufficient certainty', that 'Eckebert was still a Jew while acting as an ordinary member of the community's council and only became mayor later after his baptism.' Among 'many other things', Hoeniger regarded this as a sign of 'the original constitutional cooperation of Jews in the community and in court', 'with the result that Cologne conditions in the first half of the twelfth century would have to be regarded as the last trace of previously unlimited civil equality.'[125] Accordingly, this scholar—and after him Aronius[126]—assumed that all other mentions of Ekkebret with the addition of *Iudeus* described his status before baptism. This would mean that Ekkebret—just like *Thiderich Iudeus*—was included as a Jew among the *cives*, even ahead of several clearly Christian persons,[127] in the lists of witnesses for legal transactions among Christians and, in one case, between Jews and Christians,[128] in the community of St Lawrence.

Such an assumption, however, would run against the common practice that Jews received a Christian name on converting, as was demonstrably the case in Cologne-St Lawrence.[129] Conspicuously, Ekkebret's son, Fordolf, was not labeled as *Iudeus*; thus no family name arose from this root. To argue against the existence of a family name, we must also consider the fact that Ekkebret had indeed been a Jew. Therefore, the closest assumption is that, in any case for Ekkebret, the addition of *Iudeus* merely served as a short formula for his Jewish background even though he was already baptised.[130] Accordingly, he was already a Christian when he held his position in the community, although he was still frequently labeled as *Iudeus*. The same must also be true of Thiderich. The use of Christian names like Henry[131] or even Gerard[132] by Jews is not affected by this; they were never mentioned in the lists among the *cives*.

Writing around 1197, the author of the *Chronica regia Coloniensis* refers to another baptised Jew in Cologne around the middle of the twelfth century, who appears in a miracle story dated 1153. Actually, it was not the convert but his son who was still Jewish—*quidam Iudeus ex patre Iudeo set converso*—who was the occasion for this miracle of the Host. In this story, the son is supposed to have received communion at Easter and afterwards buried the Host in the graveyard by the church. Thereupon, a priest opened the 'burial site' and found the figure of a child there. When he went to carry this to the church, a heavenly light appeared and the child's form slipped from the priest's hands and traveled with the light to Heaven. The *Recensio II* written a few decades later gave this story a bias against baptised Jews. By omitting the word *Iudeus* from the description of the son, the scribe suggested that even the Christian son of a baptised Jew was unworthy of receiving communion and had committed a sin against the Host.[133]

The Benedictine monk Arnold of Lübeck also included the miraculous baptism of a Jew in his *Chronica Slavorum* (finished in 1209). It was

set in Cologne at the time of Archbishop Philip (1167–91). The beginning of this conversion lay in the Cologne Jew's visit to the church on
Easter Saturday when, according to Church tradition, children were
baptised.[134] He had come out of curiosity and now his eyes were opened
and he saw the Holy Spirit in the form of a dove above the baptised infant.[135] This 'revelation' allowed him neither fully to believe in the divine mystery nor to doubt it. Even the words he often heard about the
glory of that dove could not overcome the Jewish *perfidia*.[136] A year
later, while visiting the synagogue on Good Friday, the same Jew allegedly saw how the Jews in accordance with their 'custom' were crucify-
ing the wax figure used to represent the Saviour and—as in the Passion
Story—tormenting it in other ways.[137] Now he believed, and immediately after his visit to the synagogue he consulted the archbishop, to be
baptised on Easter Saturday (without even so much as a hint of the
three-day period which was demanded before baptism).[138]

The tale is evidence of the ideas Christians held about Jewish customs at Purim. In this case the mocking of Haman is transferred onto
Christ and the date shifted to Good Friday.[139] Accordingly, the Jews did
not commit the killing of Christ out of blindness but with conscious
hatred;[140] they perpetrate not a 'real' murder but a 'figurative' repetition
of this deicide every Good Friday. However, in this tale this had 'real'
effects, as it led to a baptism.[141]

Probably, the Benedictine abbot learnt the starkly anti-Jewish story
in Lübeck either directly or indirectly from a man who either posed as a
baptised Jew or may actually have been a convert, looking for sympathy
or support from his Christian audience with this version.[142] In Lübeck,
where there was certainly no Jewish community at this time, the narrator must have reckoned that his depiction of the anti-Christian Jewish
'cult of the synagogue' could not be exposed as false. It is therefore very
doubtful that the conversion, if there was one, occurred in Cologne or
that the story was told in the Rhineland center.[143] As in similar narratives, no missionary aim by clerics is mentioned.[144] Rather, the crucial
effect was based on the contrasting perceptions of the Jew regarding the
Christian and Jewish cults and on empathy with the Passion of Christ
in particular.[145] Arnold's story does not offer any reliable guide to
Christian-Jewish relations at Cologne.

The relatively large amount of other evidence concerning baptised
Jews in the lower Rhine center comes almost exclusively from the ex-

ceptional documentation of chest books ('Schreinsbücher') that sets in around 1130. In particular, they are preserved in the admittedly fragmentary remains from the parish and civic community of St Lawrence, which surrounded the Jewish quarter and was also central to the wider urban structure. Elsewhere, this type of documentation is unknown before the end of the twelfth century, when it first appears at Andernach, which belonged to the church of Cologne, and at Metz.[146] Therefore, any attempt to generalize from the findings at Cologne for other cities with large Jewish communities will result in mere speculation. Indeed, even in Cologne with this unusual (though fragmentary) evidence, at most a handful of Jewish converts can be identified who remained Christians for any length of time during the twelfth century, mostly in the decades around 1150.

As for the 'Jude'/'Iudeus' family of councillors and patricians at Cologne, which can be traced back to the twelfth century, it is impossible to prove that it descended from a baptised Jew.[147] The same is true for families thus labeled since the thirteenth century in Worms, Mainz, Passau, and Strasbourg (1236), as well as other towns like Frankfurt, Hamburg, Überlingen (1253),[148] and also Minden,[149] not to mention certain rural settlements.[150] In regard to the twelfth century, we can only infer that the epithet 'Judeus' was not generally openly detrimental to social status, even for those who belonged to the close circle of municipal leaders and lower aristocratic families. They accepted it as the mark of their family, even though that meant their ancestry, real or assumed, were thought or surmised to have been converted Jews.

V

Evidence of completed voluntary baptisms is otherwise only found in the story concerning Josua-Bruno, the doctor of the archbishop of Trier mentioned above, and that of the conversion of the Cologne Jew, Judah ben David ha-Levi of Cologne, alias Hermannus quondam Judaeus. These sources are of varying credibility. The few lines in the *Gesta Treverorum* accord fewer problems. Their author at least cannot have invented the baptism of such a prominent Jew by Archbishop Bruno.[151] In the case of the *Opusculum de conversione sua* of Hermannus (whose career certainly did not go beyond the Premonstratensian monastery of Cappenberg),[152] I follow the suggestion recently made by Jean-Claude Schmitt. He proposed that this record was written toward the end of the twelfth century in Cappenberg by one of the monks—in no way need it have been Hermann himself—based on oral traditions within the monastery.[153]

Both stories have one thing in common. They tell of the baptism of a prominent Jew after a long period of preparation in the court of an archbishop or a bishop. Both had spent considerable time in these surroundings. Judah stayed for about twenty weeks,[154] while Josua was in permanent contact with the archbishop, since he was one of the archbishop's doctors. At the court, Josua held intense discussions, some of them based on the *divina volumina*,[155] in a friendly, or at least benevolent, atmosphere. Both stories therefore present an antithesis, indeed they stand in stark contrast, to the enforced baptisms or any speedy conversion which was brought about some other way.[156] Both are examples of successful conversion, for which the Premonstratensian monk recommends reference to the *vetus testamentum*.[157] This way, via the bishop's court, was no doubt only appropriate for the conversion of a very small number of Jews. However, these must have been prominent Jews, considering their close link to that court, and they must also have belonged to the élite of their community.

The dangers arising from the conversion of prominent Jews met a strong response in Jewish tradition. The community of Mainz and the court of the archbishop stand at the center of the legend which grew up around the Rabbi Amnon. He was described as a member of a rich family and as 'a great man of his generation' (*Gedol ha-Dor*). By the end of the twelfth century the legend was introduced, probably by Ephraim of Bonn, into a tradition which has had a continuous influence ever since.[158] Reportedly, the archbishop, who had close relationships with Amnon, out of esteem demanded repeatedly over a long period that the Jew confess Christianity. Amnon, however, persistently refused. The Church dignitary's insistence one day led the Jew as far as making the request for a three-day period to think about it—in accordance with the norms set in the imperial Jewish rights. Amnon immediately regretted his behaviour, allowed the three days to pass, and, having been forced to appear before the archbishop once more, confessed his faith publicly. The dignitary maimed him so cruelly that Amnon 'vanished' soon after in the synagogue of Mainz at Rosh ha-Shanah.

The effectiveness of this legend, again based on older motifs, was significantly reinforced by the fact that three days after his death, Amnon is supposed to have conveyed to Kalonymus ben Meshullam in a dream the text of the piyyut, 'Let us describe the greatness of the Holiness of this day'—a much older prayer that no doubt already had a central significance at Rosh ha-Shanah in most Ashkenazic communities by the twelfth century. The festival, and the prayer now coming from the mouth of a martyr temporarily resurrected in a dream, thereafter spread the story of the temptation and martyrdom of the Jew who, despite close ties to the court of the archbishop, remained—as his name suggests—faithful. They also helped to deepen the urgency of the theme in the collective memory. Thus a warning memorial was raised on a prominent place, so to speak, of the threat to the existence of Judaism.

The legend touches an ominous sore spot at the center of Jewish relations with the Christian world, which was for Jews indispensable. In this perspective, the respect for Jews shown by bishops as embodiments of Christianity, and by their circles, appears as an underhanded device of conversion, which if refused could only be averted by martyrdom. All the more persistent is the warning against getting entangled in the human nets in high Christian circles—which yet remained indispensable for Jews. In fact, the authors both of the *Gesta Treverorum* and of the *Opusculum de conversione sua* stress this very connection between sympathy and conversion. Their aim, however, was to demonstrate the voluntary nature of the conversion of individual, highly regarded Jews. Again, Jewish and Christian traditions coincide as they concentrate on members of the Jewish élite.

VI

The conversion of Jacob, son of the rich Jew, Ysaac of Regensburg, owner of much money and gold from a loan business, is the theme of a story from the pen of an anonymous monk at the Benedictine monastery of Egmond, situated on the North Sea coast.[159] His annals also contributed—as we have seen[160]—to the early transmission in writing of the motif of the 'corrupting' love between a cleric and a Jewish girl. He dates the events in Regensburg to some time during the reign of Konrad III

(1138–1152),[161] but did not write the story down until some decades later, between 1170 and 1180,[162] placing it immediately after the description of the dedication of two altars at Egmond in 1136 and after short reports from 1137. The details concerning the altar dedications indicate the author's great admiration for relics and, in particular, those of martyrs.[163]

Not without reason, the author characterised the 'circumstances' of his monastery,[164] where at the beginning of the twelfth century Cluniac influence took effect, as *in extremo margine mundi*.[165] No doubt, no member of the convent would ever have seen a Jew, let alone known a Jewish community. The author explicitly claimed to have learnt his story from the mouth of a certain well-known *iudeus christianus* from the city on the Danube, whom he considered extremely reliable. The man from Egmond refers much more clearly therefore to his 'source' than the urban Benedictine, Arnold of Lübeck. He also had much more cause to do so; after all, the events he described and confirmed in this way would have been much more spectacular than those from the pen of the Lübeck abbot.[166] There are grounds for suspicion that the source presented himself at the Egmond monastery with his 'story' in order to ask for support in the most effective way. Perhaps the *iudeus christianus* also produced a letter of recommendation, either genuine or faked.[167]

In fact, the material poverty of converted Jews forms the first leitmotif in the story. The youthful Jew, described as comely and highly moral, had already honored the Christian faith in secret, but did not want to become a Christian publicly because he was afraid of his father and worried about life as a beggar, in which he had seen many *iudeos christianos* suffering. Thus, he gathered a considerable amount of gold without his father's knowledge, in order to be able to provide later for his living costs and also to support other Jewish converts.[168] Thus, the son's theft from his Jewish father was justified by his willingness to ease the poverty of baptised Jews.[169] He contacted the *archidiaconus civitatis* in his father's absence, asked to be baptised, and entrusted him with the treasure. They agreed that after his baptism and separation it would be returned to him. Greed, however, made the archdeacon break the agreement, delay the baptism, and make a deal with the father to secure for himself the deposited money and further money which the son had stolen, in return for handing him over.[170] The fortune, which was hoarded for converted Jews by a Jew seeking baptism, was sacrificed in this way to the greed of a high cleric, whose duty made him responsible for spiritual care but who made money a motive for delaying a baptism.

Just as telling is the other message from this story. It lies in the ensuing description of how Jacob, handed back to his rich father, Ysaac, resisted the daily attempts by his parents to induce him to renounce his faith in Christ. This continued until his father, under cover of night, secretly chained his son's legs, weighted his feet with lead, and sank him in the Danube. The river waters, which the Jew considered deadly,[171] became baptismal water for his son whose desire for baptism had been foiled. Jacob was not driven into the flood waters by Christians to be baptised—as was the case for his fellow Jews in 1096[172]—but rather by his own father, who therefore caused the baptism for which his son had longed. The baptism thus became 'a baptism of blood' in the water.[173]

Ysaac's crime against Jacob did not remain secret. The martyrdom was eventually discovered by a blind widow, who—as is described with a delight for detail—by wetting her eyes with the water of the Danube became able to see and discover the corpse in midstream, surrounded by heavenly light. She immediately reported this miracle to others, with the result that the bishop finally learnt of it via a chain of informants and led a solemn procession of monks and clerics to the 'place of the discovery'. The *corpus sanctum* was thus translated to the cathedral. On the next day, almost the whole town gathered there. No one knew, however, where the dead man was from or who he was. He was eventually identified by the Jews who were present and this was reported to the bishop. However, Ysaac denied that the dead man was his son, Jacob, whom he had sent *secundum consuetudinem iudeorum* to study in Spain.[174] However, he finally had to reveal all the facts to the bishop because of the testimonies and oaths of the other Jews. As a result, the archdeacon was 'demoted', sentenced to death, and burnt by the castellan. The body of the martyr, on the other hand, was honorably buried and shone forth by signs and miracles. For this reason his father and mother and a large number of Jews believed in Christ (the father's crime seems to have been forgotten). This Christian martyrdom inflicted by a Jew on his son became for Jews in this area, as it says in the conclusion, *causa et fomes in Christi credendi*, that is, the cause and a powerful impetus for their faith in Christ.[175]

These spectacular events or even the Christian saint of Jewish background are not mentioned in any other source. However, the dramatic
plot of a serious conflict between a son seeking baptism and his parents
was passed on elsewhere. One need only remember the two stories by
Caesarius of Heisterbach about young Jewish women seeking baptism,
and the *Opusculum de sua conversione*. The motif apparently had a basis
in historical fact, for which further evidence can be found in Christian
sources about the serious pogrom of 1241 in Frankfurt.[176]

Moreover, the story, which allegedly originated from the mouth of a
baptised Jew, clearly alludes to the motif of *Kiddush ha-Shem* which
Ysaac performed on Jacob.[177] Here too, the killing was done to avert
baptism, for which the murdered man was expressly striving. Thus,
Kiddush ha-Shem appears in its Christian reflection as a crime to prevent
baptism which had long been desired. The motive of Jewish martyrdom
was reevaluated as a motive for Christian martyrdom. The procedure
shows a clear parallel with the description of an alleged Jewish ritual as a
reason for conversion.[178] This type of allusion to *Kiddush ha-Shem* is
surely inexplicable without the reporter's knowledge of this practice
among Ashkenazic Jews during pogroms, especially from 1096. On the
other hand, the excuse given by the father, that it was usual for Jews to
send their sons *in Hispaniam* for study, implies that we can conclude he
was not acquainted with Judaism in German lands. Therefore, it is more
likely that the Egmond monk's source impressed a story on the author
and his wider audience which met their assumptions about contemporary Judaism. In order to do so, he used central motifs which were imagi-
nable for the monks in that remote monastery.

VII

Placing the action in distant Regensburg protected the source and the
author in the Egmond story from attempts at local verification, and this
was also the case in the story told by Arnold of Lübeck. It left enough
room for further details of the scenario. At the same time, the distance
away from the setting of the alleged events and the audience's poor
knowledge of Jewish life encouraged the spread of anti-Jewish tendencies and motifs. Accordingly, the reports of conversion both in the *Gesta*

Treverorum and in the *Opusculum de sua conversione*, while differing in genre, are far less anti-Jewish because they must reckon with a knowledgeable audience.

In the *Opusculum*, the narrator himself is a converted Jew (or so he claims) who necessarily represents his original faith and religious community more negatively than the Christian. However, he is not intent on spreading anti-Jewish attitudes. In the two other cases, baptised Jews serve to lend credibility to reports with biases clearly directed against Judaism and Jewish practice. The question remains whether these witnesses were only 'pieces' in a literary game or if indeed they were Jewish converts appearing far from any Jewish settlements, in regions where they were readily accepted as such because of their 'statements'. Whether they actually came from this background or were only pretending was secondary to the anti-Jewish impact far away from home.

Significantly, such appearances of converted Jews are not recorded during the twelfth century near to Jewish settlements and in towns with larger Jewish communities. The few cases attested of Jewish converts who stuck permanently by their new faith and who lived in a town with Jewish residents are exclusively from Cologne and do not contain an anti-Jewish strain. Even when such converts were labeled as baptised Jews by parts of, or additions to, their names, this does not allow any conclusions as to widely held anti-Jewish attitudes. To the contrary, such descriptions were only bearable for Christians so named, a number of whom held respected positions in Christian society, if no condemnation of Jewish descent was combined with it in their immediate surroundings.

This benign view contrasts with the negative characterisations of Jewish converts written from other Christian positions by religious authors whose attitudes toward Judaism applied equally to baptised Jews, and who thus questioned the effects of baptism. This opinion of Christian authors overlapped—with values reversed—with Jewish estimations of positive Jewish characteristics which were irrevocable even through baptism. In contrast, baptism was held to extinguish the guilt even of a serious crime previously committed, as in the view of the Egmond monk. Among Jews, too, views toward Jewish converts were by no means uniform, as we can see from the variance in evaluating enforced baptism.

The evidence concerning baptised Jews in the *Regnum Teutonicum* during the twelfth century therefore presents very different impressions about the position of converted Jews in the Christian community as well as in the Jewish community. These impressions cannot be forced into a uniform picture for either side, Jewish or Christian, and they are just as impossible to arrange according to an underlying trend. Their indications for Judeo-Christian relations are correspondingly ambiguous. On one side, these are characterised by the murder and enforced baptism of Jews by Christians, among whom those who professed crusading motives and who usually came from elsewhere were the main instigators. Furthermore, the relations are defined by the mutual polemic which, in the wake of the pogroms, became more acute during the twelfth century. It aimed at the devaluation or redefinition of the opposing religion, its symbols, and its rituals.[179] Prevailing negative prejudices and stereotypes on both sides also characterise this end of the scale of attitudes and behavior. On the other end of the scale, one can find love and sexual relationships between high clerics and Jewish women, mutual respect if not friendship between Jews and Christians around court, and even continual contacts between influential clerics and Jews in the home of a Jewish family. This type of evidence admittedly only appears in Christian sources as a backdrop for the description of the conversion and baptism of a Jew.

On the whole, it was fundamental that Jews and Christians were living together in close quarters in urban places where both religions and cultures had their centers. This cohabitation increased during the twelfth century within German lands in old and new Jewish settlements, with the result that more Christians than ever before met with Jews or at least attained a clearer picture of them, and the same was true of Jews with Christians. This meant that relations between Jewish and Christian communities gained greater significance, so that mutual links gained a broader basis, one which was partly strengthened by institutional ties.

The impact of growing contacts and other changes in the ways of life—in particular, the religious movements among Jews and especially Christians, leading to a hitherto unknown diversity—can only be appraised with difficulty as a whole, and even more specifically with regard to the baptism of Jews.[180] In any case, they multiply the need for further differentiations in describing Judeo-Christian relations. This means that the differences among Jews and those among Christians will need to be investigated more closely than has hitherto been the rule, such as those between their respective areas of life and their formative religious and cultural factors. In this way, a view will be opened toward a picture full of facets and nuances, of the lives shared by people who came from religions and cultures that were different but still based on common ground.

Notes

The translation of this essay was produced by Andrew Terrington, Belfast, and completely revised by Christoph Cluse; the footnotes were translated by Ulrike Flach. I am especially grateful to my friend Israel Jacob Yuval, Hebrew University of Jerusalem, for his many suggestions. To him, to Yacov Guggenheim, Jerusalem, and to Eva Haverkamp, Rice University, I owe thanks for their essential support in dealing with Hebrew sources and literature. I am also obliged to Gerd Mentgen and Christoph Cluse for various suggestions as well as for their support in producing the printed version.

1. Still essential regarding our topic is Peter Browe, S.J., 'Die Judenbekämpfung im Mittelalter,' *Zeitschrift für katholische Theologie* 62 (1938): 197–231, 349–384; idem, 'Die kirchenrechtliche Stellung der getauften Juden und ihrer Nachkommen,' *Archiv für katholisches Kirchenrecht* 121 (1941): 3–22, 165–191; idem, *Die Judenmission im Mittelalter und die Päpste*, Miscellanea Historiae Pontificiae 6 (Rome, 1906), especially 138ff.; Bernhard Blumenkranz, 'Jüdische und christliche Konvertiten im jüdisch-christlichen Religionsgespräch des Mittelalters,' 1966, reprint in idem, *Juifs et Chrétiens, patristique et Moyen Age* (London, 1977), no. xiv, and especially Jacob Katz, *Exclusiveness and Tolerance: Studies in Jewish-Gentile Relations in Medieval and Modern Times,* Scripta Judaica 3 (Oxford, 1961), especially 67–76. For a comparative examination, see Jeremy Cohen, 'The Mentality of the Medieval Jewish Apostate: Peter Alfonsi, Hermann of Cologne, and Pablo Christiani,' in *Jewish Apostasy in the Modern World,* ed. Todd M. Endelman (New York, 1987), 20–47; Robert C. Stacey, 'The Conversion of Jews to Christianity in Thirteenth-Century England,' *Speculum* 67 (1992): 263–283, and Joshua Starr, 'The Mass Conversion of Jews in Southern Italy (1290–1293),' *Speculum* 21 (1946):203–211. On the later Middle Ages, cf. the two studies, offering different perspectives, by Joseph Shatzmiller, 'Jewish Converts to Christianity in Medieval Europe,' in *Cross*

Cultural Convergences in the Crusader Period: Essays Presented to Arye Graboïs, ed. Michael Goodich, Sophia Menache, and Sylvia Schein (San Francisco, 1995), 297–318, and, with many new sources and insights, Gerd Mentgen, 'Jüdische Proselyten im Oberrheingebiet während des Spätmittelalters. Schicksale und Probleme einer "doppelten" Minderheit,' *Zeitschrift für Geschichte des Oberrheins* 142 (1994): 119–139.

2. Robert Chazan, *European Jewry and the First Crusade* (Berkeley, 1987), especially 192 ff., is right to distinguish among the different sectors regarding the question of the 'watershed' of 1096. See also the earlier study by Jeremy Cohen, *The Friars and the Jews: The Evolution of Medieval Anti-Judaism* (Ithaca, N.Y., 1982) and more recently, Anna Sapir Abulafia, *Christians and Jews in the Twelfth-Century Renaissance* (London, 1995), and Daniel J. Lasker, 'Jewish-Christian Polemics at the Turning Point: Jewish Evidence from the Twelfth Century,' *Harvard Theological Review* 89 (1996): 161–173, both with a focus on the religious and theological. Thoughtful *résumés* have recently been offered by David Berger, *From Crusades to Blood Libels to Expulsions: Some New Approaches to Medieval Antisemitism*, Second Annual Lecture of the Victor J. Selmanowitz Chair of Jewish History (New York, 1997), and Jeremy Cohen, *Living Letters of the Law: Ideas of the Jew in Medieval Christianity* (Berkeley, 1999).

3. See the contributions by Avraham Grossman, Jeremy Cohen, Eva Haverkamp, Friedrich Lotter, Rudolf Hiestand, and Israel Yacob Yuval which mostly originated as papers read at the Spring Conference 1996 of *the Konstanzer Arbeitskreis für mittelalterliche Geschichte*, published in *Juden und Christen zur Zeit der Kreuzzüge*, ed. Alfred Haverkamp, Vorträge und Forschungen 47 (Sigmaringen, 1998), and those of a Jerusalem conference published in *Facing the Cross: The Persecution of Ashkenazic Jews in 1096*, ed. Yom-Tov Assis, Jeremy Cohen, Ora Limor, and Michael Toch, Yearbook of the Dinur Centre for Jewish History (Jerusalem, 1998). See also Eva Haverkamp, 'Hebräische Berichte über die Judenverfolgungen während des Ersten Kreuzzugs,' Ph.D. diss. (Konstanz, 1999), forthcoming in MGH, series for Hebrew sources.

4. Here, I shall for the most part exclude the duchy or kingdom of Bohemia, which remained only loosely connected with the empire for a long time and which offered many different conditions to the Jews, especially regarding aspects of ruling and rights. As a more recent overall view, orientated toward legal history, see Jiri Kejr, 'Böhmen und das Reich unter Friedrich I.,' in *Friedrich Barbarossa. Handlungsspielräume und Wirkungsweisen des staufischen Kaisers*, ed. Alfred Haverkamp, Vorträge und Forschungen 40 (Sigmaringen, 1992), 241–289.

5. Alfred Haverkamp, '"Heilige Städte" im hohen Mittelalter,' 1987, reprinted in Haverkamp, *Verfassung, Kultur, Lebensform: Beiträge zur italieni-*

schen, deutschen und jüdischen Geschichte im europäischen Mittelalter, ed. Friedhelm Burgard, Alfred Heit, and Michael Matheus (Mainz, 1997), 361–402; idem, 'Leben in Gemeinschaften: alte und neue Formen im 12. Jahrhundert,' in *Aufbruch–Wandel–Erneuerung: Beiträge zur "Renaissance" des 12. Jahrhunderts,* ed. Georg Wieland (Stuttgart, 1995), 11–44, and also idem, *Aufbruch und Gestaltung: Deutschland 1056–1273,* 2d rev. ed. (Munich, 1993); in the English version this aspect is given less consideration: *Medieval Germany, 1056–1273,* 2d ed. (Oxford, 1992). On the religious situation in the twelfth century see the work by Giles Constable, *The Reformation of the Twelfth Century* (Cambridge, 1996), written from extensive experience and with the broad view required.

6. Based on the results of the *Germania Judaica I,* ed. Ismar Elbogen et al. (Breslau, 1934; reprint, Tübingen, 1963), Michael Toch, 'The Formation of a Diaspora: The Settlement of Jews in the Medieval German Reich,' *Aschkenas* 7:1 (1997): 57, recently published a map on places of Jewish residence up to 1100. Some of the allocations remain at issue because of the state of documentation. Evidence of the existence of Jewish communities around 1100 exists only concerning the archiepiscopal metropolises of Cologne, Mainz, and Trier, as well as for the cities of Worms, Speyer, Regensburg, and Prague. Regarding the archiepiscopal center of Magdeburg, a continuity of Jewish settlement is probable. The same can be said of the city of Merseburg, but with less cogent arguments. Further entries in Toch's map appear to me at least questionable: The evidence for a Jewish community in the episcopal city of Bamberg is not convincing. This applies even more to Halle an der Saale (see Eva Haverkamp, 'Hebräische Berichte' [as in note 3]), and also to Xanten (see below, note 12) and Bonn.

7. In addition to the 'classic' by Jean Schneider, *La ville de Metz aux XIIIe et XIVe siècles* (Nancy, 1950), see Marianne Pundt, *Metz und Trier: Vergleichende Studien zu den städtischen Führungsgruppen vom 12. bis 14. Jahrhundert,* Trierer Historische Forschungen 38 (Trier, 1998).

8. In contrast to some versions of the well-known travel report by Benjamin of Tudela (cited in *Germania Judaica I* [as in note 6], 232) there is no evidence for a continuity of the Jewish community in the numerous sources from Metz; see Jean-Luc Fray, 'La présence juive en Lorraine au Moyen Age: Continuités et ruptures,' *Archives juives* 27:2 (1994): 25–38, and Pundt, *Metz und Trier* (as in note 7).

9. See the seminal work by Gerd Mentgen, *Studien zur Geschichte der Juden im mittelalterlichen Elsaß,* Forschungen zur Geschichte der Juden, A 2 (Hannover, 1995), 30, 125 ff.

10. For the evidence see most recently Bernhard Schimmelpfennig, 'Christen und Juden im Augsburg des Mittelalters,' in *Judengemeinden in*

Schwaben im Kontext des Alten Reiches, ed. Rolf Kiessling, Colloquia Augustana 2 (Berlin, 1995), 23–38.

11. In contrast to *Germania Judaica I* (as in note 6), 266, I consider the document of 1210 as a rather strong proof of the existence of a larger group of Jews in Passau; see *Monumenta Boica*, vol 28:2 (Munich, 1829), 137 f., no. 31, and also the comments by Julius Aronius, *Regesten zur Geschichte der Juden im fränkischen und deutschen Reiche bis zum Jahre 1273* (Berlin, 1887–1902), 167 f., no. 380.

12. In contrast to Toch, 'Settlement' (as in note 6), 58 (with a map for the time between 1100 and 1200) and 68, I regard the evidence concerning Königswinter, Neuß, and Aschaffenburg as too weak. Until 1200 only a Jewish cemetery, dating back to the massacre of Cologne Jews there in 1096, can be found at Xanten, which does not necessarily imply that there was also a local Jewish settlement.

13. For all Jewish settlements on the Middle Rhine see the seminal work by Franz-Josef Ziwes, *Studien zur Geschichte der Juden im mittleren Rheingebiet während des hohen und späten Mittelalters*, Forschungen zur Geschichte der Juden, A 1 (Hannover, 1995).

14. Nürnberg and Erfurt are not taken into account for the period up to 1200 by Toch, 'Settlement' (as in note 6).

15. This also applies to Xanten and Aschaffenburg, where Jewish presence at this time is doubtful; cf. above, note 12.

16. Bernhard Töpfer, 'Kaiser Friedrich I. und der deutsche Reichsepiskopat,' in *Friedrich Barbarossa* (as in note 4), 389–433, and further contributions to the same volume.

17. Ferdinand Opll, *Stadt und Reich im 12. Jahrhundert (1125–1190)* (Vienna, 1986), 135 ff.

18. William Chester Jordan, *The French Monarchy and the Jews: From Philip Augustus to the Last Capetians* (Philadelphia, 1989), 31 ff.

19. *Die Urkunden Friedrichs I.*, 5 vols., ed. Heinrich Appelt, MGH Diplomata 10 (Hannover, 1975–1990), 4:43 f., no. 833 (see there, too, for a "not quite impossible" dating around 3 June 1183). The charter is only preserved in an incomplete insertion into another document. In its arenga, the legal decree is justified with the claim that it was the emperor's duty and a demand of equity according to law and reason, that the emperor render justice to every one of his *fideles*—not only to those following the Christian religion, but also to those who differed from it and lived according to their ancestral tradition: "Offitium est imperatoriae maiestatis nostrae et iuris equitas atque rationis hortatur, ut unicuique fidelium nostrorum, non solum christianae relligionis cultoribus, verum etiam a fide nostra discolis ritu paternae traditionis suae viventibus, quod suum est, equitatis examine conservemus. . . ."

20. Cf. Peter Hilsch, *Die Bischöfe von Prag in der frühen Stauferzeit* (Munich, 1969).

21. On this topic and for information on the state of recent research, also on other aspects, see Haverkamp, *Aufbruch* (as in note 5).

22. For more information see Simon Schwarzfuchs, *Kahal: La communauté juive de l'Europe médiévale* (Paris, 1986) (including older literature); Israel Jacob Yuval, 'Heilige Städte, heilige Gemeinden—Mainz als das Jerusalem Deutschlands,' in *Jüdische Gemeinden und Organisationsformen von der Antike bis zur Gegenwart*, ed. Robert Jütte and Abraham Kustermann, Aschkenas, Beiheft 3 (Vienna, 1996), 91–101; and Alfred Haverkamp, '"Concivilitas" von Christen und Juden in Aschkenas im Mittelalter,' ibid., 103–136.

23. Though covering a different period, the work by Herbert Fischer, *Die verfassungsrechtliche Stellung der Juden in den deutschen Städten während des 13. Jahrhunderts*, Untersuchungen zur deutschen Staats- und Rechtsgeschichte, alte Folge 140 (Breslau, 1931; reprint Aalen, 1969), 7 ff., is still essential. (After his immigration into Israel in 1949 Herbert Fischer adopted the name Arye Maimon).

24. Attilio Milano, *Storia degli ebrei in Italia* (Torino, 1963), 69 ff.: According to Benjamin of Tudela, larger Jewish settlements were only to be found in Pisa and Lucca (about twenty to forty families); cf. also Shlomo Simonsohn, *History of the Jews in the Duchy of Mantua*, Publications of the Diaspora Research Institute 17 (Jerusalem, 1977), 2 f. Michele Luzzati (Pisa) is preparing a volume on Lucca for the series *A Documentary History of the Jews in Italy*, which will contain much hitherto unpublished material.

25. See Jean Stengers, *Les Juifs dans les Pays-Bas au Moyen Age*, Mémoires de l'Académie Royale de Belgique. Classe des Lettres et des sciences morales et politiques 2.45 (Brussels, 1950), and the doctoral dissertation by Christoph Cluse, *Studien zur Geschichte der Juden in den mittelalterlichen Niederlanden*, Forschungen zur Geschichte der Juden, A 10 (Hannover, 2000), ch. 1.

26. See Fischer, *Stellung* (as in note 23); Haverkamp, '"Concivilitas"' (as in note 22).

27. Michael Toch, 'Wirtschaft und Verfolgung: Die Bedeutung der Ökonomie für die Kreuzzugspogrome des 11. und 12. Jahrhunderts. Mit einem Anhang zum Sklavenhandel der Juden,' in *Juden und Christen* (as in note 3), 258–266, argues with good reasons against overestimating the Jewish money-lending 'in isolation'.

28. Alexander Pinthus, *Die Judensiedlung der deutschen Städte: Eine stadtbiologische Studie* (Berlin, 1931); Alfred Haverkamp, 'The Jewish Quarters in German Towns during the Late Middle Ages,' in *In and Out of the Ghetto: Jewish-Gentile Relations in Late Medieval and Early Modern Germany*, ed. Ronnie Po-chia Hsia and Hartmut Lehmann (New York, 1995), 13–28.

29. The context of settlement history which I have sketched deserves greater attention when discussing the Jews' relationship to the imperial court. On the state of research see Alexander Patschovsky, 'Das Rechtsverhältnis der Juden zum deutschen König. Ein europäischer Vergleich,' *Zeitschrift der Savigny-Stiftung für Rechtsgeschicthe, Germanistische Abteilung* 110 (1993): 331–371, who is the first to also take the Western European evidence into account; for a shorter English version see idem, 'The Relationship between the Jews of Germany and the King (11th–14th Century): A European Comparison,' in *England and Germany in the High Middle Ages*, ed. Alfred Haverkamp and Hanna Vollrath (Oxford, 1996), 193–218.

30. Cf. the still important work by Karl Bosl, *Die Reichsministerialität der Salier und Staufer*, 2 vols., Schriften der MGH 10 (Stuttgart, 1950–1951).

31. *Die Urkunden Heinrichs IV.*, vol. 2, ed. Dieter von Gladiss, MGH Diplomata 6.2 (Weimar, 1959), 543ff., no. 411 (Speyer), 547ff., no. 412; Aronius, *Regesten* (as in note 11), 71ff., no. 170f. Concerning the document for Worms, also see the preliminary remarks on the 1157 charter by Frederick I in *Die Urkunden Friedrichs I.* (as in note 19), 284, no. 166. The works by Sara Schiffmann are still useful, especially 'Die Urkunden für die Juden von Speyer 1090 und Worms 1157,' *Zeitschrift für die Geschichte der Juden in Deutschland* 2 (1930): 28–39; and 'Heinrichs IV. Verhalten zu den Juden zur Zeit des ersten Kreuzzuges,' ibid., 3 (1931): 39–58. Further studies are quoted in Haverkamp, '"Concivilitas"' (as in note 22), 110, note 27.

32. Cf. Friedrich Lotter, 'Imperial versus Ecclesiastical Jewry Law in the High Middle Ages: Contradictions and Controversies concerning the Conversions of Jews and their Serfs,' *Proceedings of the Tenth World Congress of Jewish Studies*, vol. B I, ed. David Assaf (Jerusalem, 1990), 53–60; idem, 'Talmudisches Recht in den Judenprivilegien Heinrichs IV.? Zu Ausbildung und Enticklung des Marktschutzrechts im frühen und hohen Mittelalter,' *Archiv für Kulturgeschichte* 72 (1990): 23–61.

33. On the long-term impact cf. Klaus Lohrmann, *Judenrecht und Judenpolitik im mittelalterlichen Österreich* (Vienna–Cologne, 1990), 53ff.; Friedrich Lotter, 'Geltungsgsbereich und Wirksamkeit des Rechts der kaiserlichen Judenprivilegien im Hochmittelalter,' *Aschkenas* 1 (1991): 23–64.

34. Ziwes, *Studien* (as in note 13), 67–73. Their preeminence was largely based on the legal decrees issued by the three communities (the *takkanot ShU"M*); cf. Louis Finkelstein, *Jewish Self-Government in the Middle Ages* (New York, 1924; rev. ed., 1964), 56ff., 218ff.

35. Otto of Freising, *Gesta Friderici I. imperatoris*, ed. Georg Waitz and Bernhard von Simson, MGH Scriptores rer. Germ. 46 (Hannover–Leipzig, 1912), 28; Bischof Otto von Freising und Rahewin, *Die Taten Friedrichs oder*

richtiger Cronica, ed. Franz-Josef Schmale, trans. Adolf Schmidt, Ausgewählte Quellen zur deutschen Geschichte des Mittelalters 17 (Darmstadt, 1974), 152 f.

36. See the appeal by bishops and secular leaders from eastern Saxonia around 1107/08: Friedrich Lotter, *Die Konzeption des Wendenkreuzzuges*, Vorträge und Forschungen, Sonderband 23 (Sigmaringen, 1977), 59 ff.

37. See the older literature collected in *Heidenmission und Kreuzzugsgedanke in der Ostpolitik des Mittelalters*, ed. Helmut Beumann, Wege der Forschung 7 (Darmstadt, 1963). As a guide to more recent literature, see Hans-Dietrich Kahl, 'Die weltweite Bereinigung der Heidenfrage—ein übersehenes Kriegsziel des zweiten Kreuzzuges,' in *Spannungen und Widersprüche: Gedenkschrift für František Graus*, ed. Susanna Burghartz et al. (Sigmaringen, 1992), 63–89; idem, 'Crusade Eschatology as Seen by St. Bernard in the Years 1146 to 1148,' in *The Second Crusade and the Cistercians*, ed. Max Gervers (New York, 1992), 35–47. Jürgen Miethke, 'L'engagement politique: la seconde croisade,' in *Bernard de Clairvaux: Histoire, mentalités, spiritualité*, Sources chrétiennes 380 (Paris, 1992), 472–503, argues against Kahl's thesis that 'missionary crusade was a product of sybilline eschatology'. Bernard's call for the crusade, which is at the center of this discussion, is accorded a different weight by Lotter, *Konzeption* (as in note 36) and 'The Crusading Idea and the Conquest of the Region East of the Elbe,' in *Medieval Frontier Societies*, ed. Robert Bartlett and Angus MacKay (Oxford, 1989), 267–306. See also Rudolf Hiestand, 'Juden und Christen in der Kreuzzugspropaganda und bei den Kreuzzugspredigern,' in *Juden und Christen* (as in note 3), 153–208.

38. For an extensive discussion of the canonical norms and with an approach concerning the practice which has not remained unchallenged, cf. Friedrich Lotter, '"Tod oder Taufe": Das Problem der Zwangstaufen während des ersten Kreuzzugs,' in *Juden und Christen*, 107 ff.

39. See the additamentum to the *Gesta Treverorum* (around 1132) on alleged plans by the archbishop of Trier in 1066: Eva Haverkamp, '"Persecutio" und "Gᵉzerah" in Trier während des Ersten Kreuzzugs,' in *Juden und Christen*, 35 f.

40. Otto von Freising and Rahewin, *Die Taten Friedrichs oder richtiger Cronica*, (as in note 35), 206, 208. Otto describes Radulf's aim as killing the Jews. For further Latin sources see Wilhelm Bernardi, *Konrad III.*, Jahrbücher der deutschen Geschichte 16 (Berlin, 1883; reprint, 1975), 522 ff. Lotter, *Konzeption* (as in note 36), 30–34. According to Ephraim bar Jacob, Radulf preached revenge on the local Jews by the Christians for the crucifixion of Christ. During the persecutions near Cologne, near Burg Stahleck, in Aschaffenburg, and elsewhere, the Jews were faced with the choice of either baptism or death. During the pogrom in Würzburg in February 1147 this alternative was

given only to one woman. According to Ephraim's report, there is only one case during the pogroms in France, which took place around the same time, in which this alternative was given. See *Hebräische Berichte über die Judenverfolgungen während der Kreuzzüge*, ed. Adolf Neubauer and Moritz Stern, trans. S. Baer (Berlin 1892), 58ff., 64 (German: 187ff., 196), and the English translation in *The Jews and the Crusaders: The Hebrew Chronicles of the First and Second Crusades*, trans. Shlomo Eidelberg (Madison, 1977), 121ff., 131. On Ephraim see Robert Chazan, 'Ephraim Ben Jacob's Compilation of Twelfth-Century Persecutions,' *Jewish Quarterly Review* 84 (1994): 397–416.

41. *Annales Herbipolenses*, ed. Georg Heinrich Pertz, MGH Scriptores 16 (Hannover, 1859), 3, on the persecution of Jews in 1146/47 in general: "Omnes ad locum ubi steterunt pedes Iesu Christi properant, signo crucis vestimenta non improbaliter sed presumptuose signant, Iudeos in omni fere transitu inventos baptizari cogunt, reluctantes sine dilatione interfitiunt. Und factum est, ut nonnulli Iudeorum necessitate compulsi fonte baptismatis abluerentur, at alii in fide suscepta perseverarent, alii pace reddita, quasi canes ad vomitum, ita denuo ad obscenas legitimorum suorum observationes redirent." On the incidents in Würzburg see below, note 56.

42. See, with different emphases, David Berger, 'The Attitude of St. Bernard of Clairvaux toward the Jews,' *Proceedings of the American Academy for Jewish Research* 40 (1974): 106f., which concludes 'that he was an unusually strong opponent to the destruction of Jews, yet an equally strong spokesman for anti-Jewish stereotypes and prejudices,' and further (103): 'Bernard was not led to violence by his prejudices, but the hatred which he preached was fanning the flames of violence in lesser men,' and more recently, Jeremy Cohen, '"Witnesses of Our Redemption": The Jews in the Crusading Theology of Bernhard of Clairvaux,' in *Medieval Studies in Honour of Avrom Saltman*, Bar-Ilan Studies in History 4 (Ramat-Gan, 1995), 67–81, as well as Friedrich Lotter, 'The Position of the Jews in Early Cistercian Exegesis and Preaching,' in *From Witness to Witchcraft: Jews and Judaism in Medieval Christian Thought*, ed. Jeremy Cohen, Wolfenbütteler Mittelalter-Studien 11 (Wiesbaden, 1996), 173ff. See also p. 259 and note 70, on Bernard's view of Anaklet II.

43. In studying the events in western continental Europe, the persecutions under the Almohads in Northern Africa, especially those between 1141 and 1148, and later on in Andalusia, during which Jews and Christians were given the choice of conversion to Islam or death, have been given too little consideration. See Salo Wittmayer Baron, *A Social and Religious History of the Jews*, 2d ed., vol. 3 (New York, 1957), 124ff.; *The Encyclopedia of Islam*, new ed., vol. 7 (Leiden, 1993), 801ff. (citing more recent literature). Insofar as Christians were affected by these events, the news are likely to have been spread also to the Christian West.

44. *Hebräische Berichte* (as in note 40), 73f., 209f.; see *Germania Judaica I* (as in note 6), 243–245.

45. *Hebräische Berichte*, 69, 203f.; *Germania Judaica I*, 61–63. On the further events in Speyer, Boppard, and Vienna in 1196 see Gerd Mentgen, 'Kreuzzugsmentalität bei antijüdischen Aktionen nach 1190,' in *Juden und Christen*, 287–326.

46. During the pogrom in Blois, the Jews who had been accused of an alleged ritual murder were in vain offered to save their lives through baptism: *Hebräische Berichte*, 66ff., 199ff. Cf. the contribution by Israel Jacob Yuval, 'Christliche Symbolik und jüdische Martyrologie zur Zeit der Kreuzzüge,' in *Juden und Christen*, 94ff.; the essay by Jean-Paul Savage, 'Le massacre des juifs à Blois, en 1171,' *Mémoires de la Société des sciences et lettres de Loir-et Cher 49* (1994): 5–20, gives no more than a compilation of the sources in translation. When in 1192 the Jews in Bray-sur-Seine or Brie-Comte-Robert were accused of an allegedly unjustified execution of a Christian on Purim, at least the more respected Jews are said to have been offered to save their lives through baptism but, again, in vain: *Hebräische Berichte*, 70, 205f. See Robert Chazan, 'The Bray Incident of 1192: Realpolitik and Folk Slander,' *Proceedings of the American Academy for Jewish Research 37* (1969): 1–18, and idem, *Medieval Jewry in Northern France: A Political and Social History* (Baltimore, London, 1973), 69f.; for references as to the place of these events see idem, 'Ephraim' (as in note 40), 402. On the boys who were 'spared' in Blois and Bray see below, note 51.

47. The author of the 'Continuatio' (written around 1132) to the *Gesta Treverorum, Additamentum et continuio prima*, ed. Georg Waitz, MGH Scriptores 8 (Hannover, 1848), 190, a Trierer collegiate cleric, is repeatedly referring to the canon law. He explicitly names the Jews in Trier who had been forced to baptism and who had returned to their faith in 1097 as *apostantes*. See Eva Haverkamp, 'Hebräische Berichte' (as in note 3).

48. See above note 1 and below note 51.

49. On the recent state of research see Ivan G. Marcus, 'Die politischen Entwicklungen im mittelalterlichen deutschen Judentum, ihre Ursachen und Wirkungen,' in *Judentum im deutschen Sprachraum*, ed. Karl E. Grözinger (Frankfurt/Main, 1991), 61–88; Joseph Dan, 'Das Entstehen der jüdischen Mystik im mittelalterlichen Deutschland,' ibid., 127–172; Ithamar Gruenwald, 'Normative und volkstümliche Religiosität im Sefer Chasidim,' ibid., 117–126 (including criticism of Marcus concerning the characterization of the Hasidim as a sectarian movement), and Eli Yassif, 'Entre culture populaire et culture savante: Les *exempla* dans le Sefer Hassidim,' *Annales HSS 49* (1994): 1187–1222.

50. See Josef Hacker, 'On the Persecutions of 1096' [Hebrew], *Zion 31* (1966): 230, who suggests relating these 'cases' to the events at Regensburg in 1096, but this is by no means necessarily so, considering the illustrative

character of *Sefer Hassidim*. Here, too, I follow the suggestion and advice of my friend Israel Yuval.

51. See Chazan, *Medieval Jewry* (note 46), 85 ff.; Eva Haverkamp, 'Hebräische Berichte' (note 3). In addition, see the evidence (a letter from the community of Orléans) for 'sparing' and forcibly baptising the boys at Blois during the pogrom in 1171 (revoked later, after payment of ransom, mediated by the archbishop of Sens), and for the 'release' of the boys under thirteen years of age in Bray in 1192 (according to Ephraim bar Jacob): *Hebräische Berichte*, 34, 150 and 70, 206.

52. *Die Urkunden Heinrichs IV.* (as in note 31), 2:546f., no. 411, for the Jews of Speyer: "Nullus filios aut filias eorum invitas baptizare presumat et, si coactus aut furtim raptos aut vi captos baptizaverit, XII libras auri ad erarium regis aut episcopi persolvat. Si autem aliqui eorum sponte baptizari velint, triduo reserventur, ut integre cognoscatur, si vere christiane religionis causa aut aliqua illata iniuria legem suam abnegent; et sicut patrum legem reliquerunt, ita eciam et possessiones eorum." The charter by Henry IV for the Jews of Worms (ibid., 548f., no. *412) and the corresponding charter by Frederick I (*Die Urkunden Friedrichs I.* [as in note 19], 1:285, no. 166) leave out the phrase saying that the fine of 12 pounds of gold could also be paid to the *erarium . . . episcopi*. Concerning the time limit of three days, see Friedrich Lotter, 'Geltungsbereich' (as in note 33), 45 ff. Apparently, the time limit was employed as early as the year 576, during the forced conversions in Clermont; see Dietrich Claude, 'Gregor von Tours und die Juden: Die Zwangsbekehrungen von Clermont,' *Historisches Jahrbuch* 111 (1991): 131–147, and Günter Stemberger, 'Zwangstaufen von Juden im 4. bis 7. Jahrhundert—Mythos oder Wirklichkeit,' in *Judentum—Ausblicke und Einsichten: Festgabe Kurt Schubert*, ed. Clemens Thoma, Günter Stemberger, and Johann Maier (Frankfurt/Main, 1993), 93. The norm implies that a third party check the willingness to be baptised during this time limit.

53. Lotter, 'Jewry Law' (as in note 32), 59; idem, 'Geltungsbereich' (as in note 33), 27, 55, regarding the differences between late classical Roman law and the internal norms of the Jewish community the order of Henry IV was following.

54. See *Germania Judaica I*, 330, 336.

55. See above, note 47.

56. On the incidents in Würzburg see *Annales Herbipolenses* (as in note 41), 4. According to this most of the Jews (*senes cum iunioribus, mulieres cum parvulis*) were killed by the citizens and *peregrini*: "Pauci fugam ineuntes salvantur, pauciores spe evadendi baptizantur, paucissimi postmodum reddita pace in fide perseverasse noscuntur." According to Ephraim bar Jacob some of the Jews

were able to take refuge with their Christian neighbours and to escape to a fortress the next day: *Hebräische Berichte*, 62, 195; Eidelberg, *Jews* (as in note 40), 127f. See Karlheinz Müller, 'Bildungsrang und Spiritualität der Würzburger Juden,' in *Unterfränkische Geschichte*, vol. 2, ed. Peter Kolb and Ernst-Günther Krenig (Würzburg, 1992), 381ff. On the discussion of the ritual murder motif connected with the Würzburg incidents, see Israel Jacob Yuval, 'Vengeance and Damnation, Blood and Defamation: From Jewish Martyrdom to Blood Libel Accusations' [Hebrew, *Zion* 58 (1993): 79–81; versus Gerd Mentgen, 'Über den Ursprung der Ritualmordfabel,' *Aschkenas* 4 (1994): 406f. (first published in Hebrew in *Zion* 59 [1994]: 343f.); most recently, the contributions by John M. McCulloh, 'Jewish Ritual Murder: William of Norwich, Thomas of Monmouth, and the Early Dissemination of the Myth,' *Speculum* 72 (1997): 728–732, and Berger, *Crusades* (as in note 2).

57. *Hebräische Berichte*, 64, 196; Eidelberg, *Jews*, 131: 'Those who had been forcibly converted in the various communities returned to the true path in that same year [4]907 [1147].' An unnamed 'priest' (*kômer*) is supposed to have 'guided them to the land of France (*eretz Tsarfat*) and other lands, so that they might return to their Torah and remain in those places until their defilement had worn off.' As far as I know, there is no mention of this deed anywhere else. Besides, it is hardly feasible.

58. On the scope for defining *vis* for the purpose of converting the Jews in the early Middle Ages, see Claude, 'Gregor von Tours' (as in note 52), 146f.; recently and in great detail, Lotter, '"Tod oder Taufe"' (as in note 38), 115–122.

59. Essential for the early Middle Ages is Arnold Angenendt, 'Der Taufritus im frühen Mittelalter,' in *Segni e riti nella chiesa altomedievale occidentale*, 2 vols., Settimane di studio del Centro italiano di studi sull'alto medioevo 33 (Spoleto, 1987), 1:275–321; more generally, cf. Andreas Stenzel, *Die Taufe: Eine genetische Erklärung der Taufliturgie* (Innsbruck, 1958), and Bruno Kleinheyer, *Sakramentliche Feiern I: Die Feiern der Eingliederung in die Kirche*, Gottesdienst der Kirche. Handbuch der Liturgiewissenschaft 7.1 (Regensburg, 1989).

60. Cf. Andreas Heinz, 'Eine Hildesheimer Missalehandschrift in Trier als Zeuge hochmittelalterlicher Taufpraxis (BATr Abt. 95, no. 404),' *Jahrbuch des Vereins für Heimatkunde im Bistum Hildesheim* 52 (1984): 39–55.

61. Heinz, 'Missalehandschrift,' 45; idem, 'Die Feier der Firmung nach römischer Tradition,' *Liturgisches Jahrbuch* 39 (1989): 67–88; Kleinheyer, *Feiern* (as in note 59), 121ff. Also see below, p. 270 and note 134, on the baptism of children on Easter Saturday *iuxta morem ecclesie*.

62. Aronius, *Regesten* (as in note 11), 319f., no. 757; *Germania Judaica II: Von 1238 bis zur Mitte des 14. Jahrhunderts*, 2 vols., ed. Zvi Avneri (Tübingen, 1968), 2:680.

63. Cohen, *Friars* (as in note 2), 229 ff.

64. *Hebräische Berichte*, 28, 137; Eidelberg, *Jews*, 67.

65. See the thorough survey of the manuscript sources by John Gilchrist, 'The Canonistic Treatment of Jews in the Latin West in the Eleventh and Early Twelfth Centuries,' *Zeitschrift der Savigny-Stiftung für Rechtsgeschichte, Kanonistische Abteilung* 75 (1989): 70–106, especially 75–77; recently Lotter, '"Tod oder Taufe"' (as in note 38).

66. See L[eopold] Lucas, 'Judentaufen und Judaismus zur Zeit des Papstes Innozenz III.,' in *Beiträge zur Geschichte der deutschen Juden: Festschrift Martin Philippson* (Leipzig, 1916), 25–38. Cf. Innocent's reply to an inquiry by the bishop of Metz in 1206 on the baptism of a Jew in the face of death who, surrounded only by Jews, had baptized himself by saying the baptismal formula and throwing himself into water: ibid., 33 f. = Aronius, *Regesten*, 163 f., no. 369.

67. Shlomo Simonsohn, *The Apostolic See and the Jews*, vol. 1, *Documents: 492–1404*, Studies and Texts 94 (Toronto, 1988), 80 f., no. 77; cf. Lotter, 'Judenprivilegien' (as in note 33), 52.

68. For further literature, cf. Ulrich Horst and Barbara Faes de Mottoni, 'Die Zwangstaufe jüdischer Kinder im Urteil scholastischer Theologen,' *Münchener Theologische Zeitschrift* 40 (1989): 173–199.

69. *Hebräische Berichte*, 29, 138; Eidelberg, *Jews*, 67.

70. In connection with his request to the emperor to ward off the fury of the schismatics (*rabiem schismaticorum*) against the Church, Bernhard relates the struggle against the 'usurper' Roger II to the case of Anaclete II who, as a Jewish brood (*iudiaca soboles*), occupied Peter's place to the disgrace of Christ (*in Christi . . . iniuriam*): *Sancti Bernhardi Epistolae I. Corpus Epistolarum 1–180*, ed. J. Leclerq and H. Rochais, S. Bernhardi Opera 7 (Rome, 1974), 335, no. 139 (dated early [?] 1136); *Regesten des Kaiserreiches unter Lothar III. und Konrad III.*, part 1: *Lothar. III.*, newly revised by Wolfgang Petke and J. F. Böhmer, Regesta Imperii 4.1 (Cologne, 1994), 296, no. 462.

71. See Mary Stroll, *The Jewish Pope: Ideology and Politics in the Papal Schism of 1130*, Brill's Studies in Intellectual History 8 (Leiden, 1987), 156 ff., especially 160; Mentgen, 'Proselyten' (as in note 1), 118 (with further literature); on 'racist' tendencies in Bernard of Clairvaux, see also Manfred Kniewasser, 'Die antijüdische Polemik des Petrus Alfonsi (getauft 1106) und des Abtes Petrus Venerabilis von Cluny († 1156),' *Kairos*, neue Folge 22 (1980): 51, and Cohen, '"Witnesses"' (note 42), 75.

72. See above, note 47.

73. "Hunc maiori prae ceteris familiaritate et dilectione idem Bruno sibi annectebat, satagens, ut quomodo ille ipsum carnaliter medicaretur, ita ipse illi salutem animae operaretur. Cum hoc saepissime de divinis disputabat volu-

minibus, semper illum ad conversionem deprecans et exhortans; in quo tandem Domino largiente optatum tenuit effectum. Nam consiliis eius acquievit et ab ipso baptizatus est": *Gesta Treverorum* (as in note 47), 195. On friendship as a foundation for attempting conversion see David Berger, 'Mission to the Jews and Jewish-Christian Contacts in the Polemical Literature of the High Middle Ages,' *American Historical Review* 91 (1986): 581 f.

74. See Blumenkranz, 'Konvertiten' (as in note 1), 264, citing two letters of recommendation for a Jewish convert by Anselm of Canterbury to the prior and archdeacon of Canterbury and to the bishop of Rochester: *Anselmi Cantuariensis archiepiscopi Opera omnia*, vol. 2, ed. Franciscus Salesius Schmitt (Stuttgart, 1968), 323 f., nos. 380 f.

75. Following the quotation above (note 73): "Cui Bruno suum nomen inposuit, et in cunctis bonis adiuvit, cunctis fidelibus suis ipsum commendans, et petens, quia genus illud hominum multum est in fide instabile semperque desiderat in vitae necessariis habundare, quatinus ubicumque ille ipsis manentibus superveniret, providerent ei necessaria cum caritate." On the status of this account within the chronicle and on the author's intention see Eva Haverkamp, "'Persecutio'" (as in note 39), 43 ff.

76. *Die Chronik der Böhmen des Cosmas von Prag*, ed. Bertold Bretholz, MGH Scriptores rer. Germ. n.s. 2, 2d ed. (Berlin, 1955), 230 f.; Aronius, *Regesten*, 101 f., no. 220; cf. *Germania Judaica I*, 29 f., and Heinz Schreckenberg, *Die christlichen Adversus-Judaeos-Texte (11.–13. Jh.)* (Frankfurt/Main, 1988), 97 ff.

77. See Hans-Georg von Mutius, 'Das Apostasieproblem im Lichte jüdischer Rechtsgutachten aus Deutschland, Frankreich und Italien vom Ende des 10. bis zum Ende des 11. Jahrhunderts,' in *Vorträge zur Justizforschung: Geschichte und Theorie*, vol. 2, ed. Heinz Mohnhaupt and Dieter Simon, Rechtsprechung 7 (Frankfurt/Main, 1993), 2 f., 15. See also Katz, *Exlusiveness* (as in note 1), 67–81.

78. See David Levine Lerner, 'The Enduring Legend of the Jewish Pope,' *Judaism* 40:2 (1981): 148–170; Abraham David, 'Bemerkungen zur Legende vom jüdischen Papst,' *Freiburger Rundbrief: Beiträge zur christlich-jüdischen Begegnung* 37/38 (1985/86), 150–153 (citing recent editions and translations). I am following the conclusion of the second version, whereas according to the first version Elhanan leaves a 'written condemnation of Christianity' after his 'descent' from the papal see, and secretly returns to Mainz where he becomes a "highly-esteemed Jew in the eyes of the people" (David, 152). I would like to thank my friend Israel Yuval for his important hints and support in dealing with this record.

79. See Israel Yuval, 'Heilige Städte' (as in note 22), 95 ff.

80. Lerner, 'Legend' (as in note 78), 150. On the practice of *Kiddush ha-Shem* see the recent contributions by Simha Goldin, 'The Socialisation for

Kiddush ha-Shem among Medieval Jews,' *Journal of Medieval History* 23 (1997): 117–138, and with new conclusions, Avraham Grossman, 'The Cultural and Social Background of Jewish Martyrdom in Germany in 1096,' in *Juden und Christen*, 73–86.

81. Yuval, 'Heilige Städte,' especially 94.

82. This attitude can also be seen with the author of the *Annales Herbipolenses*; see note 41.

83. In addition to the relevant works by Browe und Blumenkranz (see note 1), see Berger, 'Mission' (as in note 73), especially 583; Robert Chazan, *Daggers of Faith: Thirteenth-Century Christian Missionizing and Jewish Response* (Berkeley, 1989), 14f.

84. Concerning England in the twelfth century cf. Stacey, 'Conversion' (as in note 1), 266.

85. This source has been edited with insufficient commentary by Virgil Fiala, 'Ein Fragment des Traditionsrodels der Cisterzienserabtei Neuburg im hl. Forst,' *Cistercienserchronik*, neue Folge 61 (1954): 28. I owe this reference to Mentgen, 'Proselyten' (as in note 1), 120.

86. In a document by Frederick I, which presumably can be dated back to the fall of 1174, Burchardus is listed among the witnesses as *vicedominus Argentinensis* directly after Bishop Rudolf of Strassburg and before the abbot of St. Gregorien. The latest possible dating of this document is the deposition of Rudolf in March 1179: *Die Urkunden Friedrichs I.* (note 19), 3:126f., no. 631. According to this Burchard must have got this position in Strassburg under Bishop Rudolf, who himself had been imperial chaplain and provost of St. Thomas in Strasbourg (before 1163); cf. Josef Riedmann, 'Studien über die Reichskanzlei unter Friedrich Barbarossa,' *Mitteilungen des Instituts für Österreichische Geschichtsforschung* 76 (1968): 91. In a document by the provost and convent of St. Thomas from 1182, Burchardus is explicitly called *vicedominus et frater noster*: *Urkundenbuch der Stadt Straßburg*, vol. 1, ed. Wilhelm Wiegand (Strasbourg, 1879), 98, no. 118, line 18; he also appears as *vicedominus* in the list of witnesses, line 27; see ibid., 99, no. 119, line 36 (also before 1182). Further mentions as *vicedominus*, ibid., 104, no. 127, and *Die Urkunden Friedrichs I.*, 4:282, no. 993, lines 34f. (of 1189); *Urkundenbuch Straßburg*, 1:106, no. 130, line 28 (1192, on house-owning in Strasbourg) = *Die Regesten des Kaiserreiches unter Heinrich VI.*, revised by Gerhard Baaken and J. F. Boehmer, *Regesta Imperii* 4.3 (Cologne, 1972), 86f., no. 210; *Urkundenbuch Straßburg*, 1:109, no. 132, line 14 (of 1193), and ibid., 109, no. 133, lines 25f. (of 1194); presumably still among the *canonicis Argentinensis ecclesie*: ibid., 105, no. 128 (of 1190), and apparently to be distinguished from the *canonici*: 109, no. 133, line 26 (of 1194). It remains unclear if Burchardus *clericus in Argentina*, who held the im-

perial church in Balbronn in 1192, is identical with the *vicedominus: Regesta Imperii* (as above), 4.3:88f., no. 214. See also the studies by Paul Scheffer-Boichorst, 'Der kaiserliche Notar und der Strassburger Vitztum Burchard, ihre wirklichen und angeblichen Schriften,' 1889, reprinted in idem, *Gesammelte Schriften*, vol. 2 (Berlin, 1905), 225–247, and the survey in Hans-Walther Klewitz, *Geschichte der Ministerialität im Elsaß bis zum Ende des Interregnums* (Frankfurt/Main, 1929), 77.

87. See Hannes Möhring, *Saladin und der Dritte Kreuzzug: Aiyubidische Strategie und Diplomatie im Vergleich vormehmlich der arabischen mit den lateinischen Quellen*, Frankfurter Historische Abhandlungen 21 (Wiesbaden, 1980), 93ff., 125ff., 134f.

88. See Rainer Maria Herkenrath, *Die Reichskanzlei in den Jahren 1174 bis 1180*, Österreichische Akademie der Wissenschaften, phil.-hist. Klasse, Denkschriften 130 (Vienna, 1977), 45ff.; *Die Urkunden Friedrichs I.*, 5:46f., 66–68. It can only be presumed that Burchard is involved in no. 639 of 21 May 1175; no. 643 of 10 November 1175 was 'composed under the influence' of Burchard, judging by 'some of the wordings.' No. 649, 'composed and written by Burchard,' is not dated clearly: 'probably summer 1176.' Burchard can be verified with certainty in no. 653 of 29 July 1176 in Pavia. Of course this hypothesis on the identity of the *vicedominus* and the *capellanus*, which has already been discussed in previous research, will have to be further examined.

89. The report has been preserved in Arnold of Lübeck, *Chronica Slavorum*, ed. Georg Heinrich Pertz, MGH Scriptores rer. Germ. 14 (Hannover, 1868), bk. 7, ch. 8, 264–277, 266f. (on Alexandria), 269 (on Cairo, *In qua habitant Sarraceni, Iudei et christiani. Quelibet natio suam legem colit*), 273 (on Damascus). On how Burchard's report may have passed from the imperial court to Arnold of Lübeck, see Franz-Josef Schmale, *Deutschlands Geschichtsquellen im Mittelalter: Vom Tode Kaiser Heinrichs V. bis zum Ende des Interregnums*, vol. 1 (Darmstadt, 1975), 440.

90. See *Germania Judaica I*, 341 and notes 224–228; as far as I can tell, the article by E. Rosenthal on 'Kalonymos als Bankier Kaiser Friedrichs I.,' which was announced for the *Neues Archiv*, was never published. In addition Marcus, 'Entwicklungen' (as in note 49), 66f., 77.

91. On the philosophical context see Georg Wieland, 'Symbolische und universale Vernunft: Entgrenzungen und neue Möglichkeiten,' in *Friedrich Barbarossa* (as in note 4), 533–549.

92. Fiala, 'Fragment' (as in note 85), 28: ". . . quod dominus Burchardus Argentinensis ecclesie uicedominus allodium quoddam in Dunne\<he\>im L. scilicet et duos agros cultos et tres curtes cum prato et cellerario in cimiterio LXIIIIor \<lib\>ris ab ipso comparatum gloriose uirgini Marie et honorabili in

Christo abbati . . . fratribusque . . . contradidit. . . ." The editor (29) erroneously
took the price to be an estimate.

93. See Karl Leyser, 'Friedrich Barbarossa—Hof und Land,' in *Friedrich
Barbarossa*, 525f.

94. According to the first municipal charter for Strasbourg from around
1130, the value of one *quartale frumenti* is equal to one *ama vini*: *Urkundenbuch
Straßburg* (as in note 86), 1:471, no. 616, line 3. One *ohm* amounted to *c.* 45 to
50 liters; see Medard Barth, *Der Rebbau des Elsass und die Absatzgebiete seiner
Weine. Ein geschichtlicher Überblick*, 2 vols. (Strasbourg, Paris, 1958), 1:325f. (I
am grateful to Dr. Lukas Clemens, Trier, for this reference).

95. Fiala, 'Fragment': "Illud etiam sane memorie commendandum est,
quod ipse ad eternam illumina<tio>nem anime sue comparandam statuit ut de
eodem censu coram altari beate Marie singulis noctibus <la>mpa ardeat. Pro
huiusmodi beneficiis gloriose uirgini et fratribus ab ipso collatis in consortium
plenari<um fr(ater)>nitatis ipse et domina Anna deuotissime ab ipsis recepti
sunt et participes facti sunt omnium orationum <et> elemosinarium suarum et
pro eis tam uiuis quam defunctis sicut pro abbate monacho et fratre omnibus
<ro>getur et in anniverariis eorum secundum dispositionem abbatis priorum et
seniorum de ipso allodio caritate <su>e administrabitur. . . ."

96. On Burchard's property in Strasbourg see above, note 86.

97. Caesarius of Heisterbach, *Dialogus Miraculorum*, 2 vols., ed. Josephus
Strange (Cologne, 1851), 1:92–94. On the author and the *Dialogus*, probably
written between 1219 and 1223, see Fritz Wagner, 'Studien zu Caesarius von
Heisterbach,' *Analecta Cisterciensia* 29 (1973): 79–95; idem, 'Caesarius von
Heisterbach,' in *Lexikon des Mittelalters*, vol. 2 (Munich, 1983), cols. 1363–1366
(giving further literature); idem, 'Der rheinische Zisterzienser und Predigt-
schriftsteller Caesarius von Heisterbach,' *Cistercienser Chronik* 101 (1994):
93–111. Concerning the aspects discussed here, Ivan Marcus, 'Jews and
Christians Imagining the Other in Medieval Europe,' *Prooftexts* 15 (1995):
217ff. and (partly identical) idem, 'Images of the Jews in the *Exempla* of
Caesarius of Heisterbach,' in *Witness to Witchcraft* (as in note 42), 247–256, offers new insights. See also Ludger Tewes, 'Der Dialogus Miraculorum des
Caesarius von Heisterbach. Beobachtungen zum Gliederungs- und Werk-
charakter,' *Archiv für Kulturgeschichte* 79 (1997): 13–30.

98. See p. 273f.

99. Caesarius, *Dialogus*, 1:92; on the idea of a 'flux of blood' (*fluxus sangui-
nis*) from which the Jews were said to suffer on Good Friday, see the recent contribution by Willis Johnson, 'The Myth of Jewish Male Menses,' *Journal of
Medieval History* 24 (1998): 273–295, especially 287, and Cluse, *Studien* (as in
note 25), 321ff.

100. Caesarius, *Dialogus*, 1:93: "Episcopus . . . eidem suasit ac persuasit, ut puellam a se defloratam, per baptismi, gratiam renovatam, legitime duceret, malens illum, sicut vir pius et iustus, ecclesiasticis carere beneficiis, quam illam multis expositam periculis in paternis manere delictis. Clericus . . . conversus est postea in ordine nostro, similiter et eius instinctu puella."

101. The history of research is too complex to survey here; I have followed the recent contribution by J. P. Gumbert, 'Een en ander over het handschrift van de Egmondse Annalen,' in *Heiligenlevens, Annalen en Kronieken: Geschied-schrijving in middeleeuws Egmond*, ed. G. N. M. Vis, M. Mostert, and P. J. Margry (Hilversum, 1990), 55–69, especially 65. On the annals, see also p. 273.

102. 'Annales Egmundenses,' in *Fontes Egmundenses*, ed. Otto Oppermann (Utrecht, 1933), 158, give the following didactic introduction: "Item eiusdem regis Fritherici temporibus in festivitate paschalis gaudii maximum Dominus misericordie sue dedit indicium et dilectionis quam habet ad populum christane religionis, de cuius rei veritate nulli fidelium est dubitandum. In civitatibus ori-entalis Francie circa Renum constitutis habundant synagoge iudeorum, in quarum una puella fuit iudea. . . ." Presumably, it is still the eastern Frankish empire or the *Regnum Teutonicum* which is meant by 'orientalis Francia.'

103. Ibid., 160: "Quo Dei viso beneficio et audito, diaconus et ipse prostra-tus epicopi pedibus confessus est facinus suum, et ab omnibus in commune christianis et iudeis clamoribus, gemitibus, oblationibus glorificatum est nomen Christi, quod est super omne nomen benedictum."

104. Caesarius, *Dialogus*, 1:94f.; Aronius, *Regesten*, 187, no. 418.

105. Caesarius, *Dialogus*, 1:95–98; Aronius, *Regesten*, 184–186, no. 414. See Browe, 'Kirchenrechtliche Stellung' (as in note 1), 6; further references in Cluse, *Studien* (as in note 25).

106. See notes 31–32.

107. Caesarius, *Dialogus*, 1:98f.: "Praedictus miles, cum sit aetate iuvenis, nec tamen multum dives, virginem loco filiae nutrit, volens illam tradere viro, vel in aliquo monasterio tradere." Aronius, *Regesten*, 186, no. 417; *Germania Judaica I*, 159f.

108. *Kölner Schreinsurkunden des 12. Jahrhunderts*, 2 vols., ed. Robert Hoeniger, Publikationen der Gesellschaft für Rheinische Geschichtskunde 1 (Bonn, 1884–1894), 1.3.4, 241, no. 6, dating around 1161 = Aronius, *Regesten*, 125, no. 288. Robert Hoeniger, 'Zur Geschichte der Juden Deutschlands im frühern Mittelalter,' *Zeitschrift für Geschichte der Juden in Deutschland* 1 (1886): 76 note 2, has a different reading in the last line of this document which was erased. According to this the brothers of Sophia had given their *testimonium*. On 'Jewish law and German or Cologne law' with respect to the principle that Jewish daughters 'could only inherit when the deceased had left neither a son

nor any surviving progeny of a son', see Adolf Kober, *Grundbuch des Kölner Judenviertels, 1135–1425*, Publikationen der Gesellschaft für Rheinische Geschichtskunde 34 (Bonn, 1920), 46ff.

109. See the evidence in the index of Hoeniger, *Schreinsurkunden* (as in note 108), 2.2:114, who merely presumed he might have been identical with Gerhard Unmaze, ibid., note 1; Paul Strait, *Cologne in the Twelfth Century* (Gainesville, 1974), 81ff., identifies him as Gerhard Unmaze; cf. Sonja Zöller, *Kaiser, Kaufmann und die Macht des Geldes: Gerhard Unmaze von Köln als Finanzier der Reichspolitik und der 'Gute Gerhard' des Rudolf von Ems*, Forschungen zur Geschichte der älteren deutschen Literatur 16 (Munich, 1993), who also identifies Unmaze as a model for the key figure in *Der guote Gêrhart*. Her sometimes daring theses have attracted some right criticism, notably by Manfred Groten, *Köln im 13. Jahrhundert. Gesellschaftlicher Wandel und Verfassungsentwicklung*, Städteforschung A 36 (Cologne, 1995), 17f., and Anke Kleine, '"Der Gefährte im Paradies": *Der guote Gêrhart* und die jüdische Überlieferung,' *Jiddistik-Mitteilungen* 17 (April 1997):6f.

110. See Hoeniger, 'Geschichte' (as in note 108), 76f.; Klaus Cuno, 'Namen Kölner Juden,' *Rheinische Heimatpflege*, neue Folge 4 (October–December 1974): 278–291. According to the index in Hoeniger, *Schreinsurkunden*, 2.2:217, no. 122, Sophia is only used for definitely Christian women in the ten other cases mentioned.

111. Ibid., 232, no. 27 of c. 1147–1165 = Aronius, *Regesten*, 127, no. 297. Nathan had bought the house he was living in for his sons Gerard (the following names Natai and Abraham have been crossed out) and Iosep between 1140 and 1165, so that the brothers could freely dispose of it: Hoeniger, *Schreinsurkunden*, 1:231, no. 23.

112. Probably, Petrus is named after the patron saint of the cathedral, which would imply a baptism under the influence of one of the members of the cathedral chapter or the archiepiscopal court. On the other hand, the Christian name Petrus Alfonsi for the Jewish court physician Moses was determined by his conversion on the holiday of Peter und Paul and by King Alfonso I being his *patronus*; see Cohen, 'Mentality' (as in note 1), 23f.

113. Both Hoeniger, 'Geschichte,' 76, and Aronius, *Regesten*, 125, no. 288, speak of the only case of a 'mixed marriage' mentioned in the documents from the chests of Cologne.

114. See Gerold Bönnen, Alfred Haverkamp, and Frank G. Hirschmann, 'Religiöse Frauengemeinschaften im räumlichen Gefüge der Trierer Kirchenprovinz während des hohen Mittelalters,' in *Herrschaft, Kirche, Kultur: Beiträge zur Geschichte des Mittelalters. Festschrift für Friedrich Prinz*, ed. Georg Jenal (Stuttgart, 1993), 369–415. Especially the necrologies have only rarely been

dealt with. No evidence is to be found in material from convents rather remote from the major Jewish settlements, recently studied by Elsanne Gilomen-Schenkel, 'Das Doppelkloster—eine verschwiegene Institution. Engelburg und andere Beispiele aus dem Umkreis der Helvetia Sacra,' *Studien und Mitteilungen zur Geschichte des Benediktiner-Ordens und seiner Zweige* 101 (1990): 197–211.

115. See notes 85, 105. The problems connected with both choices are discussed in *Sefer Hassidim* (ms. Parma, no. 262; ed. Bologna, no. 703), whose author appears to favor the convent: Jehudah ben Chemouel le Hassid, *Sefer Hassidim: Le guide des Hassidim*, trans. Édouard Gourévitch, Patrimoines: Judaïsme (Paris, 1988), 63 f. I owe this reference to Christoph Cluse, Trier.

116. New results are presented in Ludger Horstkötter, 'Zweifel an der Gleichsetzung des Propstes Hermann von Scheda mit dem jüdischen Konvertiten Hermann von Cappenberg,' *Analecta Praemonstratensia* 71 (1995): 52–76. Horstkötter does not consider the controversy on the historicity of *Hermannus quondam Judeus*, on which see note 153.

117. They are (a) the provost *Herimannus Israelita* (attested in 1170), whom Horstkötter, 'Zweifel' (as in note 116), would allocate at the convent of Bredelar; (b) a canon and priest at the collegiate church of St Cassius in Bonn (attested in 1149 and 1153, here *Herimanni presbiteri nomine Judei cognominati, eiusdem ecclesie canonici*); (c) *Hermannus Iudaeus*, canon of St Mary *ad gradus* in Cologne (attested between 1172 and 1181); and (d) the canon *Godefridus Iudeus* attested at Cappenberg in 1199.

118. Horstkötter, 'Zweifel,' 68 ff.

119. See note 147.

120. According to the edition of the note concerning this handover, the otherwise unknown Konrad of Mergersdorf "delegavit super aram S. Nycolay . . . quemdam Judeum Henricum ad censum quinque denariorum singulis annis persolvendum": Maximilian Fischer, *Merkwürdigere Schicksale des Stiftes und der Stadt Klosterneuburg aus Urkunden gezogen*, 2 vols. (Vienna, 1815), 2:85, no. 140, also in *Codex traditionum ecclesiae collegiatae Claustroneoburgensis*, ed. Maximilian Fischer, Fontes rerum Austriacarum 2.4 (Vienna, 1851), 86, no. 398. Aronius, *Regesten*, p. 145, no. 323a, as well as *Germania Judaica I*, 143 f., have merely noted an unspecified tax. But the legal act recorded was a transfer of the person; it is by no means—as Aronius thought—a 'parallel to the situation at Würzburg,' where only tranfers of possessions by Jews are attested. It is impossible that the *delegatio* concerned a Jew. These problems could be overcome if *quemdam* were a wrong reading of *quondam*, but this is not the case: Professor Dr. Floridus Röhrig, Can. Reg. and archivist at Klosterneuburg has kindly informed me that one has to read *quendam* instead of *quemdam* and that

iudeum was added, 'apparently by a different, albeit not much younger hand,' above *Heinricum*. The only possibility is that the scribe was rendering the name of the tax-payer more precise by adding *iudeum*. I would not regard this addition as a family name, given the palaeographic evidence and the social context. (Dr. Gerd Mentgen later pointed out to me that Lohrmann, *Judenrecht* [as in note 33], 46f., note 129, has already discussed this evidence, to which there is no reference in the book's index). *Ernustus Judeus* was certainly a Christian, he appears in a list of witnesses before *Adalramus advocatus de Perge*, *Wichart de Frondorf*, and *Adelsbertus de Werde Herosolimitanus* (the latter was certainly a crusader) of a note on a donation to the Augustinian chapter of Berchtesgaden in 1136: *Germania Judaica I*, 149f. Here I can only hint at further evidence of various persons with non-Jewish names who are called 'Jews' in ibid., 159 (concerning the Cistercian convent Raitenhaslach) and 155 (on Leibnitz in Steiermark). See further in this essay for evidence from Cologne and from the thirteenth century.

121. Cf. Alfred Haverkamp, 'Das Bambergische Hofrecht für den niederbayerischen Hochstiftsbesitz,' *Zeitschrift für bayerische Landesgeschichte* 30 (1967): 423–506. On the concept of 'Zensualität,' which is little known in Anglo-American research, see also Michael Matheus, 'Forms of Social Mobility: The Example of *Zensualität*,' in *England and Germany* (as in note 29), 357–369.

122. Aronius, *Regesten*, 132, no. 310.

123. In a document by archbishop Arnold for the Cologne Benedictine abbey of St. Martin, which was closely connected to the municipal ruling classes, Everhardus is mentioned on the extensive list of witnesses, distinguished according to clergymen, *liberi*, *ministeriales*, and *burgenses*. Everhardus is in the fifth place, followed by his brother Walter, who is not described any further (. . . *et frater eius Walterus*). The list gives another seven names. Cf. Aronius, *Regesten*, 114, no. 250; cf. Richard Knipping, *Die Regesten der Erzbischöfe von Köln im Mittelalter*, vol. 2, Publikationen der Gesellschaft für rheinische Geschichtsforschung 21 (Bonn, 1901), 78, *regestum* no. 457 (of late 1147), based on the original, with reference to older editions.

124. Hoeniger, 'Geschichte' (as in note 108), 73; idem, *Schreinsurkunden*, 1:217f., no. 2 (dated between 1135 and 1152): The act appears as the second entry into the fragmentary chest book. It refers to the purchase of a plot of ground in a Christian's *curia* by "Vives Iudeus et Agnes uxor eius . . . presentibus parrochianis parrochie s. Laurentii etiamque potestate civitatis consistente ibi." After the testimonium of the same *parrochyani* the following text leads up to the list of witnesses: "Hoc autem totum factum est eo tempore, quo Egebreth (qui

Iudeus fuit) et Harduwic filius Geroldi erant magistri vicinorum parrochie s. Laurentii" (= Aronius, *Regesten,* 118f., no. 261). The crucial part *qui Iudeus fuit* was put in parentheses by Hoeniger. In his 'Erläuterung zu der Ausgabe' he explained: 'Parentheses include all textual irregularities such as additions above the line or in the margins, later additions over erasures, etc.'

    125. Hoeniger, 'Geschichte,' 74, 75f.

    126. On criticism of Hoeniger's rather cautious conclusions see Adolf Kober, *Studien zur mittelalterlichen Geschichte der Juden in Köln am Rhein, insbesondere ihres Grundbesitzes* (Ph.D. diss., Breslau, 1903), especially 13f. (including a list of other criticism voiced meanwhile), 18. In the index to *Schreinsurkunden,* 2.2:238f., Hoeniger leaves open whether the name *Iudeus* added to Theodericus, Eckkebertus, Reginbolt, and Winricus can be taken as an epithet or if it is supposed to show that they are Jews.

    127. Ibid., 1:218, IV, no. 4, a legal act among Christians dated 1135–1152: "Huius rei testes sunt Richart (prepositus) et Udilolf et Godescalc et Theodericus advocatus aliique civium magistri, Luzeman et Heriman (frater eius), Herman et frater eius Bertolfus; Thiderich (Iudeus) et Emunt, Eckebret (Iudeus) et Fordolfus (filius eius), Gerart (Ungemaz) et Hartwich (Harde), Cuno (Liginde) et Gerhart (de Kercinpuzze) et alii cives quam plures)" = Aronius, *Regesten,* 117f., no. 259. See also ibid., 220, VII, no. 7 (between 1139 and 1152): ". . . fuit presens Rutgerus nuntius iudicis nostri, fuerunt etiam magistri civium Luceman et Hermann frater eius, Thiderich (Iudeus), Emunt, Bertolf et Heriman frater suus, Eckebret Iudeus et Fordolf filius, Hertwich et Gerhart (cognatus suus) Cuno et Gerhart (de platea) allique cives communes interfuerunt."

    128. Ibid., 1:219, V, no. 3 (also between 1135 and 1152): "Hoc contigit in tempore magistrorum civium quorum nomina: Emunt, Tiderich, Hereman et filius eius Hereman, Hildewin, Berenger, Hereman Albus, Wolbero, aliique cives, Hildebrant, Heinrich Strenzebuch, Ekebret Iudeus, Wezil neldere, Marcman filius suus, et alii cives quorum nomina hic singulariter notari nequaquam poterant." = Aronius, *Regesten,* 117, no. 258. In Hoeniger, *Schreinsurkunden,* 1:221, VII, no. 9 (between 1139 and 1152, = Aronius, *Regesten,* 121, no. 272), "Eckebret et Fordolfus filius eius" are mentioned among the *cives* without any further description. Ekkebret is also mentioned in Hoeniger, 'Geschichte,' 71 ff. Concerning Tiderich, who may be identical with *Thiderich Iudeus* in the list of witnesses mentioned above, see the passages in note 127 above and also Hoeniger, *Schreinsurkunden,* 231, 2, IV, no. 15 (between 1140 and 1165): purchase of a house by a Christian from the sons of *Thioderici Iudei* = Aronius, *Regesten,* 126, no. 294 (with further references to Thiderich).

129. See above, note 112 on Ioseph-Petrus.

130. In my opinion a similar meaning of *Iudeus* can be found in the entry concerning the purchase by *magister Alelmus, fisicus*, of a porch and a barn of the house of one 'Jew named Christianus' (*testitudinem et stabulum de domo cuiusdam Iudei, nomine Cristiani*) in the community of Dilles between 1210 and 1225: This name is quite unimaginable for a Jew, despite the increasing assimilation in naming; cf. Hoeniger, *Schreinsurkunden*, 2.1:282, VI, no. 4.

131. Aronius, *Regesten*, 119f., no. 265, and 122, no. 273.

132. Ibid., 122f., no. 277f. Regarding the names *Winricus Iudeus* (between 1187 and 1200) in the parish St. Columba, and *Reginbolt (Iudeus)* on the roll of citizens, it cannot be said if the addition referred to baptized Jews of to a family name: Hoeniger, *Schreinsurkunden*, 1:366, VIII, nos. 3f., and 2:2, 22, IV, no. 88.

133. *Chronica regia Coloniensis, Annales Maximi Colonienses*, ed. Georg Waitz, MGH Scriptores rer. Germ. 18 (Hannover, 1880), 90; Aronius, *Regesten*, 122, no. 274. On the state of research see Schmale, *Geschichtsquellen* (as in note 89), 105ff.

134. Arnold, *Chronica Slavorum* (as in note 89), 169: "In sabbato quippe sancto pasche, cum parvuli iuxta morem ecclesie baptizarentur, quidam Iudeus eiusdem civitatis quasi pro curiositate cum aliis spectatoribus huic se negotio ingessit"; Aronius, *Regesten*, 148f., no. 330.

135. Also see the evidence for the *curiositas* of Juda ben David ha-Levi in Hermannus quondam Judaeus, *Opusculum de conversione sua*, ed. Gerlinde Niemeyer, MGH Quellen 4 (Weimar, 1963), 73f., 76.

136. See quotation below, note 144.

137. Arnold, *Chronica Slavorum*: "Siquidem Iudeis quedam est detestabilis consuetudo, ut inplentes mensuram patrum suorum quovis anno ad contumeliam Salvatoris ymaginem ceream crucifigant. Quam dum more suo contumeliis afficerent et cetera, que in passione eius leguntur, flagellando. . . ." Note that only an annual date is mentioned, not specifically fixed during Holy Week.

138. Ibid., p. 170: "Relicta enim synagoga, statim ad archiepiscopum cucurrit, que gesta sunt nunciavit, et abrenuncians infedilitati synagoge in sabbato sancto lavacrum regenerationis accepit et non solum angelis Dei, sed et hominibus de sua conversione gaudium fecit."

139. On 'applying' the Jewish *consuetudo* to torment a picture of Hamann on the Feast of Purim to the archbishop of Trier in a source of before or around 1130, see Eva Haverkamp, "'Persecutio'" (as in note 39), 35f.; Mentgen, 'Ursprung' (as in note 56); Christoph Cluse, 'Stories of Breaking and Taking the Cross: A Possible Context for the Oxford Incident of 1298,' *Revue d'Histoire Ecclésiastique* 90 (1995): 405ff.

140. See Jeremy Cohen, 'The Jews as the Killers of Christ in Latin Tradition, from Augustine to the Friars,' *Traditio* 39 (1983), esp. 13–16 on the twelfth century, but without mentioning Arnold of Lübeck.

141. Cf. the following argument for the credibility of the story, Arnold, *Chronica Slavorum*, p. 170: "Illi inplentes mensuram patrum suorum, qui sibi suisque inprecantes dixerunt: 'Sanguis eius super nos et super filios nostros'" (Matthew 27:25, read in connection with the Passion on Palm Sunday), "ipsum sub ymagine sua contumeliis affectum crucifigentes, vere crucifigunt, non verbum vite sicut patres eorum manibus nefariis contrectantes, sed odiendo, execrando, malitie illum manibus contingentes. . . ."

142. Ibid.: "Et qui vidit testimonium perhibuit, et scimus, quia verum est testimonium eius." (Cf. John 21:24.) "Nam idem Iudeus divinitus illuminatus hec vidit et credidit." See also Aronius, *Regesten*, 149, no. 330.

143. See the parallel in the Egmond annals, and note 165.

144. The words which are perceived by the Jew have no effect, either: "Audierat sepius magnum esse christianitatis sacramentum, sed Iudaica repugnante perfidia, quicquid inde mente concipere poterat, dubie recipiebat."

145. Arnold's further explanations are focussed on this theme: *Chronica Slavorum*, 5.15, 170f.

146. Wolfgang Herborn, 'Schreinswesen, -buch, -karte,' in *Lexikon des Mittelalters*, vol. 7 (Munich, 1995), cols. 1557–1559.

147. Basically the evidence is to be found in Friedrich Lau, 'Das Kölner Patriziat bis zum Jahre 1325,' part 3, *Mitteilungen aus dem Stadtarchiv von Köln*, 26 (1895), 115–119; in addition see Strait, *Cologne* (as in note 109), 90ff., 101ff. Regarding the widow of Daniel Judeus (d. 1227), Groten, *Köln* (as in note 109), 154, has assumed that 'Sela, also called Sihardis, was perhaps a baptised Jewish woman who gave her husband that byname which his family was to keep' (which I do not find convincing).

148. For detailed evidence from his field of research see Cluse, *Studien* (as in note 25), 385ff., and Mentgen, 'Proselyten' (as in note 1), 121ff., for evidence of marking baptised Jews with *Judeus* as late as the fifteenth century; for evidence from Westphalia see Horstkötter, 'Zweifel' (as in note 116), 52–76.

149. *Germania Judaica I*, 235f (from 1214 on).

150. Ibid., 237, on Ismaning near München, between 1197 and 1212: Fridericus Judeus among 'the first witnesses' of a charter; 155 on Leibniz in der Steiermark, from 1233 ('Heinrich mit dem Beinamen Judeus').

151. See notes 73–75.

152. Most recently, Horstkötter, 'Zweifel,' 71 (without reference to the recent controversy, for which see the following note).

153. Jean-Claude Schmitt, 'La memoire des Prémontrés: À propos de l' "autobiographie" du prémontré Hermann le Juif,' in *La vie quotidienne des moines et chanoines réguliers au moyen âge et temps modernes*, ed. Marek Derwich (Wroclaw, 1995), 439–452. The authenticity has been questioned by Avrom Saltman, 'Hermann's *Opusculum de conversione sua*: Truth or Fiction?' *Revue des études juives* 147 (1988): 31–56; for arguments against regarding it as 'fiction', see Friedrich Lotter, 'Ist Hermann von Schedas Opusculum De conversione sua eine Fälschung? *Aschkenas* 2 (1992): 207–218. See also Horstkötter, 'Zweifel'.

154. Hermannus, *Opusculum* (as in note 135), 73.

155. See note 73, and the hint in Hermannus, *Opusculum* (as in note 135), 76, where Judah is said to have received books from clerics while attending their *scholae*.

156. This is almost the didactic leitmotif, as can be seen from the introductory *Epistola Hermanni* to Henry: "Non enim ea facilitate conversus sum, qua multos sepe infideles sive Iudeos sive paganos ad fidem catholicam repentina et inopinata mutatione converti videmus, ut quos heri perfidos dolebamus, hodie fideles et nostros in gratia Christi factos coheredes gaudeamus." *Opusculum*, 69, see Berger, 'Mission" (as in note 73), 587.

157. Hermannus, *Opusculum*, 73f., 80f., 104; cf. Blumenkranz, 'Konvertiten' (as in note 1), 278.

158. See Ivan G. Marcus, 'A Pious Community and Doubt: Qiddush ha-Shem in Ashkenaz and the Story of Rabbi Amnon of Mainz,' in *Studien zur jüdischen Geschichte und Soziologie: Festschrift Julius Carlebach*, ed. Hochschule für Jüdische Studien (Heidelberg, 1992), 97–113 (almost identical with the French version in *Annales HSS* 49 (1994): 1031–1047); a commented edition of the source itself also in *Tora, wer wird dich nun erheben? Pijutim Mimagenza. Religiöse Dichtungen aus dem mittelalterlichen Mainz*, ed. and trans. Simon Hirschhorn (Gerlingen, 1995), 54f.

159. Aronius, *Regesten*, 105, no. 226, lacks noticeable critical distance; *Germania Judaica I* is cautious on 23 ('to be taken with great caution'), and follows Aronius on 286. Lotter, 'Geltungsbereich' (as in note 33), 55, takes the story as the description of a real incident of 'around 1139'; idem, 'Opusculum' (as in note 153), 215 and note 22, thinks the 'Regensburg story' was so 'untypical, that it is quite possible that it was based on some real event.' The source has recently been studied by Mary Minty, 'Kiddush ha-Shem in German Christian Eyes in the Middle Ages' [Hebrew], *Zion* 59 (1994): 234ff. (cf. the English summary, XII–XIV).

160. See notes 99–100.

161. 'Annales Egmundenses' (as in note 102), 149: "Huius Conradi regis temporibus res digna relatu in civitate Bawarie Rainsburch contigit, quam ex ore cuiusdam iudei christiani eiusdem civitatis notissimi certissime comperi-

mus. Erat ibi iudeus quidam dives plurimum argenti et auri positisque in fenore nummis, qui habebat filium etate iuvenem, vultu decorum, moribus compositum et christiane fidei ab ipsis cunabilis occultum amatorem."

162. See p. 264.

163. See above note 101 and further, on the consecration of two altars in the monastery of Egmond by the bishop of Utrecht in 1136, 'Annales Egmundenses,' 149: In the altar of St Mary there are relics of two of the 11,000 Virgins of Cologne; the other altar "in honore sancti Stephani martiris, Ieronis, Laurentii, Vincentii et omnium martirum Christi, in quo continentur reliquie Fritherici martiris atque pontificis, Dionisii, Pancratii et aliorum plurimorum sanctorum."

164. For an overview, see J. Hof, *De abdij van Egmond van de anvaang tot 1573* (The Hague, 1973).

165. 'Annales Egmundenses,' 152, on the occasion of the consecration of the church in 1143. Bishop Hartbert of Utrecht is supposed to have said in his sermon: "se mirari, quod tante et tot reliquie maximorum sanctorum, apostolorum, martyrum, confessorum et virginum continerentur in extremo margine mundi."

166. See pp. 269–270.

167. See note 142 and Cluse, *Studien*, 355 ff.

168. 'Annales Egmundenses,' 149: "Quem palam christianum fieri tum timor patris sui prohibuit, tum metus mendicitatis qua iudeos christianos factos frequenter viderat coartari. Quapropter auri non modicam quantitatem patre nesciente congregavit, ex quo et se sustentaret et iudeis christianis aliquid subsidii impenderet."

169. See the phrasing in the following note.

170. 'Annales Egmundenses,' 150: "Ille autem pecunie insatiabilis et cupiditatis abyssus omni simulata benignitate puerum in sua suscepit, et omnem humanitatem ante et post baptismum permisit. Distulit autem baptizare puerum, donec veniens pater eius diligenter undique requireret eum. Cui archidiaconus puerum se redditurum spopondit, si pecuniam et omne quod filius eius furtive sustulerat daret sibi."

171. On the symbolic meaning of the motif of water see the new insights by Yuval, 'Symbolik' (as in note 46), 89–91.

172. See notes 50, 64.

173. Concerning the disussion on baptism of desire and baptism of blood in the twelfth century, see L. Scheffcyk, 'Taufe,' in *Lexikon des Mittelalters*, vol. 8:3 (Munich, 1996), cols. 496f. (including further literature); cf. above, note 66, on the emergency baptism of a Jew in water.

174. 'Annales Egmundenses,' 151: "Affuerunt etiam iudei signorum ab antiquo quesitores, et cum inquisitio multa fieret in populo, susurrabant ad invicem

hunc fuisse Iacob filium Ysaac iudei, pervenitque hoc verbum ad aures episcopi. Interrogatus ille negavit filium suum fuisse, dixitque filium suum ad studium se misisse in Hispaniam secundum consuetudinem iudeorum."

175. Ibid.: "Corpus autem martiris honorifice sepultum signis choruscat et prodigiis. Pater autem eius et mater et iudeorum copiosa multitudo in Christum credidit, et est hodie in illis locis martyrium eius causa et fomes in Christum credendi iudeis."

176. See the contribution by William Chester Jordan in this volume. For the Frankfurt events, see *Germania Judaica I*, 105f.; Aronius, *Regesten*, 226f., no. 529; Fritz Backhaus, ed., '*Und groß war bei der Tochter Jehudas Jammer und Klage . . .': Die Ermordung der Frankfurter Juden im Jahre 1241* (Sigmaringen, 1995); on the connection with the Mongol invasion see Israel Jacob Yuval, 'Jewish Messianic Expectations towards 1240 and Christian Reactions,' in *Toward the Millenium: Messianic Expectations from the Bible to Waco*, ed. Peter Schäfer and Mark Cohen, Studies in the History of Religions 77 (Leiden, 1998), 105–121.

177. Minty, 'Kiddush ha-Shem' (as in note 159), 234–237, gives a detailed analysis.

178. See p. 270.

179. Essential with regard to methodology is Yuval, 'Symbolik' (as in note 46).

180. From an analysis of different sources from a different period, Avraham Grossman, 'The Roots of Qiddush ha-Shem in Early Ashkenaz' [Hebrew], in *Sanctity of Life and Martyrdom: Studies in Memory of Amir Yekutiel* (Jerusalem, 1993), 99–130, comes to a different conclusion: He thinks that an outstandingly large number of Jews were baptized in the twelfth century because they could no longer withstand the political, economical, social, and especially religious pressure put upon them by the Christians.

Fourteen

From the *Rue aux Juifs* to the *Chemin du Roy*: The Classical Age of French Jewry, 1108–1223

GÉRARD NAHON

The model provided by the kingdom of France—the most populous region, the richest in material resources, the center *par excellence* for intellectual ferment—is particularly significant for the history of relations between Jews and Christians in western medieval Europe. Historical data regarding specific territories must be applied to general theories on the deteriorating condition of Jewry. Anna Sapir Abulafia has used Latin materials from the Judeo-Christian debate in this manner and concludes, contrary to the analysis of Jeremy Cohen and other historians, that the exclusion of Jews from medieval society begins in the twelfth century.[1]

The present essay is limited to the twelfth century, broadly speaking, and to the present-day borders of France; in other words, to the royal domain or Ile-de-France up to the reign of Philip Augustus, on the one hand, and to the great fiefs of Normandy, Champagne, Anjou, and the Midi, which would later be joined to the kingdom, on the other. The twelfth century, according to Ben-Zion Dinur, is characterized by the beginnings of Jewish enserfment in the wake of a murderous First Crusade: repressive legislation emerges, aimed at changing conditions which had been favorable. Robert Chazan, in a chapter entitled "Twelfth-Century Growth and Development," perceives a movement of expansion simultaneous with a sombering of the climate. Gilbert Dahan likewise writes: "The 12th century, a period of cultural, economic and political rebirth, remained 'open' to the Jews, but threats [to them] were heightened and multiplied." At the same time the intellectual ferment surrounding the *Tossafot* was also part of the "Renaissance of the twelfth century."[2]

It is in this context that I will consider data drawn from Latin and Hebrew sources concerning the Jewish population in its urban settlement, in its communities, and in its relations with lay and ecclesiastical lords and with the Capetians who built the kingdom: Louis VI (1108–1137), Louis VII (1137–1180), and Philip II Augustus (1180–1223).

I. DEMOGRAPHIC AND ECONOMIC EXPANSION

Demography

Did the Jewish population grow between 1108 and 1223? If so, must we assume natural growth or currents of immigration? If neither epidemics nor important persecutions took place, could a high mortality rate have motivated the *Taqqanah*, ascribed to Rabbenu Tam, stipulating the return of the dowry to the father of a bride deceased within the first year of marriage? As for possible immigration, Rigord, the historian of Philip Augustus, states that Jews were attracted by the goodwill of the kings and came in crowds to establish themselves in the kingdom. A *Taqqanah* adopted by a rabbinical synod held around the middle of the twelfth century carries the signatures of Samuel b. Meir, Jacob b. Meir, Eliezer b. Nathan, and one hundred and fifty other rabbis, which would imply a strong Jewish population in terms of laity as well as rabbis.[3]

If there was indeed an influx of immigration, where did it come from? From Jews fleeing Rhenish communities devastated by the first two Crusades, or Spanish and North African Jews driven out by the Almohad conquest? The chronicle of Ephraïm of Bonn recounts the initiative of a priest who led Jews forcibly converted during the violence of the Second Crusade in 1147 to France "so that they could return to their Law and reside [there] until their apostasy had been forgotten." In Languedoc Judah b. Saul Ibn Tibbon (c. 1120–c. 1190), a native of Granada, immigrated to Lunel; his son Samuel lived in Arles, in Béziers, and in Marseille. The disturbances which overtook Narbonne after the death of viscount Aimery II led to departures for Anjou, Poitou, and the

Ile-de-France. Meshullam b. Nathan of Narbonne thus arrived in Melun around 1150. Can the proliferation of ancient manuscripts evoked by Rabbenu Tam be explained by an influx of immigrants endowed with books? Bernard Blumenkranz noted an increase of Jewish communities in the royal domain: more than a third of those recorded before 1182 dwelt there. Aryeh Graboïs counts one hundred and thirty communities and small colonies. William Chester Jordan speaks of the existence of tens of thousands of Jews in the royal domain after 1223 as a result of the annexation of the Midi. But this was not an immigration movement. One may see the evidence of a migratory current coming from the Midi in the form of prayers conducted in a synagogue erected at Sens around 1205: "iuxta quandam ecclesiam veterem novam construxerunt sinagogam, ecclesia non modicum altiorem, in qua, non sicut olim prius quam fuissent eiecti de regno, demissa voce, sed cum magno clamore secundum ritum Iudaicum sua officia celebrantes."[4] Previously the Jews had prayed in low voices but now they raised a great clamor. Was it a case of Jews of the Sephardi rite singing the *entire* office out loud and in unison, as opposed to those of the Ashkenazi rite, whose cantor recited only the incipit of each prayer?

Herem ha-Yishuv

A *responsum* of Rabbenu Tam mentions two plaintiffs, one seeking to expel the other from his dwelling: "leave the residence which I discovered and established for myself," says the first. "You established nothing, others established it and set up house there before you as many witnesses can attest," answers the second. New communities had thus been created or reinforced. In Paris the rabbis appealed to their colleagues at Rome, begging them to resolve a conflict provoked by recourse to the *Herem ha-Yishuv*, the right of residence. These communities were numerous but lightly populated, since their members were increasingly involved in moneylending and had to spread throughout the territories of France to avoid excessive competition.[5]

Construction

A *responsum* of Rabbenu Tam deals with the permissibility of allowing a Christian mason to work Saturdays on the construction of a Jewish

house. Does the rabbi's indulgence in this matter point to intensive construction activity? Rabbenu Tam remarks that "less than ten years ago
there were no *Mezuzot* in all our kingdom [on the doors of Jewish
houses]."[6] May it then be inferred that Jewish homes had become more
visible and more numerous?

The construction of communal buildings follows private construction. The discovery in 1976 of the Rouen synagogue has provided us with
imposing architectural relics from the beginning of the twelfth century.
Around 1180 Louis VII asked Pope Alexander III—on behalf of the
Jews—for authorization to build *new* synagogues in regions where they
had never existed, "quod de novo constituant synagogas, ubi eas nul-
latenus habuerunt." The construction of synagogues went on for a long
time, since Pope Honorius III wrote to Simon, archbishop of Bourges, on
May 19, 1221, to complain, "quod Judei in tua diocesi habitantes, synagogas de novo contra sanctiones canonicas construere presumpserint."[7]

Apostates and Proselytes

An edict of Louis VII, in 1144, prescribes pain of death or mutilation for
apostates who re-embraced Judaism. If one considers this edict in light
of Rabbenu Tam's remark that more than twenty apostates' divorces had
been settled in the Ile-de-France, one sees that a high number of converts and *a fortiori* of Jewish families existed in the kingdom: another
index of demographic expansion.

Evidence of proselytism follows the same trend. It reveals expansion, and also probably immigration, since converts to Judaism—for reasons of safety—left their places of birth for cities where their Christian
past was unknown.[8]

Economic Expansion

Rigord was exaggerating, surely, when he wrote that half the city of Paris
belonged to Jews before their despoilment by Philip Augustus in 1180.
At that time the king extorted a ransom of 15,000 gold marks from the
Jews, which suggests the existence of great fortunes. During the expulsion of 1182 the king confiscated lands, houses, vineyards, olive-presses,
and granaries from the Jews—more external signs of wealth. It is strange

to hear the Jew of Abelard's dialogue say: "We are permitted to possess neither fields nor vines, nor landed estates, since there is no one to protect them for us." With landed properties came rights and revenues. At Meudon, a certain Benedictus Parvus owned a "lodging" which was the object of successive sales at the beginning of the twelfth century. The opulence of the charitable funds available to Jewish communities and their difficulties in allocating them are well known. In the Midi, Jewish landlords possessed goods and rights over Christian tenants. On March 8, 1217, Aimery IV and Margaret of Montmorency confirmed the landed possessions of the Jews of Narbonne once more, by means of a charter.[9]

Security

Demographic and economic expansion do not imply perfect integration. The impact of the Church's policies and preaching at the popular level is in fact unknown. In inhabited areas Jews lived in safety. When traveling cross-country—even in the Midi—some disguised themselves as pilgrims complete with *bourdon* [staff], *escharpe* [alms-purse], and perhaps an *esclavine* [cowled robe].[10]

Most writers note an erosion of Jewish security resulting from growing popular intolerance. Attacks by crusaders and the need for seigneurial protection were the first symptoms of this. A proliferation of popular accusations against the Jews and substitution of royal protection for the faltering support of the nobility were next. Popular hostility owed much to the work of the Church and notably to that of Peter of Cluny.[11]

II. Cities and Towns

Geography and Topography

A sizable number of Jewish communities, families, and isolated individuals lived in villages, but our data is concerned almost exclusively with cities and towns. Jews whose rural properties were disappearing would henceforth depend on cities and towns for their existence. A list of localities with a Jewish presence based on Latin and rabbinical sources would consist of the dozens of cities and towns in the Ile-de-France, such as Bray-sur-Seine, Etampes, Montlhéry, Orléans, Paris, Pontoise, and Saint-Denis; in Normandy, such as Caen, Evreux, Pont-Audemers, and Rouen; in Champagne, such as Epernay, Ramerupt, Rheims, Sens, Vitry, and Troyes; in Burgundy, such as Autun and Auxerre; in Anjou, such as Beaugency; and in the fiefs of the Midi, such as Arles, Beaucaire, Marseille, Narbonne, and Toulouse. The Jewish quarter was perceived as an integral part of the urban space as revealed by the solemn entry of Pope Innocent II to Saint-Denis on April 27, 1131. Jewish topographical expansion continued into the thirteenth century: purchases of real estate were denounced in a letter of Innocent III to William of Seignelay, bishop of Auxerre, dated May 16, 1207, decrying the fact that they had acquired estates, allods, and vineyards [villas, predia et vineas emerint].[12]

New Towns, Communes, and Municipalities

A powerful trend toward urban expansion was under way during the reigns of Louis VI and Louis VII. New towns were built and endowed with franchise charters. Communes established in older towns also received charters. Did Jews settle in these new towns? Do the communal charters mention them? What sorts of relations did municipalities maintain with their Jewish populations? Our knowledge of their demographic and geographic expansion and of the evolution of their status in the towns depends on the answers to these questions.

The question of Jewish settlement in the new towns remains a *desideratum*. Let us note a "rue des juifs" in Villeneuve-sur-Yonne in this regard. The *Chronicle of the Abbey of Saint-Pierre-le-Vif de Sens* sums up Louis VII's urban achievements in a single statement: "He made new towns; and, driven by the thirst for gold, despite the respect he owed to the faith, he granted certain liberties to the Jews—leproseries, new synagogues, and cemeteries." The same chronicle cites the example of "the cemetery of the Jews of Bray which is in the territory of Saint-Etienne de Sens. And it is for this reason that these Jews are subjects of the congregation of the cathedral of Sens."[13]

The communal charters sometimes included an article legalizing Jewish loans. Louis VII decreed at Château-Landon between March 24 and April 12, 1175, "that no Jew may receive pawned objects, except in the presence of legitimate witnesses." Article 18 of the charter of the commune of Auxerre, given at Sens in November 1194 by Count Peter of Nevers, stipulates that "if a Jew claims usurious interest from a Christian, he may exact no more than the interest for two years, as determined by legitimate Christian and Jewish witnesses": "Si judeus a christiano usuras exegerit, tantum usuras duorum annorum, per testes legitimos christiani et judei, poterit exigere."[14]

Certain municipalities received rights over the Jews of their regions. At Sens in 1180, in a charter anticipating an expulsion of the Jews (*Judaeorum expulsionem*), Count Guy of Nevers, Auxerre, and Tonnerre included revenues from Jews among the rights he granted the town of Tonnerre: "concerning the Jews it was also said that they should receive twenty *solidi* each from those who had a family and 5 *solidi* for the tenure of their house and a tithe on their wine and harvest or transactions. Foreign Jews residing in the town will be dealt with according to the other customs of the Jews of the town." Robert Chazan writes that "this, to be sure, was a rather rare occurrence." But other analogous concessions may have existed, even if we possess no documentation. Farms acquired by Jews would have placed them in constant contact with municipal authorities. In August 1209 Dieudonné de Bray purchased the right to a *tonlieu* on bread in Paris, a tax on the stalls where bread was sold.[15]

The 1150 statutes of Arles include the Latin text of a pledge which Jews had to swear before tribunals. An article in the charter granted to the city of Marseille in 1219 by its bishop allowed Jews and Saracens the same freedoms of movement, of residence, and of commerce enjoyed by Christians. Certain towns had an officer assigned to defend the interests of Jews. Thus the provost of Jews at Etampes was ordered to prosecute their recalcitrant debtors. In Article 25 of his letters regulating the police in the town of Etampes, promulgated at Paris in 1179, Louis VII restricted the powers of the provost of Jews: "Neither the provost of Jews nor any other may seize a man going to market, nor his belongings, whether he be returning from the market or found in the market on market-day, for reason of debt."[16]

The image of the Jew was tarnished in the north by the first accusations of ritual murder formulated between 1160 and 1171 at Loebes, Pontoise, Janville, Epernay, and especially at Blois. In the Midi (where the situation was far from idyllic), on the contrary, one may perceive an

improvement. At Béziers an ancient custom permitted the stoning of
Jews at Easter. In 1160 Bishop William of Béziers, at the instigation of
Viscount Raymond Trencavel, replaced this custom with a tax of 200
Melgorian *sous* and an annual rate of four pounds (in the currency of
Melgueil) to be paid by the Jews.[17]

Papal Pressure

Papal pressure was exerted directly by the Third Lateran Council
(March 5, 1179) and especially by the Fourth (November 11, 1215)
which imposed the wearing of a distinctive badge on the Jews. The
popes forbade employment of Christian servants or wet-nurses by Jews,
reduced their status as witnesses, and prohibited them from holding public office. The reissue of this prohibition betrays the extent of the practice
and the importance of servile employment in areas of dense population.
Alexander III (1159–1179) ordered the bishop of Marseilles to oblige
Jews to pay ecclesiastical tithes on lands they purchased or cultivated.
Finally, Innocent III wrote to the archbishop of Narbonne on August 15,
1198, to ensure a remission of interest due from Christians to Jewish
financiers.

Provincial councils passed through Paris on March 27, 1188,
Montpellier in December 1195, Paris again ca. 1200 with Bishop Odo
de Sully, Montélimar in June 1209, Avignon on September 6, 1209,
Pamiers on December 1, 1212, Paris again in 1213, and Melun in 1216.
What was the impact of the resulting battery of prohibitions at the town
level? A growing social rejection of Jews, the birth of accusations, harm-
ful royal policies—all were surely due to them. At Montélimar, in June
1209, Raymond VI, count of Toulouse, and the barons of the Toulousain
swore an oath to expel all Jews from the administration of public and
private affairs. The consuls of Largentière (Ardeche) took the same
oath. The despoilment of Jews in the royal domain perpetrated by Philip
Augustus took place in 1180, a year after the Third Lateran Council.
When the time required for dissemination and assimilation of news is
taken into account, one can see that these events succeeded one another directly.

On the May 19, 1221, somewhat surprisingly, Honorius III commanded Simon de Sully, archbishop of Bourges, to *destroy* the new syna-

gogues in his diocese. He invited him to place faithful Christians who opposed this policy under ecclesiastical censure.[18] Would the municipalities have supported their Jews in the event of an episcopal *Kristallnacht*?

III. The Communities

Latin texts ignore Jewish communities as such. They mention Jews or "the Jews" but do not recognize the Jewish collectivity as a juridical entity. Hebrew sources alone allow us to understand their functioning.

Is the demographic, geographic, economic, and social expansion suggested by the Latin sources confirmed at the level of Jewish communities' internal life? With respect to communal and intercommunal organization, to juridical developments, to studies, and to the general character of Jewish life in the West, what sort of physiognomy is presented by the Hebrew sources?

Community Structure

No "statutes" have survived from the French communities of the twelfth century. Nevertheless, certain communities such as the one at Troyes possessed rules concerning synagogal life and the distribution of financial charges from the eleventh century on. The arrangement of the *Herem ha-Yishuv* or right of residence was established early on at Paris. At the beginning of the twelfth century, the rabbis of Paris appealed to their colleagues of Rome when baffled by a problem of its application. The *Herem ha-Yishuv* was also invoked in areas where it had not been introduced. Aryeh Grabois concludes that the *Herem ha-Yishuv* was similar to the oaths binding members of the commune and asks "to what extent the people of the communes had studied the organization of Jewish communities before framing their own."

The Synods

The adoption of resolutions by delegates to a meeting of communities at the time of the synods held at Troyes was an innovation of the twelfth century and an indication of expansion. These synods, recorded in

numerous manuscripts, met after 1150 and served to define ambiguous
relations with the seigneurial power. At first the participants sought approval from their Roman colleagues. Later they were content with that
of French authorities and especially that of Jacob b. Meir, Rabbenu Tam.
Two major features of these synodal gatherings must be noted. A sort of
intercommunal federation brought delegates to Troyes from Dijon,
Auxerre, Sens, Orléans, Châlons-sur-Marne, Rheims, Paris, Melun,
Etampes, Normandy, perhaps Brittany, Anjou, Poitou, and Lotharingia.
They took note of the interference of seigneurial power in the internal
affairs of the community. Their resolutions forbade any *individual* recourse to royal, seigneurial, or juridical authority to resolve conflicts
between Jews. Paradoxically, one resolution anticipated *community* recourse to Christian authority in order to impose obedience to these very
arrangements. Non-Jewish power was relied upon to guarantee that of
the community.

Rabbinical Law

Eight talmudic prohibitions limited relations with non-Jews: it was forbidden to transact with them during their festivals, to keep an animal in
their homes or in the care of their shepherds, to sell livestock to them
directly, to employ their wet-nurses, to teach them Hebrew, to rent
them houses, or to associate with them. Rabbinical law in the 12th century accepted compromises on these points. Rabbenu Tam thus authorized the employment of non-Jews to fill grape vats while opposing those
who allowed Christians to press the grapes with them "just to make
them happy" (*Tosafot Avoda Zara* 55b). Is it permitted *today* to rent a
house to a non-Jew who might set up idols within? Rabbenu Haim
b. Hananel ha-Cohen (Paris, late twelfth century) answered in the affir-
mative, arguing that "the idolaters who live among us usually do not
bring idols [into their houses] unless someone dies or is on the point of
death and even then they do not adore them" (*Tosafot Avoda Zara* 21a).
Despite the prohibition of Deuteronomy 23:20–21, Rabbenu Tam au-
thorizes loans at interest to non-Jews, to Jews *with a non-Jewish intermediary*, and to apostates with no intermediary. Jacob of Orléans, a disciple
of Rabbenu Tam, even drew up a formulary stipulating the payment obligations of a Jewish debtor to a Jewish creditor under certain conditions

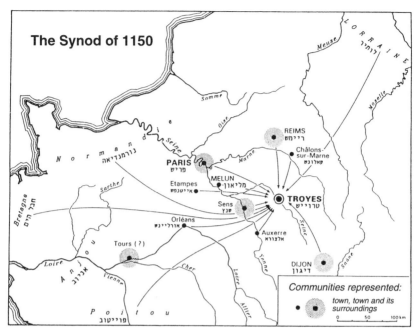

Research by C.N.R.S. Research Team 208, "Nouvelle *Gallia Judaica*" project. Map pre-pared by IMAGÉO, 1986.

of interest (*Mordechai* on *Baba Mesia* 455), while in Germany Rabbi Isaac began to forbid the use of non-Jewish intermediaries in trans-actions between Jews.[19]

Is it possible, using rabbinical sources, to elucidate the condition of Jews in France? This is once again a *desideratum*. William Chester Jordan notes an evolution of rabbinical commentaries on the biblical "rape of Dinah" episode (Genesis 34 and 49:5–7) "after the experience of the Rhenish massacres and other violent anti-Jewish incidents." Jewish commentators had originally been reserved on the subject of Jacob's sons' brutal reaction, but now they came to approve it. This evolution reflects a more somber perception of the Christian environment and corresponds to the emergence of a "martyro-centric" mentality in chronicles as well as in pietistic literature.[20]

Later on, when Jews' freedom of movement was threatened, Isaac b. Samuel of Dampierre would insist that their juridical condition was equivalent to that of knights: "In the province which surrounds us we observe the right of the Jew to reside in any place he wishes just like the knights. The law of the kingdom has [always] stipulated that the governor cannot seize the property of Jews when they leave his town. This was the practice in all the lands of Burgundy. If some lord should come along to change this right and proclaim another it would no longer be the law of the kingdom."[21]

Rabbenu Tam declares that "the children of Esau [that is, the Christians] respect Israel more than all the nations" (*Sefer ha-Yashar Novellae* 196, p. 130; cf. *Gittin* 17a); a surprising formula if one recalls that he himself suffered in the flesh the only assault known to have occurred in France at the time of the departures for the Second Crusade in 1147. Could this statement have been made before that tragic incident? All things considered, perhaps Rabbenu Tam had been informed of the massacres perpetrated in Spain and northern Africa by the Almohads and so maintained his positive appreciation of Christian society. The persecution at Blois in May 1171 proved him wrong. At the same time, by decreeing a fast to commemorate the drama, Rabbenu Tam demonstrated his authority over the communities of the realm and reinforced their integration.

A less optimistic reading of the period will be found among the Tosafists at the end of the thirteenth century. Regarding the custom of marrying off very young girls, one of them explained that "today we are in the habit of marrying off our daughters even as minors because the exile is harsher on us day by day. He who has now the means to give a dowry to his daughter [marries her off without waiting] for fear that later he will no longer have the means and that his daughter will remain a spinster forever."[22]

IV. Lay and Ecclesiastical Lordship

Lay lordship

In feudal France, the majority of Jews lived under the jurisdiction of lay or ecclesiastical lords, paying them taxes and various other forms of support. In the same locale Jews might depend on several lords: around 1100 at Troyes there were nine lords who had Jews. The lords had temporal power over them, as indicated in a letter of Innocent III to Michael de Mourize, archbishop of Arles, dated November 11, 1209.[23] How did these lords behave in their relations with Jews, given their own interests on the one hand and the interests of *their* Jews on the other?

The lords at first endeavored to attract Jews to their lands. Azriel b. Joseph, apparently a contemporary of Rabbenu Tam, reports in one consultation that "the Duke of Lorraine insisted that his Jews intercede with other Jews residing in his villages under petty lords, in order to convince them to place themselves under his power; failing which he would expel them."[24] This is a striking example of a lord's desire to increase the number of his Jews.

Lords protected their Jews from possible violence or from the encroachments of other authorities. On May 20, 1147, a band of crusaders attacked the home of Rabbenu Tam at Ramerupt, sacking it and injuring the rabbi. He only escaped death thanks to a great lord to whom he promised a horse worth five *écus*. In 1192 a royal officer killed a Jew in Bray-sur-Seine, and the countess of Champagne handed the murderer over to the Jews. As a result, Philip Augustus sent an armed force into Bray and had a large number of Jews burned. When the lord of a Jew who struck a priest neglected to punish him, Pope Innocent III instructed William de Joinville, bishop of Langres, on June 7, 1212, to apply ecclesiastical censure against the lord. In 1219 lords were asked by the pope to obtain a cancellation of interest owed by crusaders to their Jews. Certain prelates of Champagne zealously applied this measure. Countess Blanche of Champagne complained to the pope and won her case: Honorius III wrote to the abbots of Saint-Jean-des-Vignes at Soissons and to the dean of Soissons advising them to moderate the zeal of their prelates. The following year, in 1220, the same Blanche de Champagne was defending Pino, a Jew from Château-Thierry who had assaulted a cleric. Faced with the countess's attitude, James de Bazoches, bishop of Soissons, placed the entire diocese under interdict. Pope Honorius III therefore mandated the abbot and prior of Saint-Victor and the dean of the cathedral chapter at Paris to investigate the countess's case. The matter ended amicably, with Pino paying part of the expenses. Conversely, in the Blois incident of 1171, far from protecting the Jews, the count of Blois gave credence to an accusation of ritual murder and allowed thirty-two Jewish men and women to be burned alive. In this case it was not a matter of defending seigneurial Jews from another authority, but of facing a current of public opinion which was hostile to the Jews. The count of Blois gave in to the force of this public opinion and on May 26, 1171, he abandoned thirty-two of his Jews to their tragic fate.[25]

Lords granted privileges to Jews. Peter II de Courtenay, count of Nevers, permitted his Jews to sell unwanted animal parts to Christians, exempted their lands from ecclesiastical tithes, and permitted them to challenge Christian witnesses. He ignored the warnings of Hugo de Noyers, bishop of Auxerre, and thus provoked the intervention of pope Innocent III on January 17, 1208.[26]

Lords continued to entrust public offices to their Jews. On May 29, 1207, Innocent III reproached Count Raymond VI of Toulouse "for entrusting public offices to the Jews to the detriment of the Christian faith." Five years after the Fourth Lateran Council, nobles of the Bordelais continued to commit public duties in castles and rural areas to Jews. They gave certain Jews permission not to wear the distinctive badge. In a letter of April 29, 1221, Pope Honorius III enjoined William Amanien de Geniès, archbishop of Bordeaux, to constrain nobles to harden their attitudes toward the Jews, using ecclesiastical censure as needed.[27]

Finally, lords borrowed from many Jews. It will suffice to note here that among the debts of Peter, count of Nevers (ca. 1218), were 860 pounds due to Moses of Sens.[28]

Ecclesiastical Lords

Did ecclesiastical lords heed the instructions of popes and councils with regard to Jews any more than did the laity? Like lay lords, they sought first of all to have their rights recognized over the Jews of their domains. They derived very attractive revenues from these Jews, if we are to believe Abelard when he evokes the abbot of Saint Gildas of Rhuys (Morbihan), described as extorting heavier taxes from the monks than those he received from tribute-paying Jews. In October 1119 Louis VI left, among other revenues, those he possessed from Jews to the chapter of Saint-Martin de Tours. In 1122, the same king conceded jurisdiction over five Jewish houses, "as serfs of the church" with their families in the town, to Suger, abbot of Saint-Denis. At the request of the same Suger, Louis VII confirmed this jurisdiction in 1143. In the same year he confirmed revenues from their Jews to the canons of Saint-Martin de Tours. In 1157 the king confirmed the jurisdiction of Berengar, archbishop of Narbonne, over the "Jewish mount" or cemetery of the Jews. Pope Anastasius III confirmed the jurisdiction of Raymond, archbishop of Arles, over the Jews of his city on December 26, 1153. In 1190 Bartholomew, archbishop of Tours, and King Richard the Lion-Hearted arrived at an agreement to share the revenues of Tours, Chinon, Marçay, and Port d'Ablevois. Sworn witnesses declared that Bon Ami and his sons were the men of the archbishop and thus owed no tallage to the count [meaning Richard, in his capacity as count of Anjou]. Later, Philip Augustus confirmed the donations of his mother Adèle to the chapel of Jard near Melun, including a revenue of fifty pounds derived from the seal of the Jews.[29]

With the development of royal power, certain ecclesiastical lords *paid* for their jurisdiction over Jews. Thus the royal register records a sum of 200 *Provins* pounds from the abbey of Saint-Germain d'Auxerre for its Jews, in the Candlemass term of 1217.[30]

Like lay lords, ecclesiastical lords contracted loans with Jews. In his *Book of Acts Accomplished during his Administration* [*Liber de rebus in administratione sua gestis*] and in his will, Suger explains that Ursellus, a Jew from Montmorency, held a rural domain and a rent in pawn for a debt that he had authorized. Another ecclesiastical lord, Hugh, abbot of Château-Landon, owed money to Jews around 1182 when Philip Augustus intervened to cancel the debt (which had averaged a payment of forty-five pounds).[31]

During the period under consideration, the seigneurial order endeavored to retain, to protect, and to exploit Jews and thus encouraged the expansion of their activites. This analysis remains valid with one exception, that of Count Thibaut of Blois. He thought it best to abandon the thirty-two Jews who faced the pyre on May 26, 1171, to a public opinion which had been kindled white hot against them. King Louis VII on the other hand explicitly resisted the accusations fomented in his realm against the Jews of Pontoise, Epernay, and Janville. The Blois affair marked the beginning of a process at the end of which royal power would replace seigneurial power in the maintenance and defense of Jews faced with ecclesiastical repression on one side and popular opinion on the other.

V. The Monarchy: Louis VI, Louis VII, Philip Augustus

We know practically nothing concerning the relations of Louis VI with the Jews except that in 1119 he confirmed the rights of Saint-Martin de Tours over its Jews and in 1122 he granted five Jewish houses to the Abbey of Saint-Denis.

As for Louis VII, historians agree—following Achille Luchaire—that his policies were very favorable to Jews.[32] Three chroniclers, Geoffroy de Courlon, the *Chronicle of Saint-Pierre-le Vif de Sens known as Clarius*, and a historical fragment which sums up the king's life, all maintain "that he offended God by honouring the Jews beyond all measure and that, deceived by immoderate greed, he accorded them privileges contrary to himself and to his kingdom."[33] At least three caveats must be applied to this evaluation.

The first royal ordinance concerning the Jews of France to be issued in his name dates from 1144. It called for penalties of death or mutilation for relapsed Jews. But we do not know whether this ordinance was ever put into effect or if there was a persecution of converts.[34]

Louis VII ignored the violent letter of Peter the Venerable, abbot of Cluny, which advised him to allow Jews to live but to seize their goods in order to finance the Crusade.[35] Bernard of Clairvaux took up the defense of the Jews, and so they suffered no major assaults when the Crusade got underway. Did Louis VII follow his advice to cancel interest on Jewish loans contracted by crusaders?

Ephraim of Bonn wrote: "In the other French communities, we haven't heard of any Jews killed or forcibly converted in this time, but they lost a great deal of their wealth, for the king of France proclaimed: 'All volunteers for Jerusalem will have their debts to Jews canceled!' Now many of the French Jews' claims were only in writing and thus they lost their money." No such royal ordinance has survived, whether its text has been lost or whether it was simply an oral instruction given to royal officers to favour those debtors who had taken the cross.

Finally, a royal ordinance of 1179 for the police in Etampes withdrew the provost of Jews' ability to seize the goods of debtors on their way to market.[36]

Louis VII deserves some credit for resisting papal pressure, despite otherwise being a loyal servant of the Church. He had Guarin Gerard, archbishop of Bourges, intervene with Alexander III in order to allow Jews to continue employing Christian domestics and building new synagogues. The pope answered the archbishop, saying that he had already written to the king, encouraging him to give up his defense of the Jews on these points.[37] The king's benevolence is, of course, understandable given the revenues received by his officers from Jews.

Hebrew sources likewise evoke friendly relations between the king and the Jews of Paris, whose rabbis he knew. Isaac Dorbelo recounts: "At Paris one day, some apostates slandered all the Israelites before the king, saying that when they scattered dust behind them on returning from a burial this was done in order to cast a spell on the Gentiles and to make them die. The king heard the calumny and called for rabbi Moses son of rabbi Yehiel, son of rabbi Mattathias the Great of Paris. He asked him: 'What is this wicked practice I have heard of concerning you? You cast spells on the Gentiles when you return from a burial.' He responded: 'Lord king, God forbid that there should be any such thing in Israel. On the contrary, we believe that the Holy One Blessed-be-He will resurrect the dead. As scripture says concerning the dead: "May the cities see their inhabitants multiply like the grasses of the fields" (Psalm 72:16). This we recite while pulling up grasses and scattering them among the dead to affirm that we believe that God, just as with grasses which have withered and rotted in the ground, the Holy One Blessed-be-He will make them grow anew, just as the dead, once they are dead, the Lord will revive them.' [The king] said to him: 'If it be thus may your strength be maintained, you do well, this a deep and goodly belief, for you are a people blessed by the Lord your God' (Deuteronomy 7:6). Cursed be those who slander you!" One sees in this episode a theological encounter between the king and the Parisian rabbi over a dogma they hold in common, that of the resurrection.

After the tragic Blois incident of 1171, Louis VII benevolently received delegates from the community of Paris in an audience at Poissy. He rejected all the accusations made against the Jews not only at Blois

but also at Pontoise and at Janville. He condemned the actions of
the count of Blois and provided the delegates with a sealed charter of
protection.[38]

One wonders what duties R. Tam may have performed in the service
of Louis VII, given the influence of the royal model on the master from
Champagne. Could he himself be one of those Jews who "in our days
submit themselves to the kingdom to perform some mission, such as to
collect taxes or to take care of other such affairs" (*Tosafot Besa* 6a)?
Gedalia Ibn Yahya claimed to have seen an ancient *quntres* saying that
Rabbenu Tam was rich and well-thought-of at the royal court. Since
R. Tam wrote: "Even the king and all the lords know that the Jews frequently deal with the rulers of their neighbours" (*Mordechai, Baba Qama*
179), one must suppose that he himself had done so. R. Tam explained
in a letter to Joseph b. Moses of Troyes that he was completely burdened
with responsibilities, including "the business of others and the service of
the king."[39] If he had meant the service of the count of Champagne, the
ever-precise R. Tam would have used the term *Sar* [lord] in place of the
word *Melech* [king].

The *Taqqanah* signed by Rabbenu Tam concerning the return of
a dowry to the father of a young woman who died in the first year of
her marriage opens with the formula *Mi-ta-'am ha melech u-gedolaw*,
"by order of the king and his magnates," borrowed from Jonah 3:7.
According to Dinur, he was referring to the King of the universe and the
Sages of the Torah.[40] Might we not, however, admit that royal authority
may well have—on the initiative of Rabbenu Tam—given sanction to
this resolution which was voted on by delegates from Narbonne, France,
Anjou, Poitou, and Normandy?

Taking the matter one step further, the late E. E. Urbach saw the
adoption of *Taqqanot* by an intercommunal gathering as an expression of
Rabbenu Tam's grand design, to unite all the communities of France on
the model of a king extending his authority over the kingdom. He
wanted to unite the French communities in a federation, and his im-
patience sometimes showed: "I ask you," he wrote to his colleague
Meshullam of Melun, "not to make to make our kingdom *agudot agudot*,
a "scattering of grouplings." He obtained some partial success on the
liturgical level: "There were some areas in France where they sounded
the *Shofar* [between sections of the *Mussaf* (additional service) on Rosh

ha-Shanah] according to R. Jacob—may his home be covered with glory—and we also use it in all of Champagne and Normandy." On hearing the news of the tragedy at Blois in 1171, he decreed an annual fast on the 20th of *Siwan* which was accepted by *all* the communities of France, the isles of the sea [England], and the Rhineland. This was his final effort in the unification of the French communities. According to Albeck, his attempts at unification foundered in a France which was itself divided among princes.[41]

During his reign of forty-three years, Philip Augustus[42] followed a Jewish policy which alternated between despoliation, persecution, and exploitation. In 1180, he had the Jews of Paris arrested *en masse* and ransomed them for 15,000 gold marks. In 1182, he expelled the Jews from the royal domain, only to recall them in 1198. For the next twenty-five years he legislated and regulated and exploited Jewish credit, especially in his statute of September 1206 and his ordinance of February 1219. He issued a considerable number of ordinances and acts dealing with Jews, documents which Robert Chazan and William Chester Jordan have submitted to an exhaustive investigation. For Chazan his policy is characterized by three aspects: regulation, limitation, exploitation. Jordan, who was able to make use of the latest registers edited by John Baldwin, alludes to "A New Beginning" and concludes that there was a renewal of Jewish expansion in the growing empire of Philip Augustus.

On this problem of whether expansion ceased or continued at the beginning of the thirteenth century, I would insist here on three aspects of Philip Augustus' Jewish policy. The first needs no demonstration: the king wanted to extract an ever-larger profit from the Jews, and so he despoiled them, he recalled them, and he regulated their financial affairs. In his budgets, income from Jews rose from 100 pounds in 1202 to 7,550 pounds in 1217. The king therefore established and pursued a positive Jewish policy of protection and of exploitation. The second point derives from the treaties he established with the counts of Champagne and other lords. The king and the count of Champagne agreed that neither would seek to detain or to attract the Jews of the other's domain. Philip Augustus thereby expected to conserve and, if possible, to increase the Jewish population in his realm. The *Layettes du Tresor des Chartes* preserve several accords concluded with barons or with towns, in which the king inserted a clause by which he reserved the Jews to himself. One such was concluded with the abbey of Fécamp in 1211, another with the countess of Eure in 1219. The third point signals a new policy direction: the introduction of royal jurisdiction over Jews residing on seigneurial lands.[43]

Philip Augustus established the first royal statute over the Jews. This statute said nothing about their status, about their communities, or about their rights: it was concerned solely with their credit operations. In 1203–1204 the king negotiated a convention with the countess of Champagne concerning the Jew Cresselin: the king pledged not to attract Cresselin into his territory, but "nevertheless the said Cresselin may now and in the future come to lend money in the lands of the King." His accords with the countess of Champagne and other lords allowed the king to reclaim his Jews even if they had dwelt for a long time in another land. There is a list drawn up around 1204 at Mantes, of Jews who had paid a security and sworn not to leave the royal domain. A similar document contains a list of Jews who were detained at the *châtelet* at Petit Pont (Paris), though we do not know under what conditions or for what purpose.[44] The administration wanted to control as large a Jewish population as it could.

The ordinances of course included limitations on Jewish banking operations. The statute of 1206 stipulates: "No Jew may lend for a greater interest than that of two deniers to the pound per week." Far from restraining the credit practices of the Jews, however, *this in fact legalized* their operating at an annual rate of 43 percent. The document adds: "During a certain term to be defined by the king's bailiffs the Jews will be obliged to seal all their contracts with a new seal, and if they do not do so within the allotted time, then at that time their previous contracts will be void." Jewish loans thus in fact obtained legal force by means of the royal seal. The sigillographic collection of the *Archives Nationales* preserves two royal seals, that of the Jews of Pontoise (1204) and that of the Jews of Paris (1206): they depict an eagle at rest facing right, with six fleur-de-lys on a field.[45] The statute of 1206 called for the establishment of two guardians for the "seal of the Jews" in every town, to be responsible for registering loans, and a "scribe of Jewish letters" establishing acknowledgments of debts. A royal enquiry into Jewish moneylending in Normandy and the royal domain was carried out around 1210 and reveals (according to Baldwin) a total of 251,900 pounds: "that is, a sum greater than 25% of the royal revenues for 1221."[46]

The ordinance of 1219 limited loans to those who lived by the fruits of their own labor, but favored loans to knights, burghers, and merchants possessing goods or revenues which could be used as collateral. In effect it permitted pawning, mortgaging, and assignments of revenue. It funneled credit into large-scale borrowing and discouraged consumption loans. The king certainly benefited from this, but so did the Jews. In addition, the ordinances guaranteed recovery of debts by royal authority. This aspect of Philip Augustus's Jewry policy favored and encouraged Jewish immigration into royal lands or jurisdictions, and it accompanied an expansion of Jewish moneylending.

This policy of growth was carried out despite growing papal pressure, as exemplified by a lengthy letter of Innocent III to Philip Augustus dated January 16, 1205. The same pontiff wrote the king on October 9, 1208, to oblige the Jews to remit interest charges accumulated by crusaders. A letter of July 15, 1205, from the pope to Peter de Corbeil, archbishop of Sens, and to Odo de Sully, bishop of Paris, noted that he had asked the king to forbid Jews from employing Christian servants and wet-nurses. He therefore enjoined the prelates to use threats of excommunication against Christians who had commerce with Jews. In an undated pact concluded with his barons, Philip Augustus responded with a blunt refusal except on one point: "Clerics should not excommunicate those who sell to Jews or buy from them, or who work for them, but they may excommunicate those wet-nurses who suckle the children of the Jews."[47]

CONCLUSION

There was undoubtedly an offensive mounted against Jews by the papacy, and there were accusations of ritual murder at the local level which bear witness to a growing hostility toward Jews. Mentalities were evolving in a manner which threatened Jews, although the factors involved in this evolution have yet to be satisfactorily elucidated. Anna Sapir Abulafia has developed an "intellectualist" thesis, according to which changes in the clerical conception of Jews occurred slowly and passed over to the popular level by means of processes we still do not understand.[48] While this thesis may be retained in its broad outlines, it should be noted that in France the process was impeded first by lords and later by the king. The fragility of the Jewish position in the kingdom increased slowly but surely. The three crises which occurred in northern France demonstrate this. In 1147 at Ramerupt, Rabbenu Tam owed his life to the protection of a lord. While this protection was lacking in 1171 at Blois, royal protection prevented an extension of the accusations. Finally, the affair of 1198 in Bray witnessed the intervention of a king seeking to confound the protection of another lord. Henceforth the Jews' dependence vis-à-vis the royal power would increasingly marginalize them.

Despite the expulsion from the royal domain which lasted from 1182 to 1198, Jewish demographic, topographic, and financial expansion took place throughout the France of the king and of the barons. Just as Louis VII did not bow to the resolutions of the Third Lateran Council, Philip Augustus did not heed those of the Fourth. Both resisted papal pressure. At the same time, the piecemeal power of barons in the twelfth century was succeeded by a royal *dominium* over the Jews, not only those of the swollen royal domain but also those of the barons who were tied to the king by treaties. The baronial order which had been favorable to Jewish growth was succeeded by a monarchical order concerned with pushing such growth to its maximum extent, despite a social and psychological context which tended to reject Jews. In Giverny in the region of the Eure, a village made famous by the impressionist master Claude Monet, the *Rue aux Juifs* leads to the *Chemin du Roy*. This intersection is more than a symbol: it paints the portrait of an inescapable evolutionary process.

NOTES

1. On the problem of exclusion and the persecuting society, see Jeremy Cohen, The *Friars and the Jews: The Evolution of Medieval Anti-Judaism* (Ithaca and London, 1982); R. I. Moore, *The Formation of a Persecuting Society: Power and Deviance in Western Europe 950–1250* (Oxford, 1987); Gavin I. Langmuir, *History, Religion, and Antisemitism* (Berkeley and Los Angeles, 1990); idem,

Toward a Definition of Antisemitism (Berkeley and Los Angeles, 1990); Kenneth R. Stow, *Alienated Minority: The Jews of Medieval Latin Christendom* (Cambridge, Mass., 1992); Anna Sapir Abulafia, *Christians and Jews in the Twelfth-Century Renaissance* (London and New York, 1995), pp. 73 and 138.

2. Ben-Zion Dinur, *A Documentary History of the Jewish People from Its Beginning to the Present* 2d ser.: *Israel in the Diaspora*, vol. 2, bks. 1–5 (Tel Aviv and Jerusalem, 1965–1972) [Hebrew]. Salo Wittmayer Baron, *A Social and Religious History of the Jews*, 2d ed., vol. 4: *Meeting of East and West* (New York, 1957). Robert Chazan, *Medieval Jewry in Northern France: A Political and Social History* (Baltimore and London, 1973), pp. 30–62. Gilbert Dahan, *Les intellectuels chrétiens et les juifs au moyen âge* (Paris, 1990), p. 23. Charles Homer Haskins, *The Renaissance of the Twelfth Century* (Cambridge, Mass., 1927).

3. Chronicle of Ephraïm of Bonn, Abraham Habermann, ed., *Sefer Gezerot Ashkenaz we-Sarfat* (Jerusalem, 1946), p. 122; English translation in Shlomo Eidelberg, *The Jews and the Crusaders: The Hebrew Chronicles of the First and Second Crusades* (Madison, Wisc.: 1977), p. 131. Text of the *Taqqanah* in Meir b. Baruch of Rothenburg, *Responsa*, so-called Prague edition [= Budapest, 1895], fol. 159v, right col.; on these *Taqqanot* cf. Louis Finkelstein, *Jewish Self-Government in the Middle Ages* (New York, 1964), pp. 150–215, and Gérard Nahon, "Synodes et *taqqanot* en France au XIIe siècle," *Ecole Pratique des Hautes Etudes, Ve section: Sciences religieuses. Annuaire*, vol. 94 (1985–1986): 331–334; ibid., vol. 95 (1986–1987): 237–240; ibid., vol. 96 (1987–1988): 219–220.

4. Bernhard Blumenkranz, *Histoire des Juifs en France* (Toulouse, 1972), p. 17. Aryeh Graboïs, "Les juifs et leurs seigneurs dans la France septentrionale aux XIe et XIIe siècles," in *Les juifs dans l'histoire de France, Premier colloque international de Haïfa*, ed. Myriam Yardeni (Leiden, 1980), p. 11, n. 3. William Chester Jordan, *The French Monarchy and the Jews from Philip Augustus to the Last Capetians* (Philadelphia, 1989), p. 90. Shlomo Simonsohn, *The Apostolic See and the Jews, Documents: 492–1404* (Toronto, 1988), § 79, pp. 82–83.

5. S.-F. Rosenthal, ed., *Sefer ha-Yashar le-Rabbenu Tam* (Berlin, 1898), § 71, p. 167. Chazan, *Medieval Jewry in Northern France*, p. 33. Anna Sapir Abulafia notes: "This in turn encouraged the spread of numerous small communities through the eleventh and twelfth centuries in northern France," *Christians and Jews*, p. 69.

6. For Jacob b. Meir-Rabbenu Tam, see *Tosafot Shabbat* 17b–18a; Meir b. Baruch of Rothenburg, *Responsa* (Cremona edition, 1557), n. 108.

7. Simonsohn, *The Apostolic See and the Jews*, no. 59, p. 62, and no. 114, p. 118.

8. Edict of Louis VII, Archives Nationales K 23 no. 11, ed. Jules Tardif, *Monuments historiques* (Paris, 1866), no. 470, p. 256; cf. Achille Luchaire,

Etudes sur les actes de Louis VII (Paris, 1885), no. 136, p. 143; Hebrew transla-tion in Dinur, *Israel in the Diaspora*, vol. 2, bk. 1, § 12, p. 252; for cases of di-vorce, see Rosenthal, *Sefer ha-Yashar*, pp. 43–45; mention of a proselyte in an inquiry of Moses b. Abraham de Pontoise to Rabbenu Tam, ibid. no. 51 p. 107.

9. H.-François Delaborde, ed., *Oeuvres de Rigord et de Guillaume le Breton*, *historiens de Philippe-Auguste*, vol. 1 (Paris, 1882), pp. 16, 28; cf. Chazan, *Me-dieval Jewry in Northern France*, pp. 64–66. Concerning the Jew in Abelard, see R. Thomas, ed., *Dialogus inter Philosphum, Iudaeum et Christianum* (Stuttgart-Bad Cannstadt, 1970), pp. 52–53; English translation in Peter Abelard, *Ethical Writings*, tr. Paul Spade (Indianapolis, 1995), pp. 67–68. In his recent essay, "Abélard et les juifs," *Revue des études juives*, vol. 153 (1994): 253–267, Michel Lemoine does not address this oddity. Charter of 8 March 1217 in Gustave Saige, *Les juifs du Languedoc antérieurement au XIVe siècle* (Paris, 1881), no. 20, pp. 155–157.

10. Abraham b. Isaac of Narbonne, *Sefer ha-Eshkol* (Jerusalem, 1935–1938), II *Hilkhot Avoda Zara*, pp. 132–133; cf. Dinur, *Israel in the Diaspora*, vol. 2, bk. 1, pp. 161–162.

11. See Yvonne Friedman, "An Anatomy of Anti-Semitism: Peter the Venerable's Letter to Louis VII, King of France (1146)," *Bar Ilan Studies in History* (1978): 87–102; Jean-Pierre Torrell, "Les juifs dans l'oeuvre de Pierre le Vénérable," *Cahiers de civilisation médiévale*, vol. 30:4 (1987): 331–346.

12. "As in the course of the eleventh and twelfth centuries fewer and fewer Jews continued to possess land, more and more Jews depended on cities for their livelihood," Sapir Abulafia, *Christians and Jews*, p. 67. Charter in Dinur, *Israel in the Diaspora*, vol. 2, p. 98. On papal entry processions see Noël Coulet, "De l'intégration à l'exclusion: la place des juifs dans les cérémonies d'entrée solennelle au Moyen Age," *Annales*, vol. 34:4 (1979): 672–683; also in *Les chrétiens devant le fait juif* (Paris, 1979), pp. 95–109. Letter of Innocent III, Simonsohn, *The Apostolic See and the Jews*, § 86, p. 91.

13. "Villas nouas fecit; cupiditate deceptus, Iudeis, contra honestatem fidei, quasdem libertates contulit, domos leprosorum, sinagogasque nouas et cimiteria, cimiterium uero Iudeorum de Braio in territorio Sancti-Stephani-Senonensis; et ideo Iudei tenere solent consualiter a congregatione maioris ecclesie Senonensis," Gustave Julliot, ed., *Chronique de l'Abbaye de Saint-Pierre-le-Vif de Sens, rédigée vers la fin du XIIIe siècle par Geoffroy de Courlon* (Sens, 1876), pp. 476–477.

14. Château-Landon, Achille Luchaire, *Etudes sur les actes de Louis VII* (Paris, 1885), no. 658 p. 207; Auxerre charter, John Baldwin ed., *Les registres de Philippe Auguste*, with Françoise Gaspari, Michel Nortier, and Elisabeth Lalou, directed by Robert-Henri Bautier (Paris, 1992), "carte diverse" § 32, pp. 473–476.

15. Article 4 from the charter of Tonnerre, following the letters of Philip Augustus by which he confirmed customs and privileges granted to the inhabitants of Tonnerre: "De Judaeis quoque dictum est quod singuli qui familiam tenebunt, viginti solidos pro se, & quinque solidos pro fastio domus suae, & decimam partem vini et annonae si habuerint sine emptione. Judaei quoque advenae in villa remanentes secundum alias Judaeorum de villa Consuetudines erunt," in M. de Vilevault and M. de Brequigny, eds., *Ordonnances des rois de France de la troisième race*, vol. 11 (Paris, 1769), pp. 217–219. See Robert Chazan, whose interpretation of the text I do not entirely support: *Medieval Jewry in Northern France*, p. 39. On Dieudonné de Bray, see J. Monicat and J. Boussard, eds., *Recueil des actes de Philippe Auguste*, vol. 3 (Paris, 1966), no. 1091, pp. 174–175.

16. "Neque præpositus Judæorum, neque alius, hominem venientem ad forum, vel res suas, vel redeuntem de foro, vel in foro existentem, in die mercati, pro debito capiet," de Vilevaut and de Brequigny, *Ordonnances des rois*, vol. 11 (Paris, 1769), pp. 211–213.

17. For the accusations, Habermann, *Sefer Gzerot*, pp. 144–146; for Béziers, Saige, *Juifs du Languedoc*, pp. 11–12.

18. For the resolutions of the councils, see Solomon Grayzel, *The Church and the Jews in the XIIIth century: A Study of their Relations during the Years 1198–1254, Based on the Papal Letters and the Conciliar Decrees of the Period* (New York, 1966), pp. 296–313. Letters of Alexander III, "De terris vero, quas Iudaei colunt, tuae prudentiae respondemus, ut eos ad decimas persolvendas," in Simonsohn, *The Apostolic See and the Jews*, § 48, p. 50; of Innocent III, ibid., § 67, p. 71; of Honorius III, "fideles, si qui se opposuerint, per censuram ecclesiasticam, appellatione postposita, compescendo," ibid., § 114, p. 118.

19. On the *Herem ha-Yishuv*, cf. Louis Isaac Rabinowitz, *The Herem Hayyishub: A Contribution to the Medieval Economic History of the Jews* (London, 1945); the Roman consultation has been edited by Samuel David Luzzato in *Bet ha-Ozar*, vol. 1 (1847), pp. 57a–60a; see Gérard Nahon "Synodes et taqqanot en France au XIIe siècle," *Annuaire de l'Ecole Pratique des Hautes Etudes, Section des Sciences Religieuses*, vol. 95 (1986–1987): 237–240. On credit see Hayyim Soloveitchik, "Pawnbroking: A Study in *Ribbit* and of the *Halakhah* in Exile," *Proceedings of the American Academy for Jewish Research*, vols. 38–39 (1970): 203–208; see Sapir Abulafia, *Christians and Jews*, p. 68.

20. Jordan, *The French Monarchy and the Jews*, pp. 11–14 and 20.

21. *Tosafot Bava Qamma* 58a; Dinur, *Israel in the Diaspora*, vol. 2, bk. 1, p. 153, does not cite the text in question precisely. He indicates quite rightly that "the province which surrounds us" must mean Champagne. One notes that this Hebrew text corresponds very closely to a passage written on the subject by Nicolas Brussel: "La considération du grand profit que les Barons tiroient des

Juifs domiciliez dans l'étendue de leur Baronie, par le moyen des fortes tailles qu'ils levoient sur eux, fit qu'ils s'efforcèrent de se les rendre patrimoniaux. Pour cet effet, plusieurs Hauts-Seigneurs commencèrent sur la fin du XIIe siècle et dans les premières années du XIIIe à établir pour maxime, qu'il n'étoit pas libre à un *Juif* domicilié d'ancieneté dans une Baronie, de transférer son domicile dans une autre; & que si néanmoins le *Juif* essayoit de le faire, sa personne & ses effets seroient réclamables par le Baron du lieu de son ancien domicile," in Brussel, *Nouvel examen de l'usage général des fiefs en France pendant les onzième, douzième, treizième et quatorzième siècles pour servir à l'intelligence des plus anciens Titres du Domaine de la Couronne & de l'Histoire* (Paris, 1750), vol. 1, p. 570.

22. *Tosafot Qiddushin* 41a. For dating see Ephraim-Elimelekh Urbach, *The Tosaphists, Their History, Writings, and Methods*, vol. 2 (Jerusalem, 1980) [Hebrew], p. 633.

23. For this section one should refer to the article by Aryeh Graboïs, "Les juifs et leurs seigneurs dans la France septentrionale aux XIe et XIIe siècles," in *Les juifs dans l'histoire de France*, pp. 11–23. The letter of Innocent III is published in Simonsohn, *The Apostolic See and the Jews*, § 90, p. 96.

24. *Hagahot Mordekhai on Qiddushin* § 1008, cited by Dinur, *Israel in the Diaspora*, vol. 2, bk. 1, § 12, p. 156; cf. S. Kohn, *Mardochai ben Hillel, Sein Leben und seine Schriften* (Breslau, 1878), p. 101.

25. For the assault on Ramerupt, see The Chronicle of Ephraïm of Bonn in Habermann, *Sefer Gzerot Ashkenaz we-Sarfat*, pp. 120–121; English translation in Eidelberg, *The Jews and the Crusaders*, pp. 130–131. For the Bray-sur-Seine affair, see Robert Chazan, "The Bray Incident of 1192: *Realpolitik* and Folk Slander," *Proceedings of the American Academy for Jewish Research*, vol. 37 (1969): 1–18. Innocent III to William de Joinville in Simonsohn, *The Apostolic See and the Jews*, § 91, pp. 96–97; Honorius III to the abbot of Soissons in ibid., § 103, pp. 106–107; *terram in eius diocesi constitutam supposuit sentente interdicti*, Honorius III on January 15, 1221, ibid., § 111, pp. 114–115; the bishop of Soissons on the expulsion decree can be found in Grayzel, *The Church and the Jews* pp. 163–164, note a. On the Blois affair, see Robert Chazan, "The Blois Incident of 1171: A Study in Jewish Intercommunal Organization," *Proceedings of the American Academy for Jewish Research*, vol. 36 (1968): 13–31. List of victims' names in Siegmund Salfeld, *Das martyrologium des Nürnberges Memorbuches* (Berlin, 1898), pp. 16 and 17.

26. Simonsohn, *Apostolic See and the Jews*, § 88, pp. 92–94.

27. Raymond of Toulouse, *quod Judeis publica committis officia in contumeliam fidei Christiane*, in Simonsohn, *Apostolic See and the Jews*, § 87, p. 92; on the nobles of the Bordelais, ibid., § 113, p. 117.

28. John Baldwin, *Les Registres de Philippe Auguste*, p. 239, article A13.

29. Abelard, *Historia Calamitatum*, English translation in Joseph Muckle, *The Story of Abelard's Adversities* (Toronto, 1954), p. 58. On Tours, Jean Dufour, ed., *Recueil des actes de Louis VI roi de France (1108–1137)*, dir. Robert-Henri Bautier (Paris, 1992), p. 321, n. 155; on Saint-Denis, "Concedimus etiam saepe memoratæ Ecclesiae, in Burgo suo, quinque Judaeorum mansiones cum familiis suis propriorum servorum Ecclesiae absque ulla reclamatione nostra, successorumve nostrorum, liberas & quietas emancipationes, usurariorumque , & monetae falsae omnimodam justitiam et districtiones," de Vilevault and de Brequigny, *Ordonnances*, vol. 11, pp. 181–182; confirmations of Louis VII: Achille Luchaire, *Etudes sur les actes de Louis VII*, Saint-Denis, no. 111, pp. 135–136, Tours, no. 117, p. 137, Narbonne, no. 387, p. 224. Oddly enough, the disposition in the abbey's favour would be repeated in October 1353 at Saint-Denis by Jean I [or Jean II] in practically identical terms: "Concessimus etiam ut Judaei qui ad praesens sunt vel habendi sunt in Burgo seu in Castello Sancti Dionysii, usque ad quinque cum familiis suis, liberi sint ab omni Justicia nostra, & ab omni exactione nostra; tantum sub jure vel Justicia sint Abbatis," in Secousse, *Ordonnances des roys de France de la troisième race*, vol. 4 (Paris, 1734), p. 139. Arles: Simonsohn, *Apostolic See and the Jews*, § 47, pp. 48–49. "Bonus Amicus et filii sui sunt proprii homines archiepiscopi nec debent tallias comiti," John Baldwin, ed., *Les Registres de Philippe Auguste*, "charte diverse," no. 23, p. 463. Melun: *Sigillum judeorum*, op. cit., p. 224, article 344: the year 1197 indicated in the edition's note is a problem.

30. *De Abbate S. Germani Altisiodori, pro Judaeis IIC libras pruvinenses*, N. Brussel, *Nouvel examen*, p. 515.

31. Suger, *Liber de rebus in administratione sua gestis*, and *Testament*, in Albert Lécoy de la Marche, *Oeuvres complètes de Suger* (Paris, 1867), pp. 156–157 and 338–339; cf. Aryeh Graboïs, "L'Abbaye de Saint-Denis et les juifs sous l'abbatiat de Suger," *Annales*, vol. 24:5 (1969): 1187–1195; Elie Berger and H.-François Delaborde, *Recueil des actes de Philippe-Auguste*, vol. 1 (Paris, 1916), p. 63, no. 62.

32. Achille Luchaire, *Philippe Auguste et son temps (1137–1226)* (Paris, 1980), p. 90. One should also consult the excellent work of Yves Sassier, *Louis VII* (Paris, 1991), pp. 72, 141, 149–150, 154, and 470.

33. "In hoc tamen graviter Deum offendit quod in regno suo Judeos ultra modum sublimavit et eis multa privilegia Deo et sibi et regno contraria, immoderata deceptus cupiditate, sublimavit quosdam," in the *Chronique de Saint-Pierre-le-Vif de Sens, dite de Clarius. Chronicon Sancti Petri Vivi Senonensis*, ed. Robert-Henri Bautier and Monique Gilles (Paris, 1979), p. 315. Nearly identical text of the *Fragmentum historicum vitam Ludovici summatim complectens* (BN ms lat. 5002) in Léopold Delisle, ed., *Recueil des Historiens des Gaules et de la France*, vol. 12 (Paris, 1877), p. 191.

34. Paris, Archives Nationales, K 23 no. 11. Sealed original. (= Musée de l'Histoire de France AE II 154), ed. Jules Tardif, *Monuments historiques*, no. 470, p. 256; J. P. Babelon, *Archives Nationales, Musée de l'Histoire de France, II Salle du Moyen Age; Catalogue* (Paris, 1960), pl. 3.

35. Letter in Giles Constable, ed., *The Letters of Peter the Venerable*, vol. 1 (Cambridge, Mass., 1967), pp. 327–330; cf. Sapir Abulafia, *Christians and Jews*, pp. 116 and 131.

36. The account of Ephraïm of Bonn published in Habermann, *Sefer Gzerot*, p. 121, on the royal remission of crusaders' debts to Jews, uses a term that I translate as "charter," implying a written acknowledgment of debt which did not involve collateral: its cancellation thus left the creditor with an irreversible loss. Shlomo Eidelberg, however, translates the passage thus: "Most of the loans of the Jews were *on trust*, and so they lost their money," Eidelberg, *The Jews and the Crusades*, p. 131. For Etampes, see n. 16.

37. "Scripsimus itaque memorato regi, ut a defensione Iudeorum in hac parte desistat," letter of Alexander III c. 1180 to Guarin Gérard, archbishop of Bourges, in Simonsohn, *Apostolic See and the Jews*, § 59, p. 62.

38. Simha b. Samuel de Vitry, *Mahzor Vitry*, ed. Simon Halevy Hurwitz (Nuremberg, 1923), vol. 1, no. 280, pp. 247–248; cf. Shlomo Eidelberg, "Terre de sainteté, tribulation de deux coutumes," *Proceedings of the American Academy for Jewish Research*, vol. 59 (1994): 1–14 [Hebrew]. The audience is known to us through three Hebrew letters, the first coming from the elders of the community of Paris, the second from those of Troyes, and the third by Nathan b. Meshullam. Texts in Habermann, *Sefer Gzerot*, pp. 145–146; English translation Robert Chazan, ed., *Church, State and the Jew in the Middle Ages* (New York, 1980), pp. 115–117.

39. Gedalia Ibn Yahya, *Shalshelet ha-Qabbala* (Jerusalem, 1962), p. 118; S. F. Rosenthal, ed. Jacob b. Meir, *Sefer ha-Yashar* (Berlin, 1898), no. 15, p. 26.

40. Dinur, *Israel in the Diaspora*, vol. 1, p. 73.

41. Isaac Raphael, ed., Abraham ben Nathan de Lunel, *Sefer ha-Manhig, Rulings and Customs* (Jerusalem, 1978), vol. 1, p. 121. Notice of the fast by Ephraïm of Bonn in Habermann, *Sefer Gzerot*, p. 126. For the gathering cf. Shalom Albeck, "Rabbenu Tam and the Historical Problems of His Time," *Zion*, vol. 19 (1954): 104–145 [Hebrew], and Ephraim E. Urbach, *The Tosaphists: Their History, Writings and Methods*, vol. 1, pp. 60–113. On R. Tam's preoccupation with unifying the northern French communities, see Emily Taitz, *The Jews of Medieval France: the Community of Champagne* (Westport, Conn., 1994) [I owe this reference to Anne Holtmann], pp. 107–112.

42. On Philip Augustus, one may refer to the paragraph of Achille Luchaire, *Philippe Auguste et son temps (1137–1226)* (Paris, 1980), pp. 255–256,

and to the great work of John W. Baldwin, *The Government of Philip Augustus: Foundations of French Royal Power in the Middle Ages* (Berkeley and Los Angeles, 1986); especially the section on royal administration of the Jews, pp. 230–233.

43. Arch. Nat., J 211 no. 3 and J 221 no. 1; this last charter contains the following article: *quod dominus rex michi reddidit comitatum Augi, salvo sibi placito ensis, et Judeis suis;* cf. Alexandre Teulet, *Layettes du trésor des Chartes,* vol. 1 (Paris, 1863), pp. 487b–488a, no. 1360.

44. John Baldwin, ed., *Les registres de Philippe Auguste,* pp. 385 and 570.

45. Arch. Nat. S 2165 and S 2333, cf. M. Douet D'Arcq, *Inventaires et documents, Collection de sceaux,* vol. 2 (Paris, 1867), no. 4495 and 4496.

46. John Baldwin ed., *The Government of Philip Augustus,* pp. 231–232.

47. 16 January 1205: Simonsohn, *Apostolic See and the Jews,* § 79, pp. 82–83; 15 July 1205: ibid., § 82, pp. 86–87; 9 October 1208: ibid., § 89, p. 95; Eusèbe de Laurière, *Ordonnances des roys de France de la troisieme race,* vol. 1 (Paris, 1723), pp. 39–42, art. 8.

48. "This is not to say that all anti-Jewish feeling as it developed from the twelfth century onwards was purely intellectual. Much of the hatred towards Jews stemmed from totally uneducated people. . . . The history of the precise interaction between the work of the scholars we have studied and popular attitudes demands a book in its own right," Anna Sapir Abulafia, *Christians and Jews,* p. 139.

Jews and Christians in Twelfth-Century England: Some Dynamics of a Changing Relationship

ROBERT C. STACEY

The Jews of medieval England were, in many respects, an archetypical medieval Ashkenazic community. Almost all the structural features that characterized Jewish life elsewhere in twelfth- and thirteenth-century northern Europe can be found in England, but in high relief. Partly this "high relief" is accidental, the consequence of obsessive record-keeping by English governments. Yet it is not a documentary mirage. English Jews do exemplify the structural characteristics of Ashkenazic life to an extraordinary degree and in exaggerated ways. At the same time, their historical experience mirrors general developments in Jewish-Christian relations in dramatic fashion. Together, these observations lend to English Jewish history an interest and importance incommensurate with the tiny number of medieval English Jews. As a case study in Christian-Jewish relations during the twelfth century, they can scarcely be bettered.

In his recent study, *Medieval Stereotypes and Modern Antisemitism*, Robert Chazan has usefully distinguished five characteristic features of Ashkenazi Jewish communities in the period between roughly 1000 and 1300.[1] Following Chazan's lead, we might therefore argue for the Ashkenazic archetypicality of the English Jewish community on the following grounds.

First, like all Jewish communities north of the Loire, the English Jewish community was a community of immigrants. There were no Jews at all living in England prior to 1066, and no evidence that Jews elsewhere had any commercial contacts with England. When Jews finally did arrive in the country, they came in association with the Norman conquerors. Prior to 1154, the greatest number of Jews living in England had come from Normandy, although there was also some continuing immigration to and from the Rhineland.[2] In the half-century after 1154, new Jewish immigrants arrived in England from both Angevin and Capetian territories. This new wave of immigrants, however, only reinforced the "Frenchness" of English Jewish culture. French was the language of the Jewish hearth and home in post-conquest England, and seems to have remained so right up until the expulsion in 1290. No doubt most Jews learned some English—they must have done so, simply to carry on their daily lives and business dealings. But English never seems to have become their primary vernacular language. Jews continued to bear French names, usually translations of the meaning of their Hebrew names.[3] When they wrote in a vernacular language, it was invariably in French.[4] And when an unknown Christian author wrote a ritual crucifixion story involving a Bristol Jewish family, probably in the 1260s, he seems to have presumed that although the Jews of Bristol could speak English when required to do so, they customarily spoke French among themselves.[5]

Secondly, the English Jewish community was a minority community. Estimates of medieval population are notoriously unreliable, but they are somewhat less so for England than for most other places. By the mid-thirteenth century, England had a population of perhaps five million people. Of these, three thousand to five thousand were Jews. By 1290, the Jewish population had dropped to less than two thousand, while the Christian population may have grown to as much six million, its medieval peak.[6]

Third, the English Jewish community was extraordinarily dependent upon moneylending for its economic livelihood, and uniquely successful in the business. In 1240, the Jewish community's liquidable assets—that is to say, the principal owing to them on loans, plus cash in hand, jewels, and houses—were valued at approximately 200,000 marks. This sum excludes all interest charges, but still represents a third of the total circulating coin in the kingdom. In per capita terms, this works out to between forty and sixty marks for every man, woman, and child in the

English Jewish community.[7] No other Jewish community in Europe could approach this level of per capita wealth. Not unrelatedly, the Jews of England were also overwhelmingly urban. There were no Jewish agriculturalists in thirteenth-century England, and only a few small-town Jewish settlements, although the number of small settlements may have been growing in the decades prior to 1290.

Fourth, it was a community exclusively subject to royal dominion. Jewish legal status was defined by the Crown, and all Jews were directly subject to the administrative omnicompetence of the king's government. Finally, English Jews were among the first Jews in western Europe to suffer the consequences of the developing anti-Semitism of the high medieval world. England pioneered the ritual crucifixion charge, and remained its most consistent exponent. In 1290, England also became the first European kingdom permanently to expel its Jewish population. In the hundred and fifty years between these two events, the Jews of England were subjected to crippling taxation, sweeping judicial executions on charges of coin-clipping and malicious murder, and royally-sponsored conversionist campaigns. In this, too, English Jews appear as an archetypical Ashkenazic community.

Does this English evidence also suggest some general connection between the fundamental structures of Ashkenazic life—immigrant, minority communities of moneylenders, living in towns under the jurisdictional authority of kings—and the tragic history of Christian-Jewish relations in Ashkenaz? If such connections are in fact valid, England may offer us a valuable model for their working out elsewhere in medieval Europe. But it may be well to look again at this case for England's archetypicality. Some qualifications may be in order. Most importantly, not all these archetypical elements in English Jewish experience characterized the English Jewish community from its beginnings. Most emerged for the first time, or were at least dramatically accentuated, in the half century between 1144, when the ritual crucifixion charge was first adumbrated by the relatives of William of Norwich, and 1194, when Archbishop Hubert Walter reorganized the royal administration of Jewish bonds. There is, in short, an important historical dynamic at work in the shaping of English Jewry as a classic Ashkenazic community.

Let us start with immigration. Jewish immigration to England came in two waves: one under the Normans, the other during the reign of King Henry II. Jews were also, however, internal immigrants within

England. Jewish settlements spread outward from London and the southeast only during Stephen's reign, or perhaps in the last few years of the reign of King Henry I.[8] Even in the economic "boom" areas of the north and east, however, the density of Jewish settlements did not increase dramatically until the 1160s. In Lincolnshire, Yorkshire, and East Anglia, where the anti-Jewish violence of the Third Crusade was most severe, Jewish settlements were thus only about two generations old when they were attacked. The newness of these Jewish communities was certainly not the only reason they were assaulted. In 1189, expectations that the crusading King Richard would follow the example of King Philip of France and expel the Jews from the kingdom of England were widespread even in areas, like London, where Jews had resided for more than a century.[9] But in provincial England, expectations of an imminent mass expulsion in 1189–90 were also fueled by the memory of a time, not so long past, when Jews simply did not live in these areas of the kingdom.

Linguistically, Jews in medieval England were aliens in a more profound sense than perhaps anywhere else in Europe. In the immediate aftermath of the Norman conquest, the contrast between the French-speaking Jewish newcomers and the English-speaking Christian majority was, of course, an obvious one. At the same time, however, the Jews' status as fellow Francophones tended to unite them, at least in the eyes of the conquered English, with the French-speaking military aristocracy created by the Conquest. Jews in the Anglo-Norman period were thus not so isolated a linguistic minority as they would later become. By the mid-twelfth century, however, English was emerging as the first language of virtually all children raised in England, irrespective of family origins or class. By the end of the twelfth century, French was a language the English upper class learned from textbooks; and "the French of Marlborough" was already a target of Parisian derision.[10]

The linguistic contempt was of course mutual. By the mid-thirteenth century, English had become so important a marker of national identity that the followers of Simon de Montfort could treat anyone in England who did not speak English as an enemy to their cause.[11] Nor was their presumption groundless. For the fact was that by the 1260s, there were only two groups of people in England whose children were still being raised in French. One was the Jews; the other was the royal family, including the king's unpopular French relations. Both groups were perceived as foreigners, and both became targets for the patriotic wrath of the Montfortians.

By the mid-thirteenth century, French in England had thus become identified as the language of the kingdom's enemies. Attitudes toward French were of course more complex than this simple characterization allows. At the same time that French was the language of the national enemy, French remained—indeed, was increasingly—the language of high culture and aristocratic refinement, in England and on the Continent. This was, indeed, part of the appeal of French, and helps to explain why French survived as long as it did in a country where almost no one aside from Jews spoke it as their primary vernacular language. Jews were by no means immune to the cultural appeal of French culture. Their continuing allegiance to the French language made them participants (in their own eyes, at least) in an international Francophone culture that comprised both Jews and Christians. At the same time, however, there seems little doubt that for thirteenth-century English Jews, their continuing dependence upon French as their primary vernacular language alienated them from their English-speaking neighbors much more profoundly than it had done a century before.

Similar developments were taking place with regard to attitudes toward Hebrew. Interest among English Christians in Hebrew went back to at least the tenth century, but became more widespread after the Conquest, when Hebrew was studied by a few Anglo-Norman prelates as a language useful for astrology and sorcery.[12] Scholarly interest in Hebrew biblical exegesis was not entirely absent from the Anglo-Norman period, but became much more marked a feature of English intellectual life under the Angevins, especially, it appears, in the circles of Thomas Becket and William de Longchamps.[13] Interest in Hebrew biblical commentary continued throughout the thirteenth century also, particularly among the English Franciscans in the circle around Bishop Robert Grosseteste.[14] By the mid-thirteenth century, however, linguistic difference was coming to be seen as dangerous in ways it had not previously been; and Hebrew, like French, was now also being portrayed as a language that might threaten the well-being of English Christians. In the 1220s, when a Christian deacon converted to Judaism, he was induced to do so by the beauty of his Jewish lover.[15] In the 1270s, however, when another cleric, the Dominican Robert of Reading, also converted to Judaism, he was said to have been seduced into apostasy by the Hebrew language, which led him on to conversion and death.[16]

The most striking example of this sense of the threat posed by Hebrew to Christians is, however, the mid- to late-thirteenth-century account of the ritual crucifixion of Adam of Bristol.[17] Throughout this tale, the author goes out of his way to stress the differing languages his characters spoke, and the differing purposes for which they used them. The Jews in the story speak French and Hebrew, some English, but no Irish. A visiting Irish priest speaks Irish, French, and some English. His Irish servants speak only Irish, however, and so cannot understand the shouted warnings of the people of Bristol, who speak only English. A married priest of Bristol takes the confession of the Irish priest in French; and God the Father, of course, speaks Latin. God the Son, however, startles the Jewish perpetrators of Adam's murder by addressing them in Hebrew, a language unknown to any Bristol Christians (according to the tale), and therefore utilized by the Jewish characters for secret communications between themselves that they did not want their Christian neighbors to understand—in this case, of course, for their plans to murder Adam of Bristol.

Whether in fact Jews in thirteenth-century England did speak conversational Hebrew with one another is an interesting question. What matters, however, is that by the 1260s Christians in England were convinced that they did, and that they did so with nefarious intent. By the middle of the thirteenth century, both the vernacular and the learned languages of the Jews of England were seen as threatening by their English-speaking neighbors in ways that they had not been a century before. Jews had become a minority group identifiable not only by their religion, but also, increasingly, by their language.

It was also during the years between 1144 and 1194 that the Jews of England emerged as the quintessential moneylenders in the English kingdom.[18] Prior to the 1150s, moneylending in England was dominated by a closely connected group of Anglo-Saxon merchant-moneyers whose roots can in some cases be traced back to the pre-Conquest period. Monasteries also were active in the business of lending money, certainly after 1066, and probably before; and so too, after 1066, were some Jews. It was not until the 1160s, however, that Jewish involvement with moneylending began to influence the patterns of Jewish settlement within the kingdom; and not until the 1170s that evidence mounts of truly substantial fortunes in the hands of Jewish moneylenders. Both developments were, to a considerable extent, the consequence of decisions taken by the crown.

That the king deliberately built up Jewish moneylending in England so as to profit from it is a claim widespread in modern historical literature, and found even in some late-twelfth-century chroniclers. But it is mistaken. What happened, I believe, is this. The loss of Normandy between 1141 and 1144 by King Stephen disrupted the cross-channel trade between London and Rouen, a trade in which the Jews of London had for long been involved. At the same time, however, the anarchy also undermined the entire system of moneychanging and bullion-trading within England in which Jews had played a modest but important role alongside Christians. In these circumstances, Jews began moving out of London and into the eastern parts of the kingdom, especially into East Anglia, where a certain amount of foreign silver continued to be imported and exchanged, and where Stephen's royal authority was somewhat better established than elsewhere in the kingdom.[19] By 1159, there were Jewish communities outside London at Norwich, Lincoln, Cambridge, Winchester, Thetford, Bungay, Northampton, Oxford, and Bury St Edmunds, and smaller settlements at Gloucester, Worcester, and Newport in Essex. None of these provincial Jewish communities was particularly wealthy, however, and there is nothing in this pattern of settlement to suggest that it was determined by moneylending. Rather, by 1159 Jews settled in towns that were centers of minting and foreign exchange and associated with important fairs. Between 1159 and 1194, however, both the patterns of Jewish settlement within England, and the relative wealth of these provincial Jewish communities one to another, were completely transformed by the impact of moneylending.

What lay behind this sudden economic transformation was a series of decisions by the English crown. In 1158, Henry II ruined the group of Anglo-Saxon merchant-moneyers who had previously been responsible for the coinage, and who had also been one of the principal sources for small-scale loans.[20] In the mid-1160s, he confiscated the entire estate of William Cade, by far the largest moneylender in England, and a man who lent particularly to the wealthy and powerful. In less than a decade, Henry thus eliminated both the top and bottom rungs of the credit market throughout England. In London, there were plenty of Christian merchants ready to move into the credit vacuum that suddenly opened up. Some of these men had been acting already as Cade's agents. Now, they struck out on their own. In the north and east, however, where the demand for capital was especially great, Jewish lenders took over much of the market. Two axes of Jewish finance now emerged: one running north and east, from London to Cambridge, Bury, Thetford, Bungay, and Norwich; the other running north and west, from London to Oxford to Northampton to Lincoln and ultimately to York. The three nodal points in this network were Norwich, Lincoln, and London, and it was there that the greatest Jewish fortunes of the twelfth century were made. By his death in 1186, Aaron of Lincoln had become a figure even grander than William Cade; and when he died, the king thereupon confiscated his estate too.[21]

The confiscation of Aaron of York's estate in 1186 decisively altered the relationship between the English crown and Jewish moneylending. For Jews, these changes would ultimately prove catastrophic. Although Henry II had levied taxes on Jewish communities and occasional, massive fines on individual Jewish lenders, he had not previously been involved in the direct collection of debts owed by Christians to Jewish lenders. Royal officials sometimes assisted Jewish lenders in enforcing their debts, and no doubt this occasioned some resentment. But there is nothing in such procedures that would justify William of Newburgh's bitter description of the Jews of England as "the king's usurers."[22] This was a description written in the early 1190s, and it refers specifically to the circumstances that arose after 1186, when the king confiscated Aaron of Lincoln's bonds and began to collect them directly on his own behalf, using all of the coercive force of the exchequer to do so. The sums involved were prodigious. At his death, Aaron may have been owed as much as £75,000 in principal and interest on his bonds. The bulk of this sum, moreover, was owed by the magnates, knights, and monasteries of northern England. Henry's attempts to collect these debts helped to spark the massacres of 1189–90 at York, Lincoln, and Stamford. They also marked the beginning of thirty years of hostility between the Angevins and the Northerners, hostility that would culminate in the Magna Carta rebellion.[23]

To explain how Jews in England became such successful moneylenders, this essay has emphasized the consequences of royal decision-making: the disruptions of the Anarchy; the dismissal of the Anglo-Saxon merchant-moneyers; the confiscation of Cade's estate. Clearly other factors also contributed to making England a place where moneylenders could prosper. The domestic peace and administrative strength of Henry II's regime made it easier in England than in most places to collect one's debts. The litigiousness of English society and the rapacity of Angevin government increased the demand for loans, particularly among the armigerous classes. So too did inflation, the impact of which can be clearly traced from the 1180s onward, not least upon the costs of war. All these factors, with the possible exception of the inflation, bring us back to the influence of the crown itself on the fortunes of English Jewry.

This is not a new theme. As has long been recognized, no other monarchy in Europe exercised so much control over the Jewish population within its kingdom. But there were changes over time. The exclusive lordship claimed by thirteenth-century kings over all the Jews of England did not derive uninterruptedly from the Conquest. Rather, it was the product of developments that took place in this same critical half-century between 1144 and 1194.

From their beginnings, the Jewish communities at Rouen and London were under the direct and exclusive jurisdiction of the crown. That much seems clear. What, however, about Jewish communities outside the two capitals? In Normandy, there is good evidence of seigneurial Jewish communities during the 1190s, but little to document when such communities began.[24] In England the evidence is better. In 1146, when the Jews of Norwich appealed to King Stephen to do them justice against a local knight, they began by reminding him that "We are your Jews. . . ."[25] Would such a remark have been necessary if all the Jews in England were in fact under the exclusive jurisdiction of the crown at this date? The *Leges Edwardi Confessoris*, a roughly contemporary compilation of legal material, asserts the crown's exclusive jurisdiction over Jews, but in language that implies that the facts, by this date, were otherwise.

> It should be known that all Jews, wherever they are in the kingdom, ought to be under the liege guardianship and protection of the king; nor can any one of them subject himself to some powerful person without the license of the king, because the Jews themselves and all their possessions are the king's. But if someone detains them or their

money, the king shall demand [them] as his own property if he wishes and can.[26]

We may even be able to guess who some of these "powerful persons" were. By 1159, Jews were living in a number of seigneurial boroughs throughout East Anglia and the Midlands, including Bungay, Thetford, Bury St Edmunds, Castle Rising, Leicester, and possibly Coventry.[27] Bungay and Thetford were boroughs claimed by the Bigod Earls of Norfolk; Bury belonged to its abbot; Castle Rising to the Earls of Arundel; Leicester to the powerful Earl Robert; and Coventry to the Earls of Chester. In 1159, Bungay and Thetford were in the king's hands, having been confiscated from the rebellious Hugh Bigod in 1157. The Jewish communities in both towns paid tribute to the crown, therefore, in 1159.[28] In these other seigneurial boroughs, however, the Jewish communities apparently were not subject to the king's 1159 taxation. At Castle Rising, moreover, we know a little about what the Earl of Arundel's lordship over the Jewish community there entailed. Prior to 1176, when his estates fell to the crown, the earl took aids from the Jews of Castle Rising at will, and took aids from his tenants to repay loans he had contracted with Deulebeneye, Jew of Rising.[29] He did not need the king's permission to do any of this.

Henry II was, of course, committed to recovering all the rights his grandfather had enjoyed in 1135. And though the evidence is patchy, it does appear that he reasserted the crown's claim to exclusive jurisdiction over all Jews. In the mid-1170s, a revised version of the *Leges Edwardi Confessoris* was circulating around the king's court which omitted all the qualifying language of the 1140s version. It declared flatly that all Jews, in whichever kingdom they might be, were under the liege guardianship and protection of the king, and that they and all their property belonged to the king.[30] In 1179–80, the exchequer began asserting its own jurisdiction over legal cases involving Jews.[31] Further centralization occurred in 1194, when Jewish cases were apparently removed from the ordinary jurisdiction of the eyre justices and transferred instead to Westminster.[32] In the same year, the king also issued new regulations governing Jewish lending throughout England.[33] This legislation makes no acknowledgment whatsoever of the existence of any seigneurial Jewish communities in England. It applied to all Jews, irrespective of their places of residence.

Many of the seigneurial Jewish communities that existed in 1159 were gone by 1194. Their disappearance has usually been explained by reference to the massacres of 1190, which hit several of these communities quite hard. This may not, however, be the entire story. At Bury St Edmunds, for example, where some of the worst attacks took place, the Jewish community was not destroyed by the rioting. It was deliberately expelled by the abbot about six months later, on the memorable grounds "that everything in the town and within the banlieu belonged by right to St Edmund: therefore, either the Jews should be St Edmund's men or they should be banished from the town."[34] To effect this expulsion, however, the abbot had first to seek the king's permission to carry it out; and the king in turn then modified the terms of the expulsion order to permit Jewish lenders to return to the town temporarily to collect their remaining debts.

This may be the key to what was happening in other seigneurial boroughs also. The Jews of Bury were no longer welcome in the borough because Henry II and Richard I had begun to insist on the exclusivity of their royal jurisdictional rights over all Jews in England. The Jews of Bury were not the men of St Edmund because they were, now, the king's men—and as such their presence was a standing threat to the jurisdictional integrity of the Abbot's liberty of Bury St Edmunds. The same considerations may well lie behind the disappearance of Jewish communities at Bungay, Thetford, and Castle Rising. All three boroughs had been restored to their rightful heirs between October 1189 and June 1190, after decades in the hands of the crown. The last thing the Earls of Norfolk or Arundel wanted was to give the king's officials an excuse to intervene again in their newly restored lordships by permitting Jews to remain there.

Outside East Anglia, a few seigneurial Jewish communities survived rather longer. At Leicester, for example, the Jewish community lasted until 1232, in part perhaps because the town was in royal hands from 1207 until 1231. In 1232, however, when Simon de Montfort received half the town as heir to the Leicester earldom, he immediately expelled the Jews who resided there. His charter of expulsion says nothing about royal permission having been sought for his action; but it does speak explicitly of the need to protect the integrity of the borough's liberty from the threats to that liberty posed by Jews.

Happily, the Jews of Leicester did not have to move far to escape from Montfort's territory. They simply moved to the other half of the town, held by the Countess of Winchester, and so outside Montfort's jurisdiction.[35]

This essay began by arguing the case for the archetypicality of the English Jewish community within Ashkenaz. It then undermined this case by arguing for the exceptionalism of the community, suggesting that most of its archetypical elements were the product of uniquely English and Norman events that took place in the years between 1144 and 1194. I might perhaps conclude, then, by squaring this circle: it was the very archetypicality of Jewish experience in England that rendered it so exceptional. Nowhere else in Europe was there a Jewish community that was so small, so strikingly a group of immigrants and aliens, so completely dependent upon moneylending as the Jews of England became, and so astonishingly successful at it. No wonder, then, that the historical experience of this community should exhibit, in so exaggerated a form, the characteristic features of Ashkenazic Jewish history generally.

But clever though such a conclusion might be, it is not where I want to leave the argument. Structurally and culturally, Anglo-Jewry was indeed typical of many other Ashkenazic communities of the twelfth and thirteenth centuries. It was also, in important ways, quite exceptional. But what I really want to argue for is the historical contingency, even the unpredictability, of the history of the Jews in medieval England. That history did not have to turn out the way it did. It took a decisive turn between 1144 and 1194. Yet there are undeniable parallels between the changes that took place in England at this time and those occurring in other Ashkenazic communities. By all means, then, let us search for models; and let us recognize clearly how formative for medieval Jewish experience in Europe the last half of the twelfth century truly was. But in so doing, let us not lose sight of the particularity of experience that characterized these differing communities. There may not be a history of the Jews in medieval Ashkenaz. It is still too soon to tell. What there surely can be is a series of parallel histories of Jewish experience in a variety of political communities scattered unevenly across the landscape of twelfth-century northern Europe. And there are still a great many of those that remain to be written.

Notes

1. Robert Chazan, *Medieval Stereotypes and Modern Antisemitism* (Berkeley, 1997), 1–18.

2. Julius Aronius, *Regesten zur Geschichte der Juden in Frankischen und Deutschen Reiche* (Berlin, 1902), nos. 234, 264, 273, 293, 353, 354.

3. Cecil Roth, *A History of the Jews in England*, 3d ed. (Oxford, 1964), 93–95.

4. The vast bulk of the written material deriving from the English Jewish community in the Middle Ages is in Hebrew. There are a number of French letters and notations, and a few references to Jews writing in Latin, usually in connection with allegations of forgery. There are no surviving examples of any written material in English by Jews, and no references known to me referring to Jews writing in English.

5. The Latin text of this story has now been published by Christoph Cluse, "'Fabula ineptissima'. Die Ritualmordlegende um Adam von Bristol nach der Handschrift London, British Library, Harley 957," *Aschkenas: Zeitschrift fur Geschichte und Kulture der Juden* 5.2 (1995): 293–330. I am working on an edition, translation, and discussion of this text.

6. On the Jewish population of England, the calculations of Vivian D. Lipman, "The Anatomy of Medieval Anglo-Jewry," *Transactions of the Jewish Historical Society of England* 21 (1968): 4–77, remain definitive. Richard Britnell has surveyed recent calculations for the overall population of England in "Commercialisation and Economic Development in England, 1000–1300," in *A Commercialising Economy, England 1086 to c. 1300*, ed. Richard H. Britnell and Bruce M. S. Campbell (Manchester, 1995), 11–12.

7. A mark was equivalent to two-thirds of a pound sterling. For these calculations, see Robert C. Stacey, "Jewish Lending and the Medieval English Economy," in *A Commercialising Economy*, ed. Britnell and Campbell, 78–101, at 93–95.

8. Kevin T. Streit, "The Expansion of the English Jewish Community in the Reign of King Stephen," *Albion* 25.2 (1993): 177–92. I have attempted to work out the economic context for this internal migration in Stacey, "Jewish Lending," 82–87.

9. Robert C. Stacey, "Crusades, Martyrdoms, and the Jews of Norman England, 1096–1190," in *Juden und Christen zur Zeit der Kreuzzuge*, ed. Alfred Haverkamp, Vorträge und Forschungen 47 (Sigmaringen, 1998), 233–51.

10. Ian Short, "On Bilingualism in Anglo-Norman England," *Romance Philology* 33 (1979–80): 467–79; Michael T. Clanchy, *From Memory to Written Record: England 1066–1307*, 2d ed. (Oxford, 1993): 197–206; R. A. Lodge,

"Language Attitudes and Linguistic Norms in France and England in the Thirteenth Century," in *Thirteenth Century England IV*, ed. Peter R. Coss and Simon D. Lloyd (Woodbridge, 1992), 73–83; Ian Short, "Tam Angli quam Franci: Self-Definition in Anglo-Norman England," in *Anglo-Norman Studies XVIII*, ed. Christopher Harper-Bill (Woodbridge, 1996), 153–75.

11. *Flores Historiarum*, ed. H. R. Luard, Rolls Series 95 (London, 1890), 2:481; John R. Maddicott, *Simon de Montfort* (Cambridge, 1994), 231; David A. Carpenter, *The Reign of Henry III* (London, 1996), 337–38.

12. Bernhard Blumenkranz, *Les Auteurs Chrétiens Latins du Moyen Age sur les juifs et le judaïsme* (Paris, 1963), 225; Frank Barlow, *The English Church, 1066–1154* (London, 1979), 247–48, 259; R. Barrie Dobson, *The Jews of York and the Massacre of March 1190* (Borthwick Papers, 1974), 3–5.

13. Beryl Smalley, *The Study of the Bible in the Middle Ages*, 2d ed. (Oxford, 1952), 186–95, 235; Raphael Loewe, "The Medieval Christian Hebraists of England: Herbert of Bosham and Earlier Scholars," *Transactions of the Jewish Historical Society of England* 17 (1953): 225–49; Beryl Smalley, *The Becket Conflict and the Schools* (Oxford, 1973), 73–74.

14. Deeanna Copeland Klepper, "Nicholas of Lyra and Franciscan Hebraism," in *Nicholas of Lyra: The Sense of Scripture*, ed. Phillip Krey and Leslie Smith (forthcoming). I am grateful to Dr. Klepper for sending me a copy of this paper in advance of publication.

15. Frederic W. Maitland, "The Deacon and the Jewess," in *Roman Canon Law in the Church of England: Six Essays* (London, 1898), 158–79.

16. *The Chronicle of Bury St Edmunds, 1212–1301*, ed. Antonia Gransden (London, 1964), 58.

17. See note 5 above. The handwriting of the manuscript would appear to date the surviving text to the period 1260–1280. I am grateful to Paul Brand for advice on this dating.

18. For what follows in this and the next paragraph, see my "Jewish Lending," 88–93.

19. Judith Green, "Financing Stephen's War," *Anglo-Norman Studies XIV*, ed. Marjorie Chibnall (Woodbridge, 1992), 91–114, at 99–100; Edmund King, "The Anarchy of King Stephen's Reign," *Transactions of the Royal Historical Society*, 5th ser. 34 (1984): 133–53.

20. Pamela Nightingale, "Some London Moneyers and Reflections on the Organization of English Mints in the Eleventh and Twelfth Centuries," *Numismatic Chronicle* 142 (1982):34–50; "'The King's Profit': Trends in English Mint and Monetary Policy in the Eleventh and Twelfth Centuries," *Later Medieval Mints*, ed. Nicholas J. Mayhew and Peter Spufford, British Archaeological Reports, International Series 389 (Oxford, 1988), 61–75.

21. Robert C. Stacey, "Aaron of Lincoln," in *The Dictionary of National Biography: Missing Persons*, ed. C. S. Nicholls (Oxford, 1993), 1.

22. "The Chronicle of William of Newburgh," in *Chronicles of the Reigns of Stephen, Henry II and Richard I*, ed. Richard Howlett, Rolls Series 82 (London, 1885–90), 1:322–23.

23. James C. Holt, *The Northerners: A Study in the Reign of King John* (Oxford, 1961).

24. H. G. Richardson, *The English Jewry under Angevin Kings* (London, 1960), 201–12.

25. *The Life and Miracles of St William of Norwich by Thomas of Monmouth*, ed. Augustus Jessopp and Montague Rhodes James (Cambridge, 1896), 100.

26. "Sciendum est quod omnes Iudei, in quocumque regno sint, sub tutela et defensione regis ligie debent esse; neque aliquis eorum potest se subdere alicui diuiti sine licencia regis, quia ipsi Iudei et omnia sua regis sunt. Quod si aliquis detinuerit eos vel pecuniam eorum, requirat rex tanquam suum proprium, si uult et potest." Bruce O'Brien, *God's Peace and King's Peace: The Laws of Edward the Confessor* (Philadelphia, 1998).

27. *Pipe Rolls 2–4 Henry II* (Pipe Roll Society, London, 1884), 56, 127, 183; *Pipe Roll 5 Henry II* (London, 1885), 12; *Red Book of the Exchequer*, ed. Hubert Hall, Rolls Series 99 (London, 1896), vol. 2, Appendix A, cclxvii–cclxxvii.

28. *Pipe Roll 5 Henry II*, 12.

29. *Red Book*, vol. 2, appendix A, cclxvii–cclxx.

30. *Chronica Rogeri de Hoveden*, ed. William Stubbs, Rolls Series 51 (London, 1868–71), 2:231. I am grateful to Dr. O'Brien for advice.

31. The evidence is complex. The *Dialogue of the Exchequer*, completed between 1177 and 1179, says nothing to suggest that the exchequer exercised regular jurisdiction over Jews. From 1179 on, however, one finds a steady stream of Jewish legal cases being heard by the exchequer and noted on the pipe rolls: *Pipe Roll 26 Henry II*, 32, 153; *Pipe Roll 27 Henry II*, 134; *Pipe Roll 28 Henry II*, 162; *Pipe Roll 29 Henry II*, 159 (2); *Pipe Roll 30 Henry II*, 149; *Pipe Roll 31 Henry II*, 91. This change may have coincided with the appointment of Ranulf de Glanville as justiciar, replacing Richard de Lucy.

32. The evidence is mostly negative: i.e., the fairly plentiful evidence on the pipe rolls of justices on eyre hearing cases involving Jews suddenly disappears after 1193.

33. *Chronica Rogeri de Hoveden*, 3:266–67.

34. Jocelin of Brakelond, *The Chronicle of the Abbey of Bury St Edmunds*, trans. Diana Greenway and Jane Sayers (Oxford, 1989), 41–42.

35. Maddicott, *Simon de Montfort*, 15–16.

Conclusion

MICHAEL A. SIGNER

Whearacter hen the editors of this volume issued their letters of invitation, they hoped for an assembly of articles to fill a gap in the study of northern Europe in the high Middle Ages. Pioneering studies, notably Charles Homer Haskins's *Renaissance of the Twelfth Century* (1927), still engender stimulating and rigorous reevaluation of medieval Europe, as the volume *Renaissance and Renewal in the Twelfth Century*, edited by Robert Benson and Giles Constable (1991), demonstrated. Yet neither of those studies contained any significant appraisal, beyond the nod to Jewish translators of philosophical works and Jewish moneylending, of the specific role that the tension between Judaism and Christianity played in the development of medieval culture and society.

Certainly, there is a genealogy of scholarship criticizing the erasure of Jewish-Christian relationships from "mainstream" medieval history (as the essays by Ivan Marcus and Jeremy Cohen in this volume note). Nonetheless, the specter of medievalism, the desire to shape the Middle Ages in our own perspective, haunts all students of the era between classical antiquity and the "modern." Powerful ideological considerations have shaped the syntax for the narratives that constitute the Middle Ages. Religious triumphalism and national "genius" drew historians to shade their evidence so that a particular point of view might be illuminated. A strong affinity for essentialism, with an emphasis on the purity of either Judaism or Christianity, has separated these two traditions from one another. Our authors demonstrate their awareness of this inheritance and, at times, their agnostic attitude toward the intellectual trends that bound previous generations of scholars.

Therefore, how does our collection, *Jews and Christians in Twelfth-Century Europe*, contribute to continuing efforts to discern the complex threads that constituted European society and culture during the years 1050–1215? John Van Engen's terms "intimacy" and "distance" resonate well with the terminology of Jacob Katz's "exclusiveness" and "tolerance" as the limina for Jews and Christians. Elliot Wolfson's essay carefully maps the complexity of "intimacy" and "distance" in the development of the idealization of the martyr in Ashkenazi piety by demonstrating how it draws earlier traditions of eroticism and asceticism into a new visionary literature. There were indeed boundaries between the two communities, marked by the inheritance of juridical traditions. Each community made decisions about the education of the young, communal coherence, and sanctions for those who transgressed those boundaries. Gérard Nahon, Alfred Haverkamp, and Robert Stacey uncover the intricate web of power relationships that left room for Jews and Christians to mix with one another and create a rich material environment while maintaining a strong desire to preserve separate communal identities.

The essays by Jan Ziolkowski, Jonathan Elukin, and William Chester Jordan reveal how cultural and religious tendencies within both Jewish and Christian communities recognized "limbos"—areas where personal and communal identity were not so easily decided. Herman-Judah's conversion narrative contains significant gaps which argue against an "essential" Christian or Jewish identity. Guibert of Nogent, whose name appears frequently in these essays, finds that it is precisely the neutrality of a hated nobleman, Count Jean of Soissons, that defines him as a "neutricum."

Giles Constable's *The Reformation of the Twelfth Century* (1996) provides copious evidence of the confusion within Christian society about what constituted the proper religious path. The boundaries between monk, canon, and secular clergy were far from clear; differences in Jewish and Christian exegesis further complicated distinctions. Ivan Marcus confirms Constable's model, indicating that both Jews and Christians had greater choices of behavior in the evolving society of twelfth-century Europe. John Van Engen's exploration of the problems faced by young monks reading Leviticus demonstrates that Jews were far more than a "marker" for religious heresy. They constituted part of the tapestry of religious possibilities. The subtle apologetics of Rabbi Solomon b. Isaac of Troyes that are described in my own essay open the possibility that the rapid growth of Jews in northern France required a synthesis of an earlier layer of rabbinic culture.

Several essays broaden our knowledge about conversion or apostasy, the ultimate transgression of boundaries. This area has been sorely neglected in past studies of medival Jews and Christians. Jeremy Cohen rehearses the relevant arguments of Israeli scholars such as Baer, Katz, and Ben-Sasson, who contrast the more intense Judaism of Ashkenaz, which resulted in martyrdom, with the mass conversions of Iberian Jewry. Jonathan Elukin emphasizes the many recent studies on the development of interiority in the twelfth century and contrasts the communal conversions of the early Middle Ages with the greater scrutiny given to conversion during the twelfth century. William Chester Jordan provides a further nuance by his careful investigations of the age when decisions seem to have been made to move beyond one's religion of birth. In both of these essays, the emphasis upon the narratives by Guibert of Nogent and Herman-Judah of Cologne distinguish them from previous studies.

The tension between intimacy and distance also uncovers a shared world. The editors hoped that essays focusing on vernacular literature would provide significant evidence for continuing contact. Previous studies by Blumenkranz, Banitt, and Dahan have indicated strong elements of vernacular culture among the Jews. Susan Einbinder presses the argument further as she reveals literary techniques that appear both in vernacular romance and in Hebrew. This sharing of literary techniques might portend further studies of Hebrew poetry and prose as a "vernacular" as well as sacred language. Jan Ziolkowski's study of Latin literature demonstrates the possibilities of discovering how the use of "judaizare"—"to live in the Jewish way"—might provide further evidence of the presence of "Jewishness" in those texts. Alfred Haverkamp discovers the presence of Jews in local chronicles. Shared language, however, also may be an indication of separation and boundaries, of distance rather than intimacy. Maureen Boulton convincingly argues that Old French biblical paraphrases sharpen the negative image of the Jew. Although the stereotypes in the these texts are not surprising, they indicate how the popularization of biblical narratives spread negative images of the Jews. These literary studies indicate the potential for a narrative construction of a shared culture by Jews and Christians during the twelfth century.

Our authors also have pointed toward broader trends in understanding northern Europe in the twelfth century. A number of essays underscore the fact that a significant change took place after 1150 rather than 1096; this tightening of boundaries was influenced by a significant anti-Jewish shift in Christendom. Robert Chazan argues that the *Mainz Anonymous*, written shortly after the violence in 1096, describes the events in terms of religious symbolisms as opposed to the more political considerations of the Second Crusade. The rewriting of the narratives of the First Crusade are marked by a growing sense of the Jewish community's hostility toward their immediate European environment. Building on the theme of "vengeful messianism" developed in the work of Israel J. Yuval, Chazan illustrates how Jews reframed their earlier experience in a rhetoric much more hostile to their external environment. This sharpened hostility is echoed in the development of the monumental architecture in Milan, as shown by Walter Cahn's resolution of the puzzling iconography of the Porta Romana, and in the figure of St. Ambrose as a persecutor of Jews.

Thus, this volume brings together a group of scholars deeply attuned to the nuanced plurality of urban society and its discontents in Europe. The term "anxiety" or "doubt" arises in many of the essays. They continue and augment the important work of Gavin Langmuir, R. I. Moore, and Anna Sapir Abulafia. Our authors demonstrate again and again how Jews and Christians worked to understand and control the environment in which they lived. Living with those who were different and who claimed an exclusive interpretation of divine revelation was bound to cause anxiety about the truth of an opposing position. Despite the best efforts of religious leaders, there were Jews who were attracted to Christianity and Christians who found Judaism or Jews most attractive. The resolution of doubt led to the writing of biblical commentaries, treatises on various points of doctrine, passage of legislation, and, in many cases, violence and expulsion. These forms of exclusion were seen as prophylactic to the disease of doubt. Ivan Marcus and Michael Signer demonstrate that both communities participated in building the scaffolds of defense. Christians and their leaders were led to the invention of myths, such as the myth of ritual murder, that could lead to violence.

Jews and their leaders often called upon their God to be their ultimate champion and bring about a violent end to their enemies.

It is our hope that the essays in this volume contribute to a better understanding of the complex society that developed from the British Isles to the Elbe River from 1050 to 1215. Many events that took place at the end of the first millennium may correctly be understood as portents of what would happen in the middle of the final century in that era. This volume also demonstrates the possibilities of how other narratives might be constructed. Counterfactual history was not our aim. The gathering of scholars from a variety of disciplines committed to focusing on the specificity of the religious dimensions of social and intellectual history has demonstrated that it is possible to develop a complex and subtle narrative that might lead to different directions in the future.

Contributors

Maureen Barry McCann Boulton is professor of Romance Literature at the University of Notre Dame.

Walter Cahn is professor of Medieval Art History at Yale University in New Haven, Connecticut.

Robert Chazan is S. H. and Helen Scheuer Professor of Hebrew and Judaic Studies at New York University in New York City.

Jeremy Cohen is professor of Jewish History at the University of Tel Aviv in Israel.

Susan Einbinder is associate professor of Hebrew Literature at Hebrew Union College in Cincinnati, Ohio.

Jonathan M. Elukin is assistant professor of History at Trinity University in Hartford, Connecticut

Alfred Haverkamp is professor of Medieval History at Trier University in Trier, Germany.

William Chester Jordan is professor of Medieval History at Princeton University in Princeton, New Jersey.

Ivan G. Marcus is Frederick P. Rose Professor of Jewish History at Yale University in New Haven, Connecticut.

Gérard Nahon is professor emeritus at the École pratique des Hautes Études in Paris, France.

Michael A. Signer is Abrams Professor of Jewish Thought and Culture at the University of Notre Dame.

ROBERT C. STACEY is professor of History at the University of Washington in Seattle, Washington.

JOHN VAN ENGEN is Andrew V. Tackes Professor of Medieval History at the University of Notre Dame.

ELLIOT R. WOLFSON is Abraham Lieberman Professor of Hebrew and Judaic Studies at New York University in New York City.

JAN M. ZIOLKOWSKI is professor of Classics and Comparative Literature at Harvard University in Cambridge, Massachusetts.

Index